Introducing Multilingualism

Introducing Multilingualism is a comprehensive and user-friendly introduction to the dynamic field of multilingualism. Adopting a compelling social and critical approach and covering important social and educational issues, the authors expertly guide readers through the established theories, leading them to question dominant discourses on subjects such as integration, heritage and language testing. This second edition has been fully revised and updated, featuring new chapters on multilingualism in new media, the workplace and the family. Other key topics include:

- language contact and variation
- language and identity
- the differences between individual and societal multilingualism
- translanguaging
- flexible multilingual education.

With a wide range of engaging activities and quizzes and a comprehensive selection of case studies from around the world, this is essential reading for undergraduate students and postgraduate students new to studying multilingualism.

Kristine Horner is Reader in Luxembourg Studies and Multilingualism at the University of Sheffield, where she is also Director of the Centre for Luxembourg Studies. Her upcoming publications include a new edition of *The German-Speaking World* (2018).

Jean-Jacques Weber is Professor of English and Education at the University of Luxembourg. His most recent book publications are *Language Racism* (2015) and *Flexible Multilingual Education: Putting Children's Needs First* (2014).

Introducing Multilingualism

A Social Approach

Second edition

Kristine Horner and Jean-Jacques Weber

LONDON AND NEW YORK

This edition published 2018
by Routledge
2 Park Square, Milton Park, Abingdon, Oxon OX14 4RN

and by Routledge
711 Third Avenue, New York, NY 10017

Routledge is an imprint of the Taylor & Francis Group, an informa business

First published by Routledge 2012

British Library Cataloguing in Publication Data
A catalogue record for this book is available from the British Library

Library of Congress Cataloging in Publication Data
Names: Horner, Kristine, author. | Weber, Jean Jacques, author.
Title: Introducing multilingualism / by Kristine Horner and Jean-Jacques Weber.
Description: Second edition. | Milton Park, Abingdon, Oxon ; New York, NY : Routledge, [2017] | Includes bibliographical references and index.
Identifiers: LCCN 2017016236| ISBN 9781138244481 (hardback) | ISBN 9781138244498 (peperback) | ISBN 9781315276892 (ebook)
Subjects: LCSH: Multilingualism—Social aspects. | Sociolinguistics.
Classification: LCC P115.45 .W43 2017 | DDC 306.44/6—dc23
LC record available at https://lccn.loc.gov/2017016236

ISBN: 978-1-138-24448-1 (hbk)
ISBN: 978-1-138-24449-8 (pbk)
ISBN: 978-1-315-27689-2 (ebk)

Typeset in Bembo
by Swales & Willis Ltd, Exeter, Devon, UK

To our families and especially our mothers who taught us a lot about multilingualism: Ursula Gläser Horner and Yvette Weber-Morheng

Contents

Acknowledgements xii
Getting started xiii

PART I
Theoretical and methodological considerations 1

1 Introduction 3

A social approach to multilingualism 5
A note on terminology 6
Coping with change 7
How the book is structured 9

2 Theoretical and methodological framework 15

The construction of meaning 15
Dominant vs. critical readings 16
Towards an ethnographically based discourse analysis 18
The study of language ideologies 20
Conclusion 26

PART II
Multilingualism within and across languages 33

3 What is a language? 35

Discourse models of language 35
What is standard English? 36
'English' is a mere label 37

The fuzzy boundaries of named languages 37
Consequences for teaching 42
Consequences for research 43
Conclusion 45

4 Language variation and the spread of global languages 49

African-American English 50
Caribbean 'nation language' 52
Singlish 55
The global spread of English 56
Two French youth languages 59
Conclusion 62

5 Revitalization of endangered languages 67

Australian Aboriginal languages: a history of oppression 68
Māori in New Zealand: a revitalization success story 70
Sámi and Kven in Norway: differential positionings on the success–failure continuum 71
Hebrew in Israel: the human costs of revitalization 74
Breton in France: how (not) to standardize 75
Corsican and the polynomic paradigm 76
Why Luxembourgish is not *an endangered language* 77
Conclusion 79

PART III
Societal and individual multilingualism 87

6 Societal multilingualism 89

Ukraine 90
Switzerland 91
Singapore 92
Hong Kong and China 94
South Africa 97
Nigeria 99
Conclusion 100

7 Language and identities 104

Categorization 104
Gee's four ways to view identity 106

Identity: a peach or an onion? 107
National, ethnic and racial identity 108
Code-switching and identity 110
Translanguaging identities 117
Conclusion: individual and spatial repertoires 118

8 The interplay between individual and societal multilingualism 124

The Canadian policy of bilingualism and multiculturalism 124
Some consequences for First Nations people 125
Quebec francophone nationalism 126
Individual bilingualism through institutional monolingualism 127
Exclusion through French, inclusion through English 129
Shifting ideologies 129
Conclusion: the commodification of language 130

PART IV
Multilingualism in education and other institutional sites 137

9 Flexible vs. fixed multilingualism 139

US vs. EU language-in-education policy 141
Case study 1: Luxembourg 143
Case study 2: Catalonia and the Basque Country 146
Discussion and conclusion: towards flexible multilingual education 149

10 Mother tongue education or literacy bridges? 158

The case for mother tongue education: African-American English 158
The case against mother tongue education (in four steps): South Africa 161
The problems with mother tongue education 165
Bridges into literacy 166
Conclusion: a possible solution for South Africa 168

11 Heritage language education 174

Language and heritage in the United States 175
Language and heritage in Ecuador 176
Language and heritage in England 178

The dominance of the standard language and purist ideologies 182
Discussion and conclusion: implications for the EU policy of multilingualism 184

12 Multilingualism in other institutional sites 191

Multilingualism in the workplace 191
Language use in multilingual families 196
Conclusion 200

PART V
Critical analysis of discourses 205

13 Institutional discourses on language and migration 207

The discourse of integration 207
Language testing and citizenship 216
Conclusion: unpacking the discourses of integration and language testing 220

14 Media representations of multilingualism 226

Luxembourg's PISA results and the discourse of deficit 227
Constructing the UK as an English-only space 230
The English Only movement in the US 233
Conclusion: a historical perspective on the one nation–one language ideology 236

15 Multilingualism in the new media 241

Digital ethnography 242
Language contact phenomena in digital language 243
The limited multilingualism of the Internet 246
The policing of new media language 248
Conclusion 251

16 Linguistic landscape 255

Limitations of some linguistic landscape analyses 255
Language contact phenomena on multilingual signs 257
Some basic distinctions 259
Contextualizing and historicizing linguistic landscapes 260
Exploring the context of reception 264
Discussion and conclusion: discourses in place 265

PART VI
Further directions in the study of multilingualism 275

17 Conclusion 277

Further directions in the study of multilingualism 278
Normalizing multilingualism 283

Notes on the activities 288
Notes on the quizzes 293
Author index 299
Subject index 303

Acknowledgements

We would like to thank the numerous reviewers for their most useful and perceptive comments on earlier versions of this work. Special thanks go to Jennifer Leeman, Linus Salö, Melanie Cooke, Lionel Wee and J. Normann Jørgensen, as well as our students Emily Hopper, Tímea Kádas Pickel and Angela Woodmansee for providing detailed and invaluable comments on the whole MS. Any remaining errors, of course, are our own.

Parts of the materials have been trialled in the courses we have taught over the last few years at the universities of Luxembourg, Leeds and Sheffield and we thank the many students whose contributions have shaped the text in this way. Finally, we would also like to thank Louisa Semlyen, Laura Sandford and the Routledge staff for their support and editorial expertise, and Dr Rik Vosters of the Vrije Universiteit Brussel for his kind permission to reproduce Figure 16.4.

Every effort has been made to contact copyright-holders. Please advise the publisher of any errors or omissions, and these will be corrected in subsequent editions.

Getting started

Have a look at language use on the following multilingual signs. If you are using this book in a classroom setting, you could divide into groups and discuss one or more of the signs, depending on which contexts – Asian, Australian, Canadian, European – you and the students in your group are more familiar with:

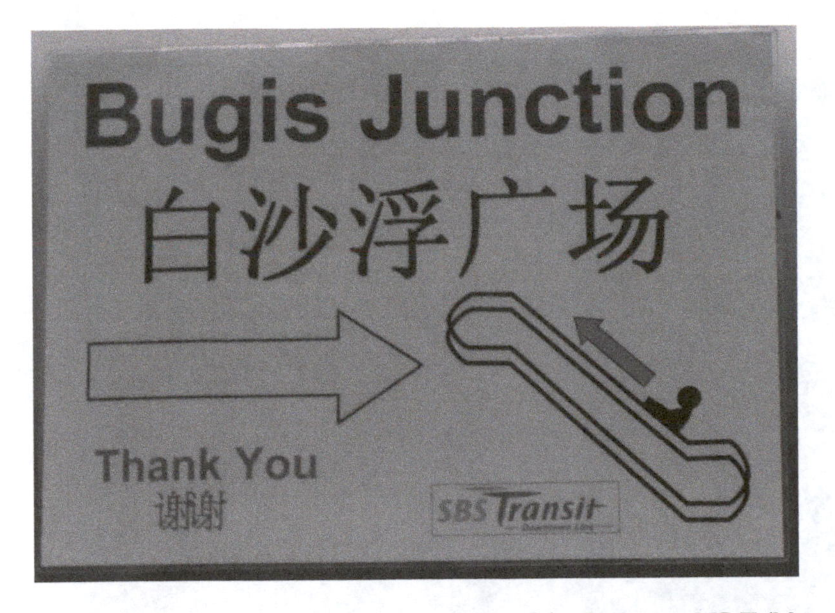

Figure 0.1 Sign in the Bugis Junction station of the Singapore MRT (Mass Rapid Transit) system

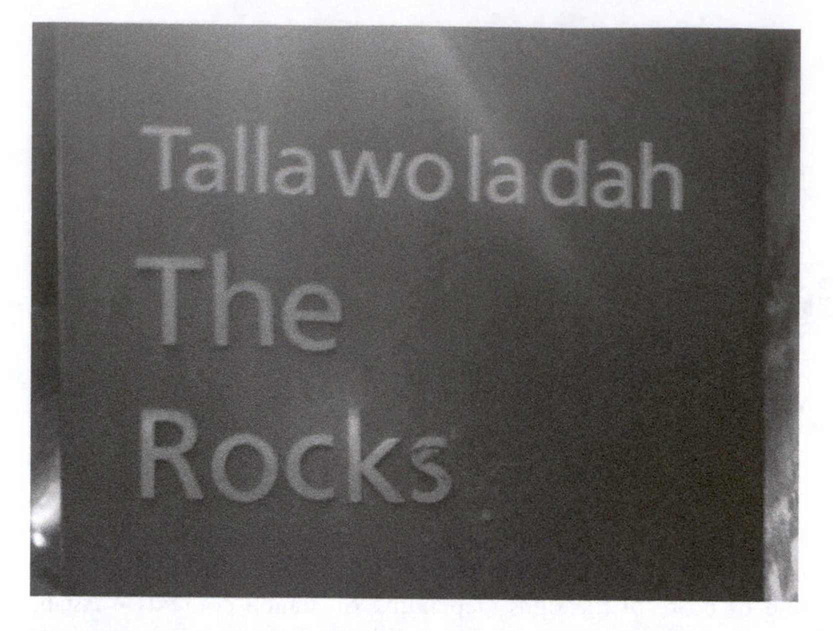

Figure 0.2 Sign in the historic 'The Rocks' area in central Sydney, Australia

Figure 0.3 Sign in the Granville Island market in Vancouver, Canada

Figure 0.4 Sign on postbox in Merano/Meran in South Tyrol/Alto Adige, Italy

Now it is your turn to take some pictures of (if possible) multilingual signs in your own area and bring them to class for discussion.

The study of the language of signs in the public space is often referred to as 'linguistic landscape'. If you are interested in this topic, you can turn to Chapter 16, where it is discussed in detail.

PART I

Theoretical and methodological considerations

CHAPTER 1

Introduction

One may as well begin with Blommaert's (2010: 102) definition of multilingualism:

> Multilingualism ... should not be seen as a collection of 'languages' that a speaker controls, but rather as a complex of *specific* semiotic resources, some of which belong to a conventionally defined 'language', while others belong to another 'language'. The resources are concrete accents, language varieties, registers, genres, modalities such as writing – ways of using language in particular communicative settings and spheres of life, including the ideas people have about such ways of using their language ideologies.

The following chapters (especially Chapter 3) will make clear why Blommaert uses scare quotes with the term 'language'. He suggests that we all have a large number of linguistic resources at our disposal, and it does not really make a difference whether they belong to only one 'conventionally defined "language"' or several of them. Hence, multilingualism is a matter of degree, a continuum, and since we all use different linguistic varieties, registers, styles, genres and accents, we are all to a greater or lesser degree multilingual. In this book, we will say that the varieties, etc. that we use constitute our linguistic repertoire. Moreover, these repertoires are not static but dynamic, since the resources in them change over time.

At the end of the above quotation, Blommaert also mentions 'language ideologies', i.e. our beliefs about what a language is (and what multilingualism is), how language works and how it is used. This book takes up Blommaert's point about the centrality of language ideologies and offers a language-ideological approach to the study of multilingualism. The concept of 'language ideology' will be fully explained in the following chapter. For instance, we will argue that seeing 'languages' as well-defined, bounded entities is the product of an ideological process.

Thus, this book is situated within a theoretical framework which problematizes even such a basic concept as 'language'. As we will see in detail throughout the following chapters, it presents an alternative view of multilingualism not in terms of 'languages' but in terms of linguistic resources and repertoires, and advocates this as a more successful way of capturing what is often an elusive and intractable linguistic reality. It takes a broad definition of multilingualism as verbal repertoires consisting of more than one variety (whether language or dialect).

Hence, also, terms such as bilingualism, trilingualism, etc. are subsumed under the term 'multilingualism'; we avoid such terms as far as possible because they are based on the problematic idea that 'languages' are easily identifiable and can be counted. In fact, however, the question of which resources in people's repertoires count as 'languages' and which do not is a socio-political rather than linguistic one – as we explain more fully in Chapter 3. Even 'multilingualism' itself is a rather problematic term because of this underlying assumption of languages as bounded entities which are countable. However, other terms which have been proposed are not unproblematic either: they, too, could be understood as being based on the same assumption or they are more restricted in their application. The former include 'plurilingualism' (Council of Europe 2005), 'polylingualism' (Jørgensen 2008), 'interlingualism' (Widdowson 2010) and even 'multiplurilingualism' (Ehrhart 2010), while the latter include Otsuji and Pennycook's (2010) 'metrolingualism', which mostly refers to urban contexts (this concept is briefly discussed in Chapter 3). While all these terms refer to the same complex linguistic phenomena, we will continue in this book to use the most widely accepted term, namely multilingualism.

FOR DISCUSSION: DESCRIBING AND COMPARING LINGUISTIC REPERTOIRES

A repertoire is the set of linguistic resources (whether 'languages' or 'dialects') which are at an individual's disposal. Can you describe as fully as possible your own linguistic repertoire: what varieties does it consist in? When, where and with whom do you use these varieties? How does your range of linguistic resources compare with those of your classmates? Make sure you include all your resources, whether you are highly proficient in them or not.

Note that repertoires are discussed in greater detail in Chapter 7.

A SOCIAL APPROACH TO MULTILINGUALISM

This book can be used for any introductory course in Multilingualism, Sociolinguistics, Applied Linguistics or Linguistic Anthropology. It can also be used for independent study – though you will find it helpful to discuss the activities with other people.

The book provides an introduction to the key social issues in the study of multilingualism. At the same time, we also hope to change the way many people think about these topics. We question deeply held assumptions about language and multilingualism (what sociolinguists and linguistic anthropologists refer to as our 'language ideologies'), and encourage readers to think critically about important social and educational issues such as the following:

- How do languages 'leak' into each other (rather than being clearly defined entities), and what implications does this have for our understanding of what a language is and what multilingualism is?
- In what sense can a language be said to be endangered, and what are the benefits and pitfalls of attempting to revitalize it?
- What is the best way of organizing a multilingual system of education which is truly open to linguistic diversity?
- What are the advantages and disadvantages of mother tongue education and heritage language education?
- How can we critically analyse (verbal and/or visual) texts such as multilingual signs, online texts and media representations of multilingualism, and how can we identify the (sometimes restrictive) assumptions and ideologies underlying them?

By tackling these and many other questions, we ultimately aim at reversing the traditional paradigm by normalizing multilingualism. In other words, we see multilingualism rather than monolingualism as the normal state of affairs. After all, far more people in the world are multilingual rather than monolingual; and if we apply the above definition of multilingualism in terms of resources and repertoires, then it is hard to imagine that there are some people left in the world who are not at least to some extent multilingual!

We add two further points here in relation to the social approach to multilingualism that we are taking. First, we think that there is a need to unpack and move beyond some of the classic and often limited concepts of structuralist sociolinguistics. To give just one example, in this book we move away from the traditional concept of **diglossia**, which has been used to describe a community where one 'dialect' or 'language' (e.g. standard German in German-speaking Switzerland) is the formal or 'high' variety used in education and government, whereas the other one (Swiss German) is the informal or 'low' variety used in everyday talk. Diglossia presupposes a stable language situation where languages can be compartmentalized and, in particular, where a neat separation can be made between a high and a low variety. However, the high vs. low distinction has been criticized, and it has been pointed out that the low variety can enjoy more prestige than the high one (as is the case in Switzerland – see the discussion of the Swiss language situation in Chapter 6). Moreover, such a binary opposition frequently simplifies and hence fails to capture the full complexity of the linguistic reality, especially in our late modern age of globalization, migration and superdiversity (Vertovec 2007; see also section below on 'Coping with change').

Second, this book deals with the social issues in the study of multilingualism, not the cognitive ones. Thus, for instance, readers will find nothing in this book about the question of whether multilingual people have a unified linguistic competence or a compartmentalized one (with knowledge of each of their languages stored separately in the brain). We might just add here that, as with many such debates, the answer probably lies somewhere in the middle, namely that multilinguals' linguistic competence is neither wholly unified nor wholly separate. Readers interested in finding out more about the cognitive aspects of multilingualism are referred to the suggestions for further reading listed at the end of this chapter.

A NOTE ON TERMINOLOGY

Of course, what we have said above about such concepts as 'language' and 'multilingualism' does not mean that we cannot use these terms any longer. It simply means that, in the case of 'languages', we need to be aware that we are dealing with socio-politically rather than linguistically defined units. Apart from 'language', we also sometimes use in this book other terms which are less than optimal such as, for instance, *migrant* children or students. The problem with this term is that it perpetuates an *us* vs. *them* distinction, which in fact needs to be overcome. What is particularly worrying is that only certain children or students tend to be perceived and categorized as 'migrants'. For instance, in a French school, a child with one French and one Belgian parent will probably not be perceived as a 'migrant', whereas a child with one French and one Nigerian parent most likely will be. Moreover, the latter child may be perceived as a 'migrant' even though she or he holds French citizenship and was born in France (and hence never migrated). As is the case with all forms of social categorization, the label 'migrant' is at least to some extent a matter of perception and thus socially constructed.

Many other terms (e.g. 'non-standard') also have negative connotations (non-standard varieties might be looked upon as inferior to standard varieties). However, in all of these cases, it is difficult to think of (widely accepted) alternative terms which avoid the negative connotations. Thus, for instance, 'vernacular varieties' does not fare much better than 'non-standard varieties' in this respect.

Another problematic distinction is the one between **minority** and **majority** groups as well as minority and majority languages. Note, first of all, that oppressed minorities can sometimes be numerically the majority group: e.g. black people in apartheid South Africa. Note also that one and the same language can be the majority language in one social context (e.g. Spanish in Spain) and a minority language in another (e.g. Spanish in the US). Following Pavlenko and Blackledge (2004: 4), the terms 'minority' and 'majority' are therefore used in this book 'not to draw attention to numerical size of particular groups, but to refer to situational differences in power, rights, and privileges'.

Finally, the term **'superdiversity'**, introduced in the previous section, refers to a diversification or intensification of (social, cultural, linguistic) diversity, as experienced specifically in Europe over the last couple of decades. According to Blommaert and Rampton (2011: 2), superdiversity is

> characterized by a tremendous increase in the categories of migrants, not only in terms of nationality, ethnicity, language, and religion, but also in terms of motives, patterns and itineraries of migration, processes of insertion into the labour and housing markets of the host societies, and so on.

However, the term, while embraced by many sociolinguists, has not gone unchallenged and has been criticized for its lack of conceptual clarity, its Eurocentric bias and its ahistorical perspective (is superdiversity a characteristic only of European societies and only in the twenty-first century?). In particular, Pavlenko (forthcoming) looks upon it as a form of academic branding rather than a substantial contribution to research.

COPING WITH CHANGE

The main reason why sociolinguistics needs to change and adapt its core concepts is that the whole world around us is changing at an ever faster rate. We live in the age of **globalization** and late modernity, and these changes affect people all over the world. As Blommaert (2010: 13) puts it,

> The term *globalization* is most commonly used as shorthand for the intensified flows of capital, goods, people, images and discourses around the globe, driven by technological innovations mainly in the field of media and information and communication technology, and resulting in new patterns of global activity, community organization and culture (Castells 1996; Appadurai 1996).

For reasons of space, we just include here a few comments on selected aspects of globalization from the perspective of what are sometimes considered the 'centre' countries, especially Europe and the USA.

In Europe, the combined processes of globalization and Europeanization have shifted boundaries to a certain degree from nation-state boundaries (e.g. Dutch vs. others) to European Union boundaries (EU citizens vs. others). Moreover, there has been a repeated redefinition of the category of 'non-EU others', as the boundaries of the EU were progressively redrawn. The result is several layers of otherness – or what Delanty and Rumford (2005: 188) refer to as 'the interpenetration of interior/exterior, self and other' – which some (many?) people may feel increasingly difficult to live with. Indeed, they find themselves living in a heterogeneous and multilingual culture which is at odds with both the official and the nationalist culture of monolingualism and monoculturalism.

In the United States, too, both the mainstream group and the immigrant minority groups could be said to potentially experience what Portes and Rumbaut (2001: 284) refer to as **reactive ethnicity**. Portes and Rumbaut use the term primarily to refer to a reaction of resistance on the part of immigrant minority groups against what is perceived as an oppressive and discriminatory mainstream, but it applies equally to the majority group: they, too, may experience social conditions as increasingly hostile and alienating. There is therefore an urgent need to find a way out of the vicious circle of reactive ethnicity engendered by xenophobic attitudes and ideologies:

> Tragically, the ideologies that hold sway among broad segments of the white middle-class electorate yield exactly the opposite results, imperiling the future of today's [immigrant] second generation and perpetuating the condition of the existing minority underclass. Results of this study point to the urgent need to enlighten the dominant majority as to where its real self-interests lie in the long run and thus build a constituency for an alternative set of policies. The future of the metropolitan areas where immigrants concentrate and of American society as a whole may well hang in the balance.
>
> (Portes and Rumbaut 2001: 286)

Many mainstream group members find the changes wrought by globalization increasingly hard to cope with. Salman Rushdie (2003: 416–17) writes about J.M. Coetzee's novel *Waiting for the Barbarians* in the following way:

> those who spend their time on guard, waiting for the barbarians to arrive, in the end don't need any barbarians to come ... they themselves become the barbarians whose coming they so feared.

In our late modern world, it is no longer just a question of being on guard against the 'barbarians' but of how to deal with their increasingly visible (and audible) presence in 'our' midst. The cognitive and behavioural patterns, however, remain the same: 'we ourselves' are in danger of becoming the barbarians whose presence 'we' are so afraid of.

HOW THE BOOK IS STRUCTURED

We have divided the book into six parts. Part I introduces important theoretical and methodological approaches in the study of multilingualism. In particular, it shows how ethnographic and discourse-analytic approaches can be combined in an eclectic framework, which is then applied in some later chapters of the book. Chapter 2 also discusses the most common beliefs about language (language ideologies).

The chapters in Part II are concerned with the difficulties of defining what a language is. Chapter 3 looks at how blurred the boundaries are, which are drawn to separate one language from another, and Chapter 4 shows that the fuzziness that exists between languages is also to be found within languages. We examine the consequences of this fuzziness for both teaching and research. Thus, it potentially relativizes such notions as 'language endangerment' and 'language revitalization', which are discussed in Chapter 5.

Part III (Chapters 6, 7 and 8) introduces the basic distinction between individual multilingualism and societal multilingualism, and investigates the complex interplay between them. The study of individual multilingualism is interested in the connections between language and identity, looking at such multilingual strategies as code-switching, translanguaging, stylization and language crossing. In the study of societal multilingualism, on the other hand, we are more concerned with how states manage their multilingualism, e.g. by adopting some languages (but not others) as their national or official language(s), or as the medium of instruction in their educational system.

The chapters in Part IV explore educational systems in much greater detail, classifying them on a continuum from fixed to flexible (Chapter 9).

Moreover, Chapter 10 examines the pros and cons of mother tongue education programmes: it criticizes the 'fixed' nature of some of these programmes and introduces the concept of the 'literacy bridge' as one way of introducing greater flexibility. Chapter 11 distinguishes between mother tongue education and heritage language education, while showing that the latter, too, can be affected by the same problems of fixedness as the former. Finally, Chapter 12 looks at the opportunities and challenges of multilingualism in other institutional sites such as the workplace and the family.

Part V illustrates the use of (critical) discourse analysis. Chapter 13 deconstructs the official discourse of 'integration' (of migrants), showing how it is informed by illiberal assumptions and ideologies that underpin current policies on migration, education and citizenship. Chapter 14 critically unpacks negative media representations of multilingualism, while Chapter 15 explores the use of multilingualism more specifically in social media. Chapter 16 extends the analysis to multimodal texts (in particular, multilingual signs which combine both verbal and visual elements).

Last but not least, the book uses a highly practical approach, and each chapter includes a number of activities asking you to apply the new concepts and to develop your understanding of the issues under discussion. The exercises are divided into three types:

- **Activity**, which asks you to carry out a well-defined task with the help of materials available in the chapter itself.
- **For discussion**, which aims to get you to think about some fundamental issues in the study of multilingualism.
- **Project work**, which requires you to go beyond the textbook and to do some extra reading or other research.

We do not necessarily expect you to do all these exercises, but we hope that you will choose the ones that you are most interested in. A few of them are followed by discussion notes at the very end of the book; however, it is important here to remember that we are not dealing with mathematical problems but with open-ended questions of interpretation: our hints and suggestions are really and truly only hints and suggestions intended to make you think, and certainly do not constitute the final word on these questions!

Before we embark on our study of multilingualism, we invite you to test your own knowledge of language and multilingualism by taking the quiz at the end of this chapter. Suggested answers are given at the end of the book, and moreover most of the questions touch upon issues that are discussed in the following chapters. Note that further quizzes can be found at the end of each Part of the book.

REFERENCES AND SUGGESTIONS FOR FURTHER READING

Defining multilingualism

Blommaert, Jan (2010) *The Sociolinguistics of Globalization*, Cambridge: Cambridge University Press.

Council of Europe (2005) *Rapport du groupe d'experts: Grand-Duché de Luxembourg: Profil des politiques linguistiques éducatives*, Strasbourg: Division des politiques linguistiques.

Ehrhart, Sabine (2010) 'Pourquoi intégrer la diversité linguistique et culturelle dans la formation des enseignants au Luxembourg?', in S. Ehrhart, C. Hélot and A. Le Nevez (eds) *Plurilinguisme et formation des enseignants*, Frankfurt/Main: Peter Lang, 221–37.

Jørgensen, Jens Normann (2008) 'Polylingual languaging around and among children and adolescents', *International Journal of Multilingualism*, 5: 161–76.

Otsuji, Emi and Pennycook, Alastair (2010) 'Metrolingualism: Fixity, fluidity and language in flux', *International Journal of Multilingualism*, 7: 240–54.

Pennycook, Alastair and Otsuji, Emi (2015) *Metrolingualism: Language in the City*, London: Routledge.

Widdowson, Henry (2010) 'Terms and conditions of enquiry', paper presented at International Conference on New Challenges for Multilingualism in Europe, Dubrovnik, 11–15 April 2010.

Cognitive approaches to multilingualism

Altaribba, Jeannette and Heredia, Roberto R. (2008) *An Introduction to Bilingualism*, Abingdon: Routledge.

Chin, Ng Bee and Wigglesworth, Gillian (2007) *Bilingualism*, Abingdon: Routledge.

Cook, Vivian and Li Wei (eds) (2016) *The Cambridge Handbook of Linguistic Multi-Competence*, Cambridge: Cambridge University Press.

Majority vs. minority

May, Stephen (2001) *Language and Minority Rights: Ethnicity, Nationalism and the Politics of Language*, London: Longman.

Pavlenko, Aneta and Blackledge, Adrian (2004) 'Introduction: New theoretical approaches to the study of negotiation of identities in multilingual contexts', in A. Pavlenko and A. Blackledge (eds) *Negotiation of Identities in Multilingual Contexts*, Clevedon: Multilingual Matters, 1–33.

Language and superdiversity

Arnaut, Karel, Blommaert, Jan, Rampton, Ben and Spotti, Massimiliano (eds) (2016) *Language and Superdiversity*, London: Routledge.

——, Karrebæk, Martha Sif, Spotti, Massimiliano and Blommaert, Jan (eds) (2016) *Engaging Superdiversity: Recombining Spaces, Times and Language Practices*, Bristol: Multilingual Matters.

Blommaert, Jan and Rampton, Ben (2011) 'Language and superdiversity: A position paper', *Working Papers in Urban Language and Literacies*, 70.

Flores, Nelson and Lewis, Mark (2016) 'From truncated to sociopolitical emergence: A critique of super-diversity in sociolinguistics', *International Journal of the Sociology of Language*, 241: 97–124.

Pavlenko, Aneta (forthcoming) 'Superdiversity and why it isn't: Reflections on terminological innovation and academic branding', in S. Breidbach, L. Küster and B. Schmenk (eds) *Sloganizations in Language Education Discourse*, Bristol: Multilingual Matters.

Vertovec, Steven (2007) 'Super-diversity and its implications', *Ethnic and Racial Studies*, 30: 1024–54.

Globalization

Appadurai, Arjun (1996) *Modernity at Large*, Minneapolis, MN: University of Minnesota Press.

Bauman, Zygmunt (1998) *Globalization: The Human Consequences*, Cambridge: Polity.

Castells, Manuel (1996) *The Rise of the Network Society*, London: Blackwell.

Coetzee, J.M. (1980/97) *Waiting for the Barbarians*, London: Vintage.

Delanty, Gerard and Rumford, Chris (2005) *Rethinking Europe: Social Theory and the Implications of Europeanization*, Abingdon: Routledge.

Portes, Alejandro and Rumbaut, Rubén (2001) *Legacies: The Story of the Immigrant Second Generation*, Berkeley, CA: University of California Press.

Rushdie, Salman (2003) *Step Across This Line: Collected Non-Fiction 1992–2002*, London: Vintage.

TEST YOURSELF QUIZ CHAPTER 1*

Language and language use are fascinating topics to study. To get you started, here is a little test about your knowledge of languages.

1. What is/are the official language(s) of the following countries: Switzerland; USA; New Zealand; Belgium?
2. Do you know the rap music of Amoc or Nash? What language(s) do they sing in?
3. Do you know about the political or sociolinguistic situation of Côte d'Ivoire, and what are the connections with former Chelsea footballer Didier Drogba?
4. What is Hindustani, and why did Gandhi try – and fail – to promote it as the national language of India?
5. In what language are these lines from Robert Burns' poem 'The Banks o' Doon' written? In English or Scots?

   Ye Banks and braes o' bonie Doon,
   How can ye bloom sae fresh and fair;
   (Doon – river in Burns' native Ayrshire; braes – slopes; bonie, bonny – beautiful; sae – so)
6. Do you know what one of the following refers to: Singlish or Verlan or Ebonics?
7. Is there a language called Chinese?
8. What language(s) may be looked upon as 'American' languages (as opposed to 'immigrant' languages) in the United States?
9. What is the difference between the English Only and the English Plus movements in the United States?
10. What language(s) is/are used on the sign in Figure 1.1 (overleaf), which you encounter as you enter the Luxembourgish village of Schengen? (Schengen has become famous because it is where the agreement on borderless Europe was signed.)

*Suggested answers can be found on page 293.

Figure 1.1 Schengen place name

CHAPTER 2

Theoretical and methodological framework

In this chapter we look at how the meaning of a text is constructed by the reader or hearer. Moreover, meaning is constructed differently by different hearers/readers, on a continuum from dominant to critical (or resisting) readings. Which position a particular hearer/reader chooses to occupy on this continuum depends to a large extent on the degree to which she or he shares the underlying assumptions, or discourse models, upon which the text is based. Then we introduce the reader to a theoretical and methodological approach combining ethnography and discourse analysis. This approach will be applied to the analysis of both verbal and visual texts throughout the textbook and primarily in the chapters of Part V. Finally, we discuss some key discourse models about language, which are widely held beliefs or ideologies about how language works and how it is used. The main language ideologies include the belief in a hierarchy of languages, the standard language ideology, the one nation–one language ideology, the mother tongue ideology and the ideology of linguistic purism. In Chapter 3, we will see how taking these language ideologies into account potentially alters the traditional understanding of multilingualism.

THE CONSTRUCTION OF MEANING

What does 'Dogs like bones' mean? Consider the following situation:

> John is watching TV. His partner Bill is preparing to cook T-bone steak in the kitchen. Their dog Pax is sleeping on a chair in the kitchen. There's a ring at the door. Their neighbour asks if they have any spare eggs. Bill brings some eggs from the kitchen, gives them to the neighbour and chats to her for a while. When he returns to the kitchen, the dish on which the T-bone steak was lying is empty.

> Bill shouts to John: 'Hey! Where's the T-bone?' John looks up and notices Pax doing something in a corner of the room. He exclaims: 'Oh no!' and adds, 'Dogs like bones!'

So, did you know that 'Dogs like bones' means something like 'Pax took the T-bone steak while you were away'? And, if uttered in a particular tone of voice, it might also suggest that Bill had been stupid to leave the T-bone steak unattended (knowing what Pax is like).

In this way, we can see that meaning is not fixed or contained within individual words, but needs to be constructed by the hearer or reader, who links the text with relevant background knowledge to make sense of it. In this case, many of us may share background assumptions about dogs and their eating behaviour which help us to understand what John meant. On the other hand, it may also be the case that you have constructed the meaning of what John said in a (slightly) different way from the way we have just done. Hence, because different readers or hearers may draw upon different background assumptions, they may come up with different interpretations of a text. There is always a range of possible interpretations, though there are also limits: indeed, it is highly unlikely that you would have constructed what John said as meaning (for instance) that crocodiles are aggressive creatures!

This has interesting implications. If you ever have a teacher or somebody else saying to you:

> This is the meaning of this text/poem/novel etc.

you can tell them that their statement just does not make sense. In fact, it can only be understood as follows:

> This is the way I (or others) have constructed the meaning of this text in a particular context at a particular time.

DOMINANT VS. CRITICAL READINGS

We use our own assumptions about the world to understand what assumptions a particular text is based upon. If the two sets of assumptions seem (to us) to be aligned, we simply go along with the writer's assumptions, we allow ourselves to be carried along by them: this is often referred to in textual criticism as the dominant reading of a text. If, on the other hand, there seems (to us) to be a clash between our assumptions and the assumptions made in or by the text, then we might well begin to question or even reject the latter: this is the resisting or critical reading (for detailed discussion, see Fetterley 1981; Montgomery *et al.* 2013: chapter 15).

ACTIVITY: THE IMPORTANCE OF BEING CRITICAL*

Here are three extracts: a newspaper headline, a sentence from a literary text and a short extract from an official language-in-education policy document. Use your own background assumptions to identify what assumptions these texts seem to be based on, and decide whether or to what extent you accept or reject these assumptions (and why):

a) As the cancer spreads.

Contextual information: In 1981, young people in Brixton, South London, demonstrated against police harassment and brutality. The street 'rioting' that ensued spread to other parts of Britain. The following day, one British tabloid published an article about these events with the headline reproduced above.

This example is taken from Fairclough (1989: 99–100) and his comments upon it are reproduced in the Notes on the activities at the end of the book.

b) Her family wished to secure me, because I was of good race.

(Brontë 1847/1985: 332)

Contextual information: This sentence is taken from Charlotte Brontë's famous novel *Jane Eyre*. Rochester, the English gentleman, is in love with the governess, Jane Eyre. Here he tells her about some of the dark secrets of his past life, in particular how he came to marry his first wife, Bertha. Bertha is a white creole, born in the West Indies as the descendant of European settlers. Rochester feels convinced that Bertha's family did everything they could to ensure that this marriage would take place, in other words that he was 'conned' into marrying Bertha.

c) *Education précoce* groups will include both Luxembourgish children and children who have learnt another L1.

(*L'éducation précoce,* Ministère de l'Education Nationale 2000: 20)

Contextual information: This sentence is taken from an official language-in-education policy document published by the Luxembourgish Ministry of Education. It deals with the organization of the first year of pre-school education, for children aged 3–4. Luxembourg has a highly heterogeneous school population (in many classrooms, especially in urban areas, non-Luxembourgish passport holders make up over 50 per cent of the schoolchildren). The national language, Luxembourgish, is spoken by most of the autochthonous children, but German and French are also officially recognized languages and widely used in the country, as well as many other languages such as Portuguese, Italian and English. (For further details about the language situation in Luxembourg, see Chapter 9.) Because of the small size of the country and the highly heterogeneous population, mixed marriages are extremely frequent and the actual linguistic reality of many families is highly multilingual.

*Brief comments on this activity can be found on page 288.

TOWARDS AN ETHNOGRAPHICALLY BASED DISCOURSE ANALYSIS

What may have made the above activity difficult for you is that you did not have much information about the context of the three examples. It is clear that the more we know about the context, the easier it becomes to understand the assumptions and implications of a text. This is why, if you want to study sites of multilingualism, it is optimal to combine the analysis of discourse with ethnographic investigation. Socioculturally and ethnographically based discourse analysis has been advocated by numerous scholars including Agar (2006), Blommaert (2005), Blommaert and Dong (2010), Bucholtz (2001) and Gee (2005, 2010).

Ethnography is a qualitative research approach in which the researcher attempts to gain access to certain people's lived realities in an endeavour to see the world through their eyes. The aim is to achieve a deep understanding – what Geertz (1973) calls a '**thick description**' – of these people's worlds, of their ways of acting and thinking. For this, the researcher needs to take a highly contextualized approach, not only analysing whatever texts (spoken or written, verbal or visual) have been collected, but also exploring their contexts of production (how and why these texts were produced) and of reception (how the texts are received) and, more generally, relating these local texts to wider social processes. The data can consist of participant observations (the researcher taking fieldnotes), (transcripts of) interviews and other spoken interactions, as well as written documents of all kinds. In the data analysis, the ethnographer looks for what Agar (2006) calls '**rich points**'. These are moments in the data where something unexpected occurs and where as a result we have difficulty in understanding:

> When a rich point occurs, an ethnographer learns that his or her assumptions about how the world works, usually implicit and out of awareness, are inadequate to understand something that happened. A gap, a distance, between two worlds has

> just surfaced in the details of human activity. Rich points, the words and actions that signal those gaps, are the unit of data for ethnographers, for it is this distance between two worlds of experience that is exactly the problem that ethnographic research is designed to locate and resolve.
>
> (Agar 2006: 7)

Moreover, Agar insists on the following two aspects:

- in ethnography, data collection and analysis are continual and dynamic;
- theory in ethnography grows out of the data in an emergent way.

The methods of discourse analysis can be applied to the data and in particular to the rich points in the data that we focus upon, to make explicit the belief systems or ideologies informing them (the way you did with the examples in the activity above). What we call here 'belief systems or ideologies' is what others have termed 'folk theories' (Agar 2006), 'mental models' (Johnson-Laird 1983), 'cultural models' or 'discourse models' (Gee 2005). Gee prefers '**discourse models**' because, though these beliefs exist in people's heads, we can only study their realization in discourse:

> We obviously do not gain our evidence for Discourse models by opening up people's heads. And we don't need to. Besides closely observing what they say and do, we look, as well, at the texts, media, social practices, social and institutional interactions, and diverse Discourses that influence them.
>
> (Gee 2005: 93)

Hence, we need to analyse our data by asking the following question:

> One way to get at people's Discourse models is ask 'What must I assume this person (consciously or unconsciously) believes in order to make deep sense of what they are saying?'
>
> (Gee 2005: 87)

It may have struck you in the last two quotations that Gee capitalizes the word 'discourse': he does this as a way of reminding us that most discourse models are not purely individual ones but can be traced across larger discourses (which Gee refers to as 'Big-D Discourses'). Thus the small-d discourse, or individual text, that we want to analyse is always part of one or more larger Big-D Discourses circulating in a particular society at a particular time. The Big-D Discourse consists of numerous small-d discourses, as in the Discourse of feminism or the Discourse of capitalism;

moreover, the Big-D Discourse consists of more than language: for example, the Discourse of punks involves not only a certain way of speaking but also a certain way of behaving, of dressing, etc. For an ethnographic, in-depth analysis the researcher needs to link the small-d discourses that she is analysing to the Big-D Discourses that they are a part of, thus shuttling between the 'micro' and 'macro' levels of the analysis and exploring the links between the two. Further examples of Big-D Discourses would be the discourse of language endangerment, as discussed at the end of Chapter 5, and the discourse of integration, analysed in Chapter 13. Note that both in the previous sentence and in the following chapters of this book we have adhered to the spirit of Gee's distinction without adopting his – slightly awkward – orthographic convention.

THE STUDY OF LANGUAGE IDEOLOGIES

A major focus of this book is people's beliefs (or discourse models) about language, their language ideologies. Language ideologies have been widely studied in linguistic anthropology and sociolinguistics. Because, like most discourse models, they usually involve simplifications, they 'can do harm by implanting in thought and action unfair, dismissive, or derogatory assumptions about other people' (Gee 2005: 72). It is therefore important to be aware of when texts rely upon such potentially stereotyped and discriminatory assumptions and ideologies.

Following Blommaert and Verschueren (1998: 25), ideology can be defined as a 'constellation of fundamental or commonsensical, and often normative, ideas and attitudes related to some aspect(s) of social "reality"'. Language ideologies are those that relate to language use and structure. Because of the potential normative power of ideologies, language ideologies, too, tend to be imbued with vested interests and can play a role in group membership and boundary negotiation, as well as social inclusion and exclusion. Irvine (1989: 255) emphasizes that language ideologies constitute 'the cultural system of ideas about social and linguistic relationships, together with their loading of moral and political interests'.

Thus, language ideologies are the cultural systems of ideas and feelings, norms and values, which inform the way people think about languages. Because ideologies constitute simplified representations of reality, such thinking often tends to be of a stereotypical manner. According to Kroskrity (2006), language ideologies are characterized by four interconnected dimensions: they represent perceptions of language and discourse that are constructed in the interests of a specific social group; they are multiple rather than fixed or unitary; people usually display varying degrees of awareness of these language ideologies; and language ideologies mediate between social structures and forms of talk.

There are many ideologies on the subject of language, which frequently complement one another. The ones that will be discussed in this book include the following (though it should be clear that they are all closely interconnected):

The hierarchy of languages

This is the belief that linguistic practices can be labelled and divided into 'languages' or 'dialects', 'patois', etc., which are then subsumed into a hierarchy, with 'languages' being looked upon as superior to 'dialects' and, additionally, certain languages being given a higher status as the 'national' or 'official' language of the state or community.

As the discussion in Chapter 3 will show, it is not possible to distinguish between language and dialect in purely linguistic terms. The most common argument put forward in support of such a distinction is the criterion of mutual intelligibility: if two varieties are mutually intelligible, they are dialects, and if not, they are languages. However, some 'languages', such as Danish, Swedish and Norwegian, are largely mutually intelligible, and some 'dialects', e.g. of Chinese, are not. As Gee (2005: 48) puts it, no rigorous distinction can be made 'between different dialects (e.g., there are dialects of German that are not mutually interpretable) and different languages (e.g., there are dialects of German and Dutch that are mutually interpretable)'.

Hence, the position advocated by numerous contemporary sociolinguists that named languages may be seen as socio-political constructs seems a more viable view. Thus, if Danish, Swedish and Norwegian or Serbian, Croatian and Bosnian are seen as separate languages, this is for socio-political rather than linguistic reasons. As Blommaert (1996: 217) argues,

> whenever some phenomenon is called 'a language', rather than 'a dialect', 'code' or other derogatory terms, ideology and politics are at play. Whenever we indulge in 'language' planning, we should be aware of the fact that we indulge in political linguistics.

The standard language ideology (Milroy and Milroy 1999)

The standard language ideology has associated axioms, in particular the belief that languages are internally homogeneous, bounded entities. Languages that have been named and thus separated off from other named languages frequently undergo a process of **standardization**. The latter process needs to be understood from a historical perspective: which variety becomes standard is mostly due to socio-political developments, and certainly not to any inherent superiority of this particular variety (as many language guardians or purists think; see Chapter 3 for discussion). In this way, the development of standardized languages is directly connected with the politics of state-making (Ricento 2006: 233). At the same time, Milroy and Milroy (1999: 19) remind us that standardization is most fully achieved in the writing system, but is never fully achieved in the spoken language; therefore, they continue,

> it seems appropriate to speak more abstractly of standardization as an ideology, and a standard language as an idea in the mind rather than a reality – a set of abstract norms to which actual usage may conform to a greater or lesser extent.

Thus they use the term 'standard language ideology' to refer to the characteristic attitudes of standard language speech communities.

According to Deumert (2003), the existence of this ideological abstraction, the 'standard language', is continuously reaffirmed through, in particular, codification rituals (the writing of grammars, dictionaries, textbooks) and pedagogical rituals (teaching it in schools). She concludes that 'these ritual practices are instrumental in creating the characteristic attitudes and beliefs of standard language speech communities, and contribute to the "normalization" of the ideological construction of standard languages' (Deumert 2003: 48).

The one nation–one language ideology

According to this ideology, language can be equated with territory, and the link between language and national identity is essential. It informs the eighteenth- and nineteenth-century discourse of modernity underlying the formation of the European nation-states which, in the words of Auer (2005: 406), is based upon the German philosopher Johann Gottfried von Herder's idea that each nation 'expresses its own character (*Volksgeist*) in and through its language'. Auer (2005: 406) argues that this is an essentialist ideology, 'since it assumes a "natural" (or perhaps God-given, *weltgeist*-derived) link between a nation and its language'.

If, on the other hand, we reconnect languages and language varieties with the speakers who actually use them, then we are faced with a potentially bewildering reality of linguistic heterogeneity and flux. For instance, as Pavlenko and Blackledge (2004: 17) point out, young people, as well as transnationals, frequently create their own hybrid communicative repertoires, located outside of the prescriptive norms of the standard language, thus configuring for themselves a '"**third space**" that enables the appearance of new and alternative identity options'. However, Auer (2005: 403) cautions that 'a rash equation of "hybrid" language use with "hybrid" social identity . . . may be as essentialist as that of nation and language which underlies traditional European language ideologies'.

Hence, the most convincing position may well be the intermediate one developed in May (2005). He argues that the link between language and (national) identity is a contingent one which, however, is very important to many speakers of the language: 'to say that language is not an inevitable feature of identity is thus not the same as saying it is unimportant' (May 2005: 330). Because it is so important to many people, they frequently develop negative attitudes towards hybrid linguistic varieties, as well as a more general fear of linguistic and cultural heterogeneity, which is perceived as a threat not only to the national language but also to the national identity. This is what Blommaert and Verschueren (1998: 362) refer to as the **dogma of homogeneism**, i.e. the view that the optimal societal structure is the one that is linguistically and culturally uniform or, in their own words, 'a view of society in which differences are seen as dangerous and centrifugal and in which the "best" society is suggested to be one without intergroup differences' (Blommaert and Verschueren 1992: 362). Underpinning this constellation, of course, is the Herderian belief in clearly definable cultures and languages that can be labelled and ranked.

The mother tongue ideology

In combination with the one nation–one language ideology, the belief that speakers have one and only one 'mother tongue' leads to such generalizations as (for instance) 'The mother tongue of the Luxembourgers is Luxembourgish', with all Luxembourgers being (erroneously) perceived as having only one mother tongue, which is or should be Luxembourgish (see example 3 in the activity above). In this connection, Deumert (2000: 395), building upon work by Skutnabb-Kangas and Phillipson (1989), wonders what the concept of 'mother tongue' could possibly refer to:

> Is your mother tongue the language(s) you learned first, the language(s) you know best or the language(s) you use most? Or does the concept of mother tongue transcend all these definitions based on origin, function and competence? Is it rather to be understood in terms of identity, that is, is your mother tongue the language you identify with?

Similarly, Holliday (2005) points to two major problems with the concept of 'native speaker': first, it leads to a negative view of non-native speakers as 'deficient' by comparison with the native speakers, and second, it assumes a norm of monolingualism in a world where the norm would rather seem to be the opposite, namely multilingualism.

For all these reasons, Leung, Harris and Rampton (1997: 555) argue that the concepts of 'native speaker' and 'mother tongue' lack explanatory adequacy and need to be broken down into three factors. They suggest

> replacing the terms native speaker and mother tongue with the notions of **language expertise**, **language inheritance** and **language affiliation** .... The term language expertise refers to how proficient people are in a language; language affiliation refers to the attachment or identification they feel for a language whether or not they nominally belong to the social group customarily associated with it; and language inheritance refers to the ways in which individuals can be born into a language tradition that is prominent within the family and community setting whether or not they claim expertise in or affiliation to that language.

Even defenders of the concept of mother tongue such as Skutnabb-Kangas and Phillipson (1989: 466), while arguing that such a concept is needed in the fight for linguistic human rights, acknowledge that it can be abused:

> Thus it may be important to differentiate between those groups, also in Europe, who because of their history are in a reactionary phase and whose emphasis on a strong identification with a language shows reactionary, nationalistic features, and those groups who are fighting for human rights for their mother tongues, as part of a more general fight for equity and justice, and for whom the mother tongue is one of the defining symbols because its oppression by the majority is so blatant.

Skutnabb-Kangas and Phillipson's (1989: 466) example illustrating the former case is the emphasis placed on the German mother tongue during the early years of the Nazi regime, as for instance reflected in the titles of many works written by supporting linguists/philologists at the time (e.g. *Liebe zur Muttersprache* ('Love of the mother tongue'), 1931; *Muttersprache im Selbsterhaltungskampf* ('Mother tongue in the fight for self-preservation'), 1932; *Volkstumskampf als Kampf der Muttersprache* ('The fight for nationhood as fight for the mother tongue'), 1936). Because of this historical legacy of the concept of mother tongue, other scholars reject it altogether. Thus Coulmas (1995: 122) calls it 'ein nationalistisch gefärbter Begriff' (a concept impregnated with nationalism), and links it to the even more problematic concept of 'race':

> Während die Rasse freilich durch die von ihren Apologeten herbeigeführte Katastrophe in der Öffentlichkeit nachhaltig diskreditiert wurde, ist uns die Muttersprache erhalten geblieben.
>
> (Coulmas 1995: 123)

> (Whereas 'race' has been thoroughly discredited due to the catastrophe engineered by its apologists, the concept of 'mother tongue' is still with us.)

The ideology of purism

Closely intertwined with the standard language, one nation–one language and mother tongue ideologies, this ideology has a powerful evaluative component, which stipulates what constitutes 'good' or 'proper' language. It is based on a denial of the linguistic 'fact of life' that language always changes, and also includes the belief that only some speakers of the language have an accent (in particular lower-class people or learners of the language as a foreign language; cf. Lippi-Green 1997).

Movements of linguistic purism tend to emerge at times of rapid social change and, depending on the situation, can target features perceived as 'non-standard' or as 'foreign'. According to Langer and Davies (2005: 5–6), it is important to distinguish

> between a purist's 'official' reason for stigmatizing a particular word or grammatical construction on the grounds that it is illogical or alien to the indigenous language, and her/his 'hidden' motivation, namely a general fear of foreign (cultural) elements or a concern that one's advanced culture might be in danger of decline due to the rise of the lower classes. Whether such a foreign invasion or general cultural decline is actually taking place is irrelevant – what matters is whether such things are *perceived* to be happening by influential members of society who will then use emotive factors and symbolic values to represent their concerns.

Horner (2005) provides a thorough account of purist ideologies in Luxembourg. She shows that it is not uncommon to come across statements expressing concern about Luxembourgish becoming an endangered language and that, in fact, there is a widespread fear of Luxembourgish dying out. She argues that this state of affairs cannot be attributed to competition from the increased use of the German language but rather from French (see the discussion of the Luxembourg language situation in Chapter 9). Yet much of the purist discourse targets so-called German lexical items. The purpose of this purist discourse is to establish a clear boundary between Luxembourgish and German, because as a language, rather than a Germanic dialect, Luxembourgish can be positioned as a valid competitor with French. Horner compares this situation to that of Corsican as described by Jaffe (1999: 132–5): indeed, Jaffe similarly argues that certain discourses construct Corsican as different from Italian, so that it is perceived as a language that can stand up against the hegemony of French.

CONCLUSION

In this chapter, we have seen that language ideologies are sets of socially shared beliefs about language, and we have listed some of the most widely held beliefs. They are in general ill-informed assumptions about language structure and language use, and we have discussed how they tend to simplify the complex linguistic reality. However, there is a need to remember that these beliefs do not exist 'out there', as it were; on the contrary, they exist in people's minds, in various degrees of specificity. All persons, whether linguists or not, hold certain beliefs about language, and it should be obvious that not everybody holds exactly the same beliefs. In any case, we have no direct access to people's minds and cannot study the beliefs as they exist in their minds. But what we can do as researchers is study the traces of these beliefs in the (both oral and written) texts that they produce. Language ideologies are emergent in talk about language; as Blackledge (2000: 26) puts it, they 'are constantly constructed and re-constructed in discursive interactions'.

Moreover, our analysis should not remain limited to the micro level of one individual's discourses, but also encompass the more macro level of the capital-D Discourses (in Gee's sense) about language that circulate in a particular society at a particular time. We are likely to find that certain language ideologies are deeply ingrained in our societies, but also that they interact in complex, often contradictory ways, and that they unfold differently in different socio-political contexts. It is therefore imperative to study each context in detail and in depth by means of an ethnographically based form of discourse analysis, as described earlier in this chapter.

We conclude with four key points to keep in mind that have arisen in this chapter:

- meaning is constructed in context;
- therefore any discourse-analytic approach is optimally complemented by an ethnographic study of the context;
- the aim of ethnographically based discourse analysis is to make as explicit as possible the discourse models (beliefs and assumptions) that inform particular texts;
- examples of such discourse models are the language ideologies which often shape the way we think about language (what a language is, how it works, how it is used).

ACTIVITY: THE LINK BETWEEN LANGUAGE AND NATIONAL IDENTITY

To some speakers the link between language and national identity is so important that it is not only essentialized but also leads to an invisibilization of all other linguistic repertoires. An example would be the following photo caption, which accompanies a newspaper article about Luxembourgish as an (allegedly) endangered language due to the rapid demographic changes and high levels of in-migration in the Grand-Duchy of Luxembourg. The text suggests that if Luxembourgish (the national language) were to die out, then Luxembourg would become 'language-less':

> Gëtt aus Lëtzebuerg a Land ouni Sprooch?
>
> (*Luxemburger Wort*, 20 February 2008, p. 15)
>
> (Will Luxembourg become a country without language?)

Analyse the language ideologies informing this text.

FOR DISCUSSION: LANGUAGE PURISM

It is important to make clear that language-ideological beliefs such as the fear of linguistic heterogeneity and ideologies of purism are not just ideas and attitudes about language, but that they also translate into social practices that can have serious consequences for whole groups of people. As Salman Rushdie (2003: 272) reminds us,

> Those who embrace difference are always in danger from the apostles of purity. Ideas of purity – racial purity, cultural purity, religious purity – lead directly to horrors: to the gas oven, to ethnic cleansing, to the rack.

And, of course, he could have added linguistic purity to his list, because public concerns about language usually are symptomatic of, or stand vicariously for, other social tensions.

Discuss Rushdie's argument and its implications.

FOR DISCUSSION: RACISM

Blommaert (2005) argues that the Flemish extreme right-wing party *Vlaams Blok* (renamed *Vlaams Belang* in 2004) subscribes to a cultural theory that could be seen as a form of Herderianism pushed to its extreme right-wing limits (see section above on the one nation–one language ideology for a discussion of Herder's ideas about language). Blommaert describes the world-view of the *Vlaams Blok* as follows:

> All cultures are equal; but all cultures function perfectly only within the confines of their historical region of origin. Transgression of cultural boundaries, for instance through migration or intermarriage,

> leads to the distortion of a natural order and therefore to conflicts. Consequently, there is no problem with the culture of the Turkish and Moroccan migrants in Belgium other than the sheer fact that they are in Belgium. Their culture is not inferior to that of the local majority, it is just not the culture that belongs in Belgium. This sophisticated line of argument allows the Vlaams Blok to avoid charges of racism (usually based on extremely narrow interpretations of racism as a theory of racial superiority).
>
> (Blommaert 2005: 199)

Discuss Blommaert's summary of the *Vlaams Blok*'s world-view in light of the following questions:

- How would you define racism?
- In what way or to what extent is the *Vlaams Blok*'s world-view racist?
- What are the links between racism and the one nation–one language ideology?

PROJECT WORK: ANALYSING DISCOURSE MODELS

Choose a country whose educational system you are not very familiar with. Collect some data, e.g. an interview with a teacher or a language-in-education policy document on the website of the Ministry of Education. Then try to identify the rich points in these texts and analyse the discourse models and language ideologies informing them.

REFERENCES AND SUGGESTIONS FOR FURTHER READING

Dominant vs. critical readings

Fetterley, Judith (1981) *The Resisting Reader: A Feminist Approach to American Fiction*, Bloomington, IN: Indiana University Press.

Montgomery, Martin, Durant, Alan, Fabb, Nigel, Furniss, Tom and Mills, Sara (2013) *Ways of Reading*, 4th edition, London: Routledge.

Ethnographically based discourse analysis

Agar, Michael (2006) 'Ethnography', in J.O. Ostman and J. Verschueren (eds) *Handbook of Pragmatics*, Amsterdam: Benjamins, 1–14.

Blommaert, Jan (2005) *Discourse: A Critical Introduction*, Cambridge: Cambridge University Press.

—— and Dong, Jie (2010) *Ethnographic Fieldwork: A Beginner's Guide*, Bristol: Multilingual Matters.

Bucholtz, Mary (2001) 'Reflexivity and critique in discourse analysis', *Critique of Anthropology*, 21: 165–83.

Coupland, Fiona, Shaw, Sara and Snell, Julia (eds) (2015) *Linguistic Ethnography: Interdisciplinary Explorations*, Basingstoke: Palgrave.

Fairclough, Norman (1989) *Language and Power*, Harlow: Longman.

Gee, James Paul (2005) *An Introduction to Discourse Analysis: Theory and Method*, London: Routledge.

—— (2010) *How to Do Discourse Analysis: A Toolkit*, London: Routledge.

Geertz, Clifford (1973) *The Interpretation of Cultures: Selected Essays*, New York: Basic Books.

Johnson-Laird, Philip N. (1983) *Mental Models*, Cambridge: Cambridge University Press.

Martin-Jones, Marilyn and Martin, Deirdre (2017) *Researching Multilingualism: Critical and Ethnographic Approaches*, London: Routledge.

Language ideologies

Blackledge, Adrian (2000) 'Monolingual ideologies in multilingual states: Language, hegemony and social justice in Western liberal democracies', *Estudios de Sociolinguistica*, 1: 25–45.

Blommaert, Jan (1996) 'Language planning as a discourse on language and society: The linguistic ideology of a scholarly tradition', *Language Problems and Language Planning*, 20: 199–222.

Irvine, Judith T. (1989) 'When talk isn't cheap: Language and political economy', *American Ethnologist*, 16: 248–67.

Kroskrity, Paul V. (2006) 'Language ideologies', in A. Duranti (ed.) *A Companion to Linguistic Anthropology*, Oxford: Blackwell, 496–517.

Mar-Molinero, Clare and Stevenson, Patrick (eds) (2006) *Language Ideologies, Policies and Practices*, Basingstoke: Palgrave.

The standard language ideology

Deumert, Ana (2003) 'Standard languages as civic rituals: Theory and examples', *Sociolinguistica*, 17: 31–51.

Milroy, James and Milroy, Lesley (1999) *Authority in Language: Investigating Language Prescription and Standardization*, London: Routledge.

Ricento, Thomas (2006) 'Topical areas in language policy: An overview', in *An Introduction to Language Policy: Theory and Method*, Oxford: Blackwell, 231–7.

The one nation–one language ideology

Auer, Peter (2005) 'A postscript: Code-switching and social identity', *Journal of Pragmatics*, 37: 403–10.

Blommaert, Jan and Verschueren, Jef (1992) 'The role of language in European nationalist ideologies', *Pragmatics*, 2: 355–75.

—— (1998) *Debating Diversity: Analysing the Discourse of Tolerance*, London: Routledge.

May, Stephen (2005) 'Language rights: Moving the debate forward', *Journal of Sociolinguistics*, 9: 319–47.

Pavlenko, Aneta and Blackledge, Adrian (eds) (2004) *Negotiation of Identities in Multilingual Contexts*, Clevedon: Multilingual Matters.

The mother tongue ideology

Coulmas, Florian (1995) 'Muttersprache: Auf Gedeih und Verderb?', *Merkur*, 49: 120–30.

Deumert, Ana (2000) 'Language planning and policy', in R. Mesthrie, J. Swann, A. Deumert and W.L. Leap (eds) *Introducing Sociolinguistics*, Edinburgh: Edinburgh University Press, 384–418.

Holliday, Adrian (2005) *The Struggle to Teach English as an International Language*, Oxford: Oxford University Press.

Leung, Constant, Harris, Roxy and Rampton, Ben (1997) 'The idealised native speaker, reified ethnicities, and classroom realities', *TESOL Quarterly*, 31: 543–60.

Skutnabb-Kangas, Tove and Phillipson, Robert (1989) '"Mother Tongue": The theoretical and sociopolitical construction of a concept', in U. Ammon (ed.) *Status and Function of Languages and Language Varieties*, Berlin: Mouton de Gruyter, 450–77.

The ideology of purism

Cameron, Deborah (1995) *Verbal Hygiene*, London: Routledge.

Horner, Kristine (2005) 'Reimagining the nation: Discourses of language purism in Luxembourg', in N. Langer and W.V. Davies (eds) *Linguistic Purism in the Germanic Languages*, Berlin: Mouton de Gruyter, 166–85.

Jaffe, Alexandra (1999) *Ideologies in Action: Language Politics on Corsica*, Berlin: Mouton de Gruyter.

Langer, Nils and Davies, Winifred V. (2005) 'An introduction to linguistic purism', in N. Langer and W.V. Davies (eds) *Linguistic Purism in the Germanic Languages*, Berlin: Mouton de Gruyter, 1–17.

Lippi-Green, Rosina (1997) *English with an Accent: Language, Ideology, and Discrimination in the United States*, London: Routledge.

Rushdie, Salman (2003) *Step Across this Line: Collected Non-Fiction 1992–2002*, London: Vintage.

TEST YOURSELF QUIZ PART I*

1. Explain the idea that meaning is constructed by the reader/hearer. Use an example of your own to illustrate this.
2. Explain and discuss the distinction between dominant and critical readings in relation to an example of your own.
3. What, in your eyes, is the essence of the ethnographic approach?
4. Explain Gee's distinction between small-d discourses and big-D Discourses.
5. Critically discuss one or two language ideologies and show how it/they involve/s a simplification of the linguistic reality.
6. Discuss the quotation from Blommaert (1996) on page 21 of the textbook.
7. Discuss the quotation from May (2005) on page 23 of the textbook.
8. Discuss your own sense of linguistic identity in relation to the concepts of language expertise, language affiliation and language inheritance.
9. Do you agree with Langer and Davies that purist ideologies are motivated by 'a general fear of foreign (cultural) elements or a concern that one's advanced culture might be in danger of decline due to the rise of the lower classes'? Why or why not?
10. Which of the language ideologies discussed in this chapter do you find particularly problematic and why?

*Suggested answers can be found on page 294.

PART II

Multilingualism within and across languages

CHAPTER 3

What is a language?

DISCOURSE MODELS OF LANGUAGE

In this chapter, we look in more detail at people's beliefs or ideologies about language (in Gee's terminology, their discourse models of language). There are two competing models of what a language is, one of which could be referred to as the 'popular' model and the other as a more 'expert' model. The popular model differentiates between 'languages' and 'dialects', and postulates a hierarchical relation between them. An evaluative dimension is tagged on to this hierarchy, with languages being perceived as better than or superior to dialects. Moreover, a 'language' tends to be automatically identified with the standard (version of the) language, as described in grammars and dictionaries.

Most of these beliefs and assumptions are rejected in the expert model, which is shared by many linguists and especially sociolinguists. According to this model, there is no purely linguistic difference between languages and dialects, and hence it would be preferable to refer to them all as linguistic 'resources' or 'varieties'. Furthermore, in linguistic terms no variety is 'better' than any other variety, and the standard variety is just one variety among many others. It is important to point out that a critical awareness is needed to keep this in mind, otherwise it is easy – also for linguists, as we will see later in this chapter – to fall back into the popular model.

Let us illustrate the expert model of language with reference to English. There are a huge number of varieties of English in the world and each 'x' in the diagram below represents one of these varieties (note that the diagram is merely indicative and the number of varieties of English outnumbers the 'x's by far):

xxxxxxxxxxxxxxxxxxxxxxxx
xxxxxxxxxxxxxxxxxxxxxxxxxx
xxxxxxxxxxxxxxxxxxxxxxxxx
xxxxxxxxxxxxxxxxxxxxxxxxxxxx
xxxxxxxxxxxxxxxxxxxxxxxx

ACTIVITY: WHAT IS ENGLISH?

Try to fill in the diagram with the names of as many varieties of English as possible (names of regional and geographical varieties, social class varieties, historical varieties, etc.).

You could do this in small teams, and the team that comes up with the highest number is the winner.

Note on the activity

Whatever names you filled in, it is important to remember that each of these varieties is not a monolithic entity but consists in turn of many 'x's which stand for regional, social or historical subvarieties. For instance, Caribbean English could be subdivided into Jamaican English, Trinidadian English, Barbadian English, etc., each of which could of course be further subdivided along regional, time or social class dimensions.

WHAT IS STANDARD ENGLISH?

In a well-known article, Trudgill (1999) shows what standard English is by going through a long list of what it is *not*. Above all, standard English is *not* a language. Trudgill argues that it is *less* than a language, in the sense that it is only one variety among many (only one 'x' in the above diagram). It is the variety normally used in writing and taught to non-native learners, but most native speakers of English are native speakers of other (non-standard) varieties.

Trudgill also argues that standard English is not (just) an accent, since varieties differ from each other not only in pronunciation but also in their vocabulary and grammar. Nor is it a style, since the full range of styles – from formal to informal – is available in standard English:

> Father was exceedingly tired subsequent to his extensive peregrination.
> Dad was very tired after his lengthy journey.
> The old man was bloody knackered after his long trip.
>
> (Trudgill 1999: 120)

All three sentences are in standard English, whereas the following sentences are in a non-standard variety (in this case, a Northern England variety of English):

> Father *were* exceedingly tired subsequent to his extensive peregrination.
> Dad *were* very tired after his lengthy journey.
> The old man *were* bloody knackered after his long trip.

So what *is* standard English? As has already been suggested above, standard English is not the whole language but only one of the 'x's in our diagram above. It is a variety of English, though it is usually considered the most important one from a social and cultural point of view, and it differs from other varieties not just in terms of accent or vocabulary but also by its grammatical forms. In other words, each variety of English has its own systematic grammar, though there will be large overlaps between these grammatical systems.

'ENGLISH' IS A MERE LABEL

If standard English is just one 'x' in the above diagram, then what is English? The English language is of course the collection of all the 'x's, all the varieties of English that exist in the world. And we regroup these varieties under a common label: English. In this way, languages are socially and ideologically constructed: the language name (English, Hindi, Swahili, etc.) is the label, behind which there is the range of varieties that are actually used by people. These varieties tend to exist on **linguistic continua**, with no clear boundaries between them, such that the varieties leak into each other. In Western Europe, for instance, there are the Romance continuum and the Germanic continuum. The latter includes such varieties as German, Alsatian, Luxembourgish, Flemish, Dutch, Frisian, English and many others. But the boundaries between these varieties or languages are unclear and fuzzy. Hence we should perhaps say that what really exists is the linguistic continua. Some scholars make a distinction here between 'language' and 'a language': thus Jørgensen (2008) argues that what we learn in childhood is 'language', and separately, as it were, we discover that the linguistic features we are learning are conventionally associated with a particular named language (e.g. English).

THE FUZZY BOUNDARIES OF NAMED LANGUAGES

Let us look at some examples taken from the Germanic linguistic continuum to illustrate the fuzzy nature of the boundaries between named languages or varieties. In the previous chapter, we reproduced a quotation by Gee in which he argues that from a linguistic point of view there is no clear boundary between Dutch and German. From a historical perspective, it is also interesting to remember that when the Germanic tribes first landed in England, their language turned from Frisian or other Germanic varieties into (Old) English, seemingly by magic! It is of course not the case that their varieties shifted overnight, but it is the political matter of how we nowadays label varieties used in the past. A further example is the shifting boundary between Luxembourgish and German: whereas in the nineteenth century Luxembourgers tended to refer to their varieties as 'our German' or 'Luxembourgish German', they now tend to perceive Luxembourgish more and more as a wholly separate language from German – in line with the 1984 language law which officially recognizes Luxembourgish as the 'national language' of Luxembourg. We can conclude that the boundaries between languages on a linguistic continuum are drawn in relation to socio-political rather than (purely) linguistic factors, and that in this sense languages are social constructs. Consequently, the development of separate languages and of their standard varieties is closely linked to the politics of state-making (see discussion of the one nation–one language ideology in Chapter 2).

Scots and Ulster-Scots: 'dialects' or 'languages'?

Scotland is institutionally bilingual in Scots and Gaelic. Scots English forms a continuum from Broad Scots (which itself consists of a large number of social and regional varieties) to standard Scottish English. The question of whether Scots is a 'language' or a 'dialect' of English is hotly debated in Scotland. As we have seen, this distinction does not really make sense in linguistic terms, but the reason that the question is debated in relation to Scots English and not in relation to, for example, Northumbrian or Yorkshire English is of course a political one. It is connected with the fact that Scotland used to be an independent kingdom, that it has a certain degree of political autonomy with its own Parliament in Edinburgh and that a referendum on the question of Scotland's sovereignty was held on 18 September 2014 (which, however, did not go through).

Thus for instance, in an article published in the *Guardian* in 2011, Brian Logan raises the question of whether Scots might become the official or national language of an independent Scotland in the not so distant future. He mentions that, when Members of the Scottish Parliament were sworn in at Holyrood, several of them took an oath to the Queen – but in Scots: 'I depone aat I wull be leal and bear aefauld alleadgance tae her majesty, her airs an ony fa come aifter her anent the laa' (*Guardian*, 20 May 2011, Part 2, page 9). He also argues that Scots will increasingly be constructed as a language separate from English as part of the movement towards independence: 'Scotland won't be the first country to emphasize (exaggerate?) its linguistic separateness as a precursor to independence' (*Guardian*, 20 May 2011, Part 2, page 9). The addition of 'exaggerate' with a question mark and between brackets suggests that 'really' (in the eyes of the journalist, or of many of his readers) Scots is just a 'dialect' of English, thus pitting the hegemonic English ideology against the ideology of Scottish (linguistic) independence.

As for Northern Ireland (Ulster), it is politically divided between Irish nationalists (often Catholic) who favour reunification with (the Republic of) Ireland and Unionists (often Protestant) who would rather keep the union with Britain. The nationalists speak a variety of English but also identify with Irish Gaelic. The variety of English spoken by the Unionists is usually referred to as Ulster-Scots, since many of them are descendants of immigrants who moved from Scotland to (Northern) Ireland. In the last few decades, Ulster-Scots has shown a development from 'dialect' to 'language' very similar to that of Scots in Scotland. Ulster-Scots was promoted by the Ulster Unionists in an attempt to set up a distinctive Ulster identity as separate from an Irish identity. The Ulster-Scots Language Society, founded in 1992, relied on a discourse of endangerment to strengthen the position of Ulster-Scots as a language. As Crowley (2007: 166) puts it,

> Ulster-Scots, a fully fledged but endangered language, gave the Unionist community precisely what the Irish language gave the nationalist community: a medium through which identity-claims and demands for civil rights could be articulated.

He concludes his discussion of the political uses of discourses of language endangerment in Northern Ireland by saying that 'given that language lies at the core of our social being, the real surprise would be if the discourses used to defend languages were not in essence a matter of politics and history' (Crowley 2007: 167).

English pidgins and creoles

The spread of English as a global language has led to the creation of numerous new varieties all over the world. Most of these World Englishes are 'hybrid' varieties mixing English with local languages. All varieties (including standard English) are of course hybrid to some extent, but varieties with a high degree of hybridity are usually referred to as **pidgins** and **creoles**. Pidgins and creoles originate in language contact situations, where speakers of different languages used a simple lingua franca for restricted communicative purposes such as trade, which later developed into a full language.

Linguists refer to these lingua francas used for limited communicative purposes as 'pidgins', and as 'creoles' once they are used as native languages by at least some of their speakers.

One widely studied creole language is Tok Pisin ('talk pidgin'), used in Papua New Guinea, an island in the south-west Pacific. It started off as a lingua franca between indentured New Guineans and their colonial masters, while they were working on plantations in Australia and elsewhere. From the mid-twentieth century onwards, Tok Pisin has begun to be perceived as a language in its own right, distinct from English. In fact, the name 'Tok Pisin' was officially adopted by Papua New Guinea in 1981, shortly after independence in 1975. Tok Pisin has now become one of the officially recognized languages of Papua New Guinea (alongside English and Hiri Motu, another creole language).

Mostly for these political reasons, Tok Pisin would not be included as an 'x' under the label 'English' but should itself be a label, separate from English. But what about all the other pidgins and creoles which are not officially recognized languages in their countries? Should Nigerian Pidgin, Cameroon Pidgin and many other such varieties be included as 'x's under English? Pennycook (2007: 107) notes that these pidgins and creoles tend to be excluded in discussions of World Englishes, because they are too hybrid and too dynamic to fit nicely into any systematic framework:

> Creole languages have to be excluded from World Englishes, therefore, since they perforce destabilize the very definitions of language and grammar that underlie this version of a global language.

For Pennycook, the important question is not whether these pidgin and creole languages should or should not be included as World Englishes, since this is a largely political matter in any case. His point is a critique of the World Englishes framework: if pidgins and creoles were included, then linguists would no longer be 'dealing with a language held in place by a core structure' (Pennycook 2007: 109). This notion of a 'core structure' is the last linguistic criterion that some traditional linguists (i.e. those subscribing to the popular model of language) hold on to in a vain endeavour to define what a language is. Without that, nothing would be left except the political dimension or, as Pennycook (2007: 109) puts it, 'a notion of language status that is not definable by interior criteria'.

Moving beyond English

What has been said so far does not just apply to a global language such as English but applies to all languages, however big or small. Languages – or rather varieties – exist on linguistic continua, and in many situations it makes little sense to distinguish between separate languages. Here is an example of a linguist writing about the languages of India:

> Classifying and labelling languages in India has proved to be a source of controversy. Part of the reason for this is that, especially among the Indo-Aryan languages, one language tends to fade into a related one with no clear break between them.
>
> (Fasold 1993: 22)

One of the examples Fasold gives is the relation between Hindi and Urdu. The two languages basically share the same grammatical system (what Pennycook calls 'a core structure'), but they have a different writing script (Nastaliq script for Urdu and Devanagari for Hindi). Hence, there is a clear distinction in written texts, whereas in spoken interactions 'the two merge into one' (Fasold 1993: 22). In fact, as we already saw in the quiz in Chapter 1, it was this vernacular mix of Hindi and Urdu that Gandhi wanted to promote under the name of 'Hindustani' as the common language that could unite Indian people. However, his proposal was rejected by Hindu nationalists who promoted instead a more 'pure' version of Hindi as one of India's official languages, thus attempting to distance Hindi from Urdu, the language associated with Pakistan.

A similar fluidity can be found in many African countries and in most other multilingual parts of the world such as Papua New Guinea. After her discussion of the language situation in Papua New Guinea, Romaine (1994: 12) concludes as follows:

> The very concept of discrete languages is probably a European cultural artefact fostered by procedures such as literacy and standardization. Any attempt to count distinct languages will be an artefact of classificatory procedures rather than a reflection of communicative practices.

As for the naming of languages, it has probably also been influenced by European (colonial) practices: indeed, many speakers in other parts of the world do not have specific names for the linguistic resources they use but simply refer to them as 'our language'.

From 'language' to 'dialect'

Just as linguistic varieties can be promoted from 'dialect' to 'language', they can also be demoted from 'language' to 'dialect' for socio-political reasons. In England, it was the 'dialect' spoken by the upper classes in the southeast of the country (the centre of political power roughly linking London to the universities of Oxford and Cambridge) which developed into what came to be looked upon as the standard 'language'. Similar political developments led to the Florentine variety becoming the national 'language' of a newly unified Italy. However, the language situation of Italy is different from that of England, in that the varieties spoken there are not varieties of Italian but, in the words of Tosi (2004: 258), 'separate and distinct Romance vernaculars, which developed from Latin, at the same time as Florentine'. These languages include northern Romance vernaculars such as Piedmontese, Ligurian, Lombard, Emilian, Venetian, as well as southern ones such as Abruzzese, Neapolitan, Pugliese, Calabrese and Sicilian. But with political unification in 1861, Florentine became the national language and the regional languages were 'officially demoted to the status of "dialects"' (Tosi 2004: 259). As a result, many Italians nowadays are at least bilingual in Italian and their 'dialect' or, more accurately, they have a complex multilingual repertoire stretching on a continuum from the local 'dialect' to the national 'language', with a wide range of less local, more regional 'dialect' forms and less national, more regional Italian forms in between (Tosi 2004: 281).

CONSEQUENCES FOR TEACHING

In the remaining sections of this chapter, we consider the consequences of this new (or alternative) understanding of what a language is, first for language teaching and second for research on multilingualism. Imagine you are a teacher of English: would you mark the following sentences as correct or incorrect?

a) I'm after eating my lunch.
b) I ain't got no money.
c) The teacher used a chalk.

All three are 'incorrect' in standard British English, but 'correct' in other, vernacular varieties of English: a) in Irish English, b) in African-American English (AAE) and c) in Indian English.

This implies that we need to be aware that when we buy a 'grammar of English', it is not a grammar of all the varieties of English but of only one of these varieties. In fact, such books should be called 'A Grammar of Standard English'. Furthermore, grammars contribute to the fixing of a language, but spoken language is something living that ultimately cannot be fixed. In McWhorter's (1998: 18) beautiful metaphor, language is like a lava lamp. Only languages such as Latin do not change much any longer. Thus there will always be variation along the dimensions of both space and time (this is the topic of the following chapter) with, moreover, different forms appropriate in different situations. However, schools tend not to be concerned with linguistic variation and situational appropriateness, but only with an absolute notion of correctness (as defined by the prescriptive grammar or textbook). School teachers often rely on this notion of correctness in their teaching and, especially, in tests. Hence, forms actually used by thousands or millions of native speakers of English are frequently marked as 'incorrect' in foreign language classroom situations!

It is therefore of the utmost importance to introduce courses on the dynamic nature of language, as well as on issues of linguistic diversity and language discrimination in all teacher training programmes. Such **'language variation' awareness programmes** are necessary to dispel the myth that 'dialects' lack grammatical rules or are inferior versions of the standard variety. Schools need to adopt an 'additive' bilingual or bidialectal approach, both encouraging students to maintain their vernacular home varieties and helping them to achieve a high level of proficiency in standard English. They need to understand that these are not exclusive choices but that, on the contrary, the best way of reaching the latter aim is via the former.

CONSEQUENCES FOR RESEARCH

L1, L2, L3, etc.

What is the study of multilingualism? Some researchers distinguish between L1, L2, L3, etc., as if there were clear distinctions between the different languages – an assumption that we have questioned in this chapter. They sometimes study purported differences between the language acquisition of bilinguals, trilinguals, quadrilinguals, pentalinguals, etc., seemingly unaware that these categories are in need of being problematized: what counts as a separate language? How do mixed codes count?

In this book, we take a more holistic view of speakers' communicative repertoires. Most speakers in the world have a repertoire of varieties at their disposal, and hence are multilingual, whether these varieties are traditionally included within the same 'language' or under separate 'languages' – as we have seen, this is primarily a socio-political distinction. From a linguistic point of view, there is no real difference between **inter-language variation** (where the boundaries between languages are drawn) and **intra-language variation** (where the boundaries are drawn between standard and vernacular varieties of a 'language').

It is important to realize that these matters are not purely theoretical but can have serious social consequences. For instance, the continuing dominance of essentializing assumptions and ideologies informs the view of migrant children as having one and only one L1 (their 'mother tongue') and can lead to the establishment of mother tongue education programmes that sometimes do more harm than good (see discussion in Chapter 10). What should be clear is that, for a form of mother tongue education to be successful, it needs to be based on the children's *actual* communicative repertoires.

For this reason, it is important to be aware of the problematic nature of such concepts as 'language', and of such terms as L1, L2, L3, etc. Otsuji and Pennycook (2010) even argue that the term 'multilingualism' is problematic, too, because of an underlying assumption that people's linguistic practices are composed of a number of discrete languages, with fixed boundaries between them. As an alternative, they suggest '**metrolingualism**', which focuses 'not on language systems but on languages as emergent from contexts of interaction' (Otsuji and Pennycook 2010: 246). They have adapted the term from Maher's (2005) concept of 'metroethnicity', which indexes (or points to) emergent forms of 'street' ethnicity, just as metrolingualism orients towards the emergence of new languages and language identities, primarily though not exclusively in metropolitan or urban spaces.

While we are highly sympathetic to Otsuji and Pennycook's argument, this does not mean that we cannot use such terms as 'multilingualism' or 'language' any longer. As we have already argued in Chapter 1, we can hardly do without such basic terms, though we need to carefully consider how we use them and be aware of the possible implications. Therefore, we will continue to use them in this book and even continue to use L1, L2 and L3, but only in connection with education systems that differentiate strictly between which 'language' is taught as L1, which one as L2, etc.

Language death

There have been a lot of sensational news reports recently about how many languages in the world are **endangered** or dying, spread by such agencies as UNESCO and reproduced by journalists. Phillipson (1992) has pointed to English as the main culprit for this, referring to it as the 'killer language'. In this way, the topics of **language shift** vs. **language maintenance** have become highly emotional ones, with languages being anthropomorphically referred to as dying or being killed by other languages. In a critical review, Block (2008) shows how prominently such metaphors of language loss and death figure in discourses. However, these metaphors presuppose the existence of distinct languages – an assumption that has been challenged in this chapter. If it is true that, as Pennycook (2004: 231) argues, languages are not 'fixed, static systems' but 'open systems' which are constantly shifting and changing, then language shift becomes a much more normal process and the whole notion of **language death** needs to be relativized. It also suggests that those who attempt to preserve one (traditional) form of linguistic diversity may not be ready to acknowledge other, newly emerging forms of linguistic diversity (such as the new mixed urban youth languages discussed in the following chapter).

In this book, we are critical of acts of linguistic purism that attempt to 'fix' a language in its authentic or pristine state and of purists who then complain that *their* (imagined) version of the language is endangered. Overall, we are much more concerned with people than with languages: after all, if languages are endangered, it is most often because the speakers of these languages are oppressed. There may therefore be a need to search for more appropriate metaphors than language death or loss to account for the dynamic patterns of development of languages. While Chapter 4 explores the dynamics of language change and variation with a special focus on youth languages, Chapter 5 discusses in much greater detail the topics of language endangerment and revitalization.

ACTIVITY: WHICH OF THESE DO YOU AGREE WITH?

a) Languages are not bounded entities (entities with clearly defined boundaries).
b) Languages are not internally homogeneous.
c) A standard language is a dialect.
d) There is a socio-political, not linguistic hierarchy on which 'dialects' are lower than 'languages'.

CONCLUSION

In this chapter, we have distinguished between two conceptions of 'language': on the one hand, named languages (e.g. English) as concepts at a socio-political, ideological level and, on the other hand, language as social action and practice. As part of this discussion, we have provided evidence in support of the statements included in the Activity 'Which of these do you agree with?':

> a + b) languages or varieties are not bounded entities, nor are they internally homogeneous. Where the lines are drawn between the 'x's (in our diagram) to separate one variety from another on a linguistic continuum is rather arbitrary from a linguistic point of view and can change because of changing socio-political developments.
>
> c + d) the standard language is just one of the 'x's. Hence, the standard language is a 'dialect' (though the term 'variety' would be preferable). However, for socio-political reasons, it is usually valued more highly than the other 'dialects' and even (erroneously) identified with the 'language' as a whole.

In the final sections of this chapter, we have discussed some important consequences for language teaching and research of this alternative understanding of what a 'language' is.

ACTIVITY: CREOLE LANGUAGES AND FUZZY BOUNDARIES

Could the creole languages below be looked upon as belonging to English or not? Compare these languages with (some of) the varieties of English discussed in this chapter and the following one.

a) Gullah, a creole language spoken along the coast of South Carolina and Georgia:
   Dem chillun gwine gone dey.
   (Those children are going to go there.)
b) Hawai'i Creole English:
   Da baby wen cry.
   (The baby cried; wen, went = past tense marker)
c) Cameroon Pidgin:
   If you no wan for register he lefam.
   (If you don't want to register him, let [me] know.)

FOR DISCUSSION: CLASSROOM LEARNING

Kamberelis (2001: 87) describes the process of classroom learning as one in which students 'make new and unfamiliar discourses their own by reaccenting them and integrating them with discourses from more familiar domains such as everyday life and public media'.

- To what extent do you agree with Kamberelis?
- How can teachers improve their students' proficiency in the standard variety by building upon their vernacular varieties?

PROJECT WORK: PIDGINS AND CREOLES

In what ways are pidgins and creoles similar to, or different from, other languages? Focus in detail on one widely used language such as Cameroon Pidgin, Nigerian Pidgin or Hawai'i Creole English. Consider both form and functions, as well as the historical development of the language. A good place to get started would be Sebba (1997) or Singh (2000). Prepare a presentation for the other students in your class.

PROJECT WORK: THE LANGUAGE SITUATION IN PAPUA NEW GUINEA

Find out as much as you can about the language situation in Papua New Guinea, which has been claimed to be the most multilingual country in the world. A good place to get started would be Romaine (1992 and 1994) or Kulick (1992). Prepare a presentation for the other students in your class.

PROJECT WORK: TEACHING TOLERANCE

In the section 'Consequences for teaching', we mentioned the importance of 'language variation' awareness programmes for teachers. One such example is the Teaching Tolerance project set up by Walt Wolfram, a professor of linguistics at North Carolina State University, together with the Southern Poverty Law Center. Its primary goal is to work towards more inclusive and equitable forms of education.

Explore the Teaching Tolerance website (www.tolerance.org/author/walt-wolfram) and comment in particular on Wolfram's text 'Everyone has an accent' (www.tolerance.org/magazine/number-18-fall-2000/everyone-has-accent). Present your findings and recommendations for good teaching practice to the other students in your class.

REFERENCES AND SUGGESTIONS FOR FURTHER READING

What is a language?

Crowley, Tony (2007) 'Language endangerment, war and peace in Ireland and Northern Ireland', in A. Duchêne and M. Heller (eds) *Discourses of Endangerment: Ideology and Interest in the Defence of Languages*, London: Continuum, 149–68.

Fasold, Ralph (1993) *The Sociolinguistics of Society*, Oxford: Blackwell.

The Guardian (20 May 2011) Brian Logan, 'The return of Scots: The language of independence', Part 2, p. 9.

Jørgensen, J. Normann (2008) *Languaging: Nine Years of Poly-Lingual Development of Young Turkish-Danish Grade School Students*, Vol. 1, Copenhagen: University of Copenhagen.

Kulick, Don (1992) *Language Shift and Cultural Reproduction: Socialization, Self, and Syncretism in a Papua New Guinea Village*, Cambridge: Cambridge University Press.

McWhorter, John (2001) *The Power of Babel: A Natural History of Language*, London: William Heinemann.

Makoni, Sinfree and Pennycook, Alastair (eds) (2007) *Disinventing and Reconstituting Languages*, Clevedon: Multilingual Matters.

Pennycook, Alastair (2007) 'The myth of English as an international language', in S. Makoni and A. Pennycook (eds) *Disinventing and Reconstituting Languages*, Clevedon: Multilingual Matters, 90–115.

Romaine, Suzanne (1992) *Language, Education, and Development: Urban and Rural Tok Pisin in Papua New Guinea*, Oxford: Oxford University Press.

—— (1994) *Language in Society: An Introduction to Sociolinguistics*, Oxford: Oxford University Press.

Sebba, Mark (1997) *Contact Languages: Pidgins and Creoles*, Basingstoke: Palgrave.

Singh, Ishtla (2000) *Pidgins and Creoles: An Introduction*, London: Hodder Arnold.

Tosi, Arturo (2004) 'The language situation in Italy', *Current Issues in Language Planning*, 5: 247–335.

Trudgill, Peter (1999) 'Standard English: What it isn't', in T. Bex and R.J. Watts (eds) *Standard English: The Widening Debate*, London: Routledge, 117–28.

Unger, Johann W. (2013) *The Discursive Construction of the Scots Language: Education, Politics and Everyday Life*, Amsterdam: Benjamins.

Consequences for teaching and research

Block, David (2008) 'On the appropriateness of the metaphor of LOSS', in P. Tan and R. Rubdy (eds) *Language as Commodity: Global Structures, Local Marketplaces*, London: Continuum, 187–203.

Cameron, Deborah (2007) 'Language endangerment and verbal hygiene: History, morality and politics', in A. Duchêne and M. Heller (eds) *Discourses of Endangerment*, London: Continuum, 268–85.

Kamberelis, George (2001) 'Producing heteroglossic classroom (micro) cultures through hybrid discourse practice', *Linguistics and Education*, 12: 85–125.

Lippi-Green, Rosina (1997) *English with an Accent: Language, Ideology, and Discrimination in the United States*, London: Routledge.

McWhorter, John (1998) *The Word on the Street: Fact and Fable about American English*, New York: Plenum.

Maher, John C. (2005) 'Metroethnicity, language, and the principle of Cool', *International Journal of the Sociology of Language*, 11: 83–102.

Otsuji, Emi and Pennycook, Alastair (2010) 'Metrolingualism: Fixity, fluidity and language in flux', *International Journal of Multilingualism*, 7: 240–54.

Pennycook, Alastair (2004) 'Language policy and the ecological turn', *Language Policy*, 3: 213–39.

Phillipson, Robert (1992) *Linguistic Imperialism*, Oxford: Oxford University Press.

CHAPTER 4

Language variation and the spread of global languages

While the previous chapter looked (among other things) at the unstable and shifting boundaries of languages (i.e. how languages leak into each other), the present chapter focuses more on variation and leakage within a language. It should be clear from our discussion in the previous chapter that there is a continuum between these two types of variation, and that all these variation types feed into multilingualism. The previous chapter focused on (named) languages as social constructs and the present one focuses on variation in time and space, mostly in English but also in French. Moreover, what the two chapters have in common is the insidious workings of the standard language ideology: just as it distorts many people's perception of what a language is, it is also responsible for their positioning of the standard variety above non-standard varieties.

Linguistic variation is inherent to all languages or varieties. In this chapter, we have chosen to illustrate it with reference to global languages such as English and French. However, this should not give the (false) impression that variation is a modern phenomenon related to postcolonialism and globalization. On the contrary, variation has always existed in all languages, however small they are. It is just that this particular focus allows us to explore different ways of conceptualizing the global spread of English, and how it has led to the development of new varieties such as Singlish (Singapore English). Similar developments have occurred with French, and our examples here are Nouchi, a hybrid urban language of Côte d'Ivoire, and Verlan, a youth language spoken in the *banlieues* (poor suburbs) of French cities. But first we start with brief examples from African-American English and Caribbean Creole to show that these languages are as systematic and rule-governed as standard English, and moreover they can enjoy high literary prestige.

ACTIVITY: LINGUISTIC VARIABLES*

Linguistic variation is ubiquitous and can occur at any level of a language. A linguistic variable can be defined as two or more ways of saying more or less the same thing, often with each variant correlating with stylistic (formal vs. informal), social (age, gender, social class, ethnic group) or geographical factors. If you are familiar with different linguistic levels (e.g. phonological, morphological, syntactic, lexical) and with the languages used in the examples below, you could try to identify the linguistic variables and the level at which variation occurs:

(a) You go to Leeds and Castleford, they take it so much more seriously. They really are, they take it so serious.
(from Tagliamonte 2006: 10)

(b) Ich komme nicht wegen des Wetters.
Ich komme nicht wegen dem Wetter.
(German; 'I'm not coming because of the weather.')

(c) Qué ha pasado?
Que pasó?
(Spanish; 'What has happened?/What happened?')

Can you think of more examples of linguistic variables in the languages that you know?

*Brief comments on this Activity can be found on page 289.

AFRICAN-AMERICAN ENGLISH

African-American English (AAE) is the variety spoken predominantly in the black community in the US and popularized all over the world through the urban black youth culture of rap and hip hop (see also Chapter 10). AAE is characterized by systematic grammatical features such as invariant or habitual *be* and double or multiple negation. Here is an example of each construction:

She be playing football.
I ain't got no money.

Invariant *be* marks habitual grammatical aspect, denoting that something happens repeatedly or regularly. As for double negation, it is frequently attacked by language purists with the claim that, as in mathematics, two negative words cancel each other out, and hence from a logical or mathematical point of view this sentence should mean that the speaker has some money. But of course such an argument is wholly erroneous: what makes sense in mathematics does not necessarily make sense in language. Indeed, to bring out the full absurdity of this position, we can simply compare English with another language such as French. In French, double negation is looked upon as the correct, standard from, upheld by the *Académie française* itself, as in:

Je n'ai pas d'argent.

while the colloquial equivalent with the single negation marker is decried as being sloppy and 'incorrect':

J'ai pas d'argent.

Moreover, it should be noted that standard French also allows multiple negation, as in:

Personne ne l'a jamais vu nulle part.
(Nobody has never seen him nowhere.)

A lot of research has focused on the linguistic structure of AAE, including the core syntactic constructions such as multiple negation and invariant *be*. The aim has been to show that the grammar of AAE is as complex and systematic as that of standard English, in response to the attacks of language mavens who look upon AAE as 'deficient' or 'illogical'. At the same time, there is a need to point out that behind the label 'AAE' there is not one single monolithic entity but a range of varieties that depend on both social and regional factors. In fact, this is a major difference compared with standard English, since standardization always involves an attempt to stop or slow down linguistic change, by 'fixing' the language in dictionaries, grammar books and textbooks. Because of the workings of the standard language ideology (as discussed in Chapter 2), the standard variety is the one that is *perceived* as the most uniform and systematic.

Finally, we note that the use of multiple negation is to be found not only in AAE but also in many other varieties, as in the following examples of Jamaican Creole taken from Sebba (1993: 152):

Im neva du notin.
(He never did nothing.)
Nobadi neva sii im.
(Nobody never saw him.)

Jamaican and Caribbean creoles are discussed in the following section, from a more socio-political and cultural perspective.

CARIBBEAN 'NATION LANGUAGE'

The US was not the only destination of the slave trade. Between four and five million slaves were brought over from Africa to work on the Caribbean plantations, especially sugar cane plantations. This number refers to those who survived the horrors of the Middle Passage; many others died or were killed and thrown overboard during the crossing. Though slavery was abolished in 1834, injustice and discrimination continued. Additionally, over half a million people were brought over as indentured workers from India to the Caribbean in the post-slavery period. Slaves and indentured workers formed the majority of the inhabitants of the British West Indies. The name itself is a misnomer: it is due to Columbus' mistake when in 1492 he thought he had reached the Indian subcontinent and called the indigenous people 'Indians'. The different territories of the British West Indies gradually gained independence from the 1960s onwards, and almost each one of them has developed a vibrant literature of its own.

Caribbean performance poetry is rooted in the African oral tradition with its subversive potential. Many of these poets use Caribbean Creole as a way of disidentifying from standard English and of challenging monolithic, restrictive conceptions of identity – whether it is Caribbean or British identity. In *History of the Voice* (1984: 13), Edward Kamau Brathwaite introduces the term 'nation language' for West Indian Creole and shows to what extent it is linked to African folk culture:

> Nation language is the language which is influenced very strongly by the African model, the African aspect of our New World/ Caribbean heritage. English it may be in terms of some of its lexical features. But in its contours, its rhythm and timbre, its sound explosions, it is not English, even though the words, as you hear them, might be English to a greater or lesser degree.

He emphasizes that the creative development of nation language is influenced not by English poetic traditions but by the rhythms of calypso, jazz, reggae, as well as religious and other rituals. Hence Caribbean poetry, unlike English poetry, tends to be sound poetry or dub poetry, meaning poetry designed to be recited or performed to reggae music. Most importantly, the language of Caribbean poetry is based on the language of ordinary people – in other words, it is demotic Caribbean – and as such, it displays an extraordinary creativity emerging out of social deprivation and poverty.

Language choice in the Caribbean is complicated by the ethnic mixture or hybridity of its population. With the virtual extinction of indigenous peoples (mostly Carib and Arawak), the majority of present-day inhabitants of the Caribbean are the descendants of slaves or indentured workers. Language choice is mostly restricted to a continuum ranging from standard English to the many creole languages. Here is the way Brathwaite describes the predicament that faced the slave:

> It was in language that the slave was perhaps most successfully imprisoned by his master and it was in his (mis-)use of it that he perhaps most effectively rebelled.
>
> (Brathwaite 1971: 237)

In an interview with Nathaniel Mackay (1995: 17), in which he was asked to comment upon this passage, Brathwaite pointed out that he did not mean language 'in terms of verbs and sentences, but the whole business of the structures, the ideological structures that are built to control the colonial, to control the slave, to control the underclasses of the western world, to control the mind'. Then as now, for the slave as for the present-day inhabitant of the Caribbean, the use of standard English can be hegemonic, whereas the use of creolized English may be considered a subversive act.

ACTIVITY: LINGUISTIC VARIATION IN TIME AND SPACE*

Discuss the main features of the following varieties of English that distinguish them from standard British or American English. Note that all the examples are literary representations of these varieties.

Old English: *Beowulf* (about eighth century)

> Hwæt we Gar-Dena in gear-dagum
> þeod-cyninga þrym gefrunon
>
> (lines 1–2)

Middle English: Geoffrey Chaucer. *The Canterbury Tales* (about 1387)

> Whan that Aprill with his shoures soote
> The droghte of March hath perced to the roote,
> And bathed every veine in swich licour
> Of which vertu engendred is the flour …
> Thanne longen folk to goon on pilgrimages,
> And palmeres for to seken straunge strondes,
> To ferne halwes, kowthe in sondry londes.
>
> (*The General Prologue*, lines 1–4 and 12–14)

Early Modern English: William Shakespeare. *Julius Caesar* (about 1599)

> Flavius: Hence! home, you idle creatures, get you home.
> Is this a holiday? What! know you not,
> Being mechanical, you ought not walk
> Upon a labouring day without the sign
> Of your profession? Speak, what trade art thou?
> 1st Citizen: Why, sir, a carpenter.
> Marullus: Where is thy leather apron and thy rule?
> What dost thou with thy best apparel on?
>
> (Act I, Scene 1, lines 1–8)

Yorkshire English, lower-class speech: Emily Brontë. *Wuthering Heights* (1847)

> The old servant [Joseph] confirmed this statement, but muttered,
> 'Aw'd rather he'd goan hisseln fur t'doctor! Aw sud uh taen tent uh t'maister better nur him – un he warn't deead when Aw left, nowt uh t'soart!'
>
> (Harmondsworth: Penguin, 1995, p. 185)

Indian English: G.V. Desani. *All About H. Hatterr* (1948)

> And I am the feller, the same feller, who salaamed the earth of your country, the same what has written this book ...
> I write rigmarole English, staining your goodly godly tongue, maybe; but, friend, I forsook my Form, School and Head, while you stuck to yours: learning reading, 'riting and 'rithmetic.
>
> (in S. Rushdie and E. West (eds) *Mirrorwork: 50 Years of Indian Writing 1947–1997*, New York: Henry Holt and Company, 1997, p. 37)

Caribbean English: Sam Selvon. *The Lonely Londoners* (1956)

> [Galahad is talking to the colour Black, as if it were a person:]
> And Galahad watch the colour of his hand, and talk to it, saying, 'Colour, is you that causing all this, you know. Why the hell you can't be blue, or red or green, if you can't be white? You know is you that cause a lot of misery in the world. Is not me, you know, is you! I ain't do anything to infuriate the people and them, is you! Look at you, you so black and innocent, and this time so you causing misery all over the world!'
>
> (Oxford: Heinemann, 1997, p. 88)

Nigerian English: Ken Saro-Wiwa. *Sozaboy: A Novel in Rotten English* (1985)

> And as I was going, I was just thinking how the war have spoiled my town Dukana, uselessed many people, killed many others, killed my mama and my wife, Agnes, my beautiful young wife with J.J.C. and now it have made me like porson wey get leprosy because I have no town again.
>
> And I was thinking how I was prouding before to go to soza and call myself Sozaboy. But now if anybody say anything about war or even fight, I will just run and run and run and run and run. Believe me yours sincerely.
>
> (Harlow: Longman, 1994, p. 181)

African-American English: William Kennedy. *Legs* (1975)

> She didn't see nothin' what I seen, what I wants to tell you 'bout. Nobody seen what I seen ... I fear 'bout those men. I know the police lookin' for me too 'cause they askin' Mr Fogarty 'bout me before he go to jail and I don't want no police, so I highfoots it up to Albany 'cause I know they got coloreds up here plenty and nobody know me.
>
> (in *The Albany Cycle Book 2*, London: Scribner, p. 613)

*Brief comments on this Activity can be found on page 289.

SINGLISH

In the activity, we have looked at variation in English along both dimensions of time and space, including some examples of postcolonial Englishes. Another example that we discuss in this section is Singapore English. Just as with Nigerian, Caribbean and Indian English – or indeed AAE – it is important to be aware that Singapore English is not a monolithic entity. On the contrary; it is a linguistic continuum with varieties ranging from standard Singapore English to colloquial Singapore English (usually referred to as Singlish), with many speakers switching between these varieties depending on who they talk to and in which context. Some of the distinguishing features of Singlish can be seen in the following example taken from Fong (2004: 98):

> Prabhudeva kena cheat in the movie lah.
> (Prabhudeva was cheated in the movie.)

They include the *kena* passive, with the main verb often used in the infinitive form, and the discourse particle *lah*, which 'indicates speaker's mood/attitude and appeals to addressee to accommodate the mood/attitude' (Wee 2004: 125). According to Deterding (2007: 66), *lah* is 'perhaps the one word that is most emblematic of Singapore English', and he suggests that the source of *lah* may be various similar particles in other languages widely used in Singapore, including Hokkien, Cantonese and Malay (Deterding 2007: 71).

Singlish is widespread in Singapore, but it is valued in very different ways by the Singapore government and by its speakers. The government started a Speak Good English movement in 2000, with the aim of getting Singaporeans to use standard English for purely instrumental reasons. Standard English, they argue, is needed for international business and science in this globalized world. As for Singlish, it is looked upon as bad English, and the government would like to eradicate it. However, it has not been very successful in this attempt, partly because it failed to realize that one can promote standard English without having to eradicate Singlish and partly because it underestimated the strength of the link between Singlish and Singaporean identity for many citizens.

Indeed, Singlish is being used by an increasing number of Singaporeans as their home language or one of their home languages. Though it is a working-class variety, it has a lot of '**covert prestige**' as the language of solidarity that binds together Singaporeans. Unlike the overt prestige of standard, national and official languages, linguistic varieties such as Singlish can have a high value attributed to them within a particular ingroup for expressing that ingroup's cultural identity. But Singlish has outgrown its association with a particular ingroup and has come to be perceived as uniquely Singaporean and as a key marker of Singaporean identity in general. As a result, code-switching between Singlish and more standard varieties of English is frequently used for all sorts of effects by members of all social classes (see Chapter 7 on code-switching).

Thus Singapore is one of many countries extensively affected by the global spread of English. English is the first language of the education system, before the so-called mother tongues (see the discussion of Singaporean language policy in Chapter 6), and bilingual education in Singaporean schools is usually referred to as English-knowing bilingualism. For this reason, Singapore is a good example to illustrate the different ideological positions that researchers have taken with reference to the global spread of English. They will be discussed in the next section in terms of the ideological frameworks identified by Pennycook (2000, 2001).

THE GLOBAL SPREAD OF ENGLISH

The global spread of English is usually interpreted as a consequence of the role of the British Empire as well as the rise in the twentieth century of the United States as a world power. Pennycook distinguishes between six ideological frameworks for understanding the global position of English, which exist on a continuum from conservative to progressive and which, for the sake of brevity and simplicity, we have reduced to three overarching theories. In our discussion, we also rely upon Lee and Norton (2009) who apply Pennycook's frameworks to the language situation of Singapore.

The first two positions identified by Pennycook and referred to as 'colonial celebration' and 'laissez-faire liberalism' together constitute the conservative stance. It involves an uncritical celebration of the spread of English which, according to Pennycook, is a direct legacy of colonialism (hence the name 'colonial celebration'). It can frequently be found within economic and ideological frameworks of 'laissez-faire liberalism' and free market capitalism. A prime example of this is the official language policy of Singapore where the government promotes the usefulness of English (standard English of course, not Singlish) as the language which will offer all Singaporeans the best possible educational and employment opportunities in a highly competitive, globalized world.

Lee and Norton (2009: 279) point to the naivety of the Singapore government's position, since it should be clear that knowledge of English will not by itself reduce social inequalities – though of course not learning English and only using the local languages will not either! Moreover, the spread of English has had unexpected or even unwanted consequences, at least from the government's point of view: namely, the use of Singlish as (one of) the home language(s) of more and more Singaporeans. As we have seen, the government would prefer English to play a purely instrumental role as the global language of business and Singaporean identity to remain linked solely to the local languages, in particular Mandarin, Malay and Tamil. There is thus an increasing gap between official language policy and the lived experience of a large number of people in Singapore who identify with Singlish, or with both Singlish and a local language.

Lee and Norton are right to argue that Singapore's official language policy illustrates Pennycook's frameworks of 'colonial celebration' and 'laissez-faire liberalism'. However, an important element, which to some extent contradicts the ideology of laissez-faire individualism, is missing from this account and needs to be added to understand the whole picture: Singapore's official policy also illustrates the desire for, and the illusion of, full top-down control and manipulation of people's linguistic repertoires (cf. Bokhorst-Heng 1999).

Two more critical positions discussed by Pennycook in relation to the global spread of English are 'linguistic imperialism' (Phillipson 1992) and 'linguistic human rights' (Skutnabb-Kangas and Phillipson 1995). They look upon the spread of English as a new form of colonialism, which poses a threat to language diversity and language rights. According to this position, each individual has (or should have) the right to use her or his mother tongue at home and also to get an education in that language.

However noble this position may be in its aims, it is based on the problematic concept of mother tongue (see discussion in Chapter 2) and on an 'essentialization of the communities purported to benefit from this framework' (Lee and Norton 2009: 281). For instance, the Chinese Singaporean families who have switched from (let's say) Hokkien to Singlish as their home language might now be told by the linguistic human rights activists that they should fight for their right to get an education in Hokkien, their presumed mother tongue, even though they do not speak Hokkien any longer – a rather absurd and counter-productive position, to say the least. The reason for this is that the 'linguistic imperialism' and 'linguistic human rights' position relies on a dichotomizing, almost Manichean perspective that sees English as all bad and local languages as all good. However, we have already seen that in fact this is not a binary opposition: more and more people in Singapore nowadays identify with both Singlish and a local language such as Hokkien or Mandarin. Hence, what would be best for their children would probably be a flexible form of bilingual education rather than education in the presumed mother tongue.

The most progressive positions in relation to the global spread of English, which move beyond a Manichean world-view, are the frameworks that Pennycook refers to as 'linguistic hybridity' and 'postcolonial performativity'. Here the focus is double: first, on how languages constantly change and adapt, mix and 'hybridize', as with Singlish, which incorporates many elements from the local Singaporean languages; and second, on how speakers appropriate and perform languages and identities in specific contexts. Thus we have already seen how Singaporeans have appropriated English – in the sense of making it their own, using it for their own ends and needs – and identify not so much with standard English but rather with their local, nativized variety of English: Singlish. Nor does this necessarily mean the loss of other languages: on the contrary, Singlish usually co-exists with both local languages and with the more standard varieties of English.

Hence, if minority languages are endangered, this is not always due solely or even primarily to the 'invasion' of a global language such as English (see Chapter 5). What is going on in a particular context is often more complex and to understand the whole picture, it is necessary to make a basic distinction between individual and societal multilingualism and to study the social issues linked to both of these aspects. Individual multilingualism is highly valued in many societies, though there is usually a clear hierarchy of languages (linked to the social hierarchy of the speakers of these languages), with standard, national or official languages at the top and immigrant minority languages at the bottom. Societal multilingualism and linguistic diversity, on the other hand, are frequently seen as a problem or challenge, and there are consequent attempts to manage and control it – which, however, are not always successful, as we have seen in the case of Singapore. We will come back to the Singaporean language situation and explore these issues further in Chapter 6.

TWO FRENCH YOUTH LANGUAGES

There may be a need to point out that Pennycook's frameworks obviously apply not just to situations involving English but also to other global or colonial languages such as French. In the final part of this chapter, we look at the global spread of French with an example from Côte d'Ivoire illustrating Pennycook's framework of postcolonial performativity, as well as an example of linguistic variation from within metropolitan France.

Nouchi in Côte d'Ivoire

Côte d'Ivoire was a French colony, which gained independence in 1990. It is a highly multilingual and multicultural country, yet – or perhaps at least partly for that very reason – French is still the official language. The country's ruling elite speaks standard French, while the vast majority of the people use one or more of the numerous local, indigenous languages, as well as speaking some French. Four of the indigenous languages have been given the status of national languages: Bete, Baoule, Malinke and Senufo. Another widely used language, Dioula, had almost become a national lingua franca. But, since the failed *coup d'état* in 2002 led to a political division between the south of the country and the (largely Dioula-speaking) north, the role of Dioula as a national lingua franca has decreased. Instead, popular varieties of French have found an ideal breeding-ground in this climate of political tension and instability. Especially in urban areas, where speakers of many languages come together, they have spread widely.

One of these varieties is Nouchi, a new urban language of young people which emerged in the capital city Abidjan in the early 1990s. Nouchi has become the language of local rap music and of radio stations targeting a young audience, and it has spread beyond Abidjan and even beyond the national borders of Côte d'Ivoire to neighbouring countries such as Mali and Burkina Faso. It is a hybrid of French and some indigenous languages such as Dioula, Baoule and Bete, together with some words of English. Here is an example of a sentence in Nouchi:

> Y a des gban-gban au campus.
> (There is trouble on the campus; *gban* means 'hot' in Dioula)

Like with Singlish in Singapore, the Ivoirian government looked upon Nouchi as bad, corrupted French and attempted to eradicate it. As Newell (2009: 170) puts it,

> The language that most people spoke in the cities of Côte d'Ivoire was considered a dangerous corrupting force upon the nation by the country's ruling elite .... [It was] argued that French should be confined to a specific governmental role and kept 'pure', while quotidian activities should be carried out in indigenous languages.

The message for people to go back to using the indigenous languages is also the one usually advocated by linguistic human rights activists. However, it amounts to no less than perpetuating the colonial status quo: the ruling elite speaks 'pure' or standard French, while the masses should stick to their indigenous languages.

It is true that there is an important difference here: the linguistic human rights activists are more progressive in that they argue that an education in the indigenous mother tongue will make it easier for schoolchildren to later acquire French as a second or foreign language. However, this corresponds less and less to the linguistic reality: many Ivoirians do not speak an indigenous language as their home language or one of their home languages; especially for the city dwellers, Nouchi is more and more often 'the language spoken at home and thus [their] first language' (Newell 2009: 158; see also the discussion of mother tongue education in Chapter 10).

In this way, Nouchi has upset the colonial hierarchy, which may explain why the government reacted so strongly against it. In less than twenty years, Nouchi has developed from the language of the uneducated poor and of criminal gangs to 'a language indexing a shared, if contested, Ivoirian popular culture' (Newell 2009: 178). Just like Singlish in Singapore, it has become a key marker of a new, modern and urban Ivoirian identity and is now increasingly being used by people of all social classes. In other words, Ivoirians are constructing and performing new languages and identities in a perfect illustration of what Pennycook refers to as 'postcolonial performativity'.

Verlan in France

We close this chapter with an example of linguistic diversity from within France itself. Despite all the French state's efforts, since the time of the

French revolution, to construct a homogeneous and monolingual community, the reality has been and is that of a heterogeneous population and of linguistic diversity. Here we discuss a language variety called Verlan, which is spoken mostly by young people in the *banlieues* (suburbs) of Paris and other big cities such as Lille, Lyon and Marseille. Many of these speakers of Verlan are marginalized youths of North African origin, frequently referred to as *les beurs* (Verlan for Arabs). But it is also spoken by young people of many other origins (including French), so that Doran (2004) interprets the use of Verlan as the performance of hybrid, multilingual and multicultural, working-class identities.

Verlan is thus a hybrid variety mixing French with other languages such as Arabic, Berber and English (especially rap music terms). Many of the French words are pronounced *à l'envers* (inversely) – hence the name Verlan, which is the inverse form of *l'envers*. To make things even more complicated, inverting words can also involve vowel alteration, as in *meuf* (for *femme*, woman) and *keuf* (for *flic*, cop).

In her ethnographic study of a group of young people living in a Parisian *banlieue*, Doran (2004) shows that Verlan is their preferred language of peer-group interaction, though it is used in alternation with other varieties such as vernacular French, standard French and home languages such as Arabic, etc. Because these youths are often perceived and stigmatized as the Others by mainstream French society, they turn the tables on the latter by positioning its representatives as the Others by means of such Verlan terms as *les Céfrans* (for *les Français*, the French). In this way, the youths distance themselves from traditional French people and their *bourge* values (from *les bourgeois*, middle and upper-class people). The values include not only negative character traits such as intolerance but also these people's language: *le français soutenu* (standard French). But at the same time, the youths also distance themselves from *la racaille* (rabble, riffraff), the street gang members involved in drug dealing and other criminal activities, who use Verlan in all contexts. Doran's youths, on the other hand, use verbal repertoires stretching from Verlan at one end to standard French at the other, by means of which they negotiate flexible identity positions similarly located on a continuum between *racaille* at one end and *bourge* at the other. In Doran's (2004: 119–20) own words, her study highlights

> the ways in which the strategic, context-specific choice of Verlan is tied to the enactment of an interstitial 'third space' – one which is neither family minority culture nor dominant French culture – in which youths can position themselves along an alternative identity continuum, outside the fixed categories available in the standard language.

The rapid spread of youth languages such as Verlan in France and Nouchi in Côte d'Ivoire is due in large part to the phenomenal popularity of hip hop and rap music. For instance, the Ivoirian rapper Nash uses Nouchi in her songs, and her best known albums are called *Ya Koi Même?* (What's Happening?) and *Ziés Dédjas* (Open Eyes). As for French rapper Diam's, her lyrics use a 'sophisticated mix of French, English, Spanish, hip hop vernacular, Verlan and Parisian slang' (Le Nevez 2008: 319). An example of Diam's' use of Verlan discussed by Le Nevez is to be found in the following line from one of her songs: *Un truc de fou renoi* (A crazy black thing), where *renoi* is the Verlan term for *noir* (black). Sefyu (Youssef Soukouna) is another French rapper whose artist's name is actually his first name in Verlan. All these artists work in politically and linguistically transgressive ways, breaking open standard French and constructing alternative, culturally different positions for young people to identify with.

CONCLUSION

Linguistic variation is a characteristic of all languages, from the smallest to the largest ones. All varieties, whether they are perceived as languages or not, are both systematic and rule-governed, and leak into each other, with no clear boundaries between them. In this chapter, we focused on global languages such as English and French, because we also wanted to look at how the spread of global languages can be conceptualized in very different ways. We introduced Pennycook's ideological frameworks for conceptualizing the global spread of English and discussed them primarily in relation to the language situation in Singapore. To some extent we prioritized the frameworks of 'linguistic hybridity' and (especially) 'postcolonial performativity', because they emphasize human agency and creativity. It is also for this reason that we have mostly drawn our examples in this chapter from literary texts and youth languages. Finally, we have shown how youth languages such as Nouchi and Verlan have spread via hip hop music and media discourse.

ACTIVITY: RAPPING IN SINGLISH

In this chapter, we have discussed the Singapore government's negative attitude towards Singlish. Yet the government itself commissioned a rap song against SARS by Phua Chu Kang, which is – at least partly – in Singlish (available on Facebook at the time of writing: https://www.facebook.com/66914677384/videos/66115693917/). The government argued that it decided to use Singlish exceptionally because it was essential to reach the whole population, including the less-educated, in its campaign to stop the spread of the Severe Acute Respiratory Syndrome (SARS) pandemic in 2003.

- What light does this throw on the role of Singlish in Singapore?
- Analyse the use of language in the following extracts from the SARS rap song:

> Some say leh, some say lah
> Spread kaya, but don't spread SARS!

The song continues with instructions about what to do and what not to do (e.g. not to go to work) when you have caught SARS:

> Don't be a hero and continue working
> Wait the whole company kena quarantine!
> (kaya – coconut spread for bread, etc., also: charm, something that attracts people's attention and/or admiration; kena – undergo, experience, also used as a passive marker; both derived from Malay)
> (quoted from Wee 2010: 107–8)

FOR DISCUSSION: MIXED LANGUAGES

- Do you or any of your classmates use mixed languages?
- Why are such mixed varieties often considered to be 'bad'? What language ideologies underlie such judgements?

FOR DISCUSSION: LINGUISTIC VARIETIES AND STUDENTS AT HONG KONG UNIVERSITIES

According to Gu (2011), local Hong Kong students and students from Mainland China studying at Hong Kong universities use different linguistic varieties: the former mostly use Cantonese and the latter Putonghua (Mandarin). Moreover, as far as English is concerned, the former tend to use a mixed English–Cantonese variety, whereas the latter use a more standard variety of English. Gu (2011: 17) concludes

> that language often plays a substantial role in achieving a sense of intimacy among group members and that the huge inherent differences, despite the umbrella of 'unity' between HK and mainland China, lead to a mutual non-identification between HK and mainland students.

What recent socio-political developments in Hong Kong might account (at least partially) for these linguistic choices and tensions? What kinds of ideological or identity positionings might be linked with these linguistic choices?

PROJECT WORK: LANGUAGE VARIATION AND POP CULTURE

Read the article in *Dazed*, the British style magazine, about Rihanna's hit song 'Work', the lyrics of which are in Barbadian English (often referred to as 'patois'). The author of the article complains about people who mocked Rihanna's lyrics and called them 'gibberish'. The author argues that such comments constitute a form of 'casual racism'.

> http://www.dazeddigital.com/music/article/30102/1/rihanna-s-patois-and-your-misinformed-memes

What language ideology or ideologies underlie these people's negative comments and judgements? Do you agree that there is a link between these language ideologies and racism?

PROJECT WORK: YOUTH LANGUAGES

Explore one of the mixed youth languages such as Kiezdeutsch (Turkish–German) in Germany, Sheng (Swahili–English) in Kenya or Tsotsitaal (mix of many languages including isiZulu, isiXhosa, Sesotho, Afrikaans and English) in South Africa. Interesting books to get started are Androutsopoulos and Georgakopoulou (2003) or Stenström and Jørgensen (2009). Prepare a presentation for the other students in your class.

For a literary representation of Kiezdeutsch ('neighbourhood German'; also referred to by the more pejorative term Kanaksprak), you could have a look at Feridun Zaimoglu's novels and Pfaff's (2005) analysis of their language. For attitudes towards this new urban dialect, see Wiese (2014).

PROJECT WORK: POSTCOLONIAL LANGUAGE SITUATIONS

In this chapter, we have illustrated Pennycook's frameworks for understanding the global spread of English with reference to the language situations in Singapore and Côte d'Ivoire. Choose another postcolonial country, where English and/or French (or another colonial language) are playing an important role in comparison to the local languages, and try to account for what is going on in terms of one or more of these frameworks.

PROJECT WORK: THE LANGUAGE OF CARIBBEAN POETRY

Analyse the use of language of Caribbean or British-Caribbean poets such as Louise Bennett, Linton Kwesi Johnson or Jean 'Binta' Breeze. You could look at poems which deal with women's struggle such as Bennett's 'Jamaica Oman' [woman] or Breeze's 'Riddym Ravings (The Mad Woman's Poem)';

as for Johnson's poems, they mostly deal with the black struggle in deprived inner-city areas of south London and are easily available in a collection entitled *Mi Revalueshanary Fren: Selected Poems* [My Revolutionary Friends] and published by Penguin (2002). Prepare a presentation for the other students in your class.

REFERENCES AND SUGGESTIONS FOR FURTHER READING

Language variation

Tagliamonte, Sali A. (2006) *Analysing Sociolinguistic Variation*, Cambridge: Cambridge University Press.

African-American English and Caribbean nation language

For African-American English, please see references at the end of Chapter 10.

Brathwaite, Edward Kamau (1971) *The Development of Creole Society in Jamaica 1770–1820*, Oxford: Clarendon.

—— (1984) *The History of the Voice: The Development of Nation Language in Anglophone Caribbean Poetry*, London and Port of Spain: New Beacon Books.

Mackay, Nathaniel (1995) 'An interview with Kamau Brathwaite', in S. Brown (ed.) *The Art of Kamau Brathwaite*, Bridgend, Wales: Seren.

Sebba, Mark (1993) *London Jamaican*, Harlow: Longman.

Singlish

Bokhorst-Heng, Wendy (1999) 'Singapore's *Speak Mandarin Campaign*: Language ideological debates and the imagining of the nation', in J. Blommaert (ed.) *Language Ideological Debates*, Berlin: Mouton de Gruyter, 235–65.

Deterding, David (2007) *Singapore English*, Edinburgh: Edinburgh University Press.

Fong, Vivienne (2004) 'The verbal cluster', in L. Lim (ed.) *Singapore English: A Grammatical Description*, Amsterdam: Benjamins, 75–104.

Lim, Lisa, Pakir, Anne and Wee, Lionel (eds) (2010) *English in Singapore: Modernity and Management*, Hong Kong: Hong Kong University Press.

Wee, Lionel (2004) 'Reduplication and discourse particles', in L. Lim (ed.) *Singapore English: A Grammatical Description*, Amsterdam: Benjamins, 105–26.

—— (2010) '"Burdens" and "handicaps" in Singapore's language policy: On the limits of language management', *Language Policy*, 9: 97–114.

——, Goh, Robbie B.H. and Lim, Lisa (eds) (2013) *The Politics of English: South Asia, Southeast Asia and the Asia Pacific*, Amsterdam: Benjamins.

The global spread of English

Lee, Ena and Norton, Bonny (2009) 'The English language, multilingualism, and the politics of location', *International Journal of Bilingual Education and Bilingualism*, 12: 277–90.

Pennycook, Alastair (1994) *The Cultural Politics of English as an International Language*, Harlow: Longman.

—— (2000) 'English, politics, ideology: From colonial celebration to postcolonial performativity', in T. Ricento (ed.) *Ideology, Politics and Language Policies: Focus on English*, Amsterdam: Benjamins, 107–19.

—— (2001) *Critical Applied Linguistics: A Critical Introduction*, Mahwah, NJ: Erlbaum.

Phillipson, Robert (1992) *Linguistic Imperialism*, Oxford: Oxford University Press.

—— (2010) *Linguistic Imperialism Continued*, Abingdon: Routledge.

Skutnabb-Kangas, Tove and Phillipson, Robert (eds) (1995) *Linguistic Human Rights: Overcoming Linguistic Discrimination*, Berlin: Mouton de Gruyter.

Nouchi, Verlan and other youth languages

Androutsopoulos, Jannis and Georgakopoulou, Alexandra (eds) (2003) *Discourse Constructions of Youth Identities*, Amsterdam: Benjamins.

Doran, Meredith (2004) 'Negotiating between *bourge* and *racaille*: Verlan as youth identity practice in suburban Paris', in A. Pavlenko and A. Blackledge (eds) *Negotiation of Identities in Multilingual Contexts*, Clevedon: Multilingual Matters, 93–124.

Hassa, Samira (2010) '*Kiff my zikmu*: Symbolic dimensions of Arabic, English and Verlan in French rap texts', in M. Terkourafi (ed.) *The Languages of Global Hip Hop*, London: Continuum, 44–66.

Le Nevez, Adam (2008) 'Rethinking diversity and difference in French language practices', *Language Policy*, 7: 309–22.

Newell, Sasha (2009) 'Enregistering modernity, bluffing criminality: How Nouchi speech reinvented (and fractured) the nation', *Journal of Linguistic Anthropology*, 19: 157–84.

Pfaff, Carol W. (2005) '"Kanaken in Alemannistan": Feridun Zaimoglu's representation of migrant language', in V. Hinnenkamp and K. Meng (eds) *Sprachgrenzen überspringen: Sprachliche Hybridität und polykulturelles Selbstverständnis*, Tübingen: Narr, 195–225.

Stenström, Anna Brita and Jørgensen, Annette Myre (eds) (2009) *Youngspeak in a Multilingual Perspective*, Amsterdam: Benjamins.

Wiese, Heike (2014) 'Voices of linguistic outrage: Standard language constructs and the discourse on new urban dialects', *Working Papers in Urban Language and Literacies*, 120: 1–25.

Linguistic varieties and students at Hong Kong universities

Gu, Mingyue (2011) 'Language choice and identity construction in peer interactions: Insights from a multilingual university in Hong Kong', *Journal of Multilingual and Multicultural Development*, 32: 17–31.

CHAPTER 5

Revitalization of endangered languages

We argued in Chapter 3 that 'language death' is a metaphor that needs to be relativized in light of the fact that all (spoken or living) languages are involved in a continuous process of change. Nonetheless, it is also true that more and more languages and varieties are endangered in our globalized world. This is due to two main factors: first, the politics of nation-state building, with states typically promoting one language as the 'national' or 'official' language, while often repressing the languages of both indigenous and immigrant minority groups. Second, because of the spread of global languages such as English with ever higher instrumental value (see Chapter 4), there are strong pressures on minority group members to drop their minority languages and to use instead the national or official language of the state plus a global language such as English.

The main criterion of language endangerment is when a minority language is no longer used in family transmission. The consequence is often language shift: thus May (2006: 257) states that 'of the estimated 6,800 languages spoken in the world today . . . it is predicted on present trends that between 20 per cent and 50 per cent will "die" by the end of the twenty-first century' – though remember the problems associated with looking upon languages as countable entities, discussed in Chapter 3. Even with this caveat, there does seem to be an urgent need to support minority groups, and a number of international organizations have taken up the fight for their rights, including minority language rights. However, there is a big difference here between indigenous minority languages, which have recently received a lot of support (especially in Europe through the EU's Charter for Regional or Minority Languages), and immigrant minority languages, which have received very little support. While immigrant minority languages are discussed in many chapters of this book, we focus in this chapter on a number of case studies illustrating more or less successful revitalization of indigenous minority languages, namely Aboriginal languages in Australia, Māori in New Zealand, Sámi and Kven in Norway, Hebrew in Israel, and Breton and Corsican in France. There is a final section on how a language (in this case Luxembourgish) is constructed as being endangered.

We argue that **language revitalization** is most successful when it is simultaneously promoted by a grassroots movement and by the state, as well as being supported by international minority rights organizations. At the same time, we also point to the human costs involved in each situation. Let us start by contrasting the dire situation of indigenous minority languages in Australia with that in New Zealand and Norway, with the last two being perhaps the two countries in the world with the most progressive policies towards indigenous minority languages.

AUSTRALIAN ABORIGINAL LANGUAGES: A HISTORY OF OPPRESSION

In Australia, there were an estimated 250 Aboriginal languages, each with its own varieties or 'dialects', spoken in the late eighteenth century, at the beginning of colonization. Of these, about 160 have died, about 70 are under threat and about 20 are likely to survive, at least in the short term (Walsh 2007: 2). The contact between Aboriginal and European people has led to the development of pidgins and creoles such as Kriol in northern Australia and Torres Strait Creole in northern Queensland and the Torres Strait Islands (situated between Queensland and Papua New Guinea). The increased contact, especially in urban areas, of speakers of different Aboriginal languages has also led to the emergence of indigenous lingua francas. These creoles and lingua francas are often used nowadays as media of instruction in bilingual (indigenous language–English) educational programmes.

Many of the Aboriginal languages disappeared as a result of Australia's forced assimilation policy in the early twentieth century, with Aboriginal children forcibly removed from their parents by welfare officers. They were brought up in white foster-families and boarding schools, where they were taught only English and punished for using their home languages. In this way, the lives – and languages – of Aboriginal people have been blighted by a long history of oppression, with a period of respite in the second half of the twentieth century. This period started in 1967, when Aboriginal people and Torres Strait Islanders were at long last granted full citizenship rights. Moreover, a far-sighted, progressive policy of linguistic pluralism and multiculturalism was set up from this time onwards. The first indigenous bilingual schools opened in the Northern Territory in 1973, though mostly only of the transitional type (transitioning children from their indigenous language to English). By 1990, Aboriginal communities were given more control over these schools and, consequently, were able to introduce more maintenance types of bilingual education.

There was an urgent need for such maintenance and revitalization programmes, as many Aboriginal languages had already disappeared or were in the process of disappearing. However, bilingual education programmes do not provide easy solutions for this issue of language shift. As has been mentioned, regional lingua francas are frequently used in these programmes, as a result of which young people may switch from the local clan language to the wider lingua franca (Lo Bianco and Rhydwen 2001: 399). This is reinforced, as Lo Bianco and Rhydwen (2001: 399) point out, by changing patterns of settlement, with people speaking different clan languages increasingly living together. The authors even conclude that clan languages are threatened by the regional lingua francas more than by English (Lo Bianco and Rhydwen 2001: 400).

Despite these challenges faced by bilingual education programmes and language revitalization movements, they have been relatively successful because of the progressive policies of pluralism and multiculturalism during the 1970s and 1980s. The largely implicit language policies of these decades eventually crystallized in the first explicit, official language policy, the 1987 National Policy on Languages. This document, also known as the Lo Bianco report (after the name of its author, the sociolinguist and language policy expert Joseph Lo Bianco), for the first time formally recognized the indigenous Aboriginal languages. It developed a far-reaching vision of social justice, and promoted access to English for all, support for Aboriginal and Torres Strait languages, and acquisition by all schoolchildren of a language other than English (see Herriman 1996: 49).

Unfortunately, however, the National Policy on Languages was replaced by a very different policy after only four years: namely, a government White Paper entitled 'Australia's Language: The Australian Language and Literacy Policy' (1991; note the highly significant change in the title from 'languages' in the plural to 'Australia's *language*' in the singular). There had been no change in government to cause this shift in language policy: the Labour Party was in power continuously from 1983 to 1996. But there was an overall shift in the policies of the Labour government, away from the earlier concerns with pluralism and multiculturalism, and towards a new politics of 'economic rationalism' combined with 'labourism' (Moore 2000: 42). The emphasis was put on much narrower concerns such as accountability, cost efficiency and employment skills. As a result, the Australian Language and Literacy Policy moves away from the broad vision of social justice articulated in the National Policy on Languages and places more emphasis on the acquisition of basic literacy skills – by which was meant exclusively literacy in the English language. As Lo Bianco and Rhydwen (2001: 418) argue, literacy became 'the Australian variant of English-only' (see Chapter 14 on English-only policies in the USA). A negative consequence of this was the large-scale restructuring of the field of English as a Second Language (ESL): from seeing ESL as a core element of bilingual education, practitioners were now forced to offer a much narrower and more instrumental form of ESL with an almost exclusive focus on literacy skills (see Moore 2000).

The backlash against pluralism and multiculturalism gained ground throughout the 1990s, fuelled by an economic crisis and rising unemployment. The second half of the 1990s saw the election of a new Liberal–National government committed to further downsizing in areas such as education, as well as the rise of Pauline Hanson's 'One Nation' party with its anti-Aboriginal and anti-immigration policies. In this hostile atmosphere, and due to the gradual reduction or even removal of funding for indigenous bilingual education programmes, it became increasingly difficult for such programmes and the associated language revitalization movements to continue their work.

One territory in particular that introduced numerous cuts in this area was the Northern Territory, as a result of which a number of bilingual programmes were discontinued and the overall quality of education decreased considerably. Ironically, though, the resulting underachievement of Aboriginal students was blamed on bilingual education and there were repeated calls, especially in the media and among politicians, for increased English language instruction. In 2008, the Northern Territory government effectively abolished bilingual education by introducing a new policy that required English to be used as the sole medium of instruction in schools during the first four hours of each day. In this way, the early 1990s marked a shift in Australia from a highly progressive to a more and more restrictive language-in-education policy. It reached its nadir with the 2008 decision of the Northern Territory government, which had first introduced bilingual education in the 1970s, but is now implementing English-only programmes that close down educational opportunities for Aboriginal children.

MĀORI IN NEW ZEALAND: A REVITALIZATION SUCCESS STORY

Māori became an official language of Aotearoa (New Zealand) – alongside English – in 1987. According to May (2001: 293), this makes New Zealand 'the *only* example where the first language of an indigenous people has been made an official state language', since other indigenous languages such as Sámi in Norway only have 'regional official status' (see following section). After a long period of colonial oppression and assimilationist policies in education, Māori had become a highly endangered language. But the introduction of Māori-medium schooling from the 1980s onwards has led to a successful revitalization of the language. In 1982 the first Māori-medium pre-schools (*Te Kōhanga Reo* **language nests**) were established, largely run by the Māori communities themselves. These pre-schools providing immersion in the Māori language were so successful that the provision of Māori-medium education was rapidly extended to primary level and beyond. In 1985, the first Māori-medium primary schools (*Kura Kaupapa Māori*, 'Māori philosophy schools') opened, and the first Māori-medium secondary schools and tertiary institutions followed in 1993–4. They, too, are at least to a certain extent under community control, and it would seem that this degree of local control is one key factor that has contributed to the programme's overall effectiveness.

All in all, the development of Māori-medium education, whose aim is for the children to achieve biculturalism and (additive) bilingualism in Māori and English, has been such a resounding success that other communities have adopted the 'language nest' teaching and learning philosophy, both in New Zealand and beyond. Thus May (2001: 305) comments as follows on the language and education provision for Pacific Islanders (Samoan, Tongan, etc.) who have migrated to New Zealand from the 1960s:

> Māori-medium education appears to have provided a template that other minority groups are moving increasingly to adopt .... These developments are reflected in the nascent emergence of comparable Pacific Islands preschool language nests (modelled on *Te Kōhanga Reo*).

Moreover, language nest education has been adopted by other language minority communities in the world, notably in Hawai'i, where Hawaiian-medium language nest pre-schools were established from 1984; similar initiatives were taken in other parts of the world for children speaking minority languages, including some other Native American languages, as well as Sámi and Karelian.

However, it needs to be added that, in spite of all these achievements, it is still a moot point whether Māori will be effectively revitalized. Indeed, because of the all-powerful position of English in New Zealand society, it is not clear whether Māori will become (one of) the home language(s) of many Māori again or whether it will remain a (mere) school language.

SÁMI AND KVEN IN NORWAY: DIFFERENTIAL POSITIONINGS ON THE SUCCESS–FAILURE CONTINUUM

Northern Norway has traditionally been a multilingual space, with languages such as Norwegian, Sámi and Kven being used. Sámi actually consists of a number of languages, the most widely spoken being Northern Sámi, whereas others, such as Inari Sámi, only have very small numbers of speakers. Norway only became an independent state at the beginning of the twentieth century; before that, it was in union with Denmark and then with Sweden. In the nineteenth and twentieth centuries, until about 1970, a policy of assimilation, or Norwegianization, was imposed upon the Sámi and Kven communities. They were subjected to linguistic and cultural oppression, as a result of which there was a gradual shift from the community languages (Sámi, Kven) to the dominant language (Norwegian). Many Sámi and Kven people have nowadays become passive bilinguals, speaking Norwegian and able to understand the community language.

Since 1988, when Sámi was recognized as a regional official language alongside Norwegian, the Sámi people have been able to implement a successful programme of language revitalization. The Sámi Language Act went into effect in 1992, and the newly created Sámi Parliament was given partial responsibilities and powers in educational matters. This allowed the Sámi community to set up bilingual Norwegian–Sámi education programmes which have gradually been extended from primary to secondary and even higher education, with some Sámi-medium programmes being offered at the Sámi College in Kautokeino.

The Kven, on the other hand, have had to wait much longer for recognition of their community as a national minority and of their language as a regional official language. Part of the reason for this is that for a long time the Kven language has been seen as a 'dialect' of Finnish; indeed, Kven people themselves sometimes refer to it as 'our Finnish' or 'old Finnish'. Moreover, the Kven people have been categorized as immigrants in Norway, even though – as Lane (2009) points out – most of them never crossed any state borders. This is because they moved from what is now northern Finland to northern Norway long before the present-day state borders were fixed. As the Kven spoke a language linguistically related to Finnish, they were looked upon with suspicion during much of the nineteenth century, and it was 'feared that Finland would use the Kven as a "bridge" to lay claim to this part of Norway' (Lane 2009: 218), which is rich in mineral resources. For this reason, an intense process of Norwegianization was imposed upon the Kven from the 1840s to the 1990s, in spite of which they continued to be regarded as not-to-be-trusted immigrants. It is this contradiction which makes Lane (2009: 219) ask the following question:

> If a group of people, recognized as a national minority, with a historical continuous presence of more than 300 years, having settled before the borders were established, is still categorized as immigrants, then one could wonder what it takes to become Norwegian?

It is true that, in spite of the long period of linguistic repression, language shift from Kven to Norwegian did not really happen in the Kven community until the 1960s onwards. The delayed onset of the shift may be due to the fact that the Kven people constitute a small, closely knit community, which encourages language maintenance despite the Norwegianization policy. However, nowadays Kven is only spoken by the older generation who, furthermore, tend to have a negative attitude towards the language. In fact, Lane (2010: 71) discovered in her ethnographic work that many older people experience a double feeling of language shame: they are ashamed of using Kven, because of the continued history of stigmatization, and they are also often ashamed of their Norwegian, which is not considered 'proper' Norwegian. Lane (2010: 73) suggests that the language shift from Kven to Norwegian, when it eventually happened, was caused by a combination of factors: not only the policy of Norwegianization but also the processes of modernity, as a result of which Kven came to be seen as the language of the past and Norwegian as the language of modernity.

Thus the process of revitalization set in much later for the Kven language than for the Sámi languages. Lane (2009) notes that Kven was finally recognized as a regional official language of Norway in 2005, even though the Kven people are still often referred to as immigrants in mainstream media discourses. Recent Kven language revitalization efforts have been positively influenced by the achievements of the Sámi language movement and by the fact that the Kven language, on top of its symbolic value as a pillar of Kven identity, has acquired some instrumental value through increasing trade with Finland.

However, the Kven language still has a long way to go to catch up with Sámi, where revitalization has been ongoing since the 1970s. Indeed, it seems that Sámi is keeping one step ahead of Kven: according to Pietikäinen (2010), Sámi is now moving from the discourses of endangerment and revitalization to the new discourses of globalization and **authenticity**. One of her examples to illustrate this point is Sámi rap music, though it is taken from the Finnish part of Sámiland (Sámiland stretches across northern Norway, Finland, Sweden and Russia). The Inari Sámi rapper Amoc relies on a language spoken by just a few hundred people in the Finnish part of Sámiland. In this way, Inari Sámi is given new value, by being moved from the very local spaces in which it is usually used to the global spaces of hip-hop music. Instead of a language of the past, it becomes the language of a vibrant youth culture and, at the same time, it points to, or indexes, the authenticity of the rapper. But in this process, the language is also transformed: because the lyrics of the rap songs are written in a hybrid language that mixes Sámi with Finnish and English – just as Amoc's traditional Sámi clothes are mixed with the more typical rapper clothes such as baggy jeans – this involves 'a subtle shift from a normative language use toward a more heteroglossic use of Sámi together with other languages and visualizations' (Pietikäinen 2010: 98).

HEBREW IN ISRAEL: THE HUMAN COSTS OF REVITALIZATION

The main language of Israel is Hebrew and it is a key symbol of the Jews' new nation-state. Yet, about a hundred years ago, Hebrew was almost a dead language, mostly used only as a sacred language for religious purposes. Thus the story of Hebrew is often presented as yet another story of successful revitalization. However, Shohamy (2008) points out that the revitalization of Hebrew took place at the expense of many other languages, including such Jewish languages as Yiddish and Ladino, which were 'perceived as threats to the revival of Hebrew' (Shohamy 2008: 208). She looks at official documents written in the 1930s and 1940s, and shows how Hebrew was imposed upon all the people. Some of these documents stress the need to eradicate all non-Hebrew newspapers, to ban theatre performances in other languages and to change people's personal names into Hebrew ones. There was even an attempt to force people to speak Hebrew at home. In 1941 the Central Committee for the Imposition of the Hebrew Language was set up, and 'Hebrew agents' were placed strategically in big companies, hospitals and other organizations. Some splinter groups such as the Militia for the Protection of the Language engaged in violent acts including breaking shop windows for displaying non-Hebrew signs or beating up people for speaking other languages in public. Moreover, home visits were made to assess people's proficiency in Hebrew and to identify language violations.

In this way, the imposition of Hebrew was accompanied by an attempt to eradicate all other languages: the Hebrew-only policy was a subtractive, not an additive, policy. It infringed many people's basic human rights; as Shohamy (2008: 215) puts it,

> The goal of reviving Hebrew was so important that all means were justified, no questions asked. The documents point to the use of strategies of threats, sanctions, and insistence on actual repairs, of insults and humiliation, of blaming and shaming of acts that were perceived as a 'violation' of the expected ideology and practices.

There was also a strong emphasis on the importance of guarding the purity of the Hebrew language, with a café owner in Jerusalem, for instance, being reprimanded for 'saying words that offended the Hebrew language' and the mayor of Tel Aviv being blamed for 'holding activities without emphasizing Hebrew purity' (Shohamy 2008: 212). Therefore, Shohamy (2008: 216) considers the following questions, which apply to such cases where the line between revitalization and oppression is a thin one:

> What about those [people] who became silent, living in constant fear of being corrected and judged about their language – not about what they had to say but about how they said it? ... And what about those who were threatened and degraded because of their language use, and what about their feelings of shame and embarrassment for not being able to acquire this new language in the short time they were required to accomplish it?

Finally, establishing Hebrew as the dominant language in Israel has led to the marginalization of the other official language, Arabic, and of its speakers, the Israeli Arabs. Arabic has a low status in contemporary Israel and is only used in areas where Arab speakers reside. Arabic is the medium of instruction in Arab schools, and students learn Hebrew as their second and English as their third language. But the students in these schools are discriminated against, in the sense that university admission depends on high proficiency in Hebrew, so that they frequently find it hard to compete with the Jewish students from the Hebrew-medium schools. Since the language tests which count as one of the main criteria for entering Israeli universities are in Hebrew, and there are no equivalent tests in Arabic, these tests 'perpetuate the dominance of Hebrew and grant no value to Arabic' (Shohamy 2006: 100).

BRETON IN FRANCE: HOW (NOT) TO STANDARDIZE

We have seen how Hebrew was deliberately transformed from the sacred (and mostly written) language of Judaism into the spoken and everyday language of Israeli citizens. Interestingly, Breton underwent a similar transformation, though the inverse one: from spoken vernacular to written standard. Breton is a Celtic language spoken in Brittany, especially the western part, and existing in a number of regional varieties. In a country where one language, namely French, is all-powerful, the number of Breton speakers has been steadily declining and the traditional forms of the language can be looked upon as endangered. Since the 1970s, the language revitalization movement has involved the creation of a new standard, usually referred to as *néo-breton*, which is now taught especially in the Diwan schools, private schools providing immersion education in Breton. *Néo-breton* is thus the educated variety mostly used by young, middle-class people in urban areas, whereas the traditional varieties are mostly spoken by older, working-class people in rural areas. Because of the considerable differences between *néo-breton* and the traditional varieties, the former is sometimes unintelligible to the native speakers of Breton and, moreover, the rural speakers of Breton sometimes (are made to) feel that their Breton is inferior, 'bad' or 'incorrect':

> There was, among these native-speakers, a growing awareness that their Breton was 'mixed' with French, a fact which 'those people' [i.e. speakers of *néo-breton*] often discussed. Their daily Breton was not really 'good Breton' … because '*deformet eo toud*' (it's all deformed).
>
> (McDonald 1989: 285)

On the other hand, the differences between *néo-breton* and the traditional varieties can also imply that that the former is looked upon as an artificial or non-authentic variety. This is something that happens quite frequently when indigenous languages are standardized: for instance, in Chapter 10, we discuss the case of standard Setswana, which is taught in schools in some parts of South Africa but which is very different from the vernacular or 'Street Setswana' spoken by most people. In this way, standardization, instead of contributing to language maintenance, can potentially reinforce the tendency towards language shift if people fail to identify with, or feel alienated from, the standard variety. As we will see, this seems to be happening with standard Setswana. As for Breton, the language activists claim that, since the traditional varieties are on the whole only spoken by older people, it was essential for language revitalization to develop a variety that schools could pass on to the younger generation. In other words, the 'price to pay' to keep Breton alive may be the disappearance of the traditional varieties of Breton. And because it is used by a new generation of young speakers, *néo-breton* may be the variety with the best chances of survival.

At the same time, it should be clear that learning Breton at school is not sufficient to ensure survival of the language. The question is whether it will also be transmitted as a home language from one generation to another. Note that this is not a matter of choosing Breton instead of French – an unlikely choice, considering the powerful position of French in France. It is much more a question of whether *néo-breton*-speaking parents will raise their children bilingually in French *and* Breton. But if it succeeds, the story of the survival of Breton will be, as Bentahila and Davies (1993) point out, not so much a story of language revitalization but of language transformation.

CORSICAN AND THE POLYNOMIC PARADIGM

In the case of the revitalization of Hebrew and Breton, we found that there are winners and losers: some speakers are included, others are excluded.

This is what Shohamy (2008) refers to as the costs of language policy. It is therefore important to make an effort to include all varieties and all speakers of a language. Our example to illustrate this is the revitalization of Corsican.

Like Breton, Corsican is an endangered regional language of France that exists in a number of varieties. But unlike with Breton in Brittany, where the revitalization movement tried to impose a new standard upon the community of speakers, Corsican has traditionally been constructed as a **polynomic** or pluricentric language. The polynomic approach involves a positive response to linguistic variation, advocating linguistic tolerance and respect for all the different varieties of Corsican and thus attempting to include all the speakers of Corsican in the revitalization project. There is no single linguistic norm that is considered to be the only 'correct' one. In this way, the ideology of polynomy is the very opposite of the standard language ideology; and as a result, the teaching of Corsican in Corsican schools, informed as it is by the former ideology, is very different from the teaching of French, which is informed by the latter.

In her ethnographic study of language ideologies in Corsica, Jaffe (2005) notes that Corsican tends to be taught in a more communicative way than French, with much less emphasis on spelling and grammar. Moreover, Corsican spelling rules are variable rules sensitive to 'dialectal' variation. In other words, the spelling of words is dependent on pronunciation: Jaffe (2005: 290) gives the example of the pronoun *we*, which in Corsican is written *noscia* if it is pronounced /noša/, but is written *nostra* if it is pronounced /nostra/. Jaffe also records that the two teachers in the classrooms that she observed always responded positively to dialectal variation in their students' oral and written productions. She argues that this may be because in teacher training the polynomic approach has been, as it were, 'normalized' for Corsican (Jaffe 2005: 296).

We would like to conclude this section by suggesting that the polynomic paradigm could usefully be applied to language teaching more generally to encourage teaching methodologies more tolerant of language variation. And this could be the case not only for endangered minority languages that are in need of revitalization but for all languages. An attitude of linguistic tolerance is the best way of empowering learners and helping them to acquire the dominant variety.

WHY LUXEMBOURGISH IS *NOT* AN ENDANGERED LANGUAGE

If a 'dialect' is constructed as a 'language' and if it is a small language, spoken by a limited number of people, then *ipso facto* it also tends to be regarded as an endangered language. In other words, a linguistic variety almost paradoxically becomes endangered through having its status upgraded to that of a 'language'. An example of this is Ulster-Scots, which was briefly discussed in Chapter 3; another example, which will be the focus of discussion in this section, is Luxembourgish. Luxembourgish has been upgraded from a 'dialect' of German to the 'national language' of Luxembourg, as enshrined in the 1984 Language Law. It is a 'small' language, relatively speaking, in the sense that it is spoken by an estimated four hundred thousand people. However, it cannot be regarded as a minority language, if this concept is used 'not to draw attention to numerical size of particular groups, but to refer to situational differences in power, rights and privileges' (Pavlenko and Blackledge 2004: 4; see Chapter 1).

This distinction – a small language but not a minority language – points to the non-prototypicality of the Luxembourgish language situation (Horner and Weber 2010). Members of linguistic minorities in Luxembourg speak languages such as Portuguese and Italian, which are official languages of other EU member-states and are bound up with norms linked to linguistic standardization. As for the dominant languages in Luxembourg (Luxembourgish, German and French), all three of them are officially recognized in the language law of 1984. But it is the first of these, which in the law is referred to as the national language of the Luxembourgers, that is the focus of explicitly framed standardization efforts and related debates. In the context of these debates, critical issues of power and inequalities have been increasingly blurred, and it is therefore essential to distinguish between languages and their speakers. When the focus is on speakers, it is clear that people who speak Luxembourgish as a home language are in no way oppressed for this reason. On the contrary, it is speakers of Portuguese and some other languages who are sometimes discriminated against because the language-in-education policy of the state largely erases their linguistic needs and forces them to go through a German-language literacy programme (see Chapter 9). On the other hand, when the focus is on languages, as it often is in language-ideological debates in Luxembourg, Luxembourgish is constructed as an endangered language that is in need not only of standardization but also of preservation and promotion.

In relation to the high level of in-migration during the last few decades, there are fears that 'Luxembourgers' might become a minority in 'their own country' in the not so distant future. As a result, a wide-ranging discourse of endangerment has proliferated, concerning not just the survival of the language but of the nation itself (cf. Duchêne and Heller 2007). In this way, discourses of endangerment can spread about powerful, societal majority languages which, objectively speaking, do not fulfil the main criteria of endangerment: indeed, Luxembourgish, the national language of Luxembourg, is widely used in family transmission. Moreover, the number of speakers has increased steadily over the last decades, with many **new speakers** of the language (i.e. mostly resident foreigners learning and using it, although for many of them the language may not be directly linked to their sense of national identity; see O'Rourke, Pujolar and Ramallo 2015 and Hornsby 2015). In the Activity below, we consider an example of the discourse of endangerment surrounding Luxembourgish.

CONCLUSION

This chapter has explored the socio-political dimensions of discourses of endangerment and revitalization. We have looked in particular at the conditions for successful revitalization, the costs of revitalization and issues of standardization in relation to minority languages. The approach throughout has been highly practical rather than theoretical, with case studies drawn from Australia, New Zealand, Israel and Europe. Furthermore, we have seen how discourses of endangerment can spread about societal majority languages, especially if they are small languages such as Luxembourgish. However, such discourses can even spread about powerful global languages, as we will see in Chapter 14, where we critically analyse discourses constructing English as a language endangered by Spanish in the United States. Thus language endangerment can be either real or (merely) perceptual to different degrees in different contexts.

ACTIVITY: THE DISCOURSE OF ENDANGERMENT*

Look at the following extracts from a letter to the editor published in a Luxembourgish newspaper and explore how, in the educational domain, the discourse of endangerment surrounding Luxembourgish tends to be connected with the discourses of standardization and purism. More particularly, analyse the ideological implications of the metaphors that the author relies upon:

> Wat um Spill steet…
> Wa mer, fir déi opgezielte Risiken net anzegoen, eis Sprooch erhalen a stäerke wëllen, misste mer eng Rei vu Bedingungen erfëllen.
> (*Luxemburger Wort*, February 2008: 15)

> (What is at stake…
> If we don't want to run the risks listed above [the danger of Luxembourgish dying out] and if we want to maintain and strengthen our language, we would have to fulfil a number of conditions.)

All of the conditions mentioned in the article, which (according to the author) need to be fulfilled to ensure the survival of Luxembourgish, concern the teaching of Luxembourgish as a full subject at school, which leads the author to address the thorny issue of standardization. Read the following extract and consider how the author attempts to construct a boundary between standardization and purism:

> Fir datt een eis Sprooch enseignéiere kann, muss se och eenegermoosse standardiséiert ginn, dat heescht, mir mussen emol festleeën, wat dann eigentlech Lëtzebuergesch ass. Beispill: Soe mir Igel, Däreldéier, Kéisécker oder déi dräi? A wann déi dräi richteg sinn, wat fir een Ausdrock ass Standard-Lëtzebuergesch, wat enseignéiere mir? Selbstverständlech wier Purismus hei feel op der Plaz; e Minimum vun Normen wier awer néideg.
>
> (*Luxemburger Wort*, February 2008: 15)

> (So that our language can be taught, it also has to be standardized to some extent; i.e. we have to decide what actually is Luxembourgish. For example: do we say *Igel* ['hedgehog', perceived German word], *Däreldéier* ['Luxembourgish' variant no. 1], *Kéisécker* ['Luxembourgish' variant no. 2], or all three words? And if the three are correct, which term is standard Luxembourgish, which term do we teach? Of course, purism would be out of place here, but we do need a minimum of norms.)

*Brief comments on this Activity can be found on page 290.

FOR DISCUSSION: SUCCESSFUL LANGUAGE REVITALIZATION

What factors promote language maintenance? What are successful revitalization strategies? How can the human costs of revitalization be minimized?

PROJECT WORK: THE REVITALIZATION OF WELSH

Investigate the contemporary language situation in Wales. In what ways or to what extent could the case of Welsh be looked upon as a story of successful revitalization? You may want to read Williams (2000), Musk (2012), Pietikäinen *et al.* (2016) or some of the chapters in the special issue of the *International Journal of the Sociology of Language* edited by Coupland and Aldridge (2009).

PROJECT WORK: IRISH IN A HISTORICAL PERSPECTIVE

Consider one or more of the following questions: How important was Irish Gaelic in Ireland's struggle for political independence from England? How important has its role been since the creation of an independent Irish state in 1921–2? How important has its role been during the Troubles in Northern Ireland? You may want to look up Crowley's *The War of Words: The Politics of Language in Ireland 1537–2004* or, more particularly, his account of language and cultural nationalism in nineteenth-century Ireland (Crowley 1996).

PROJECT WORK: THE STANDARDIZATION OF QUECHUA IN PERU

Study the debate about the standardization of Quechua in Peru and compare it with the situation of Breton. Quechua (or Kechwa) is an indigenous language spoken by over ten million people not only in Peru but also in Ecuador (where it is usually referred to as Quichua or Kichwa; see Chapter 11), Bolivia and other South American countries. You could start off by reading Hornberger (1995) or Hornberger and King (1998).

PROJECT WORK: ENDANGERED LANGUAGE REVITALIZATION

Look at the UNESCO Interactive Atlas of the World's Languages in Danger (www.unesco.org/culture/ich/index.php?pg=00206). Choose a particular country that you are interested in and an endangered language in this country. Then carry out some research on this language: has there been an attempt to revitalize it? To what extent has it been successful? Is the language fully standardized, and if not, has there been an attempt to standardize it? What have been the 'costs' of revitalization (in Shohamy's sense of the word)? Prepare a presentation for the other students in your class.

PROJECT WORK: MĀORI AND CORSICAN LEARNING AND TEACHING PHILOSOPHIES

Explore either the learning and teaching philosophy of Māori-medium education or the polynomic approach to the learning and teaching of Corsican. For the former, you could start by looking at Berryman *et al.* (2010) and for the latter, a good place to start would be Jaffe (2005, available online in French, or Jaffe 1999, especially pages 185–90). Prepare a presentation for the other students in your class.

REFERENCES AND SUGGESTIONS FOR FURTHER READING

Language shift and language revitalization

Austin, Peter K. and Sallabank, Julia (eds) (2015) *The Cambridge Handbook of Endangered Languages*, Cambridge: Cambridge University Press.

Fishman, Joshua (ed.) (2000) *Can Threatened Languages Be Saved? Reversing Language Shift, Revisited: A 21st Century Perspective*, Clevedon: Multilingual Matters.

Grenoble, Lenore and Whaley, Lindsay (2005) *Saving Languages: An Introduction to Language Revitalization*, Cambridge: Cambridge University Press.

Hornberger, Nancy (2008) *Can Schools Save Indigenous Languages? Policy and Practice on Four Continents*, Clevedon: Multilingual Matters.

King, Kendall A., Schilling-Estes, Natalie, Fogle, Lyn, Lou, Jia Jackie and Soukup, Barbara (eds) (2008) *Sustaining Linguistic Diversity: Endangered and Minority Languages and Language Varieties*, Washington DC: Georgetown University Press.

Australian Aboriginal languages

Herriman, Michael (1996) 'Language policy in Australia', in M. Herriman and B. Burnaby (eds) *Language Policies in English-Dominant Countries*, Clevedon: Multilingual Matters, 35–61.

Lo Bianco, Joseph and Rhydwen, Mari (2001) 'Is the extinction of Australia's indigenous languages inevitable?', in J.A. Fishman (ed.) *Can Threatened Languages Be Saved?*, Clevedon: Multilingual Matters, 391–422.

Meakins, Felicity and O'Shannessy, Carmel (eds) (2016) *Loss and Renewal: Australian Languages since Colonisation*, Berlin: Mouton de Gruyter.

Moore, Helen (2000) 'Language policies as virtual realities: Two Australian examples', in T. Ricento (ed.) *Ideology, Politics, and Language Policies: Focus on English*, Amsterdam: Benjamins, 25–47.

Walsh, Michael (2007) 'Languages and their status in Aboriginal Australia', in M. Walsh and C. Yallop (eds) *Language and Culture in Aboriginal Australia* (2nd edition), Canberra: Aboriginal Studies Press, 1–13.

Māori in New Zealand

Albury, Nathan John (2016) 'Defining Māori language revitalisation: A project in folk linguistics', *Journal of Sociolinguistics*, 20: 287–311.

Berryman, Mere, Glynn, Ted, Woller, Paul and Reweti, Mate (2010) 'Māori language policy and practice in New Zealand schools', in K. Menken and O. García (eds) *Negotiating Language Policies in Schools*, London: Routledge, 145–61.

Hill, Richard and May, Stephen (2011) 'Exploring biliteracy in Māori-medium education: An ethnographic perspective', in T.L. McCarty (ed.) *Ethnography and Language Policy*, London: Routledge, 161–83.

May, Stephen (2001) *Language and Minority Rights*, London: Longman.

—— (2006) 'Language policy and minority rights', in T. Ricento (ed.) *An Introduction to Language Policy: Theory and Method*, Oxford: Blackwell, 255–72.

Sámi and Kven in Norway

Lane, Pia (2009) 'Mediating national language management: The discourse of citizenship categorization in Norwegian media', *Language Policy*, 8: 209–25.

—— (2010) '"We did what we thought was best for our children": A nexus analysis of language shift in a Kven community', *International Journal of the Sociology of Language*, 202: 63–78.

Pietikäinen, Sari (2010) 'Sámi language mobility: Scales and discourses of multilingualism in a polycentric environment', *International Journal of the Sociology of Language*, 202: 79–101.

Hebrew in Israel

Kuzar, Ron (2001) *Hebrew and Zionism: A Discourse Analytic Cultural Study*, Berlin: Mouton de Gruyter.

Shohamy, Elana (2006) *Language Policy*, Abingdon: Routledge.

—— (2008) 'At what cost? Methods of language revival and protection', in K. King, N. Schilling-Estes, L. Fogle, J.J. Lou and B. Soukup (eds) *Sustaining Linguistic Diversity*, Washington DC: Georgetown University Press, 205–18.

Breton and Corsican in France

Bentahila, A. and Davies, E. (1993) 'Language revival: Restoration or transformation?', *Journal of Multilingual and Multicultural Development*, 14: 355–73.

Blackwood, Robert (2010) *The State, the Activists and the Islanders: Language Policy on Corsica*, Dordrecht: Springer.

Hornsby, Michael (2015) *Revitalizing Minority Languages: New Speakers of Breton, Yiddish and Lemko*, Basingstoke: Palgrave.

Jaffe, Alexandra (1999) *Ideologies in Action: Language Politics on Corsica*, Berlin: Mouton de Gruyter.

—— (2005) 'La polynomie dans une école bilingue corse: bilan et défis', *Marges linguistiques*, 10: 282–300 (www.revue-texto.net/Archives/Archives.html).

McDonald, Maryon (1989) *We Are Not French! Language, Culture and Identity in Brittany*, London: Routledge.

Welsh and Irish

Coupland, Nikolas and Aldridge, Michelle (2009) 'Introduction: A critical approach to the revitalization of Welsh', *International Journal of the Sociology of Language*, 195: 5–13.

Crowley, Tony (1996) 'Forging the nation: Language and cultural nationalism in nineteenth-century Ireland', in *Language in History: Theories and Texts*, London: Routledge, 99–146.

—— (2005) *The War of Words: The Politics of Language in Ireland 1537–2004*, Oxford: Oxford University Press.

Musk, Nigel (2012) 'Performing bilingualism in Wales: Arguing the case for empirical and theoretical eclecticism', *Pragmatics*, 22: 651–69.

O'Rourke, Bernadette (2011) *Galician and Irish in the European Context: Attitudes towards Weak and Strong Minority Languages*, Basingstoke: Palgrave.

Pietikäinen, Sari, Jaffe, Alexandra, Kelly-Holmes, Helen and Coupland, Nikolas (2016) *Sociolinguistics from the Periphery: Small Languages in New Circumstances*, Cambridge: Cambridge University Press.

Williams, Colin (ed.) (2000) *Language Revitalization: Policy and Planning in Wales*, Cardiff: Cardiff University Press.

The standardization of Quechua

Hornberger, Nancy (1995) 'Five vowels or three? Linguistics and politics in Quechua language planning in Peru', in J. Tollefson (ed.) *Power and Inequality in Language Education*, Cambridge: Cambridge University Press, 187–205.

Hornberger, Nancy and King, Kendall A. (1998) 'Authenticity and unification in Quechua language planning', *Language, Culture and Curriculum*, 11: 390–410.

The discourse of endangerment and new speakers

Duchêne, Alexandre and Heller, Monica (eds) (2007) *Discourses of Endangerment*, London: Continuum.

Horner, Kristine (2005) 'Reimagining the nation: Discourses of language purism in Luxembourg', in N. Langer and W.V. Davies (eds) *Linguistic Purism in the Germanic Languages*, Berlin: Mouton de Gruyter, 166–85.

—— and Weber, Jean-Jacques (2010) 'Small languages, education and citizenship: The paradoxical case of Luxembourgish', *International Journal of the Sociology of Language*, 205: 179–92.

Hornsby, Michael (2015) 'The "new" and "traditional" speaker dichotomy: Bridging the gap', *International Journal of the Sociology of Language*, 231: 107–25.

O'Rourke, Bernadette, Pujolar, Joan and Ramallo, Fernando (2015) 'New speakers of minority languages: The challenging opportunity', *International Journal of the Sociology of Language*, 231: 1–20.

TEST YOURSELF QUIZ PART II*

1. With reference to the diagram on page 36, explain what a language is. Please use as your example one or more languages other than English. Make sure you also consider the concepts of dialect and standard language.
2. Can languages be counted? Discuss this in relation to the quotation from Romaine (1994) on page 41.
3. Do 'dialects' lack grammatical rules? Think of a 'dialect' you are familiar with and consider some of the ways in which it differs from the standard variety of the language in terms of grammar.
4. Do you think that English is a 'killer language'? Can you think of some examples that either support or contradict this view?
5. Focus on either Nouchi or Singlish. Is it a dialect or a language? Discuss.
6. Discuss the links between a variety such as Verlan and particular values and identities.
7. Discuss the influence of rap and hip hop on language. You could also look at specific examples from some song lyrics.
8. Is it important to try and revitalize endangered minority languages? Why or why not?
9. Discuss the advantages and disadvantages of standardization in the process of revitalization of an endangered minority language.
10. Is teaching an endangered minority language at school sufficient to ensure the survival of the language?

*Suggested answers can be found on page 294.

PART III

Societal and individual multilingualism

CHAPTER 6

Societal multilingualism

In this chapter we explore the language situation in a number of countries that officially recognize themselves as multilingual states. Many of these countries are situated outside the Western world, though there are a few exceptions. Indeed, most EU member-states officially recognize only one language, which is often directly linked to national identity: hence, the stereotyped generalizations that Italians speak Italian, Germans speak German, Danes speak Danish, etc., to the point where we have sometimes had students extending this (very European) assumption to other countries such as India and in all seriousness claiming that 'Indians speak Indian'.

India, however, is an officially multilingual state that recognizes as its official languages Hindi, English, as well as twenty-two regional standards. It uses a trilingual system of education (English, Hindi and a regional standard); it needs to be added that this is often not a form of mother tongue education (see Chapter 10), because many children use other local languages as their home languages. In fact, the three-language formula used in education is a – sometimes rather successful and other times less successful – way of coping with the immense linguistic diversity of the country. In some ways, it can be compared with the EU's language-in-education policy of 'mother tongue plus two other European languages' as a way of achieving the vaguely defined goal of 'unity in diversity'. After all, in EU policy, too, 'mother tongue' is usually interpreted as the standard variety of a European language, which may be more or less different from the varieties actually spoken by many children as their home languages (see Chapters 9–11).

What is important to be aware of is that the distinction between officially monolingual and multilingual states is not a fixed binary opposition but a dynamic and shifting continuum: depending on their language policies, states move on this continuum towards more monolinguality or more multilinguality. Thus, for instance, the EU policy on giving more rights to speakers of regional minority languages such as Welsh in the UK or Catalan in Spain has opened up new spaces for multilingualism in these areas. In this way, Spain and the UK have moved from more monolingual to more multilingual states, granting new rights to Catalan or Welsh, as well as their speakers. For instance, it is now possible to take the UK citizenship test not only in English but also in Welsh or Scottish Gaelic. In Catalonia, the 'catalanization' of state education (using Catalan rather than Castilian Spanish as the primary medium of instruction) has led to widespread Catalan–Castilian Spanish bilingualism since the 1980s.

While Spain and the UK have moved on the continuum from being more monolingual to more multilingual, other states have moved or are moving in the opposite direction. For instance, Ukraine has recently adopted a policy of de-Russification, thus turning the country into a more and more monolingual, Ukrainian-only space. Another example is officially trilingual Luxembourg, one of the smallest EU member-states, where the new citizenship test requires applicants to take a language test in only one language, namely Luxembourgish. This has effected a shift away from the traditional perception of Luxembourg as trilingual (Luxembourgish, German, French) to a new perception of it as a more monolingual, Luxembourgish-speaking country.

In this chapter, we explore such shifts which have recently affected the language policy balance within officially multilingual states. In particular, we look at how the global spread of English (see also Chapter 4) has upset the traditional language policy balance in a number of states. We discuss the language situation in Switzerland, the changing roles of Singlish and Mandarin Chinese in Singapore, as well as the postcolonial role of English in Hong Kong and China, South Africa and Nigeria. But first we briefly comment on shifting patterns of bilingualism in Ukraine.

UKRAINE

Ukraine was part of the USSR (Union of Soviet Socialist Republics) and as such subject to Soviet occupation. The increasing influence of the Russian language during this period is frequently interpreted nowadays as an oppressive policy of Russification (Pavlenko 2011). Since its independence in 1991, Ukraine has reversed this tendency and has implemented the opposite policy of de-Russification. Ukrainian is now the sole official language, and there is increasing social pressure to use Ukrainian not only in informal but also formal settings. One consequence of the shift from

Russian to Ukrainian is a tendency on the part of many speakers to mix the two linguistically related languages; however, such language mixing is often stigmatized, and there is an insistence on standard Ukrainian and linguistic correctness as a way of differentiating Ukrainian from Russian in the ongoing process of nation-building (Bilaniuk 2005). A number of laws were passed to increase the use of Ukrainian, especially in education and the media, though many of these laws were not fully implemented. For instance, in the domain of the media, the 1993 Law on Television and Radio Broadcasting stipulated that 50 per cent of broadcasts must be in Ukrainian, the 2004 regulation demanded that state companies must broadcast only in Ukrainian and a 2007 law required all foreign language (i.e. including Russian language) movies to be translated into Ukrainian, either dubbed or with subtitles.

As a result of these policies, as well as the tensions exacerbated by the civil strife in its eastern part, Ukraine has become, officially speaking, a more monolingual, Ukrainian-only country. Russian is perceived more and more as a 'foreign' language, or even 'the language of the enemy', and as such, is losing out to English, which has been pushing in strongly as the language of modernity and globalization. Because of the demand for English, many schools have reduced or even stopped their teaching of Russian and recruited large numbers of English teachers. As a result, young Ukrainians nowadays tend to be bilingual in Ukrainian and English rather than Ukrainian and Russian.

SWITZERLAND

Switzerland's multilingualism is based on a strict principle of territoriality: the four national languages, German, French, Italian and Romansch, are official regional languages in different parts of the country. In their education system, the Swiss traditionally learn the official language of their territory as L1 and another Swiss national language as their L2 – though we will see that this is in the process of changing.

Thus, for instance, in the German-speaking part of Switzerland, schoolchildren traditionally learn L1 German and L2 French. The complicating factor in the German-speaking part of Switzerland is the widespread use of a non-standard German variety usually referred to as Schwyzertüütsch (Swiss German). According to Watts (1999: 69), Swiss German has served as the most powerful marker of local Swiss identity at least since World War II, and its symbolic value is perceived to be much higher than that of standard German in all domains except the written medium. Many Swiss Germans look upon Swiss German as their mother tongue, while they refer to *Schriftdeutsch* (written or standard German) as their first foreign language.

Watts reaches the interesting conclusion that there is no danger of the Swiss German varieties dying out and that

> it is the oral forms of language which guarantee survival, not the written forms. In fact, Switzerland might even give the lie to the hypothesis that only a written standard can guarantee the survival of a language.
>
> (Watts 1999: 95)

At the same time, however, the Swiss German varieties are seen as obstacles to communication in the other parts of Switzerland. For instance, the French Swiss usually learn standard German as their L2, yet they often find it easier to communicate with the German Swiss in English (usually learnt as their L3). This is because many German Swiss resent using standard German and prefer to use their Swiss German varieties which, however, are difficult to understand for the French Swiss. So it is not surprising that English finds it easy to grow in such a situation.

Yet it was not in French Switzerland but in the heartland of German Switzerland that the initiative was first taken that upset the Swiss language policy balance. At the beginning of the twenty-first century, the canton of Zurich introduced English as the first foreign language in its primary schools (instead of French), thus giving priority to English over the Swiss national languages. The effect has been a deep shock leading to a major **language-ideological debate** frequently referred to as the *Sprachenstreit* (language strife; see Stotz 2006). According to Grin and Korth (2005: 79–80), questions such as the following were raised as part of these debates: Will English become the lingua franca of Switzerland? Will this undermine Swiss national unity? Is the future of the country endangered?

SINGAPORE

Just as in Switzerland, the language policy balance set up by the Singapore government over the last few decades is in the process of being broken up by the forces of globalization, though we will see that here it is not just the global role of English but also that of Mandarin that are the catalysts for change.

When Singapore gained independence from British colonialism in 1965, it was initially a member of the Malaysian Federation. This explains why the national language of Singapore is Malay, though it now recognizes four co-official languages: Malay, Mandarin, Tamil and English. The population is divided into three main ethnic groups, to each of which an official mother tongue is assigned:

ethnic group	*official mother tongue*
Chinese	Mandarin Chinese
Malay	Malay
Indian	Tamil

This policy essentializes both ethnicity and language use (see Chapter 7), whereas the reality is far more complex than the official representation of it (Bokhorst-Heng 1999): thus, concerning language use, many Chinese Singaporeans are speakers of other Chinese languages such as Cantonese, Hokkien, Teochew, etc.; many Malay Singaporeans are speakers of Javanese, Boyanese, etc.; and many Indian Singaporeans are speakers of Hindi, Gujerati, Punjabi, Urdu, Bengali, etc.

During the colonial period, vernacular-medium education in Chinese, Malay or Tamil was the most common form of education, while English-medium education was reserved for a small elite. After independence, more and more parents enrolled their children in English-medium schools, and there were fewer and fewer students in the Chinese, Malay or Tamil-medium schools. As a result, from 1987, the government introduced a state-wide system of bilingual education, with English being taught as L1, and the official mother tongue as L2. Thus, for instance, Chinese Singaporeans go to Chinese schools where they are taught first English and then Mandarin. The language-in-education policy is frequently described as 'English plus mother tongue bilingualism'.

English is seen primarily as the global language of business and science, but at the same time also as a carrier of decadent Western values. Therefore the officially assigned mother tongues play an important role as repositories of traditional Asian values. However, as already pointed out above, one major obstacle faced by the government in the realization of its language policy aims has been the fact that many Singaporeans speak other languages than the official mother tongues as their home languages. It is for this reason that the government launched a language policy campaign addressed to the Chinese Singaporeans, who constitute by far the largest ethnic group in Singapore: namely, the Speak Mandarin campaign. The Chinese Singaporeans who were speakers of other Chinese varieties or languages were encouraged to switch over to Mandarin. However, language policies seldom turn out exactly the way the policy-makers expect them to. In this case, large numbers of Chinese Singaporeans actually switched from their variety of Chinese to a variety of English, often to better prepare their children for the school system, in which after all English (as the L1) plays a more important role than Mandarin (the L2).

The result has been the development of a Singaporean variety of English known as Singlish (or Singaporean English; see Chapter 4). Singlish has spread so much that it has become, in Rubdy's (2001: 347, 352) words, an 'icon of national identity', a 'language of solidarity, identity and pride' and 'the glue that binds Singaporeans'. However, as Rubdy points out, this does not fit into the government's ideal of economic development, which is based upon the use of standard English as the global lingua franca of international trade. Hence, they have attempted to stigmatize Singlish as 'English corrupted by Singaporeans' (Rubdy 2001: 348) and have launched a new campaign aiming to promote standard English and to eradicate Singlish: the Speak Good English movement.

While the government relentlessly pursues its language policy goals, though – as we have seen – not always with the intended success, global economic developments can easily upset the precarious language policy balance that has been achieved. The most important of these developments has doubtlessly been the rise of mainland China as an economic power. As a result, Mandarin has acquired more instrumental value because of Singapore's extensive trade links with China. Mandarin has thus become more important than the other official mother tongues, Malay and Tamil. This has upset the delicate balance between the three official mother tongues, which were supposed to be equally important as the bearers of Asian cultural values and identities. However, not only has Singlish taken over at least partly this role of a marker of Singaporean identity, but moreover Mandarin is now breaking through its traditional role as official mother tongue and acquiring new instrumental value alongside English (see Wee 2008). Because of these shifts in the roles of the different languages in Singapore, many non-Chinese parents are now demanding the right for their children to learn Mandarin at school. (For the moment, the Malay ethnic group have to send their children to a school where they learn English as L1 and Malay as L2, and Indian ethnic children learn English L1 and Tamil L2.) All this obviously undermines the government's official language planning and disrupts the balance it had endeavoured to construct between English and the official mother tongues. It could mean that, even while there is no doubt that Singapore will remain multilingual, its educational system might in the long term evolve into a largely bilingual English–Mandarin one.

HONG KONG AND CHINA

In 1997 Hong Kong changed its status from a British colony to a Special Administrative Region of China. Two languages are recognized as official: Chinese and English, where Chinese is normally understood to refer to Modern Standard Chinese as the written version and Cantonese as the spoken one. At the same time, Putonghua (Mandarin), the spoken form of Modern Standard Chinese, which is the national language of China as a whole, has been vigorously promoted since the 1997 changeover of sovereignty. The official policy is for all Hong Kongers to become biliterate and trilingual: biliterate in Chinese and English, and trilingual in Cantonese, Putonghua and English.

As for English in Hong Kong, it has played a highly controversial role as the colonial language. As in many other countries of the world, the colonial language was reserved for a small elite of local administrators who were allowed privileged access to an English-medium education, whereas all other colonial subjects were only given access to frequently second-rate types of vernacular Chinese education. According to Pennycook (2002), the British colonial government in Hong Kong promoted vernacular Chinese education as a way of inculcating the conservative ideals of Confucian ethics and thus enhancing the colonial domination of its subjects: 'Conservative Chinese education was the colonial route to the making of docile bodies' (Pennycook 2002: 108). Pennycook's analysis of vernacular education as a form of governmentality and surveillance leads him to the following important conclusion which foreshadows our discussion in Chapter 10:

> This understanding of increased modes of surveillance brings into question [the] widely held view of language policy that mother tongue or vernacular education is necessarily preferable to education in other languages.
>
> (Pennycook 2002: 108)

It is this historical background, as well as the continuing socioeconomic importance of English in Hong Kong society, that explains why English-medium education is in such high demand nowadays. Yet, after Hong Kong's return to China in 1997, the government introduced a streaming system channelling large numbers of students into Chinese-medium education. Lin (2001) argues that this policy reproduces social stratification in Hong Kong society: only the children of the English-oriented elite gain access to the prestige English-medium schools. As a result, there is a widening gap between a wealthy elite, whose children study at English-medium schools, and most other parents, who are forced to send their children to Chinese-medium schools. In this way, the present system perpetuates the social injustices of the colonial system. Therefore Lin (2001) advocates instead a more flexible, bilingual English–Chinese educational system for all students at all levels of education. In fact, the Hong Kong government has to some extent responded to these criticisms by allowing more English-medium instruction in the Chinese-medium schools since September 2010.

Just as in Hong Kong, there is also an enormous and ever-increasing demand for English in the rest of China. Official policy has responded to it by introducing English as a primary school subject from third grade. Before this reform, implemented on a gradual basis from 2001 onwards, English had on the whole only been taught at secondary level. As a result, nowadays the majority population, the Han Chinese, are expected to be bilingual in standard Chinese (Putonghua 'Common Language') and English, while the numerous minority groups are expected to be at least bilingual in standard Chinese and their own minority language (which usually functions as an additional official language within its autonomous administrative region, such as Tibetan in Tibet or Mongolian in Inner Mongolia).

However, as Lam and Wang (2008) show, the actual linguistic reality of China is far more complex than the official bilingual policy, with most people not only using standard Chinese and English but also a range of local or regional Chinese 'dialects' as well as minority languages. Lam and Wang discuss in detail the circumstances of a number of Han Chinese and minority group members. Their vignettes of minority group members include, for instance, Mei whose home language is Yao (a minority language that she still uses for ingroup communication). At school she learnt Putonghua but also picked up the local Guilin 'dialect' used by most of her schoolmates. At later stages, she moreover learnt two foreign languages (English and Japanese). As for Ma, he used the Dong language at home and also learnt the Zhuang language, two minority languages spoken in the area where he grew up. At school, he learnt both the Guiliu 'dialect' and Putonghua, as well as a number of foreign languages (mainly English). As for the Han Chinese group members that Lam and Wang interviewed, they used Putonghua, one or more local or regional 'dialects' and one or more foreign languages, though none of them had learnt any of the minority languages. On the whole, minority group members tended to be even more multilingual than the Han Chinese majority population, as all of them, apart from their home language(s), also learnt one of the Chinese 'dialects' as a kind of 'intermediary code' (Lam and Wang 2008: 166) before learning Putonghua.

Yet behind this remarkable linguistic diversity, there is also a strong ideology of homogeneity and uniformity focused on Putonghua, as Dong (2009) shows. Thus, not speaking Putonghua is sometimes even identified with being poorly educated. As one of Dong's informants says, complaining about the fact that she could not understand a Chinese man who had recently migrated from the countryside to Beijing: 'What kind of education did he have if he couldn't even speak Putonghua?' (Dong 2009: 117).

Whereas the informant was a local Beijing woman, her male interlocutor was from Hubei province in the middle of China and could only speak his regional vernacular. Another of Dong's examples involves a discussion among primary schoolchildren in Beijing about the differences between rural and urban origins. At one point in the discussion, one of the migrant (or rural-origin) children says: 'Isn't it enough that we are all *Chinese*? Look, we all speak *Putonghua*' (Dong 2009: 119; the italics reflect the speaker's emphasis on the words 'Chinese' and 'Putonghua'). Dong comments that the child is here overlaying her own (stigmatized) rural identity with a national identity – being Chinese – which is constructed around the use of Putonghua. This reveals the prevalence of the one nation–one language ideology even among ten-year-old children.

SOUTH AFRICA

After the Anglo-Boer war (1899–1902), the defeated Afrikaners became British citizens and South Africa a 'dominion' of the British Empire (like Canada and Australia). The majority of whites were Afrikaans-speaking, so that this Dutch creole (rather than English) became the language frequently associated with white supremacy. This was particularly the case after 1948, when the National Party gained power and the white Afrikaner nationalists began to set up the apartheid system (the whites formed about 20 per cent of the total population). Some of the major events in the history of anti-apartheid resistance include the following: in 1960 the anti-pass law campaigns gathered momentum and led to brutal government retaliation culminating in the Sharpeville massacre, where police shot sixty-nine demonstrators and injured many others; in 1976, during the Soweto rising, schoolchildren protesting against the imposition of Afrikaans in schools were massacred; the following year Steve Biko, an activist of the Black Consciousness movement and a hero of anti-apartheid resistance, died in custody from police brutality. The other great hero, Nelson Mandela, was released in 1990 after twenty-seven years of imprisonment. This important event heralded the end of the apartheid system and the gradual change from a racist to a democratic political regime. Indeed, in the elections of April 1994, an ANC (African National Congress) government was elected and Mandela became its President. Under Mandela, South Africa developed into a multiethnic 'rainbow nation'.

Just as in Singapore and Hong Kong, vernacular or mother tongue education had been used for the purpose of social domination in South Africa during the period of apartheid. In 1953, the apartheid government introduced the Bantu Education Act, which enforced compulsory mother tongue education for all blacks and blocked their access to English. This was rightly seen by the black population as an attempt by the apartheid government to imprison them within a second-rate education and to ensure that black schoolchildren would not reach a high command of English. Among the black population, this has led to negative attitudes towards the indigenous African languages, as well as negative attitudes towards Afrikaans as the language of the oppressors. On the other hand, many South Africans now demand access to English and, through English, to better educational and employment opportunities.

After the transition from apartheid to democracy, Nelson Mandela's government voted a new constitution which recognizes eleven official languages: English, Afrikaans, isiZulu, isiXhosa, Sepedi, Setswana, Sesotho, Xitsonga, siSwati, Tshivenda and isiNdebele. The government has endeavoured to revitalize the indigenous African languages by promoting them as media of instruction, so that education is often trilingual with the African 'mother tongue' as L1, English L2 and Afrikaans L3. However, as we will see in Chapter 10, the revalorization of indigenous languages has been fraught with problems.

The relative failure of official language policy is due primarily to people's perception of English as the key to upward social mobility. In fact, more and more black South Africans are nowadays bilingual in both English and an African language such as isiZulu or isiXhosa. Others use mixed codes such as Tsotsitaal or Isicamtho, which incorporate linguistic material from indigenous languages as well as English and Afrikaans, as informal means of wider communication, especially in urban communities. Fortunately, in the new democratic South Africa, the education system has been flexible: as Probyn (2005: 157) puts it,

> in metropolitan areas such as around Johannesburg in the centre of the country, African schools reflect the mix of indigenous home languages in their communities and so have tended to introduce English medium instruction even earlier, from Grade 1, to accommodate the wide range of home languages in the classroom.

At the same time, Probyn insists that this is not a matter of replacing African languages by English: on the contrary, most parents value both their indigenous home language and English, and want their children to learn both at school. Teachers, too, frequently rely on code-switching between English and the indigenous languages (see e.g. Setati *et al.* 2002). In this way, we reach the same conclusion again as in our discussion of Hong Kong: namely, that the best system of education might be a flexible system of additive bilingual education, giving children access to both English and indigenous languages.

NIGERIA

Nigeria shares a number of features with South Africa, though it is even more multilingual with its approximately 500 indigenous languages. Just as in South Africa, English shares official status with three of these indigenous languages: Hausa, Yoruba and Igbo. French was declared as the second official language by former President Abacha, though only as a political means of counteracting the boycott imposed upon him at the time by the US, the UK and the Commonwealth countries because of his extremely poor record on human rights. In fact, French is spoken by very few Nigerians. English, on the other hand, is spoken by the educated elite and, just as in South Africa, is spreading fast, especially in urban areas. In this way, English is the only national lingua franca (even though it is only spoken by a minority of the population), whereas all the indigenous languages – including Hausa, Yoruba and Igbo – are regional languages limited to particular areas of the territory.

The Nigerian National Policy on Education has two main linguistic pillars (though not implemented everywhere in the country): the mother tongue-medium policy and the multilingual policy. The former states that as far as possible the children's first language should be used in pre-school and early primary education. In practice, however, the medium of instruction at school is often not the children's home language but the dominant language of the area (Adegbija 2004: 216–17). As for the multilingual policy, on the one hand it provides for a switch in medium of instruction from the indigenous 'first language' to English about halfway through primary education and, on the other hand, it expects all students to learn another indigenous language (usually Hausa, Yoruba or Igbo) at secondary level. Ideally, students would then be trilingual in English and two indigenous languages, though in practice, again, this policy is seldom fully implemented. What is clear, though, is the strong emphasis on English, which at this level is both medium of instruction and a core subject.

There is one other language that is widely spoken in the country but which is not officially recognized and plays no (official) role in education: namely, Nigerian Pidgin English. It is often used as an inter-ethnic lingua franca in urban interactions, as the language of trade in the marketplaces and as the language of entertainment and culture in the media and literature. In this book, there is an example of it in the Activity in Chapter 4, where an extract from Nigerian writer Ken Saro-Wiwa's novel *Sozaboy* is reproduced.

As with Singlish in Singapore, more and more people actually speak Nigerian Pidgin English as their first language, yet it is stigmatized as 'bad' English and has a low status, because it is associated with mostly poor and uneducated speakers. According to Adegbija (2004: 226), it is a 'solidarity and intimacy language' and 'the most effective language of national mobilization and motivation at the grassroots level'. He therefore concludes that, given its 'widespread and far-ranging functions in the nation, Nigerian Pidgin deserves mention in Nigeria's language policy provisions' (Adegbija 2004: 227). Wolf and Igboanusi (2006: 346) are even more explicit in stating that for many children the use of Nigerian Pidgin as a first language in early education would be a pedagogically sound measure. Indeed, it is important to take into account all the children's home linguistic resources and to build the best possible education system upon these foundations.

CONCLUSION

In this chapter we have looked at a number of officially multilingual states including Switzerland, Singapore, Hong Kong, China, South Africa and Nigeria. We have focused in particular on how global socio-political developments can affect the multilingual policy arrangements in a state. We need to add that the language policy issues in all of these states are no different and no greater than in most officially monolingual states, which are affected in very similar ways by global processes. Hence, any remaining fear of societal multilingualism seems wholly unjustified. For school systems, for instance, the solution advocated in this chapter (as well as in Chapter 9) is a flexible system of additive bi/multilingual education building upon the children's actual home linguistic resources – and this is the best solution not only for officially multilingual but also officially monolingual states. In the following chapter, we examine in greater detail the nature and full complexity of multilinguals' verbal resources and repertoires.

ACTIVITY: FOR OR AGAINST PUTONGHUA AS STANDARD CHINESE

The imposition of Mandarin (Putonghua) as the standard has not gone unchallenged in China. Thus, in July 2010, protests against Putonghua and in favour of Cantonese took place in Guangzhou and Hong Kong (areas where Cantonese is widely used). Official proposals to restrict the use of Cantonese on Guangzhou TV and to replace it with Putonghua sparked off the protests in defence of Cantonese.

The following is a brief extract from a comment about these protests posted on Chinese-forums.com on 26 July 2010 (http://www.chinese-forums.com/index.php?/topic/26982-pro-cantonese-protest-in-guangzhou).

Analyse the writer's comment and the underlying language ideologies, as discussed in Chapter 2:

> What do you guys think? I'm surprised to see a group of people care so much about their dialect.

FOR DISCUSSION: THE EFFECTS OF GLOBALIZATION

In what ways have the processes of globalization affected the language and language-in-education policies of a country that you are familiar with? Or have official policies remained relatively unchanged, even while socio-linguistic practices have changed considerably? Also consider the role of English in these changes.

PROJECT WORK: LANGUAGE-IDEOLOGICAL DEBATES

According to Blommaert (1999), a language-ideological debate occurs at a moment in time when questions of language are highly salient in a particular society. Carry out some research to find out more about one of the key language-ideological debates in a country that we looked at in this chapter:

- the debates about de-Russification in Ukraine (Bilaniuk 2005; Pavlenko 2011)
- the *Sprachenstreit* (language strife) in Switzerland in 2001 (Grin and Korth 2005; Stotz 2006)
- the debates surrounding the Speak Mandarin campaign and/or the Speak Good English movement in Singapore (Bokhorst-Heng 1999; Rubdy 2001; Wee 2008; Lim, Pakir and Wee 2010)
- the debates surrounding mother tongue education in South Africa or Nigeria (Probyn 2005; Setati *et al.* 2002; Adegbija 2004; Wolf and Igboanusi 2006; see also Chapter 10 in this book about mother tongue education).

PROJECT WORK: LANGUAGE POLICY SHIFTS

Choose a state where there has been an official shift in language policy (or in language-in-education policy), whether due to political independence, globalization or other social and economic factors. Read as much as you can about the language situation in this state to achieve a deeper understanding of the language-ideological debates that have been going on. If at all possible, do some ethnographic work to find out in what ways or to what extent the top-down policy decisions have been implemented (or not) by social actors on the 'ground', whether this is in classrooms or any other social spaces potentially affected by the language policy.

REFERENCES AND SUGGESTIONS FOR FURTHER READING

Ukraine

Bilaniuk, Laada (2005) *Contested Tongues: Language Politics and Cultural Correction in Ukraine*, Ithaca, NY: Cornell University Press.

Pavlenko, Aneta (2011) 'Language rights versus speakers' rights: On the applicability of Western language rights approaches in Eastern European contexts', *Language Policy*, 10: 37–58.

Switzerland

Grin, François and Korth, Britta (2005) 'On the reciprocal influence of language policies and language education: The case of English in Switzerland', *Language Policy*, 4: 67–85.

Stotz, Daniel (2006) 'Breaching the peace: Struggles around multilingualism in Switzerland', *Language Policy*, 5: 247–65.

Watts, Richard J. (1999) 'The ideology of dialect in Switzerland', in J. Blommaert (ed.) *Language Ideological Debates*, Berlin: Mouton de Gruyter, 67–103.

Singapore

Bokhorst-Heng, Wendy (1999) 'Singapore's *Speak Mandarin Campaign*: Language ideological debates and the imagining of the nation', in J. Blommaert (ed.) *Language Ideological Debates*, Berlin: Mouton de Gruyter, 235–65.

Lim, Lisa, Pakir, Anne and Wee, Lionel (eds) (2010) *English in Singapore: Modernity and Management*, Hong Kong: Hong Kong University Press.

Rubdy, Rani (2001) 'Creative destruction: Singapore's Speak Good English movement', *World Englishes*, 3: 341–55.

Stroud, Christopher and Wee, Lionel (2012) *Style, Identity and Literacy: English in Singapore*, Bristol: Multilingual Matters.

Vaish, Viniti, Gopinathan, S. and Liu, Yongbing (eds) (2007) *Language, Capital, Culture: Critical Studies of Language and Education in Singapore*, Rotterdam: Sense Publishers.

Wee, Lionel (2008) 'Linguistic instrumentalism in Singapore', in P. Tan and R. Rubdy (eds) *Language as Commodity: Global Structures, Local Marketplaces*, London: Continuum, 31–43.

Hong Kong and China

Dong, Jie (2009) '"Isn't it enough to be a Chinese speaker?": Language ideology and migrant identity construction in a public school in Beijing', *Language and Communication*, 29: 115–26.

Feng, Anwei (ed.) (2011) *English Language Education across Greater China*, Bristol: Multilingual Matters.

Lam, Agnes and Wang, Wenfeng (2008) 'Negotiating language value in multilingual China', in P. Tan and R. Rubdy (eds) *Language as Commodity*, London: Continuum, 146–70.

Li, David C.S. (2017) *Multilingual Hong Kong: Languages, Literacies and Identities*, Dordrecht: Springer.

Lin, Angel (2001) 'Symbolic domination and bilingual classroom practices in Hong Kong', in M. Heller and M. Martin-Jones (eds) *Voices of Authority: Education and Linguistic Difference*, Westport, CT: Ablex, 139–68.

Pennycook, Alastair (2002) 'Language policy and docile bodies: Hong Kong and governmentality', in J. Tollefson (ed.) *Language Policies in Education: Critical Issues*, Mahwah, NJ: Erlbaum, 91–110.

Pérez-Milans, Miguel (2013) *Urban Schools and English Language Education in Late Modern China: A Critical Sociolinguistic Ethnography*, London: Routledge.

Tsung, Linda (2009) *Minority Languages, Education and Communities in China*, Basingstoke: Palgrave.

South Africa

Hibbert, Liesel (2016) *The Linguistic Landscape of Post-Apartheid South Africa: Politics and Discourse*, Bristol: Multilingual Matters.

Orman, Jon (2008) *Language Policy and Nation-Building in Post-Apartheid South Africa*, Dordrecht: Springer.

Probyn, Margie (2005) 'Language and the struggle to learn: The intersection of classroom realities, language policy, and neo-colonial and globalization discourses in South African schools', in A. Lin and P. Martin (eds) *Decolonization, Globalization: Language-in-Education Policy and Practice*, Clevedon: Multilingual Matters, 153–72.

Setati, Mamokgheti, Adler, Jill, Reed, Yvonne and Bapoo, Abdool (2002) 'Incomplete journeys: Code-switching and other language practices in mathematics, science and English language classrooms in South Africa', *Language and Education*, 16: 128–49.

Nigeria

Adegbija, Efurosibina (2004) 'Language policy and planning in Nigeria', *Current Issues in Language Planning*, 5: 181–246.

Omoniyi, Tope (2003) 'Language ideology and politics: A critical appraisal of French as second official language in Nigeria', *AILA Review*, 16: 13–25.

Wolf, Hans-Georg and Igboanusi, Herbert (2006) 'Empowerment through English – a realistic view of the educational promotion of English in post-colonial contexts: The case of Nigeria', in M. Pütz, J.A. Fishman and J. Neff-van Aertselaer (eds) *'Along the Routes to Power': Explorations of Empowerment through Language*, Berlin: Mouton de Gruyter, 333–56.

Language-ideological debates

Blommaert, Jan (ed.) (1999) *Language Ideological Debates*, Berlin: Mouton de Gruyter.

CHAPTER 7

Language and identities

In this chapter we move our focus from the more macro level of various countries' official recognition of themselves as multilingual states (societal multilingualism) to the more micro level of people's multilingualism (individual multilingualism). It should be clear that all the languages or varieties that we use have both instrumental and identity functions. However, in any given place and time, some languages will be perceived as being more useful resources than others, with immigrant minority languages often at the bottom of this hierarchy. It always depends on the particular context we are in: a highly valued resource in one society does not necessarily keep this value when we move to another. At the same time, a negatively valued language can have a highly positive identity function associated with it for a particular group of people. In this chapter, we try to understand this identity function of language and how, in multilingual situations, identity may be linked to more than one language. Before we undertake this investigation, we first need to understand how identity works. Let us therefore start by looking at how other people influence our identity through processes of categorization.

CATEGORIZATION

We constantly categorize other people; we label, reify and objectify them. Labelling is a way of trying to fix somebody's identity, reducing it to a single core element that sums up her or his identity in our eyes: e.g. somebody *becomes* a 'foreigner' or an 'immigrant'. In this way, naming, categorizing and labelling are political acts. We need to be aware of this and make a conscious effort to resist and deconstruct stereotypical attributions and **categorizations**.

Thus categories such as 'foreigner' and 'immigrant' are socially constructed, and the important question is perhaps the one of power: who can impose her or his categories? Who defines where the boundaries between categories lie? Who controls 'the discourses that establish, justify and maintain relations between categories' (van Lier 2007: 51)? Another important point that emerges out of this discussion is the key distinction in social constructivist accounts of identity between ascribed or imposed identities (how people categorize us) and assumed or achieved identities (how we see ourselves). It is in and through a constant process of negotiation between ascribed and achieved identities that we construct our identity (Gee 2001; Pavlenko and Blackledge 2004). Palmer (2007: 281), relying on Gee's (2001) identity-theoretical framework, explains this process as follows:

> On one side, the person may be recognized as she or he desires to be identified – an achieved identity. And on the other side, others may disregard the achieved identity and continue to assign an identity through recognition to that individual – an ascribed identity. The individual may accept or reject the ascribed identity from others and/or the individual may continue in her or his endeavours to gain recognition of her or his achieved identity.

Thus individuals have agency but only within limits, as there also structural constraints that operate on these processes, in the sense that only certain identities are available to particular individuals in particular social contexts at particular historical moments. These processes involve a hegemonic element which reproduces social inequality, as Gee (2001: 113) explains in terms of what he calls discourse-identities (or D-identities):

> The elites often define or make sense of themselves (that is, fashion their achieved D-identities) in opposition to nonelites, to whom they ascribe inferior properties (ascribed D-identities) that contrast with the elites' more positive properties. This, historically, leaves nonelites with ascribed D-identities, which they may either 'internalize' (and, in a sense, accept) or oppose .... In modern capitalist societies, nonelites are 'encouraged' to accept the inferior identities elites ascribe to them in talk and interaction (ascribed D-identities) as if they were the actual achieved identities of these nonelite people, achieved on the basis of their lack of skill, intelligence, morality, or sufficient effort in comparison with the elites.
>
> At the same time, nonelites are encouraged to see the 'superior' identities of the elites as achieved D-identities rooted in their efforts within a fair and open system of competition.

Gee's description of the social pressure to internalize ascribed inferior (discourse-)identities applies to the attitude of many mainstream societies towards the migrant or transnational people living in their midst. This idea will be taken further in later chapters (especially Chapter 13); in this chapter we first explain Gee's concept of 'discourse-identities' and then turn to the two basic ways of conceptualizing identity: the essentialist and the social constructivist view, with the latter represented by such scholars as Gee and the others referred to in this section.

GEE'S FOUR WAYS TO VIEW IDENTITY

There is a need to briefly expound Gee's identity-theoretical framework and to situate his notion of discourse-identities within it. Gee (2001: 100f.) distinguishes between four ways to view identity:

- nature (N)-identities as states developed from forces in nature (e.g. being an identical twin): we are what we are primarily because of our 'natures';
- institution (I)-identities as positions authorized by authorities within institutions (e.g. being a US citizen or a university professor): we are what we are primarily because of the positions we occupy in society;
- discourse (D)-identities as individual traits recognized in and through our interactions with other people (e.g. being a charismatic person): we are what we are primarily because of our individual accomplishments as they are interactionally recognized by others;
- affinity (A)-identities as experiences shared in the practice of 'affinity groups' (e.g. being a 'Trekkie' or Star Trek fan): we are what we are primarily because of experiences we have had within affinity groups.

Gee (2001: 101) argues that, roughly speaking, Western society can be looked upon as having moved historically from foregrounding the first perspective through the second and third to the fourth one which, he maintains, is 'gaining prominence in the "new capitalism"' – though of course 'all of these perspectives coexist'. Gee (2001: 116f.) applies this framework to the US school system, showing how it reproduces social stratification in that African-American children are often ascribed an I-identity as 'at risk' students, whereas white children are often 'invited' to take on an A-identity as the future elites of the new capitalism. Gee's framework also helps us to understand how and why identity can be conceptualized in different ways: if you believe in the importance of N-identities, then you will tend to take an essentialist perspective on identity, whereas if you believe in the greater importance of I-, D- and

A-identities, you will take a more constructivist perspective. The following section explores this distinction in greater detail.

IDENTITY: A PEACH OR AN ONION?

How do you see your identity: more like a peach or more like an onion (to use two metaphors derived from classical Chinese philosophy)? If you see it as more like a peach, then you take an **essentialist** perspective, viewing the self as continuous and fixed. You believe in a 'true', 'deep' or 'real' self which, just like the stone in the middle of the peach, constitutes your core identity. The remaining parts of your identity are less central and liable to change over time. If, on the other hand, you see identity as more like an onion, then you believe in the possibility of having multiple and changing selves. Just like an onion, the self has many layers, some more central (inner) layers and others more peripheral (outer) ones, but all of them are subject to change over time and none of them forms an essential and fixed core (like the stone in the middle of the peach). The 'onion' view of identity is the dominant one in the social sciences nowadays, and it is referred to as '**social constructivist**' because it looks upon people as actively constructing (or co-constructing) their identity in society. We have added 'co-constructing', since we have already seen in a previous section that identity does not only depend on how we see ourselves but also on how others see us. Thus the social constructivist perspective on identity puts more emphasis on human agency, while the essentialist perspective is a more deterministic one.

The difference between essentialist and social constructivist perspectives is also reflected and constructed in the way we talk about identity. When we talk about *having* an identity, or about the danger of *losing* our identity, we take an essentialist perspective: we look upon identity as a kind of object that can be possessed or lost, like the stone in the middle of the peach. With the onion metaphor, on the other hand, a different understanding of identity comes to the fore: we may lose perhaps one or more layers of our identity, but this is part of the normal process of change, and new layers will replace the old ones. This suggests a view of identity as a process rather than an object; for this reason, some scholars prefer to talk about 'identification' rather than 'identity'. Hence, when we take a social constructivist view of identity, we will talk about identity being *constructed* and *negotiated*, or *performed* in 'acts of identity' (Le Page and Tabouret-Keller 1985). We also emphasize the multiplicity of identity layers by using plural forms as in, for example, 'repertoire of identities'.

While the point here is not to decide whether one or the other view of identity is the correct one, it is clear that most contemporary social scientists tend towards the social constructivist perspective. Indeed, a major issue with the essentialist perspective is that it would require us to specify what the 'stone' in the middle of the peach consists in; in other words, we get into the thorny philosophical and psychological question of what parts of our self are inborn and what parts are due to the process of socialization. To make this even more confusing, some of the deepest and innermost layers of our identity can be perceived or experienced as if they were essential. We may feel very strongly about them, which is why Williams (1977) refers to them as **structures of feeling**. As Rampton (2006: 345) puts it,

> Williams' 'structure of feeling' offers an account of more stable dimensions of subjectivity, related to particular aspects of socio-historical experience, but this is nevertheless incessantly recoloured, and at least potentially open to reshaping, amidst the pressures and contingencies of everyday practice.

NATIONAL, ETHNIC AND RACIAL IDENTITY

One of the deepest layers of identity that many people feel strongly about is their ethnic or national identity. The **ethnic identity** of the dominant group in a particular state is often equated with 'national' identity, while minority (or dominated) groups are considered to be 'ethnic'. In fact, both of these operate in a similar fashion and both involve ethnicity. As Jenkins (1997: 160) puts it, **national identity** is 'the ethnicity to which nationalist ideological identification refers'.

Moreover, the use of the term 'national identity' is highly ambiguous in that it can refer either to citizens of a political state or members of an 'imagined' nation (Anderson 1991). We therefore need to make a clear distinction between state and nation: the state is the political entity, whereas a nation is a group of people who *perceive* themselves as sharing certain elements such as the following:

- common descent
- common historical memories
- common culture
- homeland
- desire for political self-determination.

(based on Guibernau 1996)

The verb *perceive* is important in this definition of what a nation is: it emphasizes that these elements are not actually shared, but they need to be perceived as if they were. Depending on the socio-historical context, different elements will be foregrounded and become the key symbols of nationhood. For example, in Northern Ireland religion has played a major part in constructing boundaries between social groups, whereas in Belgium it is language that plays a more important role. These are among the different ethnic layers of identity that can bring out deep-seated feelings in people and that nationalist movements can use or abuse for their own ends. Hence, ethnicity, too, needs to be seen as something malleable and constructed, as de Fina (2007: 373–4) points out:

> As theorized by Barth (1969), ethnicity is used to define boundaries within and between groups, and therefore any aspect of social reality, from food to accent, can be used to symbolically index ethnic affiliation. Thus, there are no unified criteria that can universally define ethnic boundaries; rather, these are creatively invoked and negotiated by individuals and groups in response to their evolving social roles and circumstances.
>
> If ethnicity is seen as a process, then the close analysis of the negotiation of ethnicity within and between different groups becomes central to our understanding of its role in the construction of identities.

Finally, we should note that the concepts of race and **racial identity** are widely used in societies such as the USA, but they, too, are socially constructed. Thus, if 'black' and 'white' were natural categories, we would expect a continuum with a cut-off point in the middle:

white <-----------------------------/----------------------------> black

In fact, however, during the era of colonialism and in the Jim Crow states of the US, the rule that applied was the 'one-drop rule': one drop of 'black' blood was sufficient for a person to be categorized as black. In other words, the cut-off point was almost completely on the left of the continuum:

white <-/---> black

This shows how racial categories are not natural but socially constructed and, moreover, constructed differently in different societies at different times. Garner (2010: 4) gives the example of a person with a white mother and a black father, who might be categorized as black or mixed race in the UK, African-American or bi-racial in the US, red or yellow in Jamaica, and Coloured in South Africa at the time of apartheid. He emphasizes that these racial classifications are a function of unequal power relations and in each society they have different implications for access to resources such as education, housing and employment.

CODE-SWITCHING AND IDENTITY

Problems with the term 'code-switching'

We have seen that although the language–identity link is not essential, it is very important for many people. They frequently perceive their national identity as being linked to the national language. However, in multilingual situations it may be linked to more than one language. In the remainder of this chapter, we explore how the use of more than one linguistic variety connects with identity matters. This brings us to a key topic in research on multilingualism: namely, the study of code-switching.

The main concern of structural sociolinguistics has been to distinguish between various types of code-switching, between **code-switching** and **code-mixing**, or between code-switching and borrowing. Our concern here is not to classify but to understand what is going on. If we do introduce some traditional distinctions (e.g. between 'we-code' and 'they-code', or between situational and metaphorical code-switching), it is largely to get us to think about both the usefulness and limitations of these terms.

A problem with 'code' and the idea of switching between 'codes' is that it presupposes the existence of separate, bounded languages or varieties – something that our discussion in Chapter 3 has shown is not the case. It would be preferable to talk about people's communicative repertoires. If we understand code-switching in this more fluid and holistic way, it means that, whether we are traditionally seen as 'monolinguals' or 'multilinguals', we all switch between varieties, using to the full all the linguistic resources at our disposal. And it does not really make a difference whether we switch between varieties such as Bavarian and standard German or between 'languages' such as Dutch and German.

For all these reasons, sociolinguists have recently started to use terms which are less linked to the assumptions of structuralist linguistics. The most widely used terms that have been proposed include 'translingual practice' (Canagarajah 2013) and 'translanguaging' (García and Li Wei 2014). Otheguy, García and Reid (2015: 281) define **translanguaging** as 'the deployment of a speaker's full linguistic repertoire without regard for watchful adherence to the socially and politically defined boundaries of named (and usually national and state) languages'. Translanguaging practices, and their links with identity, are discussed in the final section of this chapter;

translanguaging – in preference to code-switching – is also the term that we will use most frequently in the following chapters of this book.

Deconstructing the 'we-code' vs. 'they-code' distinction

Gumperz (1982) distinguishes between **we-code** and **they-code**, where the former is often a societal minority language used at home and among peers (ingroup code), and the latter a societal majority language used in talk with outsiders (outgroup code). Therefore, the former is frequently associated with values such as solidarity and closeness, whereas the latter is associated with power and authority. While capturing a basic insight into the nature of code-switching, Gumperz' 'we-' vs. 'they-code' distinction has been criticized for being too fixed and essentialist. Bailey (2002: 132), for instance, argues that such 'associations between language varieties and social identities are not static or pre-set, but are negotiated in talk'. Sebba (1993) also insists that it is crucial to analyse specific interactions in specific contexts. He shows that for the Caribbean population in London both London Jamaican (or 'Creole') and London English tend to be 'we-codes', associated with the values of closeness and intimacy. He notes that a switch from London Jamaican to London English is often used

> to change from the main theme of the conversation to some kind of subroutine or secondary material: a check on shared information, a search for a missing name or date, a comment indicating how the adjacent material should be interpreted.
>
> (Sebba 1993: 123)

A switch from London English to London Jamaican, on the other hand, often corresponds with a highly emotional or affect-laden moment. He concludes that London Jamaican could be considered to be more of a 'we-code' than London English:

> If the 'we' code is taken to be the one which is closer to the 'heart and mind' of the speaker, and hence the one which imparts greatest salience to a given message, then Creole, even though used sparingly, does indeed seem to fulfil the 'we code' function for speakers in this community.
>
> (Sebba 1993: 123)

Thus, the 'we-' vs. 'they-code' binary opposition needs to be reconceptualized as a linguistic continuum along which speakers move in highly fluid ways as they construct fluid identities for themselves.

Situational and metaphorical code-switching

Gumperz (1982; Blom and Gumperz 1972) also distinguishes between **situational** and **metaphorical code-switching**. In the case of situational code-switching, the linguistic behaviour of the bi- or multilingual interlocutors changes when the situational circumstances (setting, participants) of their conversation change. An example would be the case of some French customers in an Irish pub in Paris who use French among themselves but switch into English when ordering drinks from the Irish bar attendant. A much more complex example of situational code-switching can be found in Meeuwis and Blommaert (1998), who discuss the language use of Congolese or Zairian immigrants in Belgium. French is the official language of the Democratic Republic of the Congo (formerly Zaire), though most people speak one or more of the national languages, the most important of which include Lingala (spoken especially in the capital, Kinshasa) and Swahili (mostly spoken in eastern parts of the country). These national languages are hardly ever used in their 'pure' form but almost always as 'code-switched' varieties (mixed with French). Meeuwis and Blommaert (1998: 84) note that 'pure' Lingala or Swahili is only used in highly restricted contexts such as religious services and often found to be 'nearly unintelligible' by many lay people.

The main language of communication between Congolese immigrants in Belgium is a code-switched Lingala-French variety, except among those from the eastern parts, who use Swahili-French in their ingroup. Meeuwis and Blommaert (1998: 86) insist that both Lingala-French and Swahili-French are 'single and autonomously existing code-switched codes'; in other words, they are 'fully-fledged "languages" in their own right'. Meeuwis and Blommaert (1998: 89–90) quote from a conversational interaction between three immigrants in Brussels: A is from Kinshasa (habitual language = Lingala-French), and B and C from eastern parts (habitual language = Swahili-French). Together they converse in Lingala-French, but comments limited to B and C are made in Swahili-French:

(1) B *Nani – ile soko iko* **fatigue**.
(what – that market is exhausting)

(2) A hein?
(sorry?)

(3) B zando wana eza **fatigue**.
(that market is exhausting)

(4) A ah. **heureusement qu'**okei lelo **dimanche**!
(you're lucky you went today Sunday!)

(Lingala in plain text; Swahili in italics; French bold)

In (1) B addresses a comment in Swahili-French to C, which A interrupts in (2), presumably because she wants to be involved in the conversation. B then repeats the same sentence in Lingala-French (3), and the conversation continues in Lingala-French (4). Hence, what we find here is a 'conversational alternation of languages, which are themselves code-switched codes' (Meeuwis and Blommaert 1998: 89). Meeuwis and Blommaert refer to this phenomenon as 'layered code-switching', or 'code-switching within code-switching', with the choice of code dependent on who is selected as interlocutor and not on any 'local identity negotiation' (Meeuwis and Blommaert 1998: 92).

In a metaphorical code-switch, on the other hand, the speaker uses a linguistic switch to invoke (and potentially renegotiate) particular values and to index a particular identity. **Indexicality** is the process whereby the speaker's use of certain linguistic forms 'points to' a specific social identity. Linguistic forms are thus ideologically associated with sets of social and cultural beliefs, values, norms and assumptions. An example from an excellent study by Bailey (2002) should make these relationships clearer: Bailey (2002: 132) investigates language use and the negotiation of identity among second-generation Dominican Americans and shows how particular language varieties can be 'used as metaphorical extensions of specific sociocultural interpretive frameworks, institutions, understandings, and activities, as described by Blom and Gumperz (1972) in their original distinction between situational and metaphorical code switching'. He is careful to point out that switches between the varieties

> do not follow simple dichotomies in which Spanish represents a Dominican 'we' and English represents a United States 'they', however. In the following example, Spanish is used to represent the voice of a stigmatized Dominican Other (as opposed to Dominican American).
>
> (Bailey 2002: 132)

In Bailey's example, Isabella, a Dominican American teenager, tells her friend Janelle that she is going to break up with Sammy, a recent Dominican immigrant to the US, because he talks 'like a hick'. She stylizes certain linguistic forms that Sammy uses, in particular Dominican Spanish terms of endearment such as *loca* and *niña*:

> He talks so much Spanish … I tell him, speak English, speak English … (wrinkled face) *lo::ca*, *lo::ca* ['honey']. He goes, you know, *ni:ña* ['girl'], and you know, and I don't want to hear it.
>
> (Bailey 2002: 133–4)

According to Bailey (2002: 135), Isabella's stylization of these forms

> serve[s] to index negative attributes: a stereotyped island Dominican backwardness that is inappropriate for an American urban youth context, and, perhaps, traditional Dominican gender roles associated with island Dominican male identities .... For Isabella, Sammy's addressing her as *loca* and *niña* may invoke a traditional Dominican social framework for their relationship, a framework that she wishes to avoid.

In this case, Isabella clearly distances herself from Spanish, which we might have expected to be her 'we-code'. Bailey's example thus highlights the importance of avoiding stereotyped attributions and the need to study language use in specific contexts to understand how speakers position themselves (and how they are positioned by other interlocutors), how they perform their own identities and how they stylize the identities of other social groups.

Voice and stylization

Examples of metaphorical code-switching such as the one discussed in the previous section about how Isabella distances herself from Sammy can also be analysed in terms of the Bakhtinian notion of **voice**. The Russian linguist and philosopher Mikhail Bakhtin (1981) has highlighted the multi-voiced nature of language, such that utterances are always in 'dialogue' with other voices or utterances. In particular, we frequently use code-switching to quote or represent other people's voices in our speech. According to Bakhtin, such **stylization** of somebody else's voice can be either **uni-directional** or **vari-directional**: in the former case, the evaluative positions of the speaker and of the person whose voice is being stylized are aligned, whereas in the latter case, they are in opposition (as in irony or parody). In uni-directional stylization, we admiringly or approvingly quote somebody else's words, for instance former US President Barack Obama's 2008 election campaign phrase 'Yes, we can'. In vari-directional stylization, on the other hand, we often construct, or co-construct and reinforce, a stereotype of a particular outgroup which we assume to be shared by our interlocutors (the ingroup) – as Isabella does in relation to what she sees as Sammy's traditional Dominican values.

Here is another example of vari-directional stylization taken from Kotthoff (2007), in which the speaker switches from standard German into the Alemannic 'dialect' to represent another person's voice. This other person had warned the speaker against marrying an Eastern European woman, thus drawing on a stereotype prevalent in 1990s Germany about Eastern

European women only wanting to marry German men for their money (Kotthoff 2007: 452):

> *Es war der Hammer.* Bisch wahnsinnig? Kannsch net mache. Menschenskinder, die Frau du, ha wennsch dere langweilig isch, got die Eikaufe, dann hot die Schuh du für tausend Mark.
>
> (*It was the last straw*. Are you crazy? You can't do that. Good God, the woman, when she is bored, she'll go shopping, then she will have shoes for a thousand marks.)
>
> (standard German: italics; Alemannic German: plain)

Kotthoff (2007: 453) comments that the Alemannic variety serves here 'as a marker of backward attitudes': namely, the attitudes of someone who is not only stingy but also 'hopelessly prejudiced against women from Eastern Europe, maybe against women in general'. In this way, a particular linguistic variety (Alemannic) becomes indexical of a particular (prejudiced) identity.

Language crossing

A form of metaphorical code-switching that has been much discussed in recent sociolinguistic literature is **language crossing**, which Rampton (2009: 287) defines as

> the use of a language which isn't generally thought to belong to the speaker. Language crossing involves a sense of movement across quite sharply felt social or ethnic boundaries.

In his study of language crossing among young people in a small town in the south Midlands of England, Rampton (1995) found examples of white and Asian adolescents using Caribbean Creole, black and white adolescents using Panjabi, and all of them stylizing Asian English. He interprets this language crossing as a reworking of ethnic and social class boundaries. Asian English was devalued because in this local setting it was associated with recent Bangladeshi immigrants, who were looked upon by the youngsters as being linguistically deficient in English and as occupying the lowest socioeconomic rank on the class ladder. Such examples of stylized Asian English as 'I no understanding English' (Rampton 2010: 138) were used in a clearly derisive way by youths intent on distancing themselves from this identity position. On the other hand, the position that many of them affiliated with was Caribbean Creole, which was valorized as the language of urban youth culture:

> Creole was widely seen as cool, tough and good to use. It was associated with assertiveness, verbal resourcefulness, competence in heterosexual relations, and opposition to authority. It was scarcely represented at all in the official school curriculum, and it occupied a dominant position in popular music and performance youth culture.
>
> (Rampton 2010: 137)

Finally, the inter-ethnic use of Panjabi was mostly limited to a small set of taboo words connected with such topics as sex, violence and drinking. Thus we can see that the language crossing examples can be interpreted on a continuum from affiliative uses (identifying with a particular group) to disaffiliative uses (maximizing distance from another group). Moreover, Rampton argues that language crossing allowed the youths to destabilize traditional, fixed ethnic identities and to construct new inter-ethnic identities for themselves.

In a second major study, Rampton (2006) investigates young people's language use in a multilingual and multiethnic inner-London secondary school. He looks at the stylization of social class or, more particularly, the adolescents' crossing into exaggerated 'posh' and Cockney accents, i.e. accents traditionally associated with the English upper class and the London working classes. He notes that such stylized acts tend to occur in moments of transition across social, spatial or interactional boundaries; hence stylized posh and Cockney are linked to the negotiation of boundaries (who's in and who's out? and how are the lines drawn interactionally?), and the fact that the students invoke traditional British class 'dialects' shows their sensitivity to these lines and boundaries. More specifically, the stylization of posh and Cockney introduces an orientation to 'high' vs. 'low'.

Rampton pushes the analysis further by arguing that such displays of classed sensitivity contain more pervasive or enduring elements including a psycho-social schema constructed around the high–low, mind–body, reason–emotion binary with a long history in English class society. Through their stylizations of posh and Cockney, the students reproduced this well-established 'cultural semantic', which associates posh with 'high', mind and reason and Cockney with 'low', body and emotion. As Rampton (2006: 344) puts it,

> The 'high-low' schema constitutes a relatively stable element in these youngsters' classed subjectivity, but rather than just a predefined mental template available for the interpretation of experience, it is always being animated, respecified and inflected in practical action tuned to the circumstances on hand.

In their acts of stylization, the students brought to consciousness a classed sensitivity which embodied deeper structures of feeling such as the historically grounded, high–low, mind–body, reason–emotion binary. Thus we can see that there is something deep-seated about these social class identity positions, even while the youngsters destabilized the traditional British class identities and constructed more fluid identities for themselves.

TRANSLANGUAGING IDENTITIES

In this section, we reconnect the notion of linguistic identity with the discussion of categorization at the beginning of the chapter. We have seen that most speakers in the world are multilingual to different degrees, and many of these multilingual speakers tend to mix their languages almost seamlessly. Their flexible and dynamic multilingual practices, which are usually referred to as 'translanguaging' in the scholarly literature, refract their complex and fluid linguistic identities (e.g. García and Li Wei 2014; Li Wei and Zhu 2013). Other speakers make a conscious effort to compartmentalize their languages. Different facets of their identity may be linked to the different languages they speak: they often feel that they are a different person depending on the language they speak in. This may be because they feel less confident when speaking in what is a second or foreign language for them, or that they associate each of their languages with different people, situations and cultural practices (see the discussion of Koven 2007 in Chapter 17).

We need to remember that, according to the definition given in Chapter 1, multilingualism involves not only being able to speak in different socially constructed 'languages' (such as English, French, German, . . .) but also in different varieties of the same 'language' (such as Yorkshire English, African-American English, . . .). Hence, also, we can see people as translanguaging among all the languages and varieties that they are familiar with. In this sense, multilingualism and translanguaging are the norm, and everybody translanguages to different degrees. For example, a speaker who translanguages among Yorkshire English and standard British English may feel that she is moving between a local or regional and a national identity, and may also be perceived as such by the hearer. Political issues may be more prominent with a speaker translanguaging between Scots and standard British English: what may be involved here could be a balancing of, or perhaps a tension between, national identities (Scottish vs. British), and the hearer, too, may react differently depending on the hearer's own political affiliations (e.g. pro- or anti-independence). In yet other cases, a 'racial' dimension may be linked to translanguaging practices: thus, an African-American speaker's switches from African-American English to standard American English may be interpreted by his African-American hearers as indexing an increasingly strong affiliation with white America and a betrayal of his own community, and hence his linguistic behaviour may be evaluated negatively and he may be accused of 'acting white'. In the borderlands of the US Southwest, it is the use of particular varieties of Spanish and English (standard Spanish, Chicano Spanish, Mexican Spanish, standard English, Chicano English, Spanglish) that indexes different kinds of border identities and differentiates one group of Latinas/os from another. As Bejarano (2005: 145–6) shows, Chicanas/os may refer to recently immigrated Mexicanas/os as 'wetbacks', especially if the Mexicanas/os lack fluency in English, while Mexicanas/os may call Chicanas/os 'agringado' (acting like an Anglo), especially if the Chicanas/os lack fluency in Spanish. In this way, we see how the translanguaging practices of people, as they are flexibly moving among different 'languages' or among varieties of the same 'language', are part and parcel of the ongoing, everyday process of identity construction and negotiation, and how they frequently lead to acts of other-categorization.

CONCLUSION: INDIVIDUAL AND SPATIAL REPERTOIRES

In the first part of this chapter, we have argued that any discussion of identity needs to take into account two aspects: how others see us (ascribed or imposed identities) and how we see ourselves (assumed or achieved identities). We have put forward arguments in favour of a more social constructivist understanding of identity. In the second part, we have explored how identity is constructed and negotiated through such multilingual strategies as code-switching, stylization and language crossing. Finally, we have discussed translanguaging practices and identities, and how they in turn link up with acts of categorization.

This chapter has also illustrated how sociolinguists are constantly searching for 'better' terms – translanguaging rather than code-switching and code-mixing – to move away from thinking of languages or codes as discrete, bounded entities. Therefore, when they study individual multilingualism and translanguaging practices, they consider not just a small number of named languages but the whole range of the individual's languages, varieties, genres, registers and styles, even if she (or he) masters these resources to very different degrees. Sociolinguists refer to the totality of these linguistic resources as a **repertoire**. Since repertoires have been biographically assembled, they are dynamic, constantly changing and never 'complete', as it were. For this reason, Blommaert and Backus (2013: 28) refer to them as 'indexical biographies', with the different resources indexing various aspects of people's language learning experiences and life trajectories.

According to Busch (2017), people's repertoires are linked to their 'lived experience of language'. The study of individual repertoires thus provides an insight into the nature of late modern, superdiverse subjectivities (Blommaert and Backus 2013). At the same time, however, we should not think of resources and repertoires as being purely individual; they are also closely linked to specific social spaces, in which particular speakers participate, each of which has its own linguistic norms. Therefore, Pennycook and Otsuji (2014: 166) talk about **spatial repertoires** as being the 'available and sedimented resources that derive from the repeated language practices of the people involved in the sets of activities related to particular places'. An example making clearer how the concept of spatial repertoire usefully complements that of individual repertoire can be found in the Activity that follows.

ACTIVITY: SPATIAL REPERTOIRES*

The interaction reproduced below takes place in the kitchen of a pizza restaurant in Sydney, Australia. The two Polish employees, Krzysztof and Aleksy, speak in English. At one moment, Krzysztof trips up in his search for the English word *cheese* and uses the Italian *formaggio* instead:

K: I'll bring formaggio (.) formaggi (.) whatever whatever it is!
A: Cheese
K: Yes

(Pennycook and Otsuji 2014: 174)

Since this is a part of a dialogue between two bilingual Polish–English employees, we might have expected them to switch into Polish. How then can we explain Krzysztof's use of the Italian word for cheese?

*Brief comments on this Activity can be found on page 290.

ACTIVITY: THE STORY OF THE DIFFICULT CUSTOMER*

Investigate language use and translanguaging in the following text taken from Sebba's (1993: 119–20) study of the Caribbean population in London. Here a British-born Caribbean adolescent tells his friend (also British-born Caribbean) a story about what happened in the shop where he works as a cashier. A Caribbean man came in to buy a bottle of Lucozade, for which the shop normally refunds the deposit when the customer returns the empty bottle. In this case, the man drank the bottle of Lucozade in the shop and asked for an immediate refund:

> [He] ask(d) for the money back (see man) *me want me money now*. He goes (pnk) (I'm on) the till guy (.) hhh (I jus) (.) I jus' look round at 'im (.) I said well you can't 'ave it (.) I said I 'ave to open the till (w) wait till the next customer comes (.) *'now! open it now and gi' me de money'* (.) I said I can't (.) the man just *thump 'is fist down* an' (screw up dis for me) (.) (s no man) the manager just comes (.) 'would you leave the shop before I call the security' hh the man *jus' take the bottle an' fling it at me* an (I) jus' catch it at the (ground)
>
> (London English in plain text; London Jamaican in italics; (.) = pause; (text) = insecure transcription)

Analyse the switches between London English and London Jamaican in this extract. Can you account for the language alternation in terms of Gumperz' distinction between 'we-' and 'they-code'?

*Brief comments on this Activity can be found on page 290.

ACTIVITY: TRANSLANGUAGING AND STYLIZATION*

Analyse translanguaging in the following extract from a conversational interaction between three Turkish-Danish adolescents in a Copenhagen school. They are working together on a geography project (English – bold; Turkish – italics; Danish – plain; data taken from Jørgensen 2005: 399):

Ali: **oh shit**
Eda: *Atlanta yok mu Atlanta*
(isn't Atlanta there? Atlanta?)
Asiye: hold din kæft Eda
(shut up Eda)
Ali: jorden
(earth)
Asiye: du skal snakke dansk
(you must speak Danish)
Eda: *Asiye bak şimdi aya ğımın altına alırsam görürsün şimdi seni*
(Asiye, if I take you under my foot you will see)
Asiye: *oh o kadar kolaymıymıç*
(ha as if that was so easy)

Do you find an example here of the young people quoting (or stylizing) somebody else's voice? Do you think it might be an example of uni- or vari-directional stylization?

*Brief comments on this Activity can be found on page 291.

FOR DISCUSSION: LANGUAGE AND IDENTITY

How do you see your own identity? How strong is the link with one (or more) particular language(s)? In what sense could it be described as a 'trans-languaging identity'?

FOR DISCUSSION: NATIONAL IDENTITY

- Many nationalist movements desire to achieve nation-state congruence: in other words, they believe that all citizens of a state should also be members of one (imagined) nation. Discuss to what extent or in what ways this 'core nationalist doctrine' (Smith 1971) can lead to social exclusion, xenophobia, racism or ethnic cleansing.
- The desire to protect national identity frequently involves the desire to protect (i.e. purify, keep pure) the national language. Discuss to what extent and in what ways language purist movements are connected with nationalist agendas.

PROJECT WORK: EXPLORING PEOPLE'S MULTILINGUALISM

Study the language use of a particular group of people who have multilingual repertoires. If possible, conduct short interviews with a few members of the group. Analyse the interviews to see whether Gumperz' 'we-' vs. 'they-code' distinction provides an insight into how these people use their various languages.

Moreover, try to record some conversational interactions between members of the group (use a digital voice recorder, and seek informed consent beforehand). Analyse the examples of code-switching in this data (if any). Are there examples of situational or metaphorical code-switching? Are there examples of uni-directional or vari-directional stylization? Are there examples of language crossing?

REFERENCES AND SUGGESTIONS FOR FURTHER READING

The construction of identity

Edwards, John (2009) *Language and Identity*, Cambridge: Cambridge University Press.

Evans, David (ed.) (2016) *Language and Identity: Discourse in the World*, London: Bloomsbury.

Gee, James Paul (2001) 'Identity as an analytic lens for research in education', *Review of Research in Education*, 25: 99–125.

Le Page, Robert and Tabouret-Keller, Andrée (1985) *Acts of Identity*, Cambridge: Cambridge University Press.

Liebscher, Grit and Dailey-O'Cain, Jennifer (2013) *Language, Space and Identity in Migration*, New York: Palgrave.

Palmer, John D. (2007) 'Who is the authentic Korean American? Korean-born Korean American high school students' negotiations of ascribed and achieved identities', *Journal of Language, Identity and Education*, 6: 277–98.

Paris, Django (2011) *Language across Difference: Ethnicity, Communication, and Youth Identities in Changing Urban Schools*, Cambridge: Cambridge University Press.

Pavlenko, Aneta and Blackledge, Adrian (eds) (2004) *Negotiation of Identities in Multilingual Contexts*, Clevedon: Multilingual Matters.

Preece, Siân (ed.) (2016) *The Routledge Handbook of Language and Identity*, London: Routledge.

Van Lier, Leo (2007) 'Action-based teaching, autonomy and identity', *Innovation in Language Learning and Teaching*, 1: 46–65.

Williams, Raymond (1977) *Marxism and Literature*, Oxford: Oxford University Press.

National, ethnic and racial identity

Anderson, Benedict (1991) *Imagined Communities: Reflections on the Origin and Spread of Nationalism*, London: Verso.

Barth, Frederik (1969) *Ethnic Groups and Boundaries*, Boston, MA: Little, Brown.

De Fina, Anna (2007) 'Code-switching and the construction of ethnic identity in a community of practice', *Language in Society*, 36: 371–92.

Garner, Steve (2010) *Racisms: An Introduction*, London: Sage.

Guibernau, Montserrat (1996) *Nationalisms: The Nation-State and Nationalism in the Twentieth Century*, Cambridge: Polity Press.

Jenkins, Richard (1997) *Rethinking Ethnicity: Arguments and Explorations*, London: Sage.

Smith, Anthony (1971) *Theories of Nationalism*, London: Duckworth.

Code-switching and identity

Bailey, Benjamin H. (2002) *Language, Race and Negotiation of Identity: A Study of Dominican Americans*, New York: LFB Scholarly Publishing.

Bakhtin, Mikhail M. (1981) 'Discourse in the novel', in M. Holquist (ed.) *The Dialogic Imagination: Four Essays by M.M. Bakhtin*, Austin, TX: University of Texas Press, 259–422.

Blom, Jan Petter and Gumperz, John J. (1972) 'Code-switching in Norway', in J. Gumperz and D. Hymes (eds.) *Directions in Sociolinguistics*, New York: Holt, Rinehart and Winston, 407–34.

Gumperz, John J. (1982) *Discourse Strategies*, Cambridge: Cambridge University Press.

Jørgensen, J. Normann (2005) 'Plurilingual conversations among bilingual adolescents', *Journal of Pragmatics*, 37: 391–402.

Kotthoff, Helga (2007) 'The humorous stylisation of "new" women and men and conservative others', in P. Auer (ed.) *Style and Social Identities*, Berlin: Mouton de Gruyter, 445–75.

Meeuwis, Michael and Blommaert, Jan (1998) 'A monolectal view of code-switching: Layered code-switching among Zairians in Belgium', in P. Auer (ed.) *Code-Switching in Conversation: Language, Interaction and Identity*, London: Routledge, 76–98.

Sebba, Mark (1993) *London Jamaican*, London: Longman.

Language crossing

Rampton, Ben (1995) *Crossing: Language and Ethnicity among Adolescents*, London: Longman.
—— (2006) *Language in Late Modernity: Interaction in an Urban School*, Cambridge: Cambridge University Press.
—— (2009) 'Crossing, ethnicity and code-switching', in N. Coupland and A. Jaworski (eds) *The New Sociolinguistics Reader*, Basingstoke: Palgrave, 287–98.
—— (2010) 'Crossing into class: Language, ethnicities and class sensibility in England', in C. Llamas and D. Watt (eds) *Language and Identities*, Edinburgh: Edinburgh University Press, 134–43.

Translanguaging

Bejarano, Cynthia L. (2005) *¿Qué onda? Urban Youth Culture and Border Identity*, Tucson, AZ: University of Arizona Press.
Canagarajah, Suresh (2013) *Translingual Practice: Global Englishes and Cosmopolitan Relations*, London: Routledge.
García, Ofelia and Li Wei (2014) *Translanguaging: Language, Bilingualism and Education*, Basingstoke: Palgrave Pivot.
Li Wei and Zhu, Hua (2013) 'Translanguaging identities and ideologies: Creating transnational space through flexible multilingual practices amongst Chinese university students in the UK', *Applied Linguistics*, 34: 516–35.
Otheguy, Ricardo, García, Ofelia and Reid, Wallis (2015) 'Clarifying translanguaging and deconstructing named languages: A perspective from linguistics', *Applied Linguistics Review*, 6: 281–307.

Individual and spatial repertoires

Blommaert, Jan and Backus, Ad (2013) 'Superdiverse repertoires and the individual', in I. de Saint-Georges and J.-J. Weber (eds) *Multilingualism and Multimodality: Current Challenges for Educational Studies*, Rotterdam: Sense Publishers, 11–32.
Busch, Brigitta (2017) 'Expanding the notion of the linguistic repertoire: On the concept of *Spracherleben* – the lived experience of language', *Applied Linguistics*, 38 (3): 340–58.
Pennycook, Alastair and Otsuji, Emi (2014) 'Metrolingual multitasking and spatial repertoires: "Pizza mo two minutes coming"', *Journal of Sociolinguistics*, 18: 161–84.

CHAPTER 8

The interplay between individual and societal multilingualism

In this chapter we explore the complex interplay between individual and societal multilingualism. Our example here is Canada and we rely upon one of the prime examples of ethnographic fieldwork in sociolinguistics, namely the work carried out by Monica Heller and her team of co-researchers in a French-medium school, the Ecole Champlain, in the anglophone province of Ontario. The study shows how Quebec as well as francophone communities in anglophone Canadian provinces attempted to achieve individual (French–English) bilingualism through an official policy of societal or institutional monolingualism (in French). It also reveals the ideological faultlines of such a policy, and how both francophone Canada as a whole and the Ecole Champlain in particular were forced to adapt to the new global economy of services and communication. But first of all we provide some general information about the language situation in Canada.

THE CANADIAN POLICY OF BILINGUALISM AND MULTICULTURALISM

According to the 2001 census data (as reported in Duff 2008: 74), Canada has about 30 million inhabitants, 17.4 million of whom have English as their L1 and 6.7 million have French as L1. Other important 'mother tongues' include Chinese (various varieties of Chinese), Italian and German. The largest indigenous languages are Cree (about 70,000 speakers) and Inuktitut (about 29,000 speakers). Canada has a federal government and is divided into ten provinces and three territories. The provinces have jurisdiction over education, and the territories, too, have gradually gained the right to deal with matters of education. The fact that English and French are the official languages goes back to a history of colonization by Britain and France.

In the 1960s, Quebec, the French-speaking province, started the 'Quiet Revolution' movement to gain more power and control for francophones. This led to the passing of the Canadian Official Languages Act in 1969, which enshrined French–English bilingualism, required all federal institutions to provide services in both of the official languages and ensured the right to L1-medium education for francophone minorities outside Quebec as well as anglophone minorities in Quebec. Since the 1970s, Canada has also pursued a policy of multiculturalism, which eventually led to the passing of the Multiculturalism Act in 1988. Canada thus sees itself in terms of the 'mosaic' metaphor rather than the US metaphor of the 'melting pot'. Whereas the melting pot metaphor suggests assimilation, the Canadian metaphor of a cultural mosaic reflects (nominally at least) an ideology of cultural pluralism within the official bilingual framework. It should be noted that these official policies have often been accused of being rather superficial and merely celebratory (see e.g. Bannerji 2000; Haque 2012).

In the area of education, French immersion programmes have been implemented throughout the country since the 1960s. One of the aims is to allow anglophone majority group children to learn French, using a CLIL type of instruction (Content and Language Integrated Learning; see Chapter 9), with various school subjects such as biology, history, etc. taught through the medium of French. As a way of validating the official policy of multiculturalism, such immersion programmes were gradually extended to the indigenous languages. Children are frequently taught with the indigenous language as the primary medium of education during the first few years of education or, if they no longer speak it at home, immersion programmes are used in an attempt to revitalize the language (see Burnaby 1996).

SOME CONSEQUENCES FOR FIRST NATIONS PEOPLE

Patrick (2001) discusses the language situation of the Inuit in Arctic Quebec (Nunavik). For historical reasons going back to English colonialism, these communities are mostly bilingual in English and their indigenous language, Inuktitut. However, because they are now part of Quebec, a French-speaking province, French has gained in importance in social life. Since the 1970s, many schools have offered Inuktitut as a medium of instruction in early education, and a switch to dual-medium (Inuktitut-English) instruction later on. Nowadays, however, more and more schools offer a choice of either English or French as L2, and many parents enrol their children in the French-language streams. This is mostly due to the increasing instrumental value of French, which is required for more and more jobs. But at the same time Nunavik continues to be a primarily bilingual Inuktitut–English community, and French is not (yet) widely used outside schools. For this reason, students of French get little practice in their out-of-school lives and often find it difficult to acquire the language. Patrick (2001: 313–14) concludes that the new 'trilingual language market and the resulting trilingual language policy in schools in Arctic Quebec have placed significant pressure on residents as they try to decide what the best education for their children is'.

QUEBEC FRANCOPHONE NATIONALISM

French is the majority language in Quebec, but a minority language in Canada as a whole. As a result, many Quebeckers feel that French is endangered and needs to be protected against English and to be defended in what some of them see as hostile anglophone surroundings. For this reason, Quebec has opted for a policy of French monolingualism, which goes against the federal Canadian policy of bilingualism and multiculturalism. The rise of Quebec francophone nationalism has taken place since the 1960s, often with a separatist agenda. Two referenda were held on the question of Quebec's sovereignty in 1980 and 1995, but neither of them went through.

In the 1970s Quebec adopted restrictive language policies to preserve and promote the use of French. In particular, Bill 101 (the Charter of the French language, 1977) included a number of restrictive clauses, for instance forcing new immigrants (whose mother tongue was neither French nor English) to enrol their children in French-medium schools and requiring all commercial signage to be in French only. These clauses were sources of tension and led to legal challenges, as a result of which some aspects of Bill 101 were ruled to be unconstitutional. Consequently, some of the language restrictions were gradually relaxed in the 1990s (see May 2001: 229).

According to May, the nationalists believe that societal (or institutional) monolingualism in French is necessary in Quebec for French to have a chance of survival. They think that, because of the all-powerful position of English in Canada as a whole, people will acquire English in any case and thus achieve individual bilingualism in French and English. As May (2001: 231) puts it,

> Advocates of Bill 101 argue that the only way that individual bilingualism can be maintained and fostered is by, counterintuitively, setting strict limits on the extent of institutional bilingualism.

In the following section, we will find the same ideology at work in the educational setting of a French-language school in anglophone Ontario.

INDIVIDUAL BILINGUALISM THROUGH INSTITUTIONAL MONOLINGUALISM

Heller and her co-researchers have carried out a thorough ethnographic investigation of French-language minority education in Ontario. Such schools use French as the medium of instruction and rely on an ideology of institutional monolingualism, turning the schools into French-only environments. In a way, Quebec's territorial nationalism is here appropriated but simultaneously transformed into a form of institutional nationalism, via the creation of institutions (schools) run by and for francophones.

The ultimate aim is to develop in the students individual bilingualism in French and English, with the assumption that they will acquire English in any case through living in an anglophone society, even if it is only taught as one subject among many others at school. Moreover, French–English bilingualism is understood as double monolingualism, with the students encouraged to keep the two languages separate, to avoid translanguaging and, in particular, to cut all anglicisms out of their French.

In the Ecole Champlain, a French-language high school in the Toronto area, Heller found a highly heterogeneous school population consisting of the following three groups:

- speakers of French as their L1;
- middle-class anglophones wanting to become bilingual in English and French because such linguistic capital provides access to desirable jobs, especially in the public sector;
- new immigrants from Somalia, Haiti, etc., who are speakers of French as their L1 or L2.

The school offered two streams: a more advanced one, where many of the middle-class francophone and anglophone students could be found, and a more vocational or 'general' stream, attended by many working-class French-Canadians, as well as Somalis, Haitians and other new immigrants. The school tried to enforce the use of French, though this resulted in students frequently using English in 'backstage' events (i.e. not to the teachers but among themselves); in Heller's (2001: 389) words, English became 'available as a means of contesting [the school's] authority'.

However, there was also a clear difference between advanced and 'general' classes. In the latter classes, a much wider range of vernacular and contact varieties of French was used, and there was frequent switching into English by both students and teachers. In fact, it was only in the advanced-level French classes that the school ideology of institutional monolingualism in French was strictly adhered to. Indeed, in these classes, teachers were found to insist on the 'right' kind of French: namely, standard Canadian French, while both 'the old imperialist-imposed standard of European French and the still-stigmatized Canadian French vernaculars' (Heller 2001: 391) were rejected. Heller (2001: 391) comments as follows upon this situation:

> The new standard is as harsh in its judgments of interference from English as was the old one. The major difference lies in who has control of the definition of legitimate form, and here the purpose is clearly to place that control in the hands of the new, educated, and mobilized elite .... Schools are important sites for the construction of this standard and for its deployment in gatekeeping and credentialing.

Thus the school relied upon the twin ideologies of monolingualism and language quality (Heller 2006: 78) in a continuing endeavour to create a French-only zone. However, the teachers, who were expected to implement the system of linguistic surveillance, were fighting a losing battle because of the importance of English in Canadian society and the school's need to accept anglophone students as a way of boosting its student enrolment. As a matter of fact, English was often used as a lingua franca among the students. In this situation, it is not surprising that the efforts of teachers of French focused primarily on eradicating all traces of contact with English. Heller refers to it as *la chasse aux anglicismes* (the hunt for **anglicisms**) and provides numerous examples of teachers correcting their students' use of English loanwords. Ironically, this could at times lead teachers into (ideologically) difficult situations where they would have to justify the use of borrowings from English, as in the following extract taken from Heller (2006: 105). The teacher, Lise, has just been talking (in French) about a message sent by fax when Saïd, one of the students, asks the following question:

Saïd:	comment on écrit 'le fax'? (how do you write 'the fax'?)
Lise:	f-a-x
Saïd:	quoi? (what?)
Abdillahi:	f-a-x
Lise:	f-a-x pas de 'e' (f-a-x no 'e')
Saïd:	non pas de 'e' (no no 'e')

Lise: c'est un mot anglais
(it's an English word)
Saïd: alors c'est pas en vrai français ça (laughs)
(so it's not in real French [laughs])
Lise: ben c'est un mot c'est un mot emprunté
(well it's a word it's a borrowed word)

EXCLUSION THROUGH FRENCH, INCLUSION THROUGH ENGLISH

In her detailed ethnographic study of this French-medium school in anglophone Toronto, Heller discusses many such tensions and contradictions between official policies and actual practices. Thus, even though the school was supposed to be a French-only monolingual zone, students who entered the school with high proficiency in French and low (or no) proficiency in English often found themselves excluded and marginalized. This was often the case of French-Canadian students from Quebec, as well as French-speaking immigrant students primarily from Somalia and Haiti. The former group found that, with the school's insistence on standard French, their own vernacular varieties of Canadian French were sometimes stigmatized both by teachers and other students. The same frequently happened with the varieties of French spoken by the Haitian and Somali students; moreover, these students' feelings of marginalization and alienation were compounded at least initially by the fact that they found it difficult to understand the Canadian French varieties used by many teachers and students.

Both the French-Canadian and the francophone immigrant groups were also surprised to discover the important role played by English among the students, at least outside the official spaces of classroom learning, and they quickly realized that they would need English to make friends. Interestingly, if bridges were built and new friendships were formed, this often happened through a shared interest in hip-hop music. Heller shows how this shared music culture not only helped the Somali students in particular to improve their English but also made it easier for these previously marginalized students to be fully included in the school community.

SHIFTING IDEOLOGIES

According to Heller (2006: 214), such contradictions reflect the overall dilemma faced by the school of how to reconcile (French-Canadian) authenticity with pluralism. The school had been born out of the ideology of linguistic nationalism, prevalent in Quebec since the 1960s, in an attempt to preserve an endangered language (French) and to resist the hegemony of English. However, the old politics of identity has been radically transformed in the new and changing global economy of services and information. As a result, the school has had to adapt to the growing heterogeneity of its student population. Thus, for instance, with the increasing number of Somali students, it became more problematic for teachers to present French as an oppressed language, since for these students it was clearly the opposite: namely, the language of oppression. But what most students seemed to share was a belief in French as a means of social advancement in Canadian society. In this way, language was commodified, and the old politics of identity was gradually replaced by a new politics of linguistic capital. The school put greater value on standard French, even at the risk of losing (some of) the authenticating value of the French-Canadian vernacular. The old vision of the *francophonie de souche* (local francophone communities with 'roots') gave way to a new vision of *francophonie internationale*.

Heller shows how the students in particular helped to push the school in the direction of a new policy of inclusiveness which could point the way for the country as a whole to move beyond the French–English cleavages into a truly multilingual and multicultural future. It is for this reason that Heller (2006: 207) concludes her study on a note of cautious optimism: she says that by 1995, which also happened to be the time that the researchers finished their fieldwork, 'many of the Somali students talked about the days of the major problems of segregation and racial discrimination at the school as a thing of the past', though she also adds that a 'general tendency towards segregation remained, and the progress made was fragile'.

CONCLUSION: THE COMMODIFICATION OF LANGUAGE

The shift from a politics of identity to a politics of linguistic capital – and the resulting **commodification** of language – has opened up new opportunities for francophone communities in English-speaking parts of Canada. Thus, Heller (2003) shows how some small francophone communities in southeastern Ontario have developed a new service economy based on tourism and communications. In this way, the community bilingualism in French and English is given a new value in that it gives access to specific service-related jobs, especially in call centres. Whereas previously they had been stigmatized for speaking French, their fluency in both French and English has now become a marketable commodity. However, Heller also points out that what is valued is bilingualism in the standard varieties of French and English, while their regional varieties continue to be denigrated. As a result, call centre operators frequently translanguage not only among English and French but also among their own local variety of French (when talking with each other) and a more standard variety (when talking to clients).

The other important growth area is heritage tourism, which involves the marketing of 'authentic' cultural artefacts, both goods and performances, which in turn inevitably involves a commodification of language and identity. In southeastern Ontario, numerous local festivals or 'heritage pageants' are being organized, which recount regional, Franco-Ontarian history 'as a saga of the heroic resistance of a marginalized community against the forces both of nature and of politically dominant centers' (Heller 2011: 151). Moreover, such performances are increasingly exported to other, primarily francophone, parts of the world. The authentic Franco-Canadian goods, too, are marketed locally and globally, and Heller (2011: 157) notes that vendors tend to be recruited depending on their ability 'to provide a (largely linguistic) performance of francophone Canadian-ness'. Thus, what matters in this case is fluency in Canadian French, while English may also be required to deal with non-francophone clients who, ironically, 'can't understand the authentic forms of communication that guarantee the legitimacy or the value of the product they are consuming' (Heller 2011: 171).

Just like the Ecole Champlain and the Quebec province as a whole, the francophone communities in southeastern Ontario illustrate a pattern that can be traced in many parts of the world: individual multilingualism is frequently valued in a positive way and viewed as 'linguistic capital' (Bourdieu 1977), while societal or institutional multilingualism is more likely to be negatively valued. At the same time, it is important to remember that Heller's research focuses on a 'somewhat unique linguistic context with two relatively high status international languages' (Baker 2001: 557) and that the issues would have been less clear-cut and even more complex if she had also considered the roles of indigenous and immigrant minority languages in Canada.

ACTIVITY: ANGLICISM OR VERNACULAR FRENCH?*

In the following extract, Ecole Champlain students are talking to their teacher about Molière's play *L'avare*. (*The Miser*; note that the word 'cassette' is here used in its seventeenth-century sense of 'purse'.) Lise is the teacher, and Ginette is a working-class French-Canadian student who speaks a vernacular variety of French:

Lise: okay, qu'est-ce que vous avez compris de l'histoire? Comment s'est terminée l'histoire?
(Okay, what did you understand of the story? How did the story end?)

Ginette: Harpagon a retrouvé sa cassette whatever.
(Harpagon found his purse whatever.)
Lise: Harpagon a retrouvé sa cassette.
(Harpagon found his purse.)

(Heller 2006: 108–9)

Heller (2006: 109) comments that 'Ginette provides an accurate answer mitigated through the attachment of "whatever"', and adds that 'whatever' is 'widespread in Canadian vernacular French, and can be used even by people who otherwise speak little English'.

What do you think the teacher is doing when she repeats Ginette's utterance but without the 'whatever'? Is this part of the Ecole Champlain's struggle against anglicisms, or part of its struggle to get students to switch from their vernacular French to standard French? What language ideologies underlie the teacher's concern with language 'quality'?

*Brief comments on this Activity can be found on page 291.

FOR DISCUSSION: LANGUAGE AS LINGUISTIC CAPITAL OR MARKER OF IDENTITY?

To what extent can languages be looked upon as linguistic capital and/or as markers of identity? Do only standard varieties and national or official languages have linguistic capital? Can minority languages also acquire a certain amount of linguistic capital, for instance as part of heritage tourism?

FOR DISCUSSION: POLICIES OF MULTICULTURALISM

Think of other countries that, like Canada, officially proclaim themselves as being multicultural. One example might be South Africa, which has constructed itself as a multiethnic rainbow nation in the post-apartheid era. To what extent could these countries' official policies of multiculturalism be looked upon as rather superficial or merely celebratory? What would need to change for such policies to become more substantial?

FOR DISCUSSION: DEFENDING FRENCH AGAINST ENGLISH

The European Union promotes a policy of (individual) multilingualism, such that every EU citizen should be proficient in her/his 'mother tongue' plus two other European languages (see also Chapter 11). Critics have argued that France has supported this EU policy of 'mother tongue plus two' as a way of bolstering the French language. How can you explain this?

PROJECT WORK: RESTRICTIVE LANGUAGE POLICIES

Consider some restrictive language policies such as Quebec's Bill 101. Can such policies be justified? What exceptional circumstances could justify them at least to some degree? An interesting book to get started is May (2001, especially chapter 6); remember also what we said in Chapter 5 of the present book about the costs of language revitalization. Another example that you might want to look at is the *Loi Toubon* (1994) in France (see the following project work).

PROJECT WORK: THE FIGHT AGAINST ANGLICISMS

The fight against anglicisms has taken place in many countries. An example from France is the *Loi Toubon* of 1994 (see e.g. Ager 1999: chapter 5). If you are more interested in Germany, you might want to look at the excellent analysis in Spitzmüller (2007). Choose France, Germany or another country where there has been such a 'hunt for anglicisms' and present your findings to the class. You may also want to include in your analysis a consideration of the metaphors used in connection with anglicisms (such as '*hunt* for anglicisms' in the previous sentence) in popular and/or media discourses.

REFERENCES AND SUGGESTIONS FOR FURTHER READING

Canada

Baker, Colin (2001) 'Review of Monica Heller. *Linguistic Minorities and Modernity*', *Journal of Sociolinguistics*, 5: 556–8.

Bannerji, Himani (2000) *The Dark Side of the Nation: Essays on Multiculturalism, Nationalism, and Gender*, Toronto: Canadian Scholars Press.

Burnaby, Barbara (1996) 'Language policies in Canada', in M. Herriman and B. Burnaby (eds) *Language Policies in English-Dominant Countries*, Clevedon: Multilingual Matters, 159–219.

Duff, Patricia (2008) 'Heritage language education in Canada', in D. Brinton, O. Kagan and S. Bauckus (eds) *Heritage Language Education*, New York: Routledge, 71–90.

Haque, Eve (2012) *Multiculturalism within a Bilingual Framework: Language, Race, and Belonging in Canada*, Toronto: University of Toronto Press.

Heller, Monica (2001) 'Legitimate language in a multilingual school', in M. Heller and M. Martin-Jones (eds) *Voices of Authority: Education and Linguistic Difference*, Westport, CT: Ablex, 381–402.

—— (2006) *Linguistic Minorities and Modernity: A Sociolinguistic Ethnography*, 2nd edn, London: Continuum.

May, Stephen (2001) *Language and Minority Rights*, Harlow: Pearson Longman.

Patrick, Donna (2001) 'Languages of state and social categorization in an Arctic Québec community', in M. Heller and M. Martin-Jones (eds) *Voices of Authority: Education and Linguistic Difference,* Westport, CT: Ablex, 297–314.

The commodification of language

Bourdieu, Pierre (1977) 'The economics of linguistic exchanges', *Social Science Information,* 16: 645–68.

Heller, Monica (2003) 'Globalization, the new economy and the commodification of language and identity', *Journal of Sociolinguistics*, 7: 473–92.

—— (2011) *Paths to Post-Nationalism: A Critical Ethnography of Language and Identity*, Oxford: Oxford University Press.

Tan, Peter and Rubdy, Rani (eds) (2008) *Language as Commodity: Global Structures, Local Marketplaces*, London: Continuum.

Anglicisms

Ager, Dennis (1999) *Identity, Insecurity and Image: France and Language*, Clevedon: Multilingual Matters.

Spitzmüller, Jürgen (2007) 'Staking the claims of identity: Purism, linguistics and the media in post-1990 Germany', *Journal of Sociolinguistics*, 11: 261–85.

Walsh, Olivia (2016) *Linguistic Purism: Language Attitudes in France and Quebec*, Amsterdam: Benjamins.

TEST YOURSELF QUIZ PART III*

1. In what sense is the term 'mother tongue' used in official Singaporean language policy and language-in-education policy?
2. Discuss the shifting role and importance of Mandarin in Singapore.
3. Why are some people afraid of societal multilingualism, even while they value individual multilingualism?
4. Explain the distinction between instrumental and identity functions of language.
5. Critically discuss the notions of categorizing, generalizing and stereotyping, and explain their connection with the notion of identity.
6. Explain the process of indexicality, if possible by giving an example based upon your own experience.
7. Discuss your own code-switching and translanguaging. Can it be explained with reference to such theoretical concepts as 'we-code' vs. 'they-code', situational vs. metaphorical code-switching, or language crossing?
8. Could some of the problems faced by the Ecole Champlain have been solved by the school adopting a policy of translanguaging (rather than a policy of strict separation of the languages)?
9. Can you think of some examples of anglicisms in a language (other than English!) that you are fluent in? Why do some people object to the use of such anglicisms?
10. What is heritage tourism? Is there a heritage tourism industry in your own country, and is it connected with a particular language?

*Suggested answers can be found on page 295.

PART IV

Multilingualism in education and other institutional sites

CHAPTER 9

Flexible vs. fixed multilingualism

In a highly entertaining poem about why cows are superior to human beings, British-Caribbean poet John Agard lists a whole set of features that distinguish between the two. The main theme of the poem is racism, and cows are described as not being racist because of the black and white hide of their skin. The characteristic that interests us most here is that cows 'never impose their language' upon others (Agard, 'Cowtalk', in *Mangoes and Bullets*, 1990, page 46, lines 34–5). For this is what human beings have been doing for centuries, whether it was European colonizers destroying their slaves' languages or modern nation-states imposing their language upon immigrants. In the colonial situation, the slave-traders and colonizers attempted to forestall the danger of a rebellion by separating the slaves in such a way that they would not be able to speak to each other in their own language. Moreover, cutting out the tongue was a frequent punishment meted out to slaves caught speaking their own language.

Attitudes of linguistic repression have also prevailed since the nineteenth century in the recently created European nation-states, most of which adhered strictly to the one nation–one language ideology and imposed their national or official language upon all the people. Immigrants were expected either to return to their countries of origin or to assimilate as quickly as possible. The alleged failure on the part of some immigrants to acquire a high enough level of proficiency in the national or official language has recently been interpreted as a lack of 'integration'. As a response to this, the latest trend at the beginning of the twenty-first century has been the introduction of all sorts of language tests, whether in education, for access to professions or for the right to enter, reside in and become a citizen of a particular state (see discussion in Chapter 13). In a way, the contemporary language testing regimes could be seen as a continuation of colonial language policies, and integration as a disturbing reincarnation of one of the most pervasive images of the discourse of colonialism: namely, that of the colonial power as the mother with the colonized people divided into two types of children, on the one hand the good ones who need to be protected and deserve to be civilized, and on the other hand the bad ones who must be dealt with harshly and deserve to be oppressed. In the twenty-first century, the good ones are the ones who successfully pass the integration and citizenship tests, whereas the bad ones fail. The progress from the colonial to the late modern system is that the latter is no longer based on the sheer exercise of power but on the results of a test allegedly providing an 'objective' or 'scientific' basis for the decisions. In this way, we can see how integration involves simultaneously an erasure of difference (the 'good' migrants are the same as 'us' and deserve to be integrated) and a maximization of difference (the 'bad' migrants are so different from 'us' that they cannot be integrated).

At the same time, it might be hoped that the recent trend away from monolingualism and towards multilingualism would counteract this ongoing history of linguistic repression. Thus, for instance, the EU is nowadays advocating multilingualism for all European citizens and has done a lot to revitalize lesser-used languages in Europe. This has allowed formerly oppressed languages such as Catalan and Basque to play more important roles again. During the dictatorship of General Franco from 1939 to 1975, monolingualism in Castilian Spanish had been brutally enforced. But Spain's return to democracy in the mid-1970s has also involved a linguistic democratization: Catalan and Basque have now become official regional languages in, respectively, Catalonia and the Basque Country.

Unfortunately, however, the shift to bi- or multilingualism does not automatically imply the abolition of linguistic repression. It might even be easier for migrants to move to a monolingual area where they just need to learn one dominant language, as opposed to moving to an officially multilingual area where they are expected (or forced) to learn two or more languages. A multilingual education system (i.e. a system that uses more than one language as the medium of instruction) constitutes 'an added challenge for immigrant students', as Lasagabaster (2009) puts it euphemistically. Thus multilingualism is not in itself the solution to the problem of linguistic repression. It all depends on how the multilingual language policy is applied: whether it is applied in a highly rigid and fixed way, without taking into account people's home linguistic resources, or in a more flexible way, building upon all the linguistic resources that people bring along with them.

In this chapter, we therefore distinguish between two ideologies of multilingualism: **fixed** vs. **flexible multilingualism**. The distinction is based on similar ones used in the literature, in particular the distinctions between homoglossic and heteroglossic multilingualism in García (2009) and between separate and flexible bilingualism in Blackledge and Creese (2010). Though the chapter starts with a brief look at US language policy, this is only as a contrast to EU policy, and the rest of the chapter focuses on Europe. We present two case studies, the first one involving one of the smallest EU member-states, Luxembourg, which has been officially bi- or trilingual since its creation in the first half of the nineteenth century, though there has recently been a shift towards a stronger perception of itself as monolingual. Spain, on the other hand, has moved in the opposite direction: from the monolingualism of General Franco's dictatorship to an awareness of itself as a multilingual state. We focus in particular on the language situation in Catalonia and the Basque Country. We look at the education systems of these states or regions, and argue that Luxembourg and Catalonia have more in common in this respect than the Basque Country. In fact, there are signs that both Luxembourg and Catalonia are moving towards the ideology of fixed multilingualism, while the Basque Country seems to be taking the opposite direction of a more flexible multilingualism. The chapter closes with a discussion of the main features distinguishing fixed and flexible multilingual school systems.

US VS. EU LANGUAGE-IN-EDUCATION POLICY

According to Wiley (2002), the main concern of the US language-in-education policy has been how to manage *societal* multilingualism. The US has traditionally seen itself as a society of immigration, with immigrants being assimilated into the American melting pot. Hence, most bilingual education programmes have been of the transitional type, with a focus on Spanish, the home language of the biggest minority group. The Hispanic or Latino students are 'transitioned' as quickly as possible from Spanish to English, with the ultimate aim of assimilation and eventual monolingualism in English. In other words, this is a type of what has been called *subtractive* bilingual education, where the language minority students are supposed to be weaned away from their minority language towards the dominant language.

The strong anti-immigration feeling and the concomitant suspicion of all forms of bilingual education in the US at the turn of the millennium have reinforced this trend. The English Only Movement (see Chapter 14) constructed Latinos – and their language, Spanish – as a threat to mainstream America. Ironically, a discourse of endangerment spread about English, the global language, which was claimed to be threatened by Spanish. Moreover, it was argued in a deliberately erroneous way that bilingual education supports minority languages (especially Spanish) *at the expense of* English. It was in this near-hysterical atmosphere prevailing in 2001 that the Republican President Bush transformed the Bilingual Education Act into the English Language Acquisition Act as part of his new No Child Left Behind policy, which introduced mandatory high-stakes testing in English for all children. As a result, many of the transitional bilingual education programmes were discontinued, Spanish was increasingly banned from the classroom and simple ESL (English as a Second Language) programmes were implemented. The results have been catastrophic for many language minority students, leading scholars to rename the Act 'No Child Left Untested' (Crawford 2004) or 'English Language Learners Left Behind' (Menken 2008).

The EU, on the other hand, has pursued a very different policy on multilingualism. As a way of managing the accelerated process of Europeanization and the abolition of border controls between many of the EU member-states, the European Commission has advocated the ideal of the multilingual European citizen, speaking her or his mother tongue as well as two other (European) languages. Thus, the EU policy of mother tongue plus two (MT + 2) aims to increase *individual* multilingualism (what the EU refers to as 'plurilingualism'), with a focus on standard, national or official European languages. The approach here is *additive* rather than *subtractive*, since the ideal European citizens should not give up their mother tongue but continue to practise it alongside the two other languages they have acquired.

To promote this 'plurilingualism' throughout the EU, the Council of Europe has developed new tools such as the Language Portfolio, the Common European Framework of Reference for Languages (CEFR) and the teaching methodology of CLIL (Content and Language Integrated Learning). They encourage the linking of all language courses to the levels of competence defined in the CEFR, which can then be recorded in the students' language portfolios. CLIL involves the type of bilingual education where the second (or third) language is used as a vehicle to teach non-linguistic content matter. In terms of the US situation described above, this would mean teaching some subjects such as history or mathematics with Spanish (and not English) as the medium of instruction – something that is less and less the case in US classrooms. It thus seems that US and EU language-in-education policies are diametrically opposed.

However, Budach, Erfurt and Kunkel (2008: 38) point out that CLIL constitutes an elite form of bilingual education in the sense that it mostly involves the global European languages such as English or French. Hence it is not surprising that it is strongly promoted by the EU, as it fits into the ideological EU framework of 'plurilingualism' with its emphasis on European languages. Immigrant minority languages, on the other hand, are largely ignored, and the dominant cultures within individual EU member-states continue to be marked by monoglossia and homogeneism. All this leads García (2009: 195) to conclude that though

> the present EU policy of promotion of plurilingualism contrasts sharply with that of the US ... it is to be noted that the European Union trails the United States in including in education the languages of immigrants and refugees that increasingly define it.

At the same time, we must not forget that, within the socio-political context of the EU, support for small, autochthonous languages has been growing over the last few decades. The European Charter for Regional or Minority Languages protects, as its name indicates, regional minority languages, though it specifically excludes immigrant minority languages. The European Bureau for Lesser Used Languages (EBLUL; discontinued in 2010), too, was concerned with the protection of regional minority languages, though not with social injustices affecting a broad range of immigrant linguistic minorities in the EU (Wright 2004: 199). Hence both the European Charter and EBLUL are based on an essentialist ideology. As Nic Craith (2003: 59) puts it, because they are 'aimed at languages spoken by nationals of a state in a particular territory', they imply 'an essential link between culture, space and place'.

Nonetheless, these trends at EU level could lead us to ask whether the emphasis on lesser-used languages does not also offer migrant students greater flexibility than in the English-dominated US. Do these EU policies not open up new implementational spaces for multilingualism? We will consider two case studies, first Luxembourg, and then Catalonia and the Basque Country, in an attempt to answer these questions.

CASE STUDY 1: LUXEMBOURG

With a population of 576,249 and a geographical size of 2,586 square kilometres, the Grand-Duchy of Luxembourg is situated between Belgium, France and Germany and is one of the six founding member-states of the EU. Luxembourg is home to the highest proportion of resident foreigners in the EU (46.7 per cent), the majority of whom are passport holders of other EU member-states. With 16.2 per cent of the total population, Portuguese passport holders currently make up the largest number of resident foreigners, followed by French (7.2 per cent), Italian (3.5 per cent), Belgian (3.4 per cent), other EU (9.5 per cent) and non-EU (6.9 per cent) residents. The number of resident foreigners climbed steadily after World War II and increased dramatically from the 1970s to the present (Statec 2016).

Luxembourg's niche for international banking and special tax schemes has propelled economic prosperity since the late 1960s. Together with the resident foreigners, 170,000 *frontaliers* (border-crossing commuters) make up a large proportion of the workforce in the Grand-Duchy. Their presence is linked to the small geographical size of Luxembourg as well as EU regulations facilitating free movement of the EU workforce. About 80 per cent of the *frontaliers* come from France and Belgium and are (primarily) French-speaking; nearly 20 per cent come from Germany and are (primarily) German-speaking (Statec 2016).

The language situation in Luxembourg is frequently referred to as 'triglossic' in reference to the three languages recognized by the 1984 language law: Luxembourgish, French and German. The distinction between spoken and written language has been pivotal to understanding long-standing norms and patterns of language use in Luxembourg, with most spoken communication among the native-born taking place in Luxembourgish and written functions carried out primarily in standard French or German. Luxembourgish language varieties are Germanic and are similar to Moselle Franconian varieties (likewise Germanic) spoken in adjacent parts of Germany, Belgium and France. For this reason, basic literacy skills are taught via standard German in state schools. French is introduced as a subject in the second year of primary school, becomes a full subject in the third year and gradually replaces German as the main medium of instruction at secondary level, particularly in the prestigious *lycée classique* or college preparatory secondary school. Based on the Education Act of 1843, practices in state schools have perpetuated elite bilingualism, or the valorization of standard German and French (Davis 1994). French, brought to the fore because of its widespread use by *frontaliers* and resident foreigners, is now used as a (supplemental) home language – as opposed to a (mere) school language – by a larger segment of the population than ever before.

In the late 1970s and early 1980s, a period marked by demographic changes due to high levels of immigration mostly from Portugal, pressure and support for the development of Luxembourgish grew. In 1984 a language law was passed, which for the first time officially recognized Luxembourgish as the national language and, in theory, as an administrative language. However, this legislation simultaneously reinforced the sociolinguistic status quo by designating French and German as legal, judicial or administrative languages, precisely the state of affairs prior to the ratification of the law even if it was previously *de facto* rather than *de jure* policy. The ratification of the 1984 law signals a shift towards explicit language policy, thus imparting on Luxembourgish a higher position in the hierarchy of languages (Horner and Weber 2008: 106f.). Luxembourgish is declared the 'national language' in Article 1, while the expression 'official language' is studiously avoided in the text of the law. This wording provides a springboard for language-ideological debates which frequently revolve around the status and use of Luxembourgish. Language-in-education debates, on the other hand, tend to focus on the 'trilingual ideal' (Horner and Weber 2008: 87), i.e. the mastery of the standard, written varieties of German and French together with the presupposed (consistent) use of spoken Luxembourgish.

Luxembourgish has traditionally been perceived as a key marker of national identity, but in the last decade it has also been promoted as the language of integration and has seen its role within the education system reinforced. The increased use of Luxembourgish has been hailed as a solution to the perceived problem of societal heterogeneity and as a way of achieving the vaguely formulated goals of 'integration' and 'social cohesion' (see Horner 2009). As it is still a spoken much more than a written language, it has found it easiest to take over pre-school education, where it has pushed out French, which had been widely used by the increasing number of romanophone children. This has created a fracture between educational policy and actual language practices, in that Luxembourgish is constructed as the sole language of integration in schools, while many migrant children live in areas where French is a widely used lingua franca.

Moreover, the fixed trilingual system of education has negative consequences for many children who speak Romance languages at home. They learn Luxembourgish in pre-school, then at the beginning of primary school they have to go through the same German-language literacy programme as the autochthonous Luxembourgish students, and only afterwards they learn French as a foreign language, while German continues to be used as the main medium of instruction (alongside Luxembourgish). Because many Romance languages speaking students do not achieve the required high level of fluency in German, they are barred from the elite *lycées classiques* and end up in the more vocationally oriented *lycées techniques*. But in the latter lycees, the focus is more on 'technical' subjects rather than languages, and as a result these students' acquisition of English, which is only taught at secondary level, is often limited to a rather rudimentary level. They are thus deprived of an important job qualification in both the national and European employment market. Indeed, Klein (2007) has shown that English is the most important language (along with French) facilitating access to the Luxembourgish labour market. In fact, it has become so important that he concludes his paper with the suggestion that, in Luxembourg among others, the EU language policy of mother tongue plus two other languages (MT + 2) should be 'guided by a "MT + English + 1" slogan', though he adds that, on the one hand, this means 'prioritiz[ing] economic rather than cultural considerations and, on the other hand, the advantages of commanding

English will tend to diminish when these competences become more and more abundant' (Klein 2007: 278). As a result, there is an increasing disjuncture between the employment market (where French and English are the most important languages) and language-in-education policy (where German is the language of basic literacy and the main medium of instruction throughout primary education).

CASE STUDY 2: CATALONIA AND THE BASQUE COUNTRY

Both Catalan and Basque are official regional languages in, respectively, Catalonia and the Basque Country, and both communities have become increasingly bilingual Catalan–Spanish and Basque–Spanish. After the linguistic repression during the dictatorship of General Franco, Catalan and Basque have progressively been rehabilitated as national symbols of their respective community. Thus, in Catalonia in the 1980s, the 'catalanization' of state education was implemented as part of the political programme of linguistic normalization (bringing the language back to its 'normal' state). However, Pujolar (2010) points out that, just as in Luxembourg, official discourse changed in response to the accelerated immigration of the 1990s: it shifted its emphasis from Catalan as national symbol to Catalan as a means of social cohesion and integration.

As a result, many migrant students are now put in reception or 'integration' classes where Catalan (rather than Spanish) is the language of instruction. Corona, Moore and Unamuno (2008) argue that this clashes with many of these students' experience of Spanish being widely used as a lingua franca in their out-of-school lives. Corona *et al.* analyse the textbooks in use in these reception programmes and show that they frequently portray Catalan as the key to social participation and belonging. But in the lived reality of the students themselves, it is often Spanish rather than Catalan that is 'the language which opens up doors to friendships' (Corona *et al.* 2008: 137). They thus experience a fracture similar to the one that exists in Luxembourg between educational policy and individuals' actual language practices: they learn Catalan at school but outside school they mostly use Spanish, just as in Luxembourg many migrant children learn Luxembourgish in pre-school but often use French outside school.

Therefore Pujolar (2010: 235) talks about a split between two types of integration: 'educational integration' that is supposed to take place through Catalan, and a 'more informal social integration' that tends to happen through Spanish. He also notes 'the absence of an explicit formulation of the role of Spanish in the design of the principles and policies of integration' (Pujolar 2010: 240). Interestingly, there is in Luxembourg a similar absence of an explicit formulation of the role of French in the integration policy. The resulting situation does not really open up new multilingual spaces for the migrant students, mainly because the language regime of the education system is a fixed rather than flexible one. The migrant students are like square pegs that have to fit into round holes. Their own home languages are largely ignored, and instead they are expected to assimilate into the fixed trilingualism of first Catalan, then Castilian Spanish and, third, usually English as a foreign language. What makes it even worse for the migrant students is that they are sometimes forced to take intensive Catalan or Spanish courses during the time that autochthonous students learn English as their L3. In this case, the migrant students may be debarred from taking English, though this is the one subject where many of them could have excelled (Escobar Urmeneta and Unamuno 2008: 246). Again, this is parallel to the situation in Luxembourg, where many migrant students in the lower streams of the technical lycees miss out almost completely on the opportunity of learning English.

Like Catalan, Basque is one of the official regional languages of Spain, and is mostly spoken in the Basque Autonomous Community (BAC). Since 1982, there have been three types of schools in the BAC, usually referred to as Model A, B and D schools (there is no letter 'C' in Basque):

- Model A schools: Spanish as the medium of instruction and Basque as second or foreign language.
- Model B schools: both Basque and Spanish as media of instruction.
- Model D schools: Basque as the medium of instruction and Spanish as second language.

Just as in Luxembourg and Catalonia, recent sociolinguistic changes in the Basque Country include increased immigration as well as the growing importance of English as the global language, with consequent pressure to use more English exerted by parents upon schools. In the face of these developments, public debate about education has become increasingly polarized between the two ideological positions of fixity and flexibility: supporters of the former position advocate retrenchment and consolidation of Basque as the endangered minority language, with more Basque in all schools for all students; the others advocate a more flexible move towards bilingual (Basque–Spanish) or multilingual (Basque–Spanish–English) education.

There are some signs that the flexibility position has already begun to influence schools. According to Cenoz (2008), the boundaries between Model A, B and D schools are becoming blurred and schools are adapting to the changing student population, with more schools also using English as a medium of instruction (alongside Basque and Spanish). Cenoz (2008: 26) argues that nowadays there is a continuum of schools from less multilingual to more multilingual ones:

> Some schools have only one language of instruction (Basque or Spanish) and can be placed towards the less multilingual end of the continuum on this variable. Other schools have two languages of instruction: Basque and English, Basque and Spanish, Spanish and English and others three languages of instruction (usually Basque, Spanish and a foreign language which is English in most cases).

An example of 'more multilingual' schools are the Ikastolas or Basque-medium schools, which also use Spanish and English as media of instruction, and which teach English already from the age of four. It would thus seem that, unlike Luxembourg and Catalonia, the BAC is moving in the direction of a more flexible education system which endeavours to respond to the children's linguistic needs and which takes into account the importance for all children of learning English as the global language.

In conclusion, we may wonder why so many Western states or regions (such as Luxembourg and Catalonia) fail to introduce a more flexible multilingual education system. Is it a fear that such a system could undermine or erode their national unity? But of course flexible multilingual education systems exist in many countries, for example South Africa, without undermining their national unity. South African schools often use an indigenous African language (such as isiZulu, isiXhosa, Setswana and others) as the medium of instruction during the first few years of primary education and then switch to English as the main medium of instruction. But in areas with a multiplicity of languages – especially in urban or metropolitan areas – more and more schools can be found where English is used as the medium of instruction from day one of primary education. Other schools try to combine the two approaches by experimenting with simultaneous bilingual English–indigenous language programmes. The important lesson to be learned here is flexibility: only flexible, local solutions can potentially meet all the children's linguistic needs in the best possible way. On the other hand, fixed policies decided upon at state level, and which are still common in European countries, are less and less adequate because of the increasing heterogeneity of their school populations in this age of late modernity and superdiversity.

At the same time, we hasten to add that it is not our intention to set up either the Basque or the South African system of education as a model of flexibility; on the contrary, as Echeverria (2010) points out, there is still a need to work towards a wider definition of Basqueness that includes not only native speakers but also second language learners of Basque; and for South Africa, we will show in the following chapter that here, too, flexibility is limited by a number of underlying attitudes and ideologies.

DISCUSSION AND CONCLUSION: TOWARDS FLEXIBLE MULTILINGUAL EDUCATION

We have seen that both in Catalonia and Luxembourg, the main reason why migrant students often find it difficult to 'integrate' into a multilingual education system is that the system's language teaching and learning regime is a fixed rather than a flexible one. The migrant students' home languages are largely ignored by the education system – though there may be some token promotion of their official 'mother tongue', which in any case frequently corresponds only partly to the children's actual linguistic resources (see discussion in Chapter 10). There is therefore an urgent need for education systems to move in the direction of greater flexibility, what García (2009) refers to as 'heteroglossic multilingualism'.

García argues that bilingual education should be more than double monolingualism or the learning of two compartmentalized monolingual codes, each as a separate, bounded system. She contrasts this monoglossic (or fixed) ideology of bilingualism and bilingual education with a more inclusive and plural, heteroglossic (or flexible) view, and paints a rather optimistic view of the development of bilingual education from the more fixed types of the past to the more flexible types of the present:

> those [types of bilingual education] that respond to a dynamic bilingual framework ... are exploding, as people increasingly understand the need for bilingualism across groups, for all children, and beyond two languages. Thus, all types of bilingual education are extending towards the last [dynamic or heteroglossic] type ... as many more groups attempt to develop trilingualism and other more flexible ways of translanguaging multilingually.
>
> (García 2009: 385)

Considering, for instance, the reality of the suppression of bilingual education in the US at the beginning of the twenty-first century, this view seems over-optimistic, and it might have been preferable to distinguish between the flexible heteroglossic language practices of individuals and the frequently monoglossic pressures exerted by the school systems, along the lines of Martin-Jones (2007), who discusses such disjunctures between educational policies and the contemporary multilingual realities of life. But even more controversial is the fact that García's prime examples of dynamic and flexible types of bilingual education include the school systems of such countries as Singapore, Brunei and Luxembourg. However, all these systems are strongly based on monolingual standards and compartmentalization of languages, and hence would seem to be more fixed than flexible. Here, for example, is what Stroud and Wee (2007: 259) say about Singapore:

> The language ideology behind the policy conceives of multilingualism in terms of (a limited set of) serially compounded monolingualisms; it recognizes only 'English plus official mother tongue' bilingualism, and according to the state, Singaporeans should ideally be *equally proficient* in both English and their official mother tongue .... This view of multilingualism promotes a conception of bilingualism as the mastery of officially designated systems, in an ethnic framework that (a) does not officially recognize cross-fertilization between ethnic groups, that is, Malays speaking Mandarin, or Indians proficient in Malay, nor (b) acknowledge the flux and flexibility of multilingual, hybrid economies of communication.

Meanwhile, Martin (2008: 214) says the following about the language-in-education policy in Brunei:

> It will be apparent from the discussion above that there is a certain tension inherent in the *Dwibahasa* system, a system which attempts to construct two parallel, but clearly demarcated, monolingual orders. The *Dwibahasa* policy is based on the principle of bilingualism through monolingualism ... that is, the use of separate languages for different subjects, as well as the use of monolingual textbooks in the classrooms. A corollary of this is the institutional pressure on classroom participants to conform to the fiction of two parallel monolingual orders.

García (2009) presents the Luxembourgish education system in particular as some kind of ideal of flexibility. However, as we have seen in this chapter, the trilingual Luxembourgish system is strongly informed by the standard language ideology and strict compartmentalization of languages, so that one wonders how it could possibly qualify as a heteroglossic or flexible type. In what follows, we list two of García's main criteria for an educational system to qualify as flexible, and briefly comment on each from the point of view of the Luxembourgish system:

(1) Building on all the children's home language and literacy practices.

In Luxembourg the largest minority group are the luso-descendant – or Portuguese-origin – students (over 20 per cent of the school population). In an ethnographic study of these children's language use, Weber (2009) found that their home linguistic practices include mostly Portuguese and French. In pre-school, however, they are taught spoken Luxembourgish (a Germanic language), in an environment where French is largely banned and Portuguese is given nominal respect (as their putative 'mother tongue'). Then, in primary school, they are taught standard German as the language of basic literacy from the first year onwards. German is also the medium of instruction for all academic subjects throughout primary school, while standard French is only taught as a subject from the second half of the second year onwards. As a result, Davis (1994: 188) looks upon this as a programme of the 'submersion' type, in the sense that many of these children 'fail to achieve the language skills necessary for classroom interaction and study'.

(2) Working towards educational equity.

The results of PISA (Programme for International Student Assessment) have shown that the Luxembourgish school system is one of those that most directly reproduce social stratification and inequality. Also the Council of Europe (2005: 48) in its report on language teaching and learning in Luxembourg refers to the present system of trilingual Luxembourgish–German–French education as a 'cause of failure and exclusion for a large part of the population, jeopardizing both the social integration of all the inhabitants and the economic competitiveness of the Grand-Duchy'. The maintenance of the present system is in part a defensive reaction against high levels of in-migration, especially from romanophone countries, during the last few decades. The system has become a gatekeeping mechanism, restricting access to educational and employment opportunities for large segments of the population and preserving the privileges of the dominant group.

Apart from these two key criteria, flexible multilingual education would also need to fulfil the following ones:

(3) Using translanguaging pedagogies (rather than an approach based on strict separation of languages).
(4) Offering a range of educational tracks with different combinations of media of instruction.
(5) Providing all students with access to the important local and global languages (including, in particular, English).

It could be argued that no school system actually fulfils all five criteria and thus lives up to the ideal of such a flexible model. However, this does not relieve policy-makers and teachers of their responsibility to work towards more flexible and equitable education systems and to bring them more in line with the fluid multilingual realities of today's world of increased mobility and globalization. To be fair to the educational actors in Luxembourg, we need to add that signs of flexibility are appearing here, too, with the new Ministry of Education requiring crèches to function bilingually in Luxembourgish and French from September 2017 onwards and a new international state school in Differdange, a town in the south of the country, offering French and English literacy tracks since September 2016. Maybe García's optimistic view of the development of multilingual education in the direction of ever greater flexibility will be proved right after all (though this can be likened to the doughnut: the optimist sees the doughnut, the pessimist sees the hole).

ACTIVITY: MONOLINGUAL VS. MULTILINGUAL PERSPECTIVES ON LANGUAGE ACQUISITION

Flexibility is not only a matter of educational programmes and systems (flexibly catering to the needs of all children) but also in our minds (need to move from a rigid monolingual to a more flexible multilingual mindset). Consider the following piece of writing by an emergent bilingual child in the US with Spanish as L1 and learning English as his L2:

> The Tree Piks
> My story is about of tree piks and I lobo feroz. The lobo tiro dawn the house of paja.
>
> (Escamilla and Hopewell 2010: 84)

Escamilla and Hopewell argue that, if judged from a monolingual perspective, this text could be seen in the following way:

- very poor piece of writing
- too much translanguaging between English and Spanish
- the child's Spanish is interfering with his English
- Spanish is the problem and needs to be eradicated so that his English can grow.

On the other hand, if judged from a bi-/multilingual perspective, we might reach very different conclusions:

- the child successfully uses bilingual strategies such as lexical borrowing (lobo for wolf, feroz for ferocious, paja for straw)
- he also uses Spanish phonetic principles to spell English words (e.g. piks for pigs)
- in this way, the child is very adept at transferring linguistic knowledge from one of his languages to the other
- teachers need to build upon these bilingual strategies
- hence, the child's Spanish is a useful resource which makes the acquisition of English easier for him.

Escamilla and Hopewell (2010: 85) conclude that the monolingual perspective 'may be underestimating the writing strengths of emergent bilinguals'.

- Do you agree with Escamilla and Hopewell's conclusion? Why or why not?
- To what extent is the shift from a monolingual to a multilingual perspective difficult for many of us because monolingual assumptions are so firmly ingrained in our minds?
- If you are familiar with (some of) the literature on second language acquisition: to what extent are monolingual assumptions prevalent in this research domain? (See Block 2003 and May 2013 for books that question many of the assumptions underlying research in second language acquisition.)

FOR DISCUSSION: FLEXIBLE MULTILINGUALISM

- How could flexible multilingualism be implemented in education? In your eyes, what are the most important characteristics of a flexible multilingual education system?
- Suppose you are moving to a bi-/multilingual country: which language(s) or variety/ies would you consider learning as the language(s) of integration and why? Examples discussed in various chapters of this book include the Basque Country and Catalonia (Spain), Côte d'Ivoire, Hong Kong (China), India, Luxembourg, Singapore, South Africa, (German-speaking) Switzerland. (See also Chapter 13 on language and integration.)

PROJECT WORK: EXPLORING LANGUAGE-IN-EDUCATION POLICIES

- Explore a bi-/multilingual setting where English is not one of the dominant languages. Do you find evidence of a split between 'educational' and 'informal social' integration of the type that Pujolar (2010) noted in the case of Catalonia? What is the role of English in the educational system? In particular, do migrant students find it difficult to achieve a high level of proficiency in English due to the priority given to the local bi-/multilingualism?

- Choose a bi-/multilingual state or region whose language policy and education system you are familiar with. Consider whether its official language-in-education policy is marked by flexible or fixed multilingualism. To what extent does this policy open up multilingual spaces for migrant students?

PROJECT WORK: US AND EU LANGUAGE-IN-EDUCATION POLICY

The presentation of US and EU language-in-education policies in this short chapter has inevitably been very sketchy. Try to find out more about US or EU language-in education policies.

For the US, find out about some of the most important court cases focused on language rights and educational access, and what their impact upon policy has been:

- *Meyer v Nebraska* (1923)
- *Lau v Nichols* (1974)
- *M.L. King Jr. Elementary School Children v Ann Arbor School District Board* (1979).

A good place to start reading about US language-in-education policies in general and more specifically about these (and other) court cases is Wiley (2002) or García (2009: chapter 8). Take notes and prepare a presentation to explain to the other students in your class what these court cases were about and what implications they had for US language-in-education policies.

For the EU, find out about one or more of the following, and what its/their impact upon policy has been:

- the Common European Framework of Reference for Languages (CEFR)
- Content and Language Integrated Learning (CLIL)
- the European Charter for Regional or Minority Languages.

A good place to start reading about EU language-in-education policy is García (2009: chapter 9) or Wright (2004: chapter 9). A detailed and useful account of CLIL can be found in Coyle, Hood and Marsh (2010). Take notes and prepare a presentation to explain to the other students in your class what these developments at EU level are about and what implications they have for language-in-education policy in EU member-states.

REFERENCES AND SUGGESTIONS FOR FURTHER READING

US language-in-education policy

Crawford, James (2004) *Educating English Learners: Language Diversity in the Classroom* (5th edition), Los Angeles: Bilingual Educational Services.

Menken, Kate (2008) *English Learners Left Behind: Standardized Testing as Language Policy*, Bristol: Multilingual Matters.

Wiley, Terrence (2002) 'Accessing language rights in education: A brief history of the US context', in J. Tollefson (ed.) *Language Policies in Education: Critical Issues*, Mahwah, NJ: Erlbaum, 39–64.

EU language-in-education policy

Budach, Gabriele, Erfurt, Jürgen and Kunkel, Melanie (eds) (2008) *Ecoles plurilingues – Multilingual schools: Konzepte, Institutionen und Akteure*, Frankfurt/Main: Peter Lang.

Coyle, Do, Hood, Philip and Marsh, David (2010) *CLIL – Content and Language Integrated Learning*, Cambridge: Cambridge University Press.

Nic Craith, Mairead (2003) 'Facilitating or generating linguistic diversity: The European Charter for Regional or Minority Languages', in G. Hogan-Brun and S. Wolff (eds) *Minority Languages in Europe: Frameworks, Status and Prospects*, Basingstoke: Palgrave, 56–72.

Wright, Sue (2004) *Language Policy and Language Planning: From Nationalism to Globalisation*, Basingstoke: Palgrave.

Luxembourg

Council of Europe (2005) *Rapport du groupe d'experts: Grand-Duché de Luxembourg: Profil des politiques linguistiques éducatives*, Strasbourg: Division des Politiques Linguistiques.

Davis, Kathryn A. (1994) *Language Planning in Multilingual Contexts: Policies, Communities, and Schools in Luxembourg*, Amsterdam: Benjamins.

Horner, Kristine (2009) 'Language, citizenship and Europeanization: Unpacking the discourse of integration', in G. Hogan-Brun, C. Mar-Molinero and P. Stevenson (eds) *Discourses on Language and Integration: Critical Perspectives on Language Testing Regimes in Europe*, Amsterdam: Benjamins, 109–28.

—— and Weber, Jean-Jacques (2008) 'The language situation in Luxembourg', *Current Issues in Language Planning*, 9: 69–128.

Klein, Carlo (2007) 'The valuation of plurilingual competences in an open European labour market', *International Journal of Multilingualism*, 4: 262–81.

Statec (2016) *Le portail des statistiques du Luxembourg*, http://www.statec.lu/.

Catalonia and the Basque Country

Arnau, Joachim (ed.) (2013) *Reviving Catalan at School: Challenges and Instructional Approaches*, Bristol: Multilingual Matters.

Cenoz, Jasone (2008) 'Achievements and challenges in bilingual and multilingual education in the Basque Country', *AILA Review*, 21: 13–30.

Corona, Victor, Moore, Emilee and Unamuno, Virginia (2008) 'Linguistic reception in Catalonia: Challenges and contradictions', in G. Budach, J. Erfurt and M. Kunkel (eds) *Ecoles plurilingues – Multilingual Schools: Konzepte, Institutionen und Akteure*, Frankfurt/Main: Peter Lang, 121–45.

Echeverria, Begoña (2010) 'For whom does language death toll? Cautionary notes from the Basque case', *Linguistics and Education*, 21: 197–209.

Escobar Urmeneta, Cristina and Unamuno, Virginia (2008) 'Languages and language learning in Catalan schools: From the bilingual to the multilingual challenge', in C. Hélot and A.-M. de Mejía (eds) *Forging Multilingual Spaces: Integrated Perspectives on Majority and Minority Bilingual Education*, Bristol: Multilingual Matters, 228–55.

Lasagabaster, David (2009) 'Multilingual educational systems: An added challenge for immigrant students', in J. Miller (ed.) *Culturally and Linguistically Diverse Classrooms: New Dilemmas for Teachers*, Bristol: Multilingual Matters, 18–35.

Newman, Michael and Trenchs-Parera, Mireia (2015) 'Language policies, ideologies and attitudes in Catalonia', *Language and Linguistics Compass*, 9: 285–94, 491–501.

Pujolar, Joan (2010) 'Immigration and language education in Catalonia: Between national and social agendas', *Linguistics and Education*, 21: 229–43.

Urla, Jacqueline (2012) *Reclaiming Basque: Language, Nation, and Cultural Activism*, Reno, NV: University of Nevada Press.

Flexible vs. fixed multilingual education

We list a wide range of publications here, though they often deal with the topics of not only Chapter 9 but also the closely related Chapters 10 and 11:

Abello-Contesse, Christian, Chandler, Paul M., López-Jiménez, María Dolores, Chacón-Beltrán, Rubén (eds) (2013) *Bilingual and Multilingual Education in the 21st Century: Building on Experience*, Bristol: Multilingual Matters.

Blackledge, Adrian and Creese, Angela (2010) *Multilingualism: A Critical Perspective*, London: Continuum.

—— (eds) (2014) *Heteroglossia as Practice and Pedagogy*, Dordrecht: Springer.

Cenoz, Jasone and Gorter, Durk (eds) (2015) *Multilingual Education: Between Language Learning and Translanguaging*, Cambridge: Cambridge University Press.

Conteh, Jean and Meier, Gabriela (eds) (2014) *The Multilingual Turn in Languages Education: Opportunities and Challenges*, Bristol: Multilingual Matters.

de Jong, Esther J. (2011) *Foundations of Multilingualism for Education: From Principles to Practice*, Philadelphia, PA: Caslon.

García, Ofelia (2009) *Bilingual Education in the 21st Century: A Global Perspective*, Chichester: Wiley-Blackwell.

——, Ibarra Johnson, Susana and Seltzer, Kate (2017) *The Translanguaging Classroom: Leveraging Student Bilingualism for Learning*, Philadelphia, PA: Caslon.

—— and Kleyn, Tatyana (eds) (2016) *Translanguaging with Multilingual Students: Learning from Classroom Moments*, New York: Routledge.

Little, David, Leung, Constant and van Avermaet, Piet (eds) (2014) *Managing Diversity in Education: Languages, Policies, Pedagogies*, Bristol: Multilingual Matters.

Martin, Peter (2008) 'Educational discourses and literacy in Brunei Darussalam', *International Journal of Bilingual Education and Bilingualism*, 11: 206–25.

Martin-Jones, Marilyn (2007) 'Bilingualism, education and the regulation of access to language resources', in M. Heller (ed.) *Bilingualism: A Social Approach*, Basingstoke: Palgrave, 161–82.

——, Blackledge, Adrian and Creese, Angela (eds) (2012) *The Routledge Handbook of Multilingualism*, London: Routledge.

Otwinowska, Agnieszka and de Angelis, Gessica (eds) (2014) *Teaching and Learning in Multilingual Contexts: Sociolinguistic and Educational Perspectives*, Bristol: Multilingual Matters.

Shin, Sarah J. (2013) *Bilingualism in Schools and Society: Language, Identity, and Policy*, New York: Routledge.

Slembrouck, Stef, van Gorp, Koen, Sierens, Sven and Maryns, Katrijn, van Avermaet, Piet (eds) (2017) *The Multilingual Edge of Education*, Basingstoke: Palgrave.

Stroud, Christopher and Wee, Lionel (2007) 'Consuming identities: Language planning and policy in Singaporean late modernity', *Language Policy*, 6: 253–79.

Weber, Jean-Jacques (2009) *Multilingualism, Education and Change*, Frankfurt/Main: Peter Lang.

—— (2014) *Flexible Multilingual Education: Putting Children's Needs First*, Bristol: Multilingual Matters.

Wright, Wayne E., Boun, Sovicheth and García, Ofelia (eds) (2015) *Handbook of Bilingual and Multilingual Education*, Chichester: Wiley.

Second language acquisition

Block, David (2003) *The Social Turn in Second Language Acquisition*, Edinburgh: Edinburgh University Press.

Escamilla, Kathy and Hopewell, Susan (2010) 'Transitions to biliteracy: Creating positive academic trajectories for emergent bilinguals in the United States', in J.E. Petrovic (ed.) *International Perspectives on Bilingual Education*, Charlotte, NC: Information Age Publishing, 69–93.

May, Stephen (ed.) (2013) *The Multilingual Turn: Implications for SLA, TESOL, and Bilingual Education*, London: Routledge.

CHAPTER 10

Mother tongue education or literacy bridges?

Mother tongue education is often advocated as the ideal system of education for all children. However, because it is informed by the mother tongue ideology, it inherits all the problems associated with the concept of mother tongue (see Chapter 2). The main problem is that mother tongue education programmes frequently ignore the dimension of intra-language variation. Therefore, this chapter provides a critique of mother tongue education, arguing that it is not always the panacea it is frequently made out to be. We point to the problems associated with mother tongue education and propose an alternative concept, namely the use of a literacy bridge (this concept will be explained later in the chapter). Our main example is Africa and in particular South Africa, as there has been a long-standing debate about what the best medium of instruction is in the educational systems of African countries: should it be a former colonial language such as English or an indigenous African language? (For a basic introduction to the language situation and educational system of South Africa, please refer to Chapter 6.) But we also consider what might be seen as a more unusual example in the context of a discussion of mother tongue education: namely, the situation of African-American children in the US system of education.

THE CASE FOR MOTHER TONGUE EDUCATION: AFRICAN-AMERICAN ENGLISH

A major controversy, usually referred to as the Ebonics debate, erupted in the US in December 1996 concerning the nature and use of AAE (African-American English) or AAVE (African-American Vernacular English). In light of the continuing difficulties of African-American children in the school system, the Oakland School Board in California put forward a proposal to use AAE as an integral part of these children's language education. The basic idea was to value the children's home variety in a positive way and to use it as a bridge, leading them to better acquisition of standard English.

However, there was a huge outcry in the media, with many voices (journalists, politicians, general members of the public) complaining that the use of what some of them referred to as 'slang' would mean condemning these children to educational failure. Actually, the Oakland Board of Education was attempting to do just the opposite: namely, to give the children better chances of educational success by building in a positive way upon their home linguistic resources. But because of the political and media outcry, they were eventually forced to withdraw their proposal.

One of the most hotly debated issues was whether AAE is a language or a dialect or merely 'slang'. The Oakland School Board had initially suggested that it was a language. Many contributors to the debate rejected this indignantly and vilified AAE by referring to it as 'wholly unintelligible', 'slang' or even 'gibberish'. What they revealed in the process was not only their prejudiced minds but also a blatant lack of linguistic understanding. Indeed, a linguistic variety cannot possibly be reduced to 'slang', which is largely a matter of vocabulary. Moreover, slang terms such as *booze* (for drink) or *dough* (for money) can of course be used in any variety of English, including standard English. Slang expressions change rapidly, and yesterday's slang terms have either disappeared or – like the two above – entered the (informal) standard vocabulary. But, even more interestingly, the whole debate illustrated what we discussed in Chapter 3: namely, how sets of linguistic resources are *constructed* as a language or a dialect. What the Oakland School Board had tried to do was to construct the children's home linguistic variety as a language, as a way of valuing it more positively and thus implementing a form of mother tongue education. But this construction was rejected as illegitimate for political reasons and the traditional construction of AAE as a 'dialect' of English was upheld.

Schmid (2001) compares the situation of African-American schoolchildren moving from AAE to standard English with that of Swiss German children moving from their Swiss German 'dialect' to standard German (see discussion of Switzerland in Chapter 6). She finds both similarities and differences between the two situations: for instance, both Swiss German and AAE are key markers of group identity but, unlike AAE, Swiss German is positively valued in society as a whole and is used by speakers of all social classes. Perhaps for this very reason, the Swiss education system is much more successful than the US one in helping children to transfer from the 'dialect' to the standard. The Swiss situation proves that the underlying idea of the Oakland School Board's proposal was a sound one:

> Mastering the standard language is easier if the differences in the vernacular and standard language are made explicit rather than ignored. This lesson was at the heart of the Oakland school board's proposal. Their educational reform that attempted to use AAVE to teach standard English is supported by the Swiss case.
>
> (Schmid 2001: 150)

In the Ebonics debate, this key issue was wholly misrepresented and distorted in the media. The Oakland School Board was accused of wanting to 'imprison' African-American children within their 'dialect', by denying them access to standard English. In fact, however, it was not an issue of whether these children should learn AAE or standard English, as if these were exclusive choices. Obviously, the Oakland School Board wanted the children to learn standard English, but the question they raised was what the best way of learning standard English for African-American children really is. The answer they suggested was the one that would be endorsed by the huge majority of applied linguists in the world: namely, by taking the children's home linguistic resources into account and valuing them positively. Thus, for instance, McWhorter (1998) makes a number of suggestions about how this could be achieved, including the following:

- train schoolteachers in the systematicity of Black English
- institute Afrocentric curricula at predominantly African-American schools
- allow young African-American students to speak in their home dialect in class.

Such a teaching methodology would, in McWhorter's (1998: 254) eyes, 'promote the fluently bicultural identity necessary for African-Americans to succeed in this country', though at the same time he reminds us that if US society really wants to solve this issue, it will also have to tackle 'the ills of poverty, drug abuse, and societal alienation' (McWhorter 1998: 255).

Both Schmid's and McWhorter's comments clearly bring out the potentially beneficial effects of a mother tongue education programme. But to be successful, such a programme must be based upon the children's *actual* linguistic resources, as it would have been in the case of the African-American children in Oakland. Sometimes, however, mother tongue programmes are much more problematic because they rely upon the targeted children's *assumed* mother tongue and fail to take into account the greater complexity of children's verbal repertoires. An example from South Africa illustrating this situation will be presented in the following section.

FOR DISCUSSION: SAVING LANGUAGES OR PEOPLE?

Mother tongue education is also frequently advocated as the best way of ensuring the maintainance of an endangered linguistic variety. However, this position has been criticized by William Labov, the *doyen* of sociolinguistic studies of AAE, in a paper titled 'Unendangered dialects, endangered people' (2008). Basically, his argument is that we should endeavour to 'save' people rather than linguistic varieties, even if the former might have the effect of endangering the latter. He illustrates his point in relation to speakers of AAE: as a way of improving social conditions for those who are trapped in the cycle of poverty and unemployment, one key measure would be to work towards a reduction of residential segregation in US inner-city areas. In turn, this could lead to more contact between speakers of AAE and speakers of other varieties, as a result of which AAE could *become* an endangered variety:

> At that point, AAVE as a whole might be in danger of losing its own distinct and characteristic forms of speech. I am sure that many of us would regret the decline of the eloquent syntactic and semantic options [of AAVE] that I have presented here. But we might also reflect at that time that the loss of a dialect is a lesser evil than the current condition of an endangered people.
>
> (Labov 2008: 235)

Discuss Labov's argument in relation to (a) AAE/AAVE and (b) other situations of endangered people and endangered languages.

THE CASE AGAINST MOTHER TONGUE EDUCATION (IN FOUR STEPS): SOUTH AFRICA

The debate about mother tongue education has been particularly virulent in relation to a number of African countries. Why should such countries as Senegal use French, the colonial language, as the medium of instruction in their educational system? And why should South Africa use English? Is it not time for Africans to 'decolonize their minds', as Ngugi wa Thiong'o (1986) famously put it? There is an urgent need to valorize the indigenous African languages, and this could be achieved by using them as media of instruction. Being educated in their own language would also offer millions of schoolchildren better chances of educational success, whereas the present system mostly aims at the social reproduction of a small English- or French-speaking elite.

These are cogent and persuasive arguments and therefore need to be taken seriously. They have led to educational reforms in many African countries, with more and more countries trying out some form of mother tongue education. They are advocated by large numbers of well-meaning scholars, who are genuinely concerned about improving educational opportunities for all. Yet, at the same time, they are highly problematic because they erase an important part of the linguistic reality in these countries. The main culprit encouraging such erasure is the mother tongue ideology, which informs these proposals.

Step 1: deconstructing the indigenous vs. colonial language distinction

A first thing to note is that, like many binary oppositions, the distinction between indigenous and colonial languages does not hold. Scholars such as Makoni, Brutt-Griffler and Mashiri (2007) point out that the so-called indigenous mother tongues are as much European or colonial constructions as the European languages. Rather than being authentic products of indigenous cultures, languages such as Setswana (in South Africa), Shona (in Zimbabwe) and many others are directly linked with the European colonial project, and their standard varieties were constructed by European missionaries and the colonial administrations. As Makoni, Brutt-Griffler and Mashiri (2007: 40) put it,

> These written languages – produced as much by colonial agency as by South African, and bearing at times little resemblance to the spoken language of the region's peoples – became, in effect, mother tongues in search of speakers.

Yet it is these artificially constructed mother tongues that have become (or should become) the basis of primary education, according to the proponents of mother tongue education.

Step 2: a widening gap between 'school' and 'street' varieties

Cook (2009) has carried out an ethnographic study of language use in Tlhabane and Phokeng in the North West Province of South Africa. In the government schools, standard Setswana is taught as the mother tongue and English as a foreign language. Yet most schoolchildren's home language is not standard Setswana but Street Setswana. Standard Setswana (also called 'pure' or 'school' Setswana) is the variety 'invented' by European missionaries during the period of colonialism, while Street Setswana is a more hybrid urban vernacular that incorporates lexical material from English, Afrikaans, isiZulu and Tsotsitaal (Cook 2009: 98). The school ideology is that only standard Setswana should be promoted and valued as being iconic of Tswana ethnic authenticity.

The consequence is that the schoolchildren often cannot follow the education which is supposed to be in their mother tongue. Cook found that in practice teachers frequently switched into Street Setswana or English during the lessons, when students did not get the point in standard Setswana. She notes that students often understand English better than standard Setswana:

> Not only are many students more familiar with certain English terms than with their standard Setswana equivalents, but they are more comfortable with English in general than standard Setswana.
> (Cook 2009: 110)

It is not surprising therefore that the school emphasis on standard Setswana discourages many students and strengthens their preference for English, which is looked upon as the language of opportunities and power.

The situation described by Cook is by no means unique. Numerous other studies have shown that this is a trend happening throughout African classrooms. There is an increasing gap in mother tongue education between the standard indigenous varieties used as school languages and the home languages spoken by many of the schoolchildren. Hence, for more and more children, the mother tongue taught in the classroom has less and less to do with their own linguistic repertoires. This is an urgent problem that needs to be addressed by mother tongue programmes in many African countries.

Step 3: the spread of urban vernaculars

This problem affecting mother tongue education has been exacerbated by such factors as accelerated migration to urban centres, which has furthered the shift from the rural indigenous varieties to pan-ethnic urban vernaculars. The widespread use of urban languages such as Wolof in Senegal, Nouchi in Côte d'Ivoire, Lingala in the Democratic Republic of the Congo or Isicamtho in South Africa both reflects and constructs new, post-ethnic urban identities (McLaughlin 2009: 13).

All these languages are hybrid in the sense that they incorporate material from a number of other languages. This is no different from the way in which a language such as English, for instance, has over the centuries incorporated huge amounts of linguistic material from French and other languages. However, because of their hybridity, the new urban languages tend to be looked down upon within most educational systems. As a result, the contradictory nature of mother tongue education consists in the fact that the true mother tongues of many children are ignored or rejected, while they continue to be taught in indigenous mother tongues that are actually foreign to them. Yet it is the new urban languages that 'more directly express the cultural legacy that is supposed to be preserved', rather than the 'colonially imposed "standard indigenous languages"' (Makoni, Brutt-Griffler and Mashiri 2007: 35).

Step 4: South Africa and the legacy of apartheid

As we have seen in Chapter 6, the apartheid government of South Africa introduced the Bantu Education Act in 1953, which instituted mother tongue education in African languages. This policy was consistent with the recommendations of the 1953 UNESCO report advocating mother tongue education, but its purpose was clearly separatist and discriminatory (Probyn 2005: 154), as it was fuelled by an ideology of white supremacy and a fear of linguistic and cultural heterogeneity. Chick (2001) links this fear to the Herderian ideology of European nation-states (see Chapter 2) and interprets the policy of apartheid South Africa as an extreme version of it. He comments upon the Nationalist Government's introduction of mother tongue instruction for indigenous language speakers in the following terms:

> Since mother tongue instruction is usually associated with multilingual policies, it is important to note that rather than a break with the ideology of European nation-states this policy reflects an extreme version of it. Rather than opening up space for historically marginalized languages, it was a key strategy in the grand apartheid goal of final exclusion of speakers of such languages i.e. their location in separate, linguistically and culturally homogeneous 'nation-states' or Bantustans.
>
> (Chick 2001: 31)

Because of this disturbing link of mother tongue education with the racist policies of the apartheid system, it is now more important than ever to respect people's linguistic choices, whether they choose to switch from indigenous varieties to urban vernaculars, or desire for their children an English-medium education, from which they themselves had been debarred under the apartheid system. Mother tongue education may continue to imprison them within fixed, reified, essentialized ethnic identities. Their choice to use the new urban languages, on the other hand, would seem to constitute a much more empowering option, as it indexes 'the coming together of different ethnic groups held separate by apartheid policy' (Brutt-Griffler 2006: 46).

THE PROBLEMS WITH MOTHER TONGUE EDUCATION

In academic literature, one still frequently finds an undifferentiated call for (the right to) mother tongue education, which – in the case of migrant or transnational students – is said to facilitate their acquisition of the majority language. It is important to realize that such a call, however valid in theoretical terms, may be counter-productive in actual practice: indeed, in our globalized late modern societies, there is usually such a wide range of (assumed) mother tongues that the state can easily opt out of its responsibilities, by means of the commonsensical argument that in any case it would be impossible to organize mother tongue education for each individual child.

A second problem with the call for mother tongue education is that it can involve a kind of arrogance on the part of the (frequently white, Western European or US American) 'expert' who tells people what is good for them – e.g. that they should keep up their minority language. As Bourne (2007: 143–4) puts it in relation to South Africa:

> Colonial education policy in Africa tended towards vernacular education for the native population, where only the children of the elite bought themselves into an English education. The apartheid years in South Africa strengthened the resistance to education in languages other than English, again seen as a way of denying access to employment opportunities and higher education.
>
> Today, despite a supportive national policy towards mother tongue education, the majority of South African parents struggle to enrol their children in English medium schools to avoid their placement in other language streams which are seen as being second class. It seems clear that it is not only that English is seen as providing social mobility, but that the motivations of those offering separate language streams are questioned: people still simply do not believe that the schools are committed to raising standards and ensuring high levels of academic success for their children. Separate language streams are viewed in post-apartheid South Africa, with some justification, as an attempt by the economic elite to exclude and marginalise some sections of society, to the benefit of their own children.

One key issue that Bourne indirectly raises in this context is the question of researcher reflexivity: as researchers, do we (or to what extent do we) collude – consciously or not – with the economic elites?

The third problem with mother tongue education that has already been discussed above is that official language policy is often based on an essentializing link with language inheritance rather than on the children's actual language expertise: Tswanas, for instance, are simply assumed to have standard Setswana as their mother tongue. The negative consequence of such essentialist categorizing is that, if the children master a non-standard variety (Street Setswana) instead of the standard variety, then their linguistic competencies are stigmatized in the classroom and they may be looked upon as deficient or even 'semilingual' (unable to speak any language proficiently).

Pennycook (2002: 11–12), who focuses on the (ab)uses of mother tongue education as part of colonial language policy, comments, tongue in cheek, that 'the mother tongue, rather like the Virgin Mary, remains something in whose direction the congregation of language educators should always genuflect' and that '"questioning the mother tongue" may well be akin to daubing paint on the Virgin Mary'. He reminds us that any discussion of mother tongue education needs to be located 'in specific linguistic, cultural, discursive, social, political, and economic contexts' (Pennycook 2002: 23), and concludes that such a contextual analysis

> might lead us to address questions of language in education rather differently, not focusing so much on reified notions of dominant languages and mother tongues as on trying to understand the complex and hybrid mixtures of semiotic tools that are actually used.
> (Pennycook 2002: 26)

This is exactly what this chapter has set out to do with respect to the language situation in the US and South Africa.

BRIDGES INTO LITERACY

A more flexible alternative to mother tongue education which would have a better chance of moving policy towards social justice and educational equity would be the establishment of **literacy bridges** between home and school. The concept is used, for instance, in Weber (2009) in relation to the language situation in officially trilingual Luxembourg, where large numbers of Romance-language-speaking children are forced to go through a German-language literacy programme (see discussion in Chapter 9). Weber argues that it would be counter-productive to call for education in the standard variety of the (assumed) mother tongue of each child, irrespective of the question of whether the children actually master this particular variety. On the contrary, it would be much more productive to look for the 'common linguistic denominator' of students whose home linguistic resources may well include varieties of French, Portuguese, Cape Verdean Creole, Italian, Spanish, Romanian, etc. and, in this case, set up a French-language literacy option for them alongside the existing German-language literacy programme. The French-language literacy option would act as a bridge into literacy by providing a link with, and building upon, these students' actual linguistic repertoires.

In this way, language-in-education policy would be based on the transnational students' full linguistic repertoires: indeed, as Weber shows, many luso-descendant children in Luxembourg, when they start school, have a repertoire that comprises various varieties of Portuguese, French and sometimes also Luxembourgish, rather than just having Portuguese as their 'mother tongue'. The school system needs to take into account this multilingual reality if its aim is to advance on the difficult path leading towards the elusive goal of educational equity. Three fundamental steps are required in this respect:

a) study the students' actual linguistic repertoires, taking into account all their linguistic varieties and not just a narrow range of standard languages;
b) find the common linguistic denominators;
c) establish the adequate literacy bridges by offering a reasonable range of medium of instruction options.

At the same time, three conditions have to be fulfilled: first, the whole programme needs to be based on the principle of additive, as opposed to subtractive, bilingualism; second, students from the different streams have to be brought together as much as possible in mixed-language groups to allow for peer teaching and learning; and third, all the streams have to be of sufficiently high quality to attract majority group children. Majority group children may indeed be attracted to different streams because these children do not constitute a fully homogeneous group; their homogeneity is imagined rather than real. In Luxembourg, for instance, the many children from mixed marriages with one francophone and one Luxembourgish-speaking parent might well consider enrolling in the French-language literacy option. Such a flexible educational programme structure would allow, in the words of Makoni and Mashiri (2007: 83), moving 'beyond a state-centric perspective of language planning' and towards a full acknowledgement of the linguistic repertoires that people actually deploy in our globalized, superdiverse societies.

In some situations, however, it may be difficult or even impossible to find a literacy bridge for a particular group of students, though possibilities usually arise as soon as one starts comparing the linguistic resources of different groups. This is because these groups are not clearly bounded but mix and interact with each other in the social spaces of urban areas. But even if one is left with a particular group where no literacy bridge seems available, other, more creative applications of the 'literacy bridge' principle may be possible. For instance, it would be possible in German primary schools to let Turkish-origin students write **identity texts** (Cummins 2006) in Turkish or Kurdish and translate them into German (and vice-versa), and in this way to develop literacy in two languages. By identity texts, Cummins (2006: 60) means written, spoken, visual, musical, dramatic or multimodal texts in which students invest their identities and 'that then hold a mirror up to students in which their identities are reflected back in a positive light'. Another example is Mehlem's (2003) discussion of an educational project where Moroccan children in Germany, whose home languages include mostly spoken Berber varieties such as Tamazight, are encouraged to write down oral narratives not in standard Arabic but in their spoken vernacular. At the same time, they are given the option of doing this using either the Arabic or Latin script. Mehlem argues that mother tongue education in standard Arabic does not really help these children because it fails to build upon their actual linguistic resources. The experimental use of writing in Berber, on the other hand, constitutes a more flexible model which acts as a kind of literacy bridge allowing children easier access to eventual literacy in standard Arabic and/or German:

> Für einen Teil der Kinder kann das Angebot, aufbauend auf spontanen Verschriftungen der Muttersprache einen Zugang zum Hocharabischen zu eröffnen, weiterhin sinnvoll sein. Andere werden vielleicht lieber die Chance der Spontanverschriftung in lateinischer Schrift – etwa im Zuge einer zweisprachigen Alphabetisierung – für eine Verbesserung ihrer deutschen Schriftlichkeit nutzen. In jedem Fall sollten die sprachlichen Ressourcen dieser Kinder endlich aus ihrem Schattendasein befreit werden.
>
> (Mehlem 2003: 116)

> (It may still make sense to offer some of the children access to standard Arabic by building upon their spontaneous writing in their mother tongue. Others may want to use their spontaneous writing in the Latin script – possibly as part of a two-language literacy development – in order to improve their literacy in German. In any case, these children's linguistic resources should no longer remain invisible.)

CONCLUSION: A POSSIBLE SOLUTION FOR SOUTH AFRICA

As in the above example of Moroccan children in Germany, a flexible biliteracy programme would probably also be best for many of the South African children whose case was considered in this chapter. Depending on the nature of the children's communicative repertoires, it will be necessary to look for local solutions, but in many contexts it might make sense to set up simultaneous biliteracy programmes in both English and an African language (often one of the new urban languages), which would form the best possible bridge with the students' actual home linguistic resources.

Indeed, since many South African children nowadays are multilingual, it is important for the school system to build upon the whole of their repertoires as far as possible. As Busch (2010: 283) puts it, implementing a mother tongue education programme would be tantamount to 'monolingualization': i.e. 'reduc[ing] the heteroglossia of individual speakers either to monolingualism or to a dichotomy between "mother tongue" and "target language"'. In such a programme, children would be perceived in exclusive terms as *either* 'Xhosa speakers' *or* 'English speakers', etc. Busch (2010: 293) talks about the 'damage inflicted by categorization according to the ascribed mother tongues', and comments on the 'monolingual habitus' of mother tongue education, which 'functions as an "engine" that reduces the complexity of students' everyday lives' (Busch 2010: 290).

At the same time, we should be careful not to reject mother tongue education *en bloc*. In many situations, it will be the best way of ensuring children's educational success. But it cannot simply be proclaimed as the ideal system of education, as some sociolinguists are wont to do. On the contrary, as we have shown in this chapter, it depends on each context and in more multilingual contexts, it is often the case that more flexible dual-medium or multiliteracy approaches will be more promising ways of building upon children's complex repertoires.

FOR DISCUSSION: TRANSLANGUAGING OR MOTHER TONGUE EDUCATION?

Typically, in many South African schools, English is taught with a lot of translanguaging into indigenous languages such as isiXhosa (widely used in the Cape Town area). Teachers use such translanguaging as a teaching strategy to support or 'scaffold' their students' learning (therefore Martin 2005: 89 calls it a 'safe' practice).

Many mother tongue education advocates, on the other hand, object to teachers' use of translanguaging and prefer 'language separation' pedagogic approaches. Mother tongue education in the Cape Town area is advocated primarily by linguists associated with PRAESA (Project for the Study of Alternative Education in South Africa) such as Carole Bloch, the coordinator of PRAESA's Early Literacy Unit. In an article titled 'Towards normalizing South African classroom life: The ongoing struggle to implement mother-tongue based bilingual education', Bloch, Guzula and Nkence (2010: 102) comment as follows on teachers' translanguaging practices:

> We observed [a particular teacher] using English mathematics textbooks, though she tried to talk in Xhosa to the children. However, her language emerged as code-mixing rather than the systematic use of one or the other language .... It will take some effort and time for teachers to stop using code-mixing as it has become common practice with many. The need to code-mix will only fade once all significant aspects of teaching are delivered as a matter of course in Xhosa.

Bloch *et al.* disapprove of the use of mixed language in classrooms, emphasize the role of *standard* isiXhosa as the 'mother tongue' and promote the teaching of isiXhosa and English as two wholly separate languages.

In light of the arguments for and against mother tongue education presented in this chapter, consider and discuss the following questions:

- What are the advantages and disadvantages of using translanguaging and mixed languages in bilingual pedagogy?
- If many children translanguage outside school, shouldn't mother tongue education reflect this (if it is to be truly based on children's actual out-of-school linguistic practices)?
- How can we ensure that the school's emphasis on standard varieties does not give children the feeling that their home varieties are bad and worthless?
- How can we ensure that the use of translanguaging and mixed languages by teachers actually helps students acquire the standard varieties and does not lead to what Blackledge and Creese (2010: 206) call 'the danger of participating in the reproduction of [the students' social] disadvantage'?

PROJECT WORK: AFRICAN-AMERICAN ENGLISH

Find out as much as possible about AAE. What are some of the systematic grammatical rules that distinguish it from standard English? What may have been the historical origins of AAE? A good place to start reading about AAE is Mufwene, Rickford, Bailey and Baugh's *African-American English: Structure, History and Use.*

PROJECT WORK: EXPLORING MOTHER TONGUE EDUCATION

Choose a country whose school system uses a form of mother tongue education, either for indigenous minority language children or for migrant children.

Remember that no mother tongue education programme is wholly good or wholly bad (except perhaps for the Bantu Education Act in apartheid South Africa). Considering both advantages and disadvantages, try and make a case for and/or against the particular mother tongue education programme that you are investigating. Make sure you also consider the important issue of intra-language variation (i.e. variation between standard and non-standard varieties).

PROJECT WORK: LITERACY BRIDGES AND SIMULTANEOUS BILITERACY

- Choose a country whose social composition and education system you are very familiar with. Try to make as comprehensive a list as possible of the schoolchildren's home linguistic varieties (including indigenous minority children and migrant children), taking into account all varieties and not just a narrow range of standard languages. What do you think might be the common linguistic denominators (if any)? What would be the possibilities of establishing adequate literacy bridges by offering a reasonable range of medium of instruction options? How does this compare with the official language-in-education policy of this state?
- Think about the feasibility of a flexible simultaneous biliteracy programme, where children are taught to read and write in two languages at the same time. A good example to get started on this topic is Budach and Bardtenschlager's (2008) article (available online in French). It describes a simultaneous biliteracy programme at a German–Italian school in Frankfurt/Main.

REFERENCES AND SUGGESTIONS FOR FURTHER READING

African-American English (AAE)

Labov, William (2008) 'Unendangered dialects, endangered people', in K.A. King, N. Schilling-Estes, L. Fogle, J.J. Lou and B. Soukup (eds) *Sustaining Linguistic Diversity*, Washington DC: Georgetown University Press, 219–38.

McWhorter, John (1998) *The Word on the Street: Fact and Fable about American English*, New York: Plenum.

Mufwene, Salikoko S., Rickford, John R., Bailey, Guy and Baugh, John (eds) (1998) *African-American English: Structure, History and Use*, London: Routledge.

Perry, Theresa and Delpit, Lisa (eds) (1998) *The Real Ebonics Debate: Power, Language and the Education of African-American Children*, Boston, MA: New Beacon Books.

Schmid, Carol L. (2001) *The Politics of Language: Conflict, Identity and Cultural Pluralism in Comparative Perspective*, Oxford: Oxford University Press.

South Africa and the politics of language in Africa

Bloch, Carole, Guzula, Xolisa and Nkence, Ntombizanele (2010) 'Towards normalizing South African classroom life: The ongoing struggle to implement mother-tongue based bilingual education', in K. Menken and O. Garcia (eds) *Negotiating Language Policies in Schools*, Abingdon: Routledge, 88–106.

Brutt-Griffler, Janina (2006) 'Language endangerment, the construction of indigenous languages and world English', in M. Pütz, J. Fishman and J. van Aertselaer (eds) *'Along the Routes to Power': Explorations of Empowerment through Language*, Berlin: Mouton de Gruyter, 35–53.

Busch, Brigitta (2010) 'School language profiles: Valorizing linguistic resources in heteroglossic situations in South Africa', *Language and Education*, 24: 283–94.

Chick, Keith (2001) 'Constructing a multicultural national identity: South African classrooms as sites of struggle between competing discourses', *Working Papers in Educational Linguistics*, 17: 27–45.

Cook, Susan (2009) 'Street Setswana vs. School Setswana: Language policies and the forging of identities in South African classrooms', in J.A. Kleifgen and G.C. Bond (eds) *The Languages of Africa and the Diaspora: Educating for Language Awareness*, Bristol: Multilingual Matters, 96–116.

Kamwangamalu, Nkonko M. (2016) *Language Policy and Economics: The Language Question in Africa*, Basingstoke: Palgrave.

McLaughlin, Fiona (ed.) (2009) *The Languages of Urban Africa*, London: Continuum.

Makoni, Sinfree, Brutt-Griffler, Janina and Mashiri, Pedzisai (2007) 'The use of "indigenous" and urban vernaculars in Zimbabwe', *Language in Society*, 36: 25–49.

Ngugi wa Thiong'o (1986) *Decolonizing the Mind: The Politics of Language in African Literature*, Oxford: James Currey.

Probyn, Margie (2005) 'Language and the struggle to learn: The interaction of classroom realities, language policy, and neo-colonial and globalization discourses in South African schools', in A. Lin and P. Martin (eds) *Decolonization, Globalization: Language-in-Education Policy and Practice*, Clevedon: Multilingual Matters, 153–72.

Mother tongue education or literacy bridges

Blackledge, Adrian and Creese, Angela (2010) *Multilingualism: A Critical Perspective*, London: Continuum.

Bourne, Jill (2007) 'Reflections and suggestions for ways forward', in J. Conteh, P. Martin and L. Helavaara Robertson (eds) *Multilingual Learning: Stories from Schools and Communities in Britain*, Stoke-on-Trent: Trentham Books, 135–44.

Budach, Gabriele and Bardtenschlager, Helen (2008) 'Est-ce que ce n'est pas trop dur? Enjeux et expériences de l'alphabétisation dans un projet de double immersion', *Glottopol*, 11: 148–70.

Cummins, Jim (2006) 'Identity texts: The imaginative construction of self through multiliteracies pedagogy', in O. García, T. Skutnabb-Kangas and M.E. Torres-Guzmán (eds) *Imagining Multilingual Schools: Languages in Education and Glocalization*, Clevedon: Multilingual Matters, 51–68.

Cummins, Jim and Early, Margaret (2011) *Identity Texts: The Collaborative Creation of Power in Multilingual Schools*, Stoke-on-Trent: Trentham Books.

Makoni, Sinfree and Mashiri, Pedzisai (2007) 'Critical historiography: Does language planning in Africa need a construct of language as part of its theoretical apparatus?', in S. Makoni and A. Pennycook (eds) *Disinventing and Reconstituting Languages*, Clevedon: Multilingual Matters, 62–89.

Martin, Peter (2005) '"Safe" language practices in two rural schools in Malaysia: Tensions between policy and practice', in A. Lin and P. Martin (eds) *Decolonization, Globalization: Language-in-Education Policy and Practice*, Clevedon: Multilignual Matters, 74–97.

Mehlem, Ulrich (2003) 'Experiment Muttersprache: Marokkanische Kinder schreiben Berberisch und Arabisch in Deutschland', in J. Erfurt, G. Budach and S. Hofmann (eds) *Mehrsprachigkeit und Migration*, Frankfurt/Main: Peter Lang, 103–17.

Pennycook, Alastair (2002) 'Mother tongues, governmentality and protectionism', *International Journal of the Sociology of Language*, 154: 11–28.

Weber, Jean-Jacques (2009) *Multilingualism, Education and Change*, Frankfurt/Main: Peter Lang.

CHAPTER 11

Heritage language education

In the previous chapters, we have advocated the use of flexible multilingual policies and pedagogies for language-minority children, as our primary concern was to find the best way of building upon children's actual out-of-school resources to help them achieve educational success. But of course there are other, equally legitimate concerns, such as a particular community's concern that children learn the community language (their 'mother tongue') even if they may not speak it at all and may have to learn it almost as a 'foreign' language. These concerns are often conflated or confused by mother tongue education advocates, and hence it is important to keep them conceptually distinct. The latter concern is frequently found in communities that have suffered from a long history of oppression, such as Native American communities, and for whom heritage language education is therefore extremely important.

This chapter examines the situation and teaching of **heritage languages**, first indigenous heritage languages in the US and Ecuador, and then immigrant heritage languages in the UK. Heritage language speakers typically have a historical link to an indigenous language (usually endangered) or an immigrant language (often also endangered within the new migration context), which is not normally taught in the mainstream school system of the host society. García (2009) feels that, like so many terms, 'heritage language' is not ideal because of its associations with a distant past – another term that is sometimes used, 'ancestral language', is even worse in this respect. She puts it as follows: 'And what connotations does the term "heritage" have? We think of old, ancient, in the past, when in fact, we are speaking about languages of the future' (García 2009: 60). However, we will follow the terminology of the researchers whose work we report on in this chapter. We first look at the situation of Navajo, a Native American language in the US, and of Quichua, an indigenous language in Ecuador, and then at a number of immigrant minority languages (especially Bengali) taught within the UK complementary school system (which will be described later on in this chapter).

LANGUAGE AND HERITAGE IN THE UNITED STATES

In the US, there are large numbers of bi- or multilingual speakers but their proficiency in languages other than English is generally not valued in society. Moreover, official language policies such as the No Child Left Behind policy (see Chapter 9) only emphasize English language proficiency and tend to look upon other languages merely as an obstacle to learning English. For this reason, many speakers of heritage languages shift to English and lose proficiency in their home language. Since the 1990s, however, there have been some signs of a revival in the learning of heritage languages, especially Native American languages. In particular, the Esther Martinez Native American Languages Preservation Act of 2006 officially recognizes the right to use indigenous languages in such contexts as education.

In this section, we look at the situation of Navajo, a Native American language used in the south-west of the US (mostly Arizona, New Mexico and Utah). Like all Native American languages, Navajo and its speakers have undergone a long history of linguistic repression:

> The present situation of Navajo is part of a larger process of language shift engulfing all Native American communities .... Of 175 Indigenous languages still spoken in the United States, only 20 are being acquired as a first language by children. The causes of language shift in Native American communities include a history of genocide, the seizure by whites of Indigenous lands, and explicit federal policies designed to eradicate Indigenous languages and to 'remake American Indian children into brown White citizens'.
>
> (McCarty, Romero-Little and Zepeda 2008: 161)

Navajo, with its almost 178,000 speakers, who are bilingual in Navajo and English, is one of the few Native American languages that are still acquired as a home language by children.

As part of their ethnographic research project, McCarty, Romero-Little and Zepeda (2008) found evidence of contradictory language ideologies on the part of Navajo speakers, in the sense that the language was simultaneously valorized and stigmatized. Young people in particular saw it as linked to their identity while feeling that it was an endangered or even dying language. They frequently used a discourse of both language pride and language shame. On the one hand, they were proud of Navajo as their own language. But, on the other hand, they also looked upon Navajo as belonging to the past; for them, it indexed lack of education, poverty and backwardness, as opposed to English, which was linked with 'modernity, opportunity, and success' (McCarty *et al.* 2008: 168). As a result, many young people actually tried to hide their proficiency in Navajo and preferred to use English instead. Yet their attitudes towards English could be equally contradictory: it was not only seen as the language of modernity but sometimes also as the language of colonization and oppression.

The research of McCarty *et al.* (2008: 170) aims at raising the status of Navajo by involving young people in local activities connected with the project:

> Carefully listening to youth discourses opens up new understandings of language shift dynamics and new possibilities for language education programs and practices. We are hopeful that these possibilities will continue to unfold and that they will actively involve youth and the generation of young parents, not only as language learners but as language planners, researchers and educators in their own right.

By working with the community in this way, it may be possible to set up flexible bilingual programmes that will foster the maintenance and revitalization of Navajo, as well as the youths' academic achievements in the dominant language, English. McCarty (2012, 2013) discusses such a programme at a highly successful K-5 public magnet school, the Bridge of Beauty (Puente de Hozho) school in Flagstaff, Arizona. The school population is made up of Native American, Latino and white students, and the school builds on the students' heteroglossic repertoires in Navajo, Spanish, English and other languages, all of which are seen as resources for learning. Unfortunately, however, most Native American and Latino children in the US are not able to develop in rich multilingual environments such as that of the Bridge of Beauty school and instead suffer from restrictive monolingual (English-only) policies.

LANGUAGE AND HERITAGE IN ECUADOR

In this section, we discuss an example from Ecuador to show that even a progressive language-in-education policy does not necessarily lead to language maintenance. A widely used indigenous language is Quichua or Kichwa (known as Quechua or Kechwa outside of Ecuador), spoken by about ten million people not only in Ecuador but also in Peru and Bolivia (King 2001: 7). However, like many indigenous languages, it is endangered as its speakers tend to shift towards greater use of Spanish.

In Ecuador, the second half of the twentieth century saw the development of bilingual education for indigenous communities. Especially in the 1980s, a progressive policy of bilingual intercultural education was adopted, with Quichua as the medium of instruction and Spanish as 'the language of intercultural relations' (King 2001: 42). However, the reality on the ground can be very different, as King (2001) found out: at least in the two indigenous communities that she studied (Lagunas and Tambopamba), the majority of the children did not have Quichua as their primary home language and were more proficient in Spanish than in Quichua; moreover, the amount of Quichua that they learnt at school was extremely limited and did not extend much beyond a purely symbolic use of the language.

Both Lagunas and Tambopamba have community-run elementary schools, with many indigenous teachers genuinely concerned about the revitalization of Quichua. Yet what King found during her fieldwork was very limited instruction of Quichua, with a focus on receptive rather than productive skills. Spanish was used almost exclusively as the medium of instruction in the schools, as well as being regularly used in both teacher–student and student–student interactions. As for Quichua, it was mostly limited to symbolic uses in greetings or short announcements – which largely reflects the way it was used in the Lagunas community. Though there was slightly more spontaneous use of Quichua among students in the Tambopamba school – reflecting these students' greater exposure to Quichua in this community – their proficiency in Quichua was also mostly of a receptive kind and was not expanded upon by the school. Hence, in both schools, the children had very limited competences in Quichua, and King (2001: 187) concludes that it is unlikely, in the current environment of both home and school, that Quichua will develop into the 'everyday, unmarked language of the community'.

In a further study, King and Haboud (2011) investigate the impact of migration upon the sending community (rather than the host community). They explore how large-scale emigration from Ecuador in the late 1990s affected the language competences and practices of those left behind. Their focus is in particular on children growing up with grandparents in the community, while the parents work in the USA or Spain, and send remittances back home. King and Haboud note that the resulting shifts in childhood patterns have an effect on the children's Quichua language maintenance and language learning opportunities.

Thanks to the remittances from abroad, many young people are now freed from traditional agricultural work and household chores. The youngsters, who are more financially independent, spend more time at school as well as hanging out in town. The result of this has been a loss of discipline and a rise of gangs, as well as alcohol and drugs abuse – at least according to the adults that King and Haboud interviewed. In these youngsters, lack of respect (especially for their grandparents) seems to be caused at least partially by the emotional hardship of being separated from their parents.

It is important to be aware of these changing patterns of childhood and adolescence to understand their implications for Quichua language maintenance and revitalization. As King and Haboud point out, it could be thought that, as the grandparents are often quite fluent in Quichua, the children would acquire the language from them. However, the opposite seems to be the case: 'rather than grandparents socializing children into ways of speaking Quichua, grandparents' influence is greatly diminished in many homes, and instead children are socializing them to use Spanish' (King and Haboud 2011: 151–2).

As a result, Quichua is being used less and less in the home and is becoming more and more just a school language. But even in the domain of the school, Quichua is increasingly sidelined, as Spanish and English increasingly dominate. For, in the eyes of many youngsters, it is Spanish and English that they will need if, like their parents, they emigrate one day in search of better educational or professional opportunities. In this way, King and Haboud (2011: 155) conclude that 'even progressive language policy to support an Indigenous language such as Quichua can be simply overwhelmed by large-scale global forces' (see also Mortimer 2016 for a comparable situation concerning bilingual Spanish–Guarani education in Paraguay).

LANGUAGE AND HERITAGE IN ENGLAND

In England, education policy related to issues of linguistic and ethnic diversity has been strongly influenced by the Swann Report, *Education for All*, published in 1985. It addressed the needs of bilingual students, especially those of Caribbean and South Asian descent, though it failed to endorse any form of bilingual education. It stressed the need to teach English as a second or additional language by relying on bilingual support staff. Thus bilingual minority students are given language support by an EAL (English as an additional language) teacher working collaboratively with the class teacher, as a way of helping them to cope with the English-only mainstream classroom (Creese 2005).

However, issues of diversity were increasingly sidelined in the early 1990s with the introduction of the National Curriculum, along with national testing for 7, 11 and 14-year-olds. Instead, more emphasis was put on the acquisition of standard English (without taking into account ethnic and linguistic diversity), and a discourse of blaming the victim became commonplace: if students did badly in the new system, it must be that they themselves were to blame for it. The New Labour government of Tony Blair, elected in 1997, raised expectations that it would at last tackle educational exclusion. In practice, however, its National Literacy Strategy of 1998, with as its centrepiece the 'Literacy Hour', only reinforced the free market ideology and the accompanying emphasis on imparting standard English. As Harris, Leung and Rampton (2002: 40) put it,

> The Literacy Hour assumes native-speaker knowledge of spoken English and cultural meaning, and in it, pupils' attention is focused on the basics of print literacy and standard English, overwhelmingly ignoring both the multi-modality of integrated communications systems and the heteroglossia and multi-lingualism of the global city.

The marginalization of minority communities and their languages is reflected in the fact that these communities have been left to themselves to organize classes in their own languages outside of the state education sector. Such community language classes, which usually run in the evenings or at the weekend, are frequently referred to in the UK as 'supplementary' or 'complementary' schools. Moreover, these complementary schools tend to see themselves as teaching not only proficiency in the community language but also the cultural values of the community. In this section, we report on the interesting results of a study of complementary schools by Blackledge and Creese (2010), who carried out ethnographic work in classrooms where community languages such as Bengali, Gujarati, Cantonese, Mandarin and Turkish were taught. We focus in particular on a number of issues about the nature of language and heritage arising in connection with Bengali, the official language of Bangladesh.

In all the complementary schools where Blackledge and Creese, together with their co-researchers, investigated linguistic practices and the construction and negotiation of identities, they found a pervasive tension between 'two ideological positions: one characterized by heteroglossic, flexible linguistic production which indexed multicultural cosmopolitanism, the other rooted in linguistic affiliation to national and cultural heritage' (Blackledge and Creese 2010: 24). They refer to these positions as flexible and separate bilingualism, a distinction which is very similar to the one we drew between flexible and fixed multilingualism in Chapter 9. Separate bilingualism tended to be the institutional ideology of the schools, with teachers and administrators looking upon the separation or compartmentalization of languages as necessary to ensure the maintenance of the minority language. However, actual classroom practices, not only of the students themselves, but also in teacher–student interactions, tended to be much more mixed, with both English and the minority language being flexibly drawn upon to get the classroom work done. And when teachers tried to enforce the ideology of separate bilingualism, this often brought out student contestation and resistance.

Blackledge and Creese (2010: 111) quote an example where a teacher insists on the students speaking Bengali 'because tumi Bangali' (because you are Bengali). But her demand meets with student resistance, with one student insisting on the right to choose between languages ('miss you can choose') and adducing the example of a member of her family who, while of Bangladeshi heritage, consistently switches into English:

> My aunty chose it, she speaks English all the time.
>
> (Blackledge and Creese 2010: 111)

This example illustrates the clash between the ideologies of separate and flexible bilingualism. What is particularly interesting here is that while explicitly adhering to the ideology of separate bilingualism, the teacher actually mixes English and the minority language in her own linguistic practice when she says, 'because tumi Bangali'.

Another interesting example given in Blackledge and Creese (2010: 173) is where a teacher pronounces a student's name in the Bengali way as /Jaara/, and one of the other students corrects him in the following way:

> Z-a-h-r-a. In school we call her Zahra, in school we call her Zahra.

/Zahra/ is the anglicized pronunciation of the name. Thus the student seems to resist the institutional ideology of keeping the minority language separate from English. In general, all these examples show that complementary schools often attempt to impose fixed, reified 'heritage identities' upon the students, but the imposition of these heritage values is sometimes contested and flexibly renegotiated by the students.

However, this is only the first half of the story. Apart from keeping the heritage language separate from English, many complementary school teachers and administrators also attempted to keep the standard variety of the heritage language separate from non-standard varieties. Bengali is the standard language, while many students actually use a non-standard language (Sylheti) as their home language (alongside English). But many teachers insisted on teaching the students what they considered to be the 'pure' form of the language, and looked down upon the variety spoken in the students' families. In this way, the complementary schools reproduced the mainstream society's ideology of purism: just as mainstream society values standard or 'proper' English above non-standard varieties, the complementary schools valued standard or 'proper' Bengali above Sylheti.

In fact, in the eyes of many teachers, standard Bengali had come to represent the 'heritage' of the Bangladeshi nation. They looked upon it as 'a vital symbol of the founding of the Bangladeshi nation' because of the tragic pro-Bengali protests back in 1952 in which

> the 'language martyrs' were killed while demonstrating against the imposition of Urdu as the national language by West Pakistan .... The historic incident, which marks the Bangladeshi calendar as 'Ekushey February', continues to be celebrated as a key moment in the collective memory of the Bangladeshi nation and in the Bangladeshi community in the United Kingdom.
>
> (Blackledge and Creese 2010: 188–9)

When Bangladesh split off from Pakistan in 1971, Bengali (also called Bangla) was chosen as the official language, although many languages are spoken in the country. As a result, the complementary school teachers felt that they had to protect the purity of Bengali by keeping it separate not only from English but also from other languages of Bangladesh such as Sylheti. One school administrator said that 'Sylheti should not be allowed to "contaminate" the standard form' (Blackledge and Creese 2010: 169). Another one insisted that 'when you talk about language it means Bengali, Sylheti is not a language' (Blackledge and Creese 2010: 170). On the whole, the representatives of the institution, who were themselves speakers of standard Bengali, emphasized the difference between Bengali and Sylheti, as well as the superiority of the former. This notion of superiority was also frequently extended to the speakers of the standard variety: they considered Bengali to be the language of educated people, while they looked down upon speakers of Sylheti as uneducated, poor and lower-class people.

Interestingly, these prejudiced assessments were contested by the speakers of Sylheti (some parents, the students themselves), who sometimes looked upon speakers of Bengali as snobs and show-offs. At the same time, the speakers of Sylheti tended to emphasize the similarities between Sylheti and Bengali, and they considered the two varieties to be more or less identical. These diverging ideological positions are thus also a good example illustrating the different ways of constructing the boundaries between languages (see our discussion in Chapter 3). In this way, Blackledge and Creese's data raises questions both about what constitutes 'a language' and what constitutes 'heritage'. On the whole, it is the young students in their study who show us the most flexible and sophisticated responses when they contest and subvert the adults' essentialized notions of language and heritage.

THE DOMINANCE OF THE STANDARD LANGUAGE AND PURIST IDEOLOGIES

Language hierarchies informed by the standard language and purist ideologies can be found not only in mainstream education but also in complementary schools, as indicated by the Bengali–Sylheti example discussed in the previous section. In this section, we provide three more examples from the literature which reveal the dominance of the standard language and purist ideologies in heritage language education. The first one comes from the same research project as the one reported on in the previous section, this time involving ethnographic work in a Turkish complementary school in London, which was attended by a large number of students with a Cypriot-Turkish background (Lytra *et al.* 2010). In one particular student–teacher interaction, the student relies on gestures to let the teacher know that she needs a pen. The teacher uses this opportunity to teach the students the Turkish word for 'pen', and praises the student for avoiding the use of the Cypriot-Turkish word *penna*. Lytra *et al.* (2010: 30) argue that the teacher here sets up a linguistic hierarchy on which *temiz Türkçe* (clean, uncontaminated or standard Turkish) is positioned above the Cypriot-Turkish variety used as a home language by most of the students:

> In this example, the teacher and pupil privilege the use of the standard Turkish word *tükenmez* over the Cypriot-Turkish equivalent *penna* for <pen>. These linguistic hierarchies are rooted in the marginalized position of Cypriot-Turkish and the stigmatization of regional varieties of Turkish, particularly regional accents, with respect to standard Turkish.

The second example is taken from Spanish language education in the US. At the higher levels of education, heritage speakers of Spanish are frequently taught together with foreign language learners. In such contexts, the vernacular varieties of Latino students are often stigmatized by their teachers as well as the other students. Valdés *et al.* (2008) show how Latino students are sometimes marginalized and can feel alienated in departments of Spanish at US universities because of the language ideologies prevalent there. These ideologies in fact reproduce the 'nation-imagining' beliefs and values of mainstream US society, a society that views itself as monolingual and English-speaking, and that is highly suspicious of bilingualism and of other languages (Valdés *et al.* 2008: 125). The Spanish departments simply transmit this ideology of monolingualism within the context of Spanish studies, in that they subscribe to the ideal of the monolingual and educated native speaker, whose standard Spanish is looked upon as the only 'correct' form of the language. As a result, many Spanish teachers feel the need to protect the language from 'contamination' by the mixed or contact varieties used by Latino bilinguals. Valdés *et al.* (2008: 127) conclude as follows:

> The teaching and study of heritage languages may not be successful if we are not able to address unexamined but central challenges to heritage language maintenance and development among second and third generation American bilinguals.

In an attempt to address these 'central challenges', Parodi (2008) argues that there is an urgent need to develop special educational programmes for heritage speakers, in which these students are not only given help with standard (written, academic) Spanish but at the same time also encouraged to maintain their vernacular (oral) home varieties. This is the only way, Parodi insists, of helping them to deal with the stigma attached to their varieties in society and to overcome their linguistic insecurity in academic contexts – a solution which is reminiscent of the flexible bilingual programmes proposed by McCarty *et al.* for Navajo maintenance and revitalization (discussed at the beginning of this chapter).

Another special educational programme for heritage language speakers is the SHALL (Studies of Heritage and Academic Languages and Literacies) project set up in Hawai'i by Davis and her colleagues. In Hawaiian schools there are a lot of speakers of indigenous languages (Hawaiian), creole languages (Hawai'i Creole English) and a wide range of immigrant languages. The SHALL programme attempts to bring about more equitable educational practices for all these students by putting them into the roles of critical researchers. Thus, for instance, in a Hawaiian high school the participating students were mostly speakers of heritage languages such as Ilokano and Samoan as well as Hawai'i Creole English (often referred to as 'Pidgin') as their first and second languages. They took combined heritage and academic English language classes and, as part of their coursework, explored the marginalization of (in particular) Pidgin in such institutional settings as the school. The aim was to help students develop their heritage, local and academic English language abilities and identities, all at the same time, through activities such as the following:

> Students engaged in textual analysis through oral history assignments in which they used their heritage language and/or Pidgin to interview family or community members. They then translated the interview into academic English and conducted analyses of the syntactic, phonological and lexical similarities and differences between their heritage language and English.

> This and other comparison and contrast assignments helped students develop metalinguistic awareness of academic English rhetoric as well as promoted new or enhanced multilingual literacy practices.
>
> (Davis 2009: 214)

In this way, participants were enabled to gradually move from 'at risk' and 'failing' to 'successful and capable' student identities.

DISCUSSION AND CONCLUSION: IMPLICATIONS FOR THE EU POLICY OF MULTILINGUALISM

This conclusion brings together our concerns of the last two chapters that both mother tongue education and heritage language education are sometimes too rigid, and we discuss this here in a more general way with reference to the EU policy of multilingualism. If our primary concern is helping all children achieve educational success, education – both mainstream and complementary – needs to respect, to include and to build upon all the children's linguistic resources, whether heritage languages such as Navajo, immigrant minority languages such as Sylheti or non-standard varieties such as vernacular Spanish. However, what we find in many educational systems is an emphasis on the national or official standard variety/ies and some token promotion of indigenous heritage languages, with other languages – in particular immigrant minority languages and non-standard varieties – being devalued and condemned to the margins. In England, for instance, this means that on the whole immigrant languages are only taught in complementary schools, but even here, as we have seen, only standard varieties are taught (e.g. Bengali and not Sylheti).

Hence, there is an urgent need for both policy-makers and teachers to break through the standard language ideology and to valorize all the different linguistic and cultural resources of all the children, including not only standard indigenous or immigrant languages, but also non-standard or not fully standardized varieties. Only in this way will it be possible to establish the most appropriate literacy bridges for the increasing number of transnational students. In the words of Barradas (2007: 102),

> as communities move forward to take up their roles in a Europe where borders are ever more fluid, the needs of bilingual/ multilingual children as eurocitizens have to be catered for. This also implies that, if we are to respect individuals within the context of a multifaceted and multicultural society, schools will have to be able to cope with new challenges.

> We have reached a point where the 'one model fits all' strategy no longer applies. As European education systems evolve to respond to a changing political and socio-economic reality, we are compelled to reflect on how these systems can include the diversified interests of the communities they serve.

Clearly, it is time for the UK (as well as other states) to rethink their 'one size fits all' educational system. But Barradas' admonition applies not only at the state level but also at the European level. There is also a need to reflect on how the official EU multilingual policy of 'mother tongue plus two' is unnecessarily restrictive and 'unrealistic' (Cabau-Lampa 2007) in its almost exclusive focus on (European) standard languages.

In an attempt to move towards an equitable policy of multilingualism, a more promising approach might be to distinguish between conversational and academic language proficiency – thus loosely building upon Cummins' (2000) distinction between basic interpersonal communicative skills (BICS) and cognitive academic language proficiency (CALP). Here we use academic language proficiency to mean mastery of the (primarily written) standard variety, whereas conversational language proficiency implies communicative (especially oral) skills in any variety, whether standardized or not.

Introducing such a basic distinction between conversational and academic language proficiency in language-in-education policies, and fully recognizing the former as *one* possible – and equally valid – aim of language learning at school would in turn allow for a less restrictive and more realistic reinterpretation of the EU policy of multilingualism: the aim for each EU citizen could be to achieve academic language proficiency in two varieties and conversational language proficiency in the third one. Indeed, in some social contexts, conversational language proficiency may be just what is required. An example would be the role of Corsican in Corsican language-in-education policy. Jaffe's (2011: 223) ethnographic study leads her to conclude that it may be necessary to

> bridge the school–society gap by modifying the school curriculum and its goals. That is, schools could decide to prioritize the kinds of Corsican language competencies ('spontaneous' oral, conversational practice) that the public can appreciate and may value most highly. One possible outcome could be a reduction or delay of the teaching of academic literacies in Corsican.

Another example, this time from a non-European context, would be the position of Mandarin Chinese in the educational system of Singapore, as described by Gupta (1997: 504):

> there have also been demands from members of the minorities for access to the learning of Mandarin. At present nearly all non-Chinese Singaporeans are debarred from learning Mandarin at school. The provision of Mandarin as a third language available to all would meet these demands. Oral Mandarin is what would seem to be needed: the Chinese writing system is intrinsically difficult to learn, and in Singapore it is at the oral level that Mandarin is privileged. If Mandarin, as seems likely, maintains or improves its position of privilege, the minorities will be increasingly marginalized unless they are given access to the learning of oral Mandarin in schools.

Such a revised policy of multilingualism would be less restrictive in that specifying conversational language proficiency as the target for one of the three languages would open the door to non-standard or not fully standardized varieties, with the language choices decided upon locally (by individual schools) rather than nationally. It would also be a more realistic aim which could be set as a minimum requirement, and member-states would have the option of going beyond it if they so wished. With such a remodelled and flexibly organized language-in-education policy, the students in the English school system whose case was considered in this chapter could, for instance, opt for academic language proficiency in English and a foreign language and conversational language proficiency in Sylheti. In this way, a minor change in the EU policy of multilingualism could potentially impact upon state-level language-in-education policies in a positive way, pave the way for more flexible and inclusive forms of multilingual learning and help with the revitalization of community or heritage languages.

FOR DISCUSSION: THE EU POLICY OF MULTILINGUALISM

While reading the final section of this chapter, you may have been wondering why Cabau-Lampa (2007) calls the EU policy of multilingualism 'unrealistic'. She discusses language teaching and learning in Sweden and claims that most students are highly motivated to learn Swedish and English but very few are interested in learning a second foreign language such as French. Hence, she suggests that 'mother tongue (MT) + 2' may be over-ambitious and that 'MT + 1' may be a more realistic goal.

In Chapter 9, we briefly discussed another suggestion that the 'MT + 2' formula should be replaced by 'MT + English + 1' (though this actually corresponds to the Swedish model which Cabau-Lampa finds unrealistic). And in the final section of this chapter, it was argued that the EU policy of multilingualism could be made more flexible by aiming at academic language proficiency in two languages and conversational language proficiency in a third one.

What do you think of all these suggestions? Can you think of other ways in which the EU policy of multilingualism could be improved?

FOR DISCUSSION: THE CONTRADICTORY ROLE OF SPANISH IN THE US

Consider the following statement which is often said to epitomize a prevalent attitude in mainstream US society:

> Using Spanish as a heritage or immigrant language is bad, but learning it as a foreign language is good.

Discuss the underlying language ideologies. Make sure you take into account the important aspect of language variation, including in particular Castilian Spanish, Latin American varieties of Spanish and the Spanish varieties of US Latinos.

PROJECT WORK: NATIVE AMERICAN LANGUAGES

Explore the present situation of Native American languages in light of the Native American Languages Act 1990, 1992 and the Esther Martinez Native American Languages Preservation Act 2006. What rights do these legal texts recognize for the use of Native American languages in education? Do you think these rights are sufficient to ensure the revitalization and survival of the languages? Why or why not?

To what extent do you agree with Schiffman's (1996: 246) assessment of the Native American Languages Act: 'now that Native-American languages are practically extinct, and pose no threat to anyone anywhere, we can grant them special status'?

PROJECT WORK: LANGUAGE-IN-EDUCATION POLICY IN HAWAI'I

What is the language situation and language-in-education policy of Hawai'i? Make a list of what you consider to be positive and negative aspects of Hawaiian language-in-education policy. Make sure you include the roles of both Hawaiian (a Polynesian language) and Hawai'i Creole English (often referred to as 'Pidgin') in your analysis. Apart from Davis (2009), you could also look at Wilson (1999).

PROJECT WORK: CHINESE COMPLEMENTARY SCHOOLS

Are there any Chinese complementary schools in the area where you reside? Find out which variety of Chinese is being taught: is it Putonghua/Mandarin, or is Cantonese (or another variety) also taught? And which written script is taught: the simplified characters in use in Mainland China, the traditional ones that are used in (e.g.) Taiwan, and/or Pinyin, the romanization system widely used internationally to teach (oral) Mandarin as a foreign language?

If possible, interview some teachers, students or parents and ask them about their reactions to the choices made by the school. How do they see the heritage that is to be transmitted by the school: more in terms of values, culture or language?

You could also read about recent research on Chinese complementary schools in Chen (2007) and Li Wei and Wu (2010).

REFERENCES AND SUGGESTIONS FOR FURTHER READING

Heritage language education

Brinton, Donna M., Kagan, Olga and Bauckus, Susan (eds) (2008) *Heritage Language Education*, New York: Routledge.

Kagan, Olga, Carreira, Maria and Chik, Claire Hitchins (eds) (2017) *The Routledge Handbook of Heritage Language Education: From Innovation to Program Building*, New York: Routledge.

Trifonas, Peter Pericles and Aravossitas, Themistoklis (eds) (2014) *Rethinking Heritage Language Education*, Cambridge: Cambridge University Press.

Language and heritage in the US

Davis, Kathryn A. (2009) 'Agentive youth research: Towards individual, collective and policy transformations', in T.G. Wiley, J.S. Lee and R.W. Rumberger (eds) *The Education of Language Minority Immigrants in the United States*, Bristol: Multilingual Matters, 202–39.

García, Ofelia (2009) *Bilingual Education in the 21st Century: A Global Perspective*, Chichester: Wiley-Blackwell.

McCarty, Teresa L. (2012) 'Enduring inequities, imagined futures: Circulating policy discourses and dilemmas in the anthropology of education', *Anthropology and Education Quarterly*, 43: 1–12.

—— (2013) *Language Planning and Policy in Native America: History, Theory, Praxis*, Bristol: Multilingual Matters.

——, Romero-Little, Mary E. and Zepeda, Ofelia (2008) 'Indigenous language policies in social practice: The case of Navajo', in K.A. King, N. Schilling-Estes, L. Fogle, J.J. Lou and B. Soukup (eds) *Sustaining Linguistic Diversity: Endangered and Minority Languages and Language Varieties*, Washington DC: Georgetown University Press, 159–72.

Parodi, Claudia (2008) 'Stigmatized Spanish inside the classroom and out: A model of language teaching to heritage speakers', in D. Brinton, O. Kagan and S. Bauckus (eds) *Heritage Language Education*, New York: Routledge, 199–214.

Schiffman, Harold (1996) *Linguistic Culture and Language Policy*, London: Routledge.

Valdés, Guadalupe, Gonzalez, S.V., Lopez Garcia, D. and Marquez, P. (2008) 'Heritage languages and ideologies of language: Unexamined challenges', in D. Brinton, O. Kagan and S. Bauckus (eds) *Heritage Language Education*, New York: Routledge, 107–30.

Wilson, William H. (1999) 'The sociopolitical context of establishing Hawaiian-medium education', in S. May (ed.) *Indigenous Community-Based Education*, Clevedon: Multilingual Matters, 95–108.

Language and heritage in South America

King, Kendall A. (2001) *Language Revitalization Processes and Prospects: Quichua in the Ecuadorian Andes*, Clevedon: Multilingual Matters.

—— and Haboud, Marleen (2002) 'Language planning and policy in Ecuador', *Current Issues in Language Planning*, 3: 359–424.

—— and Haboud, Marleen (2011) 'International migration and Quichua language shift in the Ecuadorian Andes', in T.L. McCarty (ed.) *Ethnography and Language Policy*, New York: Routledge, 139–59.

Mortimer, Katherine S. (2016) 'A potentially heteroglossic policy becomes monoglossic in context: An ethnographic analysis of Paraguayan bilingual education policy', *Anthropology and Education Quarterly*, 47: 349–65.

Language and heritage in the UK

Blackledge, Adrian and Creese, Angela (2010) *Multilingualism: A Critical Perspective*, London: Continuum.

Chen, Yangguang (2007) 'Contributing to success: Chinese parents and the community school', in J. Conteh, P. Martin and L.H. Robertson (eds) *Multilingual Learning: Stories from Schools and Communities in Britain*, Stoke-on-Trent: Trentham Books, 63–85.

Creese, Angela (2005) *Teacher Collaboration and Talk in Multilingual Classrooms*, Clevedon: Multilingual Matters.

Harris, Roxy, Leung, Constant and Rampton, Ben (2002) 'Globalization, diaspora and language education in England', in D. Block and D. Cameron (eds) *Globalization and Language Teaching*, London: Routledge, 29–46.

Li Wei and Wu, Chao-Jung (2010) 'Literacy and socializational teaching in Chinese complementary schools', in V. Lytra and P. Martin (eds) *Sites of Multilingualism: Complementary Schools in Britain Today*, Stoke-on-Trent: Trentham, 33–44.

Lytra, Vally, Martin, P., Barac, T. and Bhatt, A. (2010) 'Investigating the intersection of multilingualism and multimodality in Turkish and Gujarati literacy classes', in V. Lytra and P. Martin (eds) *Sites of Multilingualism: Complementary Schools in Britain Today*, Stoke-on-Trent: Trentham Books, 19–31.

Towards more flexible policies of multilingualism

Barradas, Olga (2007) 'Learning Portuguese: A tale of two worlds', in J. Conteh, P. Martin and L.H. Robertson (eds) *Multilingual Learning: Stories from Schools and Communities in Britain*, Stoke-on-Trent: Trentham Books, 87–102.

Cabau-Lampa, Béatrice (2007) 'Mother tongue plus two European languages in Sweden: Unrealistic educational goals?', *Language Policy*, 6: 333–58.

Cummins, Jim (2000) 'Putting language proficiency in its place: Responding to critiques of the conversational/academic language distinction', in J. Cenoz and U. Jessner (eds) *English in Europe: The Acquisition of a Third Language*, Clevedon: Multilingual Matters, 54–83.

—— (2006) 'Identity texts: The imaginative construction of self through multiliteracies pedagogy', in O. García, T. Skutnabb-Kangas and M.E. Torres-Guzmán (eds) *Imagining Multilingual Schools: Languages in Education and Glocalization*, Clevedon: Multilingual Matters, 51–68.

Gupta, Anthea Fraser (1997) 'When mother-tongue education is *not* preferred', *Journal of Multilingual and Multicultural Development*, 18: 496–506.

Jaffe, Alexandra (2011) 'Critical perspectives on language-in-education policy: The Corsican example', in T.L. McCarty (ed.) *Ethnography and Language Policy*, New York: Routledge, 205–29.

CHAPTER 12

Multilingualism in other institutional sites

In this chapter, we investigate multilingual language use in institutional settings other than educational ones (which were the topic of Chapters 9–11). Just like schools, institutions such as those providing health or legal assistance are ideological sites, where existing ideologies of power tend to be reproduced (Duchêne, Moyer and Roberts 2013: 8). We discuss a number of studies that show how these institutions are faced with new communicative challenges in our late modern age of globalization and superdiversity. Duchêne, Moyer and Roberts (2013: 9) refer to them as **sites of control**, in which social inequalities are reproduced and certain people are marginalized or excluded, often on the basis of linguistic skills. At the same time, we will also see one example where institutional norms and practices are resisted, in this case by a patient in a Barcelona health clinic. The other two sites that we look at are an immigration office, also in Barcelona, and an asylum agency in Brussels, thus shifting the focus to multilingualism in legal settings. In the second half of the chapter, we explore another institution, namely the family and in particular the multilingual family, as a further site of linguistic struggle. The studies we discuss here were carried out in Australia, Japan, Bolivia, the USA and Mexico, and they highlight the tension between language separation policies and translanguaging practices, as well as the powerful influence of peers, school and other external factors upon language practices and beliefs within the family.

MULTILINGUALISM IN THE WORKPLACE

In this section, we discuss three interesting studies carried out in different workplaces in Barcelona and Brussels. The first one is Moyer's ethnographic research on linguistic practices and services provided in a health clinic. She analyses multilingual medical encounters between physicians and their migrant patients. Below, we look at two extracts from this fieldwork which show that issues of understanding are not always satisfactorily resolved, despite the availability of different forms of support – an interpreter, or cultural mediator in the first extract and a multilingual receptionist in the second. In the first extract, a female Pakistani patient expresses her resistance to a previously prescribed medical treatment, which has not helped to improve her health and, moreover, was very expensive:

Patient:	(in Punjabi) the first time i came to her [this doctor] i took pills of two colours. then i went to the doctor upstairs and had two again. and my husband's salary isn't very certain, seven hundred rupees, eight hundred rupees, and we pay a rent of six hundred rupees, and to take pills every day, from where do i bring (money)? and now within seven days, twice i've taken medicine at six rupees each. Give me some good medicine with which i'll get well, i'm not fond of spending money every day.
Interpreter:	ahora me está hablando de temas económicos, que su marido no cobra mucho y que tiene problemas. (now she is telling me about financial matters, that her husband doesn't earn very much and that she has problems.)
Doctor:	dile que yo soy el medico y que si tiene algun problema que vaya a la asistente social y que entonces veremos. (tell her i am a doctor and that if she has any problem she should go see the social worker and then we will see.)

(Moyer 2013: 217–18)

The interpreter leaves out the information about previous medical treatments in his translation, even though this is essential information for contextualizing the patient's complaint, and only translates the part where she talks about her – and her husband's – economic difficulties. In this way, the interpreter, who clearly aligns himself with the institution rather than with the patient, is directly responsible for the doctor's lack of empathy with the patient. Ultimately, as Moyer (2013: 219) puts it, the patient is being 'delegitimized' by the interpreter (for more on the role of interpreters, see e.g. Eades 2010).

The second extract, discussed in Moyer and Rojo (2007), concerns one of the receptionists of the health centre, a Catalan woman who speaks Urdu and Punjabi, because she is married to a Pakistani man. She attempted to help the many Pakistani women and their babies who were frequent patients at the health clinic. Since communication with the nurses and doctors was often difficult for these women (as we have seen in the first example), the receptionist took the initiative of putting up posters explaining the main procedures in Urdu and Punjabi. However, these posters were soon taken down again and the receptionist was reprimanded:

> The explanation for taking the posters down offered by the person in charge of this clinic was that Catalan patients would complain about seeing signs in a language they could not understand, and that the presence of these signs would give the impression that it was a health centre only for migrants.
>
> (Moyer and Rojo 2007: 155)

Thus, of the two highly problematic arguments used by the person in charge, the first one was based on an assumption that *other* people would be linguistically intolerant, and the second one attached symbolic value to these posters (a health clinic for migrants only) rather than instrumental value (helping non-Catalan-speaking patients understand the procedures).

Moyer's examples highlight the importance of speaking Spanish or Catalan for access to health care. Codó's (2008) ethnographic study of practices in a state bureaucracy both confirm and nuance this result. Codó shows how administrations – in this case an immigration office – sometimes use language to restrict the access of migrants to key information. She explores how social inequalities are (re)produced in everyday encounters between state employees and undocumented migrants, and what role language plays in these processes of social stratification and exclusion. In particular, she notices a highly significant difference in the use of Catalan and Spanish: whereas Spanish is used as the **frontstage language** to address clients, Catalan is the **backstage language** used to address fellow colleagues in the office (Codó 2008: 190). This largely corresponds to the way Spanish is the language used with foreigners in Catalonia, while Catalan is the language of the ingroup (at least at the time when Codó carried out her fieldwork). There is thus a strict regulation of the sociolinguistic space, and any deviations from this norm are highly salient and usually disapproved of. For example, in the following interaction the Client has been speaking to Official B in fluent Spanish. Suddenly, the computer system breaks down and Official A turns to his colleague and interrupts the ongoing dialogue between Official B and the Client:

(1) Official A: bueno pues *a veure si sortim*.
(well let's see if we can get out of here.)
(2) Official B: *ara a més s'haurà bloquejat i un merder!*
(now the system will be down and it'll be a mess!)
(3) Official B (to Client): se han estropeao!
(they've broken down!)
(4) Client: *i què ha passat?*
(and what's happened?)
(5) Official A: pues a ver si vuelve
(let's see if it comes back on)
(6) Official B: los de XX [= street where central office is located] cuándo tocan allí no sé qué aquí se jode.
(those on XX, whenever they touch something there they fuck things up here.)

(Spanish in plain text, Catalan in italics;
Codó 2008: 190–1)

The two officials talk to each other in Catalan (in turns 1 and 2). In turn 3, Official B turns back to the Client and tells him in Spanish what has happened. This is where the deviation occurs when the Client, in turn 4, asks Official B a question in Catalan (rather than the expected language, Spanish). The Client may have used Catalan as a means to establish a closer rapport with the officials; however, his attempt is pointedly ignored by both officials, who continue to address him in Spanish in turns 5 and 6.

It can be inferred that, in the context of this immigration office, Spanish is the only legitimate language to be used by the clients. In the extract below, another client unexpectedly makes a comment about his own proficiency in Spanish:

(1) Official (sorting out documents): estos todavía no están – estamos por el día dieciocho de mayo.
(these are not [available] yet – we are still doing the eighteenth of May.)
(2) Client: vale
(alright)
(3) Official: estos faltan dos semanas para que estén aquí.
(these will be available in two weeks' time.)
(4) Client: vale – yo hablo español perfectamente, de verdad.
(okay – I speak perfect Spanish, honestly.)
(5) Official: bueno te lo he dicho en español no?
(okay I've said it in Spanish, haven't I?)

(Codó 2008: 197–8)

Codó suggests that the client felt the need to project a positive image of himself as a 'good' immigrant who knows the institutional norm of using Spanish in this particular context. It is through the close link between interactional norms and the institutional context that clients are socialized into behaving as 'proper' Spanish citizens (Codó 2008: 221). In fact, she concludes that both the clients and the office workers

> were socialized into ways of acting, doing and believing that reproduce practices of categorization and forms of exclusion which, in turn, feed into processes of social stratification. In the particular case of this office, those practices were informed by homogeneous views of Spanish identity, and by criteria of inclusion based on uniformity and founded on the mistrust of difference.
>
> (Codó 2008: 232)

The following extract (taken from a study by Maryns 2012) also illustrates how bureaucracies enact gatekeeping functions and how they regulate migrants' access to various rights and services. The interaction takes place at an asylum agency in Brussels, where the asylum authorities need to determine whether the applicant's account is credible and fulfils the criteria for refugee status. In this case, the applicant uses a mixed repertoire of Njala (an indigenous language of Sierra Leone), Krio (an English-based creole language widely spoken in Sierra Leone) and English, which the official finds hard to understand. The official wants to find out what the applicant's 'native language' is and questions him accordingly:

Official:	Njala language. but you told me that your parents, they speak Krio
Asylum-seeker:	they speak because we speak we speak together
Official:	yes
Asylum-seeker:	we speak together
Official:	uhum
Asylum-seeker:	so when when we sell market. speak
	...
Official:	but I asked you what is the language of your father and mother and you told me. the language of my father and my mother
Asylum-seeker:	nono
Official:	is Krio
Asylum-seeker:	no no we speak with people. we

(Maryns 2012: 302)

In a way, the official attempts to force the applicant to choose between the different resources in his mixed repertoire. His questions presuppose a **native monolingualism** (Maryns 2012: 303), in other words full proficiency in *either* Njala *or* Krio, a presupposition that is at odds with the reality of multilingualism and translanguaging in African countries such as Sierra Leone. Because the applicant first said that Krio was the language he used with his parents, but then later claimed that Njala is his home language, the official does not find his account reliable and 'expresses his doubts about the applicant's true linguistic identity' in his final report (Maryns 2012: 304). In this, he relies upon the very Western language ideology that looks upon multilingualism as full proficiency in a number of separate languages, one of which – he assumes – must be the speaker's native language or 'mother tongue'. Thus we can see how the clash between monolingual ideologies and multilingual realities can have far-reaching consequences for minority language speakers in legal contexts (see also Maryns 2006 and Jacquemet 2009).

LANGUAGE USE IN MULTILINGUAL FAMILIES

King, Fogle and Logan-Terry (2008: 907) define **family language policy** as 'explicit and overt planning in relation to language use within the home among family members'. They argue that the study of family language policy is important because these policies have an impact on children's linguistic and cognitive development and hence also their school success and, moreover, on the vitality and maintenance of the languages concerned. Spolsky (2009) proposes a tripartite model for studying family language policy, comprising language practices, language beliefs or ideologies, and language management.

First, it is important to observe actual language practices, as there may be gaps between purported and actual practices, or between policy and practice. For instance, one policy that is quite popular in multilingual families is **one parent one language** (OPOL), where each parent consistently speaks a different language to the children. In reality, however, parents who have adopted an OPOL policy frequently translanguage in practice. Second, the role of language beliefs and ideologies needs to be considered, since they influence the parents' choice of a particular policy and have an impact on the language practices in the home (e.g. Curdt-Christiansen 2016). Relevant language ideologies in this context are parents' (positive or negative) beliefs about multilingualism and translanguaging, as well as what de Houwer (1999: 83) calls **impact belief**: namely, parents' belief about the degree of control they have over their children's language development and choices. Third, parents – especially those with high impact belief – often act as 'home language managers' (Spolsky 2009: 25), who make conscious efforts to control their children's language choices. As a way of achieving this, they frequently rely on discursive and interactional strategies such as the **'minimal grasp' strategy** (Lanza 2009: 56), where the father or mother deliberately interrupts the conversation by pretending not to understand when children use the 'wrong' language (i.e. another language than the one they are expected to use with that parent).

Of the many interesting studies of family language policy, we just have space to discuss a few here. We start with two studies whose primary focus is on language use and practices: Rubino's (2014) study of two Sicilian families who migrated to Australia in the 1950s and 1960s, and Yamamoto's (2001) study of Japanese–English multilingual or, as she calls them, 'interlingual' families living in Japan. Rubino provides an important reminder: namely that when studying language practices in multilingual families, there is a need to take into account the full complexity of the linguistic dynamics within the families. Therefore Rubino considers all the varieties and resources in the family members' repertoires, which include not only Italian and English but also the Sicilian 'dialect'. As for the Italian that they use, it is mostly *italiano popolare* (popular Italian, Italian of the people), which Rubino (2014: 30) describes as a 'low' regional variety of Italian, in this case popular Sicilian Italian. The members of one family translanguage a lot between all these languages and varieties, as well as engaging in metalinguistic talk about the boundaries between in particular Sicilian and Italian. At the same time, however, they tend to have negative attitudes towards translanguaging and prefer to follow a 'one language at a time' maxim (Rubino 2014: 231). This is quite typical of many multilingual families, with parents frequently opting for the OPOL policy with their children. Indeed, many parents believe that such a policy will guarantee the children's acquisition of balanced bilingualism.

However, Yamamoto's (2001) study of Japanese–English interlingual families living in Japan shows that children do not automatically acquire a high proficiency in both languages, even in OPOL families. On the contrary; she found great variation in the degree of children's bilingualism: some children grow up as **near-balanced bilinguals** (i.e. almost equally proficient in both family languages), whereas others become **receptive bilinguals** (i.e. active competence in the socially dominant language and passive or very low competence in the other one). Among the factors that cause this variation and directly affect language use, she includes the following:

- if the child has siblings, there is a tendency towards greater use of Japanese among the siblings;
- a major factor is the language(s) that the child uses with her or his peers, who exert a strong pressure to conform (usually to mainstream societal norms, including linguistic ones);
- the child's language use also depends on the medium of instruction of the school that she/he attends (whether it is Japanese or English-medium instruction).

Finally, Yamamoto (2001: 129) mentions that her Japanese–English families may constitute a special case, due to the high status of English and the positive evaluation of Japanese–English bilingualism in Japanese society as a whole. Yet even this favourable factor did not ensure balanced bilingual development in all the children of her study.

Thus we can conclude that, even though OPOL is often seen as the 'right' way by many parents, it does not guarantee children's bilingual acquisition any more than other family language policies. It is also somewhat problematic because it is usually based on the mother tongue ideology and the idea of the 'native speaker' (see Chapter 2); moreover, as has already been mentioned above, it is impossible to maintain in practice, which often puts unnecessary pressure on parents. It is therefore important for researchers to make parents aware that translanguaging is a normal linguistic behaviour for multilinguals and hence is not to be viewed as something negative.

We conclude this section with two studies that show how children can exert a strong influence on the family language policy, even to the point of subverting it. These studies reveal the powerful influence of external factors such as the school and the peer group on language choices and practices within the family. In this way, the family can become a site of conflict, in particular when the children bring new languages – the languages of school and of peers – into the home, using them more and more in their interactions with their parents and especially with their siblings. Therefore, as Luykx (2005) argues, it is crucial not to look upon children as passive recipients of the family language policy but to study the active role they in turn can play in the language socialization of their parents. Luykx discusses rural to urban internal migration in Bolivia, with many Aymara and Quechua-speaking people settling in urban centres such as Cochabamba. In the new urban environment, the pressure to adopt and use (more) Spanish, the socially dominant language, is very strong and, because Spanish is the main medium of instruction of the school, it is often children who learn it most rapidly. As a result, parents may learn Spanish at least in part from their children, with Spanish gradually displacing the indigenous language and eventually becoming the main language of the home.

Pérez Báez's (2013) study similarly reveals the strong influence exerted on the family language policy by the school and the peer group and, moreover, it shows how children's language choices can have an effect beyond the immediate family unit. Pérez Báez investigates the diaspora community of San Lucas Quiaviní of Oaxaca, who have moved from this rural part of southern Mexico to the Los Angeles area. They are speakers of Zapotec or, more precisely, a Valley Zapotec language named Otomanguean (Pérez Báez 2013: 28). After migration to Los Angeles, the parents seem to develop a low 'impact belief' about their ability to control their children's language choices. Pérez Báez found that some parents continue to use Zapotec with their children, while others use Spanish; but, in both cases, the children shift to Spanish and English very rapidly. The first shift tends to be from Zapotec to Spanish and then, under the influence of school and the peer group, there is a second shift from Spanish to English, as one of the mothers tells the researcher:

> Question: I have noticed that a lot of people, once they have their children, they do not speak to them in Zapotec, they only speak to them in Spanish. Why do you think they do that?
>
> Answer: Rrilua ti queity queityru rcazdi ra mniny ygwe Dizhsa, nazh Ingles rgwe ra mniny. Nii negza xtada ra mniny rgwe Ingles.
> (I think because children don't want to speak Zapotec they only speak in English. That is why the fathers of the children speak English as well.)
>
> (Pérez Báez 2013: 42)

This mother emphasizes the children's influence on parental language choices: because the children usually favour English, many fathers accommodate them by also shifting to English, while many mothers continue to use Spanish, because they are bilingual in Zapotec and Spanish only.

Pérez Báez's study has a further interesting aspect in that it shows that language shift trends in a diaspora community can also have a negative impact on the home community and on the vitality of its indigenous language. In the case of the San Lucas Quiaviní community, this is due to the close transnational links between diaspora and home communities, including in particular frequent visits. When the Los Angeles-raised children, who usually only have a passive competence in Zapotec, visit in Oaxaca, they 'export' (Pérez Báez 2013: 30) their use of Spanish and English to the home community. As a result, the home community, which used to be a Zapotec-only environment (with Spanish mostly limited to its function as a school language), is increasingly becoming a bilingual Zapotec–Spanish community. Pérez Báez concludes that, with Spanish now also invading the home domain, the level of endangerment of the minority language has increased dramatically.

CONCLUSION

We have seen how the multilingual workplace and the multilingual family can be both sites of control and sites of resistance (Duchêne, Moyer and Roberts 2013: 9). Administrations and bureaucracies use language to 'control' their clients and may marginalize or exclude some of them on the basis of their linguistic skills. In the case of multilingual families, the choice of a particular family language policy is an attempt by parents to control their children's linguistic development, but the policy is frequently resisted by the children, who are under pressure from outside forces such as peers and school. The final study discussed in the previous section in fact shows that the consequences of the children's acts of resistance can at times not only be felt in the diaspora community but can extend as far as the home community.

In sum, the regulation of multilingualism in the family and the workplace has become a topic of great interest to an increasing number of researchers in the field. A major concern is whether institutions adopt a policy of linguistic tolerance, or whether diversity is seen as a problem and social inequalities are reproduced. In the chapters that follow, we investigate language use in further institutional sites, but from a more discourse-analytical perspective. Thus, in the following chapter we examine institutional discourses on language and migration, and in Chapter 14 we analyse media discourses about multilingualism.

ACTIVITY: DISCURSIVE OR INTERACTIONAL STRATEGIES*

Giulia is a 2-year-old child growing up in a mixed Italian–German family in Rome. Her father speaks Italian to her, and her mother German. Look at the following multilingual interaction between Giulia and her mother, and analyse it in terms of the mother's discursive strategy:

Giulia:	Mami *aple*.	(Mommy open)
Mother:	Wie bitte?	(What, please?)
Giulia:	Mami *aple*.	
Mother:	Wie bitte?	

Giulia:	Mami *aple*.	
Mother:	Wie?	
Giulia:	*APLEEEEEEE*!!!!	
Mother (covers her ears):	Wie bitte?	
Giulia:	Aufmachen?	(Open?)

(German: plain; Italian: italics; Taeschner 1983: 201; Lanza 2009: 57)

*Brief comments on this Activity can be found on page 291.

FOR DISCUSSION: OPOL (ONE PARENT ONE LANGUAGE)

Do you think OPOL is the best possible policy for a mixed, multilingual family? How would this work when both parents are together with their child(ren)?

FOR DISCUSSION: FACTORS CAUSING AN INDIVIDUAL'S LANGUAGE SHIFT

One of the parents in the study by Pérez Báez discussed in this chapter tells about a 13-year-old adolescent who migrated with his family from Oaxaca to Los Angeles. At the time when he arrived, he was bilingual in Zapotec and Spanish but he preferred to use Spanish in Los Angeles:

> Whenever I would see him I would speak to him in Zapotec and you could see the tension in his face, and he would answer in Spanish and I asked his mother, 'doesn't he speak Zapotec?' 'Oh no, [he does] but he doesn't want to speak it.' And what I have seen of him lately is that I will speak to him in Spanish and he answers in English.
>
> (Pérez Báez 2013: 41)

What factors do you think could possibly account for this adolescent's language choice patterns?

PROJECT WORK: HOW LINGUISTS CAN HELP

Read the 'Guidelines for the use of language analysis in relation to questions of national origin in refugee cases', put together by a number of sociolinguists and available here:

https://journals.equinoxpub.com/index.php/IJSLL/article/viewFile/555/1386

Discuss to what extent and in what ways these guidelines might help to solve some of the issues raised in the first half of this chapter (especially in relation to Maryns' work). Also consider whether the Guidelines document could be further improved.

PROJECT WORK: MULTILINGUALISM IN A MIXED FAMILY OR AN INTERNATIONAL COMPANY

Investigate the management of multilingualism in a mixed family or an international company. The most difficult part of this project may be to gain access to the site. See if you can get permission to audio-record some multilingual interactions or interview some members (or both). To what extent and in what way could this company or this family be seen as a site of linguistic struggle? In the case of the company, do they attempt to enforce a monolingual policy or have they adopted a policy of linguistic tolerance? In the case of the family, do you notice a tension between language separation ideologies and translanguaging practices?

REFERENCES AND SUGGESTIONS FOR FURTHER READING

Multilingualism in the workplace

Codó, Eva (2008) *Immigration and Bureaucratic Control*, Berlin: Mouton de Gruyter.

Duchêne, Alexandre, Moyer, Melissa and Roberts, Celia (eds) (2013) *Language, Migration and Social Inequalities: A Critical Sociolinguistic Perspective on Institutions and Work*, Bristol: Multilingual Matters.

—— (2013) 'Introduction: Recasting institutions and work in multilingual and transnational spaces', in *Language, Migration and Social Inequalities*, Bristol: Multilingual Matters, 1–21.

Eades, Diana (2010) *Sociolinguistics and the Legal Process*, Bristol: Multilingual Matters.

Jacquemet, Marco (2009) 'Transcribing refugees: The entextualization of asylum seekers' hearings in a transidiomatic environment', *Text & Talk*, 29: 525–46.

Maryns, Katrijn (2006) *The Asylum Speaker: Language in the Belgian Asylum Procedure*, Manchester: St Jerome.

—— (2012) 'Multilingualism in legal settings', in M. Martin-Jones, A. Blackledge and A. Creese (eds) *The Routledge Handbook of Multilingualism*, London: Routledge, 297–313.

Moyer, Melissa G. (2013) 'Language as a resource, migrant agency, positioning and resistance in a health care clinic', in A. Duchêne, M.G. Moyer and C. Roberts (eds) *Language, Migration and Social Inequalities*, Bristol: Multilingual Matters, 196–224.

—— and Rojo, Luisa Martín (2007) 'Language, migration and citizenship: New challenges in the regulation of multilingualism', in M. Heller (ed.) *Bilingualism: A Social Approach*, Basingstoke: Palgrave, 137–60.

Piller, Ingrid (2016) *Linguistic Diversity and Social Justice*, New York: Oxford University Press (especially chapter 5).

Roberts, Celia (2007) 'Multilingualism in the workplace', in P. Auer and Li Wei (eds) *Handbook of Multilingualism and Multilingual Communication*, Berlin: Mouton de Gruyter, 405–22.

Unger, Johann W., Krzyzanowski, Michal and Wodak, Ruth (eds) (2014) *Multilingual Encounters in Europe's Institutional Spaces*, London: Bloomsbury.

Language use in multilingual families

Curdt-Christiansen, X.-L. (2016) 'Conflicting language ideologies and contradictory language practices in Singaporean bilingual families', *Journal of Multilingual and Multicultural Development*, 37: 694–709.

de Houwer, Annick (1999) 'Environmental factors in early bilingual development: The role of parental beliefs and attitudes', in G. Extra and L. Verhoeven (eds) *Bilingualism and Migration*, Berlin: Mouton de Gruyter, 75–95.

King, Kendall A., Fogle, Lyn and Logan-Terry, Aubrey (2008) 'Family language policy', *Language and Linguistics Compass*, 2: 907–22.

—— and Lanza, Elizabeth (forthcoming) 'Ideology, agency and imagination in multilingual families' (introduction to special issue), *International Journal of Bilingualism*.

Lanza, Elizabeth (2009) 'Multilingualism and the family', in P. Auer and Li Wei (eds) *Handbook of Multilingualism and Multilingual Communication*, Berlin: Mouton de Gruyter, 45–67.

Luykx, Aurolyn (2005) 'Children as socializing agents: Family language policy in situations of language shift', in J. Cohen, K. McAlister, K. Rolstad and J. MacSwan (eds) *Proceedings of the 4th International Symposium on Bilingualism*, Somerville, MA: Cascadilla Press, 1407–14.

Macalister, John and Mirvahedi, Seyed Hadi (2017) *Family Language Policies in a Multilingual World: Opportunities, Challenges and Consequences*, London: Routledge.

Pérez Báez, Gabriela (2013) 'Family language policy, transnationalism, and the diaspora community of San Lucas Quiaviní of Oaxaca, Mexico', *Language Policy*, 12: 27–45.

Rubino, Antonia (2014) *Trilingual Talk in Sicilian-Australian Migrant Families: Playing Out Identities Through Language Alternation*, Basingstoke: Palgrave.

Schwartz, Mila and Verschik, Anna (eds) (2014) *Successful Family Language Policy: Parents, Children and Educators in Interaction*, Dordrecht: Springer.

Spolsky, Bernard (2009) *Language Management*, Cambridge: Cambridge University Press.

Taeschner, Traute (1983) *The Sun Is Feminine: A Study on Language Acquisition in Bilingual Children*, Berlin: Springer.

Yamamoto, Masayo (2001) *Language Use in Interlingual Families: A Japanese–English Sociolinguistic Study*, Clevedon: Multilingual Matters.

TEST YOURSELF QUIZ PART IV*

1. Do you think the schools in the Basque Country with three media of instruction (Basque + Spanish + English) could be seen as a model for flexible multilingual education throughout our globalized and super-diverse world?
2. Explain how CLIL (Content and Language Integrated Learnbing) works and how it could be applied in the education system of a country that you are familiar with. What would be the advantages and disadvantages of such a system?
3. Discuss the disjunctures (if any) between language-in-education policy and the contemporary multilingual realities of life, in relation to a country that you are familiar with.
4. Why is it important for teachers to build on students' home language and literacy practices?
5. Why was the construction of AAE (African-American English) as a language ideologically difficult to accept for many Americans?
6. Explain the difference between 'school' varieties (standard varieties) and 'street' varieties (urban vernaculars) in South Africa, and discuss the implications of this for education.
7. What is a 'heritage language'? Give some examples from specific contexts. Why is it important to support heritage languages?
8. What do you think of the teaching methods used as part of the SHALL project in Hawai'i? Could such teaching methods also be used in the education system of another country that you are familiar with?
9. What is the role of interpreters in medical or legal settings? What are the main challenges that they face? Can they ever be neutral mediators?
10. What can (or should) parents do to raise bilingual children successfully?

*Suggested answers can be found on page 296.

PART V

Critical analysis of discourses

CHAPTER 13

Institutional discourses on language and migration

In this chapter we examine the resurgence of linguistic repression in our late modern age of increased mobility, European consolidation and accelerated globalization at the beginning of the twenty-first century. Whereas Chapter 11 looked at attempts to maintain heritage languages (both indigenous and immigrant) by teaching them within the school system, the present chapter looks at how institutional discourses on language and migration frequently contribute to the precarious situation of immigrant heritage languages and their speakers. Official discourses usually claim that monolingual policies are necessary for social unity and cohesion. In these discourses, people who speak immigrant minority languages are looked upon as being in need of 'integration'. In line with the one nation–one language ideology, many states impose their national or official language upon these people through language testing. But behind such policies of integration, there often lurks not just a concern with social cohesion but also a deeper and more irrational fear of societal multilingualism and heterogeneity. We show this by first critically analysing the discourse of integration and then examining a number of language testing regimes.

THE DISCOURSE OF INTEGRATION

Integration has become a keyword across texts and genres, and is often uncritically embraced not only by politicians and journalists but also by academic researchers. In European discourses, it can refer both to European integration and the integration of people categorized as 'migrants' or 'foreigners'. Here, we explore how integration in the second sense is used in a range of texts from two European countries, Germany and Liechtenstein, including in particular official policy documents and academic publications. We have deliberately chosen liberal and progressive texts rather than the texts of the far right, as our objective is to show how even in liberal texts the use of the concept of integration is frequently informed by illiberal assumptions and ideologies that underpin policies on migration, education and citizenship.

We focus on two states with high levels of social and economic growth and consequently also relatively high levels of in-migration: Liechtenstein, which is not part of the EU, with over 30 per cent resident foreigners, and Germany, one of the biggest EU member-states, with a much lower percentage of resident foreigners (8 per cent, the majority of whom are of Turkish descent) but also with a highly visible migration debate. In this way, we aim to discuss both small and big European states, as well as states directly or only very indirectly affected by EU policies. For Germany, we quote primarily from the important report of the *Unabhängige Kommission 'Zuwanderung'* (Independent Commission 'Immigration'; 2001), chaired by politician and academic Rita Süssmuth (the Commission is popularly known as the 'Süssmuth Commission'), which led to the eventual adoption of new immigration legislation in 2004 after more than three years of at times turbulent debates. Because Süssmuth was a key actor in these debates, we also consider a book that she wrote on the topic in 2006. Moreover, the theme of integration came back into the news in 2009 with the publication of another controversial report by the Berlin-Institut für Bevölkerung und Entwicklung (Berlin-Institute for Population and Development). For Liechtenstein, an equally influential organization is the *Liechtenstein-Institut*, and so we examine one key policy document by Wilfried Marxer (2007) and a more critical presentation given at the Institute on 11 March 2008 by Veronika Marxer, the Equal Opportunities representative of the Liechtenstein government.

We show how the discourse of integration presupposes an asymmetrical world-view in which only the 'migrants' or 'foreigners' are perceived as a problem – though, interestingly, foreign residents with high amounts of capital are not usually included in this category. This world-view is constructed around a number of metaphors (or 'discourse models', as Gee calls them):

- the centre–periphery metaphor, which implies that only those on the periphery are in need of integration;
- the game metaphor, which is about winning or losing in the game of integration;
- the mathematical graph metaphor which, because it leaves unspecified the number of points (or whatever) needed to win the game, effectively renders successful completion of the game impossible (as with a mathematical graph which has no specified endpoint and potentially continues into infinity).

The three metaphors will be discussed in the following sections (for more detailed analysis, see Horner and Weber 2011). Then they will be contrasted with a more positive view of integration, the statistical correlations view, which derives its conclusions from a comparison of the achievements of migrants and autochthones – however ill-defined these categories may be – in such domains as education and employment, with society rather than the individual being perceived as the primary agency responsible for integration. In this way, we explore the main ideological frameworks within which the concept of integration functions and which most of the time go unnoticed precisely because the concept has become so much a part of dominant discourse and common sense. Moreover, we describe the recent shift in the discourse of integration from a more qualitative to a more quantitative paradigm.

The centre–periphery metaphor

The asymmetrical world-view of the centre–periphery metaphor is based on an 'us vs. them' discourse, looking upon 'them' as a problem that 'we' have to find a solution for (see Blommaert and Verschueren 1998; Horner 2009). 'We' are the actors integrating 'them' into 'our' society (which is conceived of as a homogeneous whole). This prototypical syntactic pattern is ubiquitous in the discourse of integration, with 'to integrate' used as a transitive verb describing a spatial process, as for example:

> Wie können wir die Menschen anderer Herkunft und Kultur in unsere Gesellschaft integrieren?
>
> (*Unabhängige Kommission 'Zuwanderung'* 2001: 199)
>
> (How can we integrate people of another origin and culture into our society?)

Another prototypical syntactic pattern is a (modalized) passive construction in which the migrants are represented as the (syntactic) patients due to undergo the process of integration:

> Reguläre Migranten und solche mit langfristigem Aufenthalt sollten vollständig in die Gesellschaft integriert werden.
>
> (Süssmuth 2006: 82)
>
> (Legal migrants and those with long-term residence permits should be fully integrated into the society.)

The centre–periphery metaphor views integration as a process in which 'we' are the principal actors: 'we' make the effort of integrating 'them' into 'our' society. However, it can easily be added, 'they', too, can and should be expected to make an effort. This idea is frequently expressed in German-language reports through the phrase *fördern und fordern* (fostering and requiring; see e.g. V. Marxer 2008). What 'we' do is not usually made explicit: as Marxer (2008: 16) argues, it is often limited to financial support by the state of the so-called 'integration' language courses:

> Der Begriff des Förderns [bezieht sich] heute in erster Linie auf eine staatliche Beteiligung an den Kurskosten. Es hat damit eine Verschiebung der Verantwortlichkeit vom Staat auf die Zuwanderer stattgefunden, denen alleine die Pflicht zur Integration aufgebürdet wird.
>
> (The concept of fostering applies nowadays above all to a financial contribution by the state to the costs of the courses. In this way, there has been a shift of responsibility from the state to the migrants, who are the only ones burdened with the duty of integration.)

Consequently, the discourse of integration is closely linked with the discourse of language learning. Language learning is represented as what smoothes the path from the periphery to the centre for the migrant, hence we find a dense cluster of lexical expressions taken from this domain. For instance, in the *Unabhängige Kommission 'Zuwanderung'* (2001) report, all of the following occur frequently: *Integrationsprogramm* (integration programme); *Integrationsangebot* (integration offer); *Integrationskurse* (integration courses); *Integrationsschulung* (integration schooling); *Integrationsunterricht* (integration teaching). Moreover, it is suggested that for integration, just as in language learning, there is a need to start early to achieve the best results. Thus the *Unabhängige Kommission 'Zuwanderung'* (2001: 233) talks about the desirability of a *frühzeitige Integration* (integration that starts early) for migrant children. The underlying assumption is that the 'problems of integration' already exist at the earliest stage of childhood.

Quantifying integration

A recent development is that integration is increasingly portrayed as something that can be measured and quantified. Indeed, the European Commission advocates the use of 'indicators of immigrant integration' as tools for 'quantifying and qualifying integration processes' and for 'better measur[ing] integration and the impact of integration policies' (European Commission 2004: 54). Such 'integration indicators' should include both objective, 'hard' indicators (e.g. employment and unemployment rates) and subjective, 'soft' indicators (e.g. feelings of belonging, respect for certain democratic values, etc.; European Commission 2004: 59). Hence, as we will see later in this chapter, multiple EU member-states have introduced language tests for citizenship based on CEFR (Common European Framework of Reference for Languages) levels, and some have developed points-based systems for measuring integration (see Wachendorff and Budach 2003). Such systems are supposed to measure the 'integrative' potential of citizenship applicants, either based primarily on their knowledge of the national or official language, or on a wider range of criteria including also such factors as age, education and professional experience (Wachendorff and Budach 2003: 162).

In this section, we identify and describe two related metaphors of integration that are an integral part of such a more quantitative view of integration: the game metaphor and the mathematical graph metaphor. In these metaphors, the centre–periphery model is reconfigured as a hierarchical model of social stratification, with the migrants placed at the bottom of the scale. Here integration is still seen as a process but the focus is now on 'them' as the principal actors, typically in a verb plus reflexive pronoun construction, as in 'they have to integrate themselves'. In the following typical instantiation of this syntactic pattern, we note that integration is not presented as an achieved state, but as something that 'they' have to make an effort to achieve:

> Dieser Integrationswille äußert sich darin, dass sich jeder Einzelne aus eigener Initiative darum bemüht, sich sozial zu integrieren.
>
> (*Unabhängige Kommission 'Zuwanderung'* 2001: 200)
>
> (This will to integrate manifests itself in the fact that every individual out of his/her own initiative makes an effort to integrate him/herself socially.)

As in the game of Snakes and Ladders, the migrant has to go up the ladders and avoid sliding down the snakes to reach the coveted goal of integration and win the game. The *Unabhängige Kommission 'Zuwanderung'* (2001) report is informed by this metaphor and hence also draws upon the discourse of success and failure, with its repeated talk of *erfolgreiche/gelungene Integration* (successful integration) and *Integrationserfolgen* (integration successes). This discourse presupposes the existence of an allegedly fair and open system of competition and thus reflects the sham of meritocracy that has become typical of late modern capitalism and that only thinly veils an underlying ideology of superiority.

The limitation of the game metaphor is due to the fact that it implies a clearly defined endpoint: you either win or lose the game. The continuum or ladder that defines the degrees of integration, on the other hand, has no clearly defined endpoint and is therefore more like a mathematical graph potentially continuing into infinity. Integration is looked upon as something that can be measured but, as the *Unabhängige Kommission 'Zuwanderung'* (2001: 250) report states, there are *politische Meinungsunterschiede über das Maß an erforderlicher Integration* (different political opinions about the level of required integration). In fact, depending on the national contexts, a wide range of sometimes even contradictory positions are put forward: for instance, learning the national or official language is portrayed as either the key to integration or as a mere prerequisite for integration. And the successful passing of the language test for citizenship together with the consequent award of nationality is seen as either the crowning event of integration or as the beginning of the process of 'real' integration (whatever that may mean). The *Unabhängige Kommission 'Zuwanderung'* (2001: 245) report is closer to the latter position when it states that *die Einbürgerung ist ein entscheidender Schritt auf dem Weg zu einer gelungenen Integration* (citizenship is a decisive step on the way to successful integration). It would seem that there is no clearly defined endpoint guaranteeing that an individual will no longer be socially or culturally marginalized and discriminated against, and that she or he will be accepted as an 'authentic' member by the host society.

This interpretation is reinforced by the lexical choices made by the authors of the *Unabhängige Kommission 'Zuwanderung'* (2001) report. They emphasize the need for a comprehensive (*umfassende*), far-reaching (*weitgehende*) and sustainable (*nachhaltige*) integration. The last adjective in particular suggests that integration is never a fully achieved state, that it may not be strong enough to last and that there is always a danger of the individual sliding back down along the mathematical graph in the opposite direction of what is called *Desintegration* (non-integration; *Unabhängige Kommission 'Zuwanderung'* 2001: 235).

Finally, it needs to be emphasized that both the game metaphor and the mathematical graph metaphor are informed by an **ideology of superiority** ('we' are superior to 'them') and a deficit model, as suggested by the repeated use of *Integrationsdefizite* (integration deficits) in the *Unabhängige Kommission 'Zuwanderung'* report (2001: 227, 260): 'they' are lacking or deficient, and hence need to have a strong will (*Integrationswille*) and make long and intensive efforts (*lange und intensive Anstrengungen*) to overcome their deficiencies (*Unabhängige Kommission 'Zuwanderung'* 2001: 200, 203).

The statistical correlations view of integration

The statistical correlations view represents a more positive approach to the quantification of integration, in which integration is no longer conceptualized as a process or movement from the outside to the inside, or from the bottom to the top, but rather as a state that is either achieved or not by a particular society. The prototypical sentence pattern here is 'a society is integrated if certain conditions are fulfilled', as in the following sentence from V. Marxer (2008: 3): *Eine Gesellschaft kann dann als integriert bezeichnet werden, wenn Chancengleichheit erreicht ist* (A society can be referred to as integrated once it has achieved equal opportunities). In other words, a society can be looked upon as 'integrated' if it achieves roughly equivalent educational results and employment rates for all its constituent groups, including the members of migrant communities. Marxer (2008: 3) expounds this view of integration in the following way:

> Es handelt sich hierbei um einen eher technischen Begriff, der wenig emotionale Anknüpfungspunkte liefert. Der Vorteil dieses Begriffs liegt jedoch darin, dass er als Instrument eingesetzt werden kann, dass Integration zu einer messbaren Grösse wird. Eine Gesellschaft kann dann als integriert bezeichnet werden, wenn Chancengleichheit erreicht ist. Und Chancengleichheit ist dann erreicht, wenn Migrantinnen und Migranten (unter Berücksichtigung ihrer sozio-ökonomischen Lage und familiären Situation) in den wichtigsten gesellschaftlichen Bereichen ähnliche Werte erreichen wie Liechtensteinerinnen und Liechtensteiner.
>
> Zu diesen Bereichen gehören:
>
> - Schul- und Berufsausbildung
> - Arbeitsmarktintegration.
>
> (This is a rather technical concept [of integration] which offers few emotional points of contact. But the advantage of this concept is that it can be used as an instrument, that integration becomes something that can be measured. A society can be referred to as integrated once it has achieved equal opportunities. And equality of opportunity has been achieved if migrants (taking into consideration their socioeconomic and family situation) achieve similar statistical values to those of native Liechtenstein people in the most important societal domains. These domains include:
>
> - education and vocational training
> - the employment market.)

Marxer points out the elements in Liechtenstein's integration and citizenship policies which are based on the statistical correlations view, while criticizing the more restrictive legislation that the government was about to introduce at that time (in 2008). The latter measures included the introduction of a compulsory and binding integration contract, specifying among others the level of mastery of German that migrants need to achieve to have their residency permits extended, as well as the requirement of *Integration im Ausland* (integration from abroad) for spouses of non-western European residents, who need to provide evidence of mastery of German at CEFR level A1 *before* they are allowed to enter Liechtenstein and join their partner already living there. Marxer argues that the new measures involve a shift of emphasis from *fördern* (promoting) to *fordern* (requiring) and, as already noted above, reduce the element of *fördern* to financial support by the state of the 'integration' language classes. The statistical correlations view, on the other hand, has a more progressive focus on all aspects of *fördern* in that it puts a large part of the onus of integration work on the host society: indeed, it expects the host society to remove all possible obstacles to ensure that migrant groups achieve the best possible results in such domains as education and the employment market.

ACTIVITY: THE BERLIN-INSTITUT REPORT ON INTEGRATION

The approach taken in the 2009 report on integration by the Berlin-Institut is resolutely quantitative, with results based on an *Index zur Messung der Integration* (Index for Measurement of Integration), itself based on twenty indicators, with an emphasis on the domains of education and the labour market. The authors calculate the *Integrationswerte* (integration values) for the different migrant groups and place them on a scale ranging from 1 (unsuccessful) to 8 (successful integration; 2009: 28).

Which of the views or metaphors of integration discussed in this chapter inform the following statements, all taken from the Berlin-Institut report?

> (1) Integration bedeutet nach dieser Lesart Gleichberechtigung und Chancengleichheit für alle in Deutschland lebenden Menschen – ganz unabhängig davon, ob sie einen Migrationshintergrund haben oder nicht.
>
> (2009: 10)
>
> (In this reading, integration means equal rights and opportunities for all the people living in Germany – independently of whether they have a migration background or not.)
>
> (2) Das Ziel, Migranten mit Einheimischen gleichzustellen, ist somit nirgendwo auch nur annähernd erreicht.
>
> (2009: 73)

(Thus the aim to accord equal status to migrants and natives has not been achieved anywhere, not even approximatively.)

(3) Der IMI [Index zur Messung der Integration] macht darüber hinaus deutlich, in welchen Bereichen, etwa Bildung oder Arbeitsmarkt, spezifische Defizite dieser Gruppen zu finden sind.

(2009: 83)

(The Index for Measurement of Integration shows clearly in which domains, such as education or the labour market, the specific integration deficits of these groups are to be found.)

(4) Auf dem Arbeitsmarkt schaffen es die türkischen Migranten kaum, derartige Bildungsdefizite auszugleichen.

(2009: 37)

(The Turkish migrants do not manage to make up for such educational integration deficits on the labour market.)

NOTES ON THE ACTIVITY

On Texts 1 + 2

The aim of the report is specified in terms of the statistical correlations view of integration. And the critical aspect of the report is based on the fact that this aim has not (yet) been achieved in Germany. At the same time, we may note the underlying presence of the 'us vs. them' discourse, on which the centre–periphery metaphor is based: though Text 1 talks about 'all the people living in Germany', Text 2 clearly divides them into 'natives' and 'migrants'.

On Texts 3 + 4

Here the authors of the report rely on the discourse of deficit associated with the game and mathematical graph metaphors. The calculation of the integration values for each migrant group leads to a discussion of well- vs. badly integrated people, with the latter talked about in terms of *Defizite* (deficits). This discourse of deficit is very different from the equal rights discourse associated with the statistical correlations view of integration, as it attributes the responsibility for these 'deficits' to the migrants themselves.

Implications

As a result of this use of the discourse of deficit, certain social groups are perceived as, and implicitly blamed for, being badly integrated: *Mit*

Abstand am schlechtesten integriert ist die Gruppe mit türkischem Hintergrund (By far the worst integrated group are the ones with Turkish background; 2009: 7). The authors of the report rely on the 'blaming the victim' strategy, even though they claim that this is not their intention: *Gleichwohl ist es nicht das Ziel dieses Reports, jene bloßzustellen, die schlecht integriert sind* (All the same, it is not the aim of this report to point a finger at those who are badly integrated; 2009: 5). Yet it was mainly this aspect of the study that was taken up by journalists, as can easily be seen by reading through the media texts published after the release of the report (available on www.berlin-institut.org/aktuelles/presseschau.html). A large number of the headlines are almost uncannily similar, stressing that the Turkish residents are 'the worst integrated' (*Spiegel*, 24 January 2009; *Oberhessische Presse*, 25 January 2009; *Basler Zeitung*, 27 January 2009), 'the least integrated' (*Süddeutsche Zeitung*, 26 January 2009), 'hardly integrated' (*taz*, 26 January 2009) or that they 'do not take part in the game of integration' (*Warum Türken bei der Integration nicht mitspielen*; *Welt*, 25 January 2009). The authors of the report may argue that they cannot be held responsible for the way in which journalists interpret and represent their results, yet it should be clear from the preceding analysis that they have encouraged or even invited such responses through the use of the deficit discourse typically associated with the game and mathematical graph metaphors.

LANGUAGE TESTING AND CITIZENSHIP

Just like integration, **citizenship** has become an increasingly important and hotly debated issue in this age of globalization and migration flows. Because citizenship is a central concept in scholarship broadly extending across the social sciences and humanities, it is unsurprising that it is explored and theorized in rather diverse ways. According to Faulks (1998: 2–4), citizenship tends to be understood in relation to legal, philosophical and socio-political criteria. Legal interpretations focus on the formal link between the individual and the state, including in particular the territorial right to residency. Philosophical lines of thought grapple with questions concerning which normative models of citizenship are fair and just with regard to the myriad relationships between individuals as well as the link between the individual and the state. Socio-political approaches zone in on issues of identity and power, providing an analysis of social practices and ideological processes in relation to state infrastructures. These three strands of research overlap in various ways; in this light, many researchers assert that citizenship involves the dynamic interface between rights and duties and also that citizenship is best understood as both legal status and social practice (see Isin and Wood 1999).

In comparison to the work of scholars in political science, law and sociology, just to name a few key fields of activity, the participation of sociolinguists in the academic discussion on citizenship does not have a lengthy tradition. However, the recent introduction (or reformulation) of language requirements and/or formalized language testing as part of citizenship legislation in many countries situated at the global 'centre' has prompted critical sociolinguists to explore this shift in language policy (cf. Shohamy 2006: 66–8). The case studies in Extra, Spotti and van Avermaet (2009b) and Hogan-Brun, Mar-Molinero and Stevenson (2009) on testing regimes – predominantly dealing with EU member-states – situate their analyses largely in relation to Kroskrity's (2000) framework on regimes of language. This line of scholarship shows how the introduction of language requirements and/or formalized tests is underpinned by intersecting language-ideological clusters that inform beliefs about the way that language and society 'should' be organized, and enable the positioning of speakers of certain languages and varieties at different points on linguistic hierarchies.

Historically speaking, there are two traditions of citizenship, one based on *ius sanguinis* (law of the blood, i.e. parental origins) and the other on *ius soli* (law of the soil, i.e. country of birth). While the former is commonly applied in European states, the latter was widely used by European colonizers to justify their claim to citizenship in countries of settlement such as the US, Australia, Canada and South Africa. The application of *ius sanguinis* in many European states has as a consequence that immigrants are largely excluded and find it difficult to be awarded citizenship. Partly as a way of justifying this position of intransigence, European politicians have had recourse to the discourse of integration, which has spread like wildfire across the EU and which we have critically analysed in the first half of this chapter. It is claimed that immigrants are not (or not sufficiently) 'integrated'; usually they are seen as *deficient*, especially in matters of language. Here it needs to be made clear that what is meant by 'language' is only the standard, official or national language of the state. Thus the foremost requirement that is imposed upon them is that they must become (more) proficient in the standard version of the dominant language. The award of citizenship is made dependent upon a number of integration or citizenship tests, whose main function is often to test language proficiency in the dominant language. The required level of proficiency is usually defined in terms of the Common European Framework of Reference for Languages (CEFR; see Chapter 9). However, Extra, Spotti and van Avermaet (2009a: 18) point out that this constitutes a 'misunderstanding or misuse' of the CEFR:

> The CEFR, which is essentially meant as a tool to promote multilingualism, is used by some policy makers as a scientific justification to promote monolingualism in official state languages and to focus more on what newcomers lack than on what they might be able to contribute and add in terms of resources to a more diverse society.

Van Avermaet (2009: 32) demonstrates that over the last decade more and more EU member-states have introduced some form of language testing with increasingly stricter conditions for the award of citizenship:

> Based on a first ALTE [Association of Language Testers in Europe] survey in 2002 only four out of fourteen countries that were included (29 per cent) officially had language conditions for citizenship. From this second ALTE survey in 2007 we see that already eleven out of eighteen countries (61 per cent) have started to involve language conditions for citizenship.

At the same time, there is still a lot of variation in the level of proficiency required in the different countries, which reveals how arbitrary this measure really is. Van Avermaet (2009: 29) points out that, in 2007, the required CEFR level ranged from A2 (in Lithuania, Estonia, the Netherlands) to B2 (in Denmark). He concludes in the following way:

> So it seems that an immigrant can be considered a legal citizen at different language levels, which is intriguing both from a theoretical and from a pragmatic point of view.
>
> (van Avermaet 2009: 29)

Hence, there may be a need to question this whole enterprise of testing and to critically examine to what extent such tests are primarily used as a means of social exclusion. As Shohamy (2009: 56) puts it,

> The implementation of language testing for citizenship regimes raises suspicions as to the 'real' intentions of the policy in the current atmosphere of anti-immigration. One wonders if these language testing policies are introduced in the name of justice or in the name of racism, purism and ethnic and migrant cleansing.

Indeed, the history of language testing as a means of immigration control shows disturbing links with racist policies. McNamara (2009b: 224) mentions the infamous Australian Dictation Test at the beginning of the twentieth century, 'where the explicitly racist White Australia Policy was enforced through a test of dictation in a language that the undesirable immigrant did not speak, thus ensuring failure on the test'. This test was a 'ritual of exclusion' (McNamara 2009b: 226), primarily aimed at Asian immigrants, though it was later extended to people who were deemed undesirable for broader political reasons:

> In a famous case in 1934, the Czech Jewish journalist Egon Erwin Kisch, who was travelling to Melbourne as an international delegate at a conference organized by Communist groups, was subjected to the test but it was difficult to find a language that he did not speak. Finally, a test in Scottish Gaelic appeared to do the trick, but on appeal this was found to be an unreasonable choice and Kisch was able to remain in Australia for six months and to complete a lecture tour where attendances were considerably boosted by the notoriety of the case.
>
> (McNamara 2009b: 226)

Shortly after this case the Australian Dictation Test fell into disuse, though it was not repealed until 1973.

Another more contemporary example of a test to regulate migration is the Dutch integration (*inburgering*) test of 2006, which combines language testing with knowledge of society. Extra and Spotti (2009: 76) report that when the test was presented to sixty-seven Dutch citizens, the pass rate was only 58 per cent. Moreover, many of their informants found the test to be rather subjective and unethical. Extra and Spotti (2009: 78) conclude as follows:

> What is demanded from Dutch newcomers [i.e. immigrants to the Netherlands] in terms of knowledge about Dutch society is certainly not common knowledge for the average Dutch citizen.

However, McNamara warns that while examples of 'unfair' tests could be multiplied, this approach might have the undesirable consequence of suggesting that such a thing as a 'fair' test is theoretically possible. For McNamara (2009a: 162) it is more important to unpack the ideology of exclusion upon which every 'testing for citizenship' policy is based:

> This concern for test fairness is a two-edged sword, because it implies that a 'fair' test (one that meets normal standards of validity and reliability) would be acceptable, when in fact the real problem is not the quality of the instrument but the policy itself.

CONCLUSION: UNPACKING THE DISCOURSES OF INTEGRATION AND LANGUAGE TESTING

In the first part of this chapter, we have distinguished between a number of different discourse models of integration, and noted the increasing trend to measure and quantify integration in late modern Europe. We have analysed mostly liberal and progressive texts that explicitly argue that efforts need to be made not only by migrants but also by the host society to achieve integration. We have shown how even these liberal texts are frequently caught within the illiberal assumptions of the centre–periphery, the game and the mathematical graph metaphors, namely the 'othering' assumption and the 'deficit' assumption: a group of people are othered and seen as constituting a 'problem' for the mainstream society, and they are perceived as being inferior and having a deficit which they need to make up. Moreover, integration is mystified as a difficult and long-lasting process with no clearly defined endpoint, like a mathematical graph potentially continuing into infinity.

The only more positive view of integration is the statistical correlations view, which rejects the deficit assumption and specifies the endpoint of the integration process: a society can be seen as integrated if it offers equal opportunities and outcomes to all the different social groups living and working there, in such domains as education and the employment market. Here, however, integration as a term becomes superfluous: statistical correlations can be established for any social group, whether defined ethnically or by social class, gender, age, etc. And we already have enough terms to deal with any disparities in this respect, such as social discrimination or inequality. Hence it is hard to see any positive uses of the term 'integration'. But because the term has become so pervasive, so commonsensical in the European context, it is important to be aware of the potentially discriminatory ideological frameworks within which it functions.

In the second part of the chapter, we have presented arguments against language testing for citizenship. Does this mean that we do not think that transnationals and migrants should learn the dominant language(s) of the state they have moved to? No, on the contrary, we think that they should be encouraged to learn the language(s) and be offered as many opportunities as possible of doing so (language courses, etc.). The only thing that we disagree with is the policy of language *testing*, because we feel convinced that such policies only exacerbate existing social inequities.

We feel convinced that the pressures of living in a new environment are such that most immigrants will *want* to acquire the dominant language(s) as quickly as possible. For instance, in the United States, it has been shown that immigrants are going through a more rapid shift to English than ever before (e.g. Torres 2010: 49), yet the *perception* of many mainstream society members is that the opposite is the case. In fact, it is a widespread but erroneous assumption that immigrants assimilated more smoothly in the 'good old days', which further problematizes the contemporary state of affairs (cf. Wilkerson and Salmons 2008). Hence, what is needed is not the implementation of language tests but a better offer of language courses as well as the convincing of mainstream society members that the huge majority of immigrants are successfully completing the language learning processes which are expected of them.

ACTIVITY: INTEGRATED SPEECH*

In an interview with 14–15-year-old Danish adolescents, the interviewer asks them about their ways of speaking (data taken from Jørgensen 2010). Analyse in particular the way in which the adolescents (who are speaking in Danish) use the word 'integration':

Interviewer: taler I ligesom jeres lærere?
(do you speak like your teachers?)
Selma: nej
(no) [laughter]
Interviewer: hvordan taler I så?
(how do you speak then?)
Selma: gadesprog nej
(street language no) [laughter]
Interviewer: hvad er gadesprog?
(what is street language?)
Lamis: vores lærere de taler rigtig meget integreret
(our teachers they speak really integrated)
Selma: vi taler sådan der nogle gange
(we speak like that sometimes)
Interviewer: integreret?
(integrated?)
Lamis: ja
(yes)

*Brief comments on this Activity can be found on page 291.

FOR DISCUSSION: LANGUAGE VARIETIES AND INTEGRATION

What is more important for purposes of integration: learning the local variety or the national standard? Discuss this in relation to a context you are familiar with and then compare with the following study of marriage-migrant women in a rural area of South Korea (Park 2016 and forthcoming).

Park's participants are women from Vietnam and Cambodia who married South Korean men and 'integrated' through learning the local variety of South Korean (the Gyeongsang dialect). But gradually they became aware that their rural variety was stigmatized in South Korean society as a whole and they felt that, to be accepted outside the local community, they also needed to become fluent in standard Korean. Here for example is what Kyung, one of Park's (2016) participants, says:

> There is already an existing boundary that separates migrant women from Koreans, but on top of this, if migrant women speak a dialect, their social status will drop even more. Because I'm used to speaking a dialect, the dialect comes out. I'm making a lot of effort to change my speech into standard Korean .... But I don't want to abandon my dialect. Whenever I get together with my husband's friends, they adore my accent and compliment me.

FOR DISCUSSION: ISLAM AND INTEGRATION

In what ways have integration policies in the EU member-states tended to focus on Muslim communities in the post-September 2001 era? To what extent have far right political movements used or abused this concern?

PROJECT WORK: LANGUAGE TESTING POLICIES

Choose a country whose education system you are familiar with. Is there a form of high-stakes testing for all schoolchildren? Can these tests only be taken in the national or official language(s)? What are the consequences if children fail these tests? Should such tests be abolished or could they be replaced by more equitable forms of multilingual testing? (Read the section on multilingual assessment in Chapter 17.)

Also try to find out whether there is a policy of testing for citizenship. Have there been major changes in this policy over the last few decades? If yes, have these changes been triggered by political, economic or educational concerns?

PROJECT WORK: THE UK LANGUAGE AND CITIZENSHIP TEST

Find out about the language and citizenship test in the United Kingdom and consider whether it constitutes a 'barrier' or an 'entitlement' for migrants (Cooke 2009). Start off by reading Blackledge (2009) and Cooke (2009).

PROJECT WORK: REFUGEES AND THE DISCOURSE OF INTEGRATION

Look for recent online media articles dealing with the integration of refugees and asylum-seekers from countries such as Syria, Iraq and Afghanistan. Carry out a discourse analysis of some of these articles to find out what has changed (if anything) about the mainstream discourse of integration, as discussed in the first half of this chapter.

PROJECT WORK: THE DISCOURSE OF DIVERSITY

Apart from 'integration', another keyword of recent EU policy is 'diversity' (as in the EU motto, 'unity in diversity'). Critically analyse the discourse of diversity as it is used in an EU policy document or in the language-in-education policy of a particular EU member-state (available on the websites of the European Commission, the Council of Europe, the Ministries of Education, etc.). Following the method of analysis applied to the discourse of integration in this chapter, try to identify and describe the ideological frameworks (what Gee calls 'discourse models') within which this keyword functions.

Alternatively, you could read an official language or language-in-education policy document and find one or more keywords which inform what the whole text is about. Then subject this keyword (or these keywords) to the same kind of critical analysis.

For additional examples of how this can be done, you could have a look at Blommaert and Verschueren (1998) on the discourse of diversity in Flanders (Belgium) or Hélot and Young (2005) on the discourse of diversity in French language-in-education policies.

REFERENCES AND SUGGESTIONS FOR FURTHER READING

The discourse of integration

Berlin-Institut (2009) *Ungenutzte Potentiale: Zur Lage der Integration in Deutschland*, Berlin: Berlin-Institut für Bevölkerung und Entwicklung. www.berlin-institut.org/fileadmin/user_upload/Zuwanderung/Integration_RZ_online.pdf.

European Commission (Directorate-General for Justice, Freedom and Security) (2004) *Handbook on Integration for Policy-Makers and Practitioners*, Luxembourg: Office des Publications officielles des Communautés européennes. http://ec.europa.eu/justice_home/funding/2004_2007/doc/handbook_integration.pdf.

Flubacher, Mi-Cha (2016) 'On "promoting and demanding" integration: A discursive case study of immigrant language policy in Basel', in E. Barakos and J.W. Unger (eds) *Discursive Approaches to Language Policy*, London: Palgrave, 231–52.

—— and Yeung, Shirley (2016) 'Discourses of integration: Language, skills and the politics of difference' (introduction to special issue), *Multilingua*, 35(6): 599–616.

Horner, Kristine (2009) 'Language, citizenship and Europeanization: Unpacking the discourse of integration', in G. Hogan-Brun, C. Mar-Molinero and P. Stevenson (eds) *Discourses on Language and Integration*, Amsterdam: Benjamins, 109–28.

—— and Weber, Jean-Jacques (2011) 'Not playing the game: Shifting patterns in the discourse of integration', *Journal of Language and Politics*, 10: 139–59.

Marxer, Veronika (2008) *Fordern und fördern: Perspektiven der liechtensteinischen Integrationspolitik*, Vortrag am Liechtenstein-Institut, Bendern. www.llv.li/pdf-llv-scg-fordern_und_foerdern_inkl._anhang_11.3.08.pdf.

Marxer, Wilfried (2007) *Migration und Integration: Geschichte – Probleme – Perspektiven*, Arbeitspapiere Liechtenstein-Institut Nr. 8, Bendern: Liechtenstein-Institut. www.liechtenstein-institut.li/Portals/11/pdf/politikwissenschaft/LIAP_08_Integration_Marxer.pdf.

Park, Mi Yung (2016) '"I want to learn Seoul speech!": Language ideologies and practices among migrant women in Korea', paper presented at Sociolinguistics Symposium 21, University of Murcia, 15–18 June 2016.

—— (forthcoming) 'Gender ideologies and Korean language learning: Experiences of rural marriage-migrants in South Korea', in K. Horner and J. Dailey-O'Cain (eds) *Multilingualism and (Im)mobilities: Language, Power, Agency*, Bristol: Multilingual Matters.

Süssmuth, Rita (2006) *Migration und Integration: Testfall für unsere Gesellschaft*, München: dtv Deutscher Taschenbuch Verlag.

Unabhängige Kommission 'Zuwanderung' (2001) *Zuwanderung gestalten – Integration fördern*, Berlin: Druckerei Conrad. www.bmi.bund.de.

Wachendorff, Ulrike and Budach, Gabriele (2003) 'Die Migrationsdebatte in Deutschland: Pressestimmen zum Bericht der Zuwandererkommission', in J. Erfurt, G. Budach and S. Hofmann (eds) *Mehrsprachigkeit und Migration*, Frankfurt/Main: Peter Lang, 147–63.

Language testing and citizenship

Blackledge, Adrian (2009) '"As a country we do expect": The further extension of language testing regimes in the United Kingdom', *Language Assessment Quarterly*, 6: 6–16.

Cooke, Melanie (2009) 'Barrier or entitlement? The language and citizenship agenda in the United Kingdom', *Language Assessment Quarterly*, 6: 71–7.

Extra, Guus and Spotti, Massimiliano (2009) 'Language, migration and citizenship: A case study on testing regimes in the Netherlands', in G. Hogan-Brun, C. Mar-Molinero and P. Stevenson (eds) *Discourses on Language and Integration*, Amsterdam: Benjamins, 61–81.

—— and van Avermaet, Piet (2009a) 'Testing regimes for newcomers', in G. Extra, M. Spotti and P. van Avermaet (eds) *Language Testing, Migration and Citizenship*, London: Continuum, 3–33.

—— (eds) (2009b) *Language Testing, Migration and Citizenship: Cross-National Perspectives on Integration Regimes*, London: Continuum.

Faulks, Keith (1998) *Citizenship in Modern Britain*, Edinburgh: Edinburgh University Press.

Hogan-Brun, Gabrielle, Mar-Molinero, Clare and Stevenson, Patrick (eds) (2009) *Discourses on Language and Integration: Critical Perspectives on Language Testing Regimes in Europe*, Amsterdam: Benjamins.

Isin, Engin F. and Wood, Patricia K. (1999) *Citizenship and Identity*, London: Sage.

Kroskrity, Paul V. (2000) 'Regimenting languages: Language ideological perspectives', in P.V. Kroskrity (ed.) *Regimes of Language: Ideologies, Polities, and Identities*, Santa Fe, NM: School of American Research Press, 1–34.

McNamara, Tim (2009a) 'Language test and social policy: A commentary', in G. Hogan-Brun, C. Mar-Molinero and P. Stevenson (eds) *Discourses on Language and Integration*, Amsterdam: Benjamins, 153–63.

—— (2009b) 'The spectre of the Dictation Test: Language testing for immigration and citizenship in Australia', in G. Extra, M. Spotti and P. van Avermaet (eds) *Language Testing, Migration and Citizenship*, London: Continuum, 224–41.

Milani, Tommaso M. (ed.) (2015) *Language and Citizenship*, special issue of the *Journal of Language and Politics*, 14: 3.

Shohamy, Elana (2006) *Language Policy: Hidden Agendas and New Approaches*, Abingdon: Routledge.

—— (2009) 'Language tests for immigrants: Why language? Why test? Why citizenship?', in G. Hogan-Brun, C. Mar-Molinero and P. Stevenson (eds) *Discourses on Language and Integration*, Amsterdam: Benjamins, 45–59.

Van Avermaet, Piet (2009) 'Fortress Europe? Language policy regimes for immigration and citizenship', in G. Hogan-Brun, C. Mar-Molinero and P. Stevenson (eds) *Discourses on Language and Integration*, Amsterdam: Benjamins, 15–43.

Language and migration

Jørgensen, J. Normann (2010) 'Education policies and minority language – superdiversity or national purity?', paper presented at Bilingual Education and Minority Languages symposium, Mondorf, 25–7 June 2010.

Torres, Lourdes (2010) 'Puerto Ricans in the United States and language shift to English', *English Today*, 26: 49–53.

Wilkerson, Miranda and Salmons, Joseph (2008) '"Good old immigrants of yesteryear" who didn't learn English: Germans in Wisconsin', *American Speech*, 83: 259–83.

The discourse of diversity

Blommaert, Jan and Verschueren, Jef (1998) *Debating Diversity: Analysing the Discourse of Tolerance*, London: Routledge.

Hélot, Christine and Young, Andrea (2005) 'The notion of diversity in language education: Policy and practice at primary level in France', *Language, Culture and Curriculum*, 18: 242–57.

CHAPTER 14

Media representations of multilingualism

Multilingualism is a real shape-shifter, at least in the media. From being perceived in the past as all bad, it is nowadays increasingly perceived as all good. From a social perspective, it was common for the media to emphasize 'the enormous evils of bilingualism – its inevitable separation of citizens into permanently antagonistic bodies' (*New York Times*, Topics of the Times, 5 June 1902), whereas nowadays it is much more common to find multilingualism linked to peace, as in media reports about the EU or the UN. From a cognitive perspective, too, a similar shift has taken place: from multilingualism being seen as a disadvantage, a deficiency or even a disease, to articles such as the following one extolling the cognitive benefits of multilingualism:

> Multilingualism has a whole slew of incredible side-effects: [Here we are given a whole list of things at which multilinguals are claimed to be 'better' than monolinguals, including scoring better on standardized tests, being better at remembering, being more perceptive, being better decision-makers, being more resistant to manipulation and even being 'more self-aware spenders'. This list builds up to a final, climactic element.] More recently, and perhaps more importantly, it's been found that people who learn a second language, even in adulthood, can better avoid cognitive decline in old age .... This is great news for anyone who is multi-lingual.
>
> (*The Atlantic*, 17 October 2014)

Interestingly, we note the use of highly similar hyperbolic language in both articles: 'enormous', 'inevitable', 'permanently' in the *New York Times* and 'whole slew of incredible side-effects', 'perhaps most importantly', 'this is great news' in the *Atlantic*. Thus, whether multilingualism is good or bad, it has to be absolutely so: all good or all bad, with nothing in between. The underlying assumption in both articles, however, remains the same: monolingualism is the norm and multilingualism is exceptional, deviant, abnormal – either all good or all bad.

This chapter deals with yet another contradiction: the fact that the new present-day positive evaluation of multilingualism in the media is hardly ever extended to the multilingual members of migrant and minority groups. We explore the media representations of three such groups: luso-descendants in Luxembourg, South Asians in the UK and Latinos in the US. In our examples, we will see how the members of these groups are marginalized and discriminated against through negative ideological constructions, and how these cultural representations are naturalized and conventionalized, to the point of becoming commonsensical. As a result, many people do not question them any longer; they do not even notice them. In fact, of course, these representations are not natural, not necessary in any way; on the contrary, they are historically constructed and highly ideological. There is therefore an urgent need to become aware of the ideological nature of such representations and, if they have pernicious effects, of the possibility of constructing alternative – hopefully less pernicious – representations.

LUXEMBOURG'S PISA RESULTS AND THE DISCOURSE OF DEFICIT

In Chapter 9, we discussed the language situation in Luxembourg, with its dual strategy of identification shifting between monolingual identification with the national language (Luxembourgish) and identification with the trilingual ideal of Luxembourgish, German and French (see Horner 2004). The latter representation of Luxembourg as an inherently tri-/multilingual and multicultural nation-state is rooted in the belief that students in Luxembourgish schools have the opportunity to acquire greater amounts of linguistic capital and thus openness to the outside world than do their counterparts in other European Union member-states. However, after the results of the first Programme for International Student Assessment (PISA) tests were publicized in December 2001, various discussions took place to try to come to terms with the fact that the scores for students in Luxembourg were third from the bottom in all three subject areas: reading, mathematics and natural science. As these results were potentially damaging to nation-building strategies based on the trilingual ideal and the related 'model' educational system, attempts were made to invalidate the results (Horner 2007). Two overarching strategies tended to be relied upon: one is based on the argument that Luxembourg cannot be compared with other countries and, thus, there is nothing to be learned from tests administered on an international level; the other strategy involves the blaming of certain groups of people within the national arena. In these discourses, civic ideals and European 'values' are often overshadowed by the desire for a homogeneous, Luxembourgish-speaking ethnic nation. The one nation–one language ideology is highly salient, and societal heterogeneity and linguistic diversity are perceived as a fundamental problem.

An example of this latter strategy can be found in the following letter to the editor published in the *Luxemburger Wort*, which is the dominant newspaper on the national market. It was written in the immediate aftermath of the publication of the PISA results. It emphasizes the high number of foreign residents in Luxembourg and claims that they not only disrupt the (alleged) cohesion of the ideal nation-state but, moreover, their children are to blame for the bad PISA results. In the extract below, the author discusses the luso-descendant children's alleged linguistic deficiencies:

> Fast 60 Prozent der Schüler in den ersten Klassen (Tendenz steigend!) sind Kinder ausländischer, zumeist portugiesischer Herkunft (43,1 Prozent), die bei Schuleintritt zu einem grossen Teil weder ihre eigene(!) noch die Landes- oder eine Drittprache (z.B. Französisch bei vielen unserer portugiesischer Mitbürger) perfekt beherrschen, was eine unentbehrliche Grundvoraussetzung für das Erlernen der mittlerweile fast zu Tode diskutierten Basics darstellt. Ohne Basics also kein 'Back to Basics' oder: '*Wou näischt ass, kann och näischt kommen*'!!
>
> (*Luxemburger Wort*, 26 January 2002, p. 26; German – plain; Luxembourgish – italics)

> (Almost 60 per cent of the pupils in the first years of primary school (with the percentage going up continuously) are children of foreign, mostly Portuguese origin (43.1 per cent), most of whom when starting school do not master perfectly either their own language(!) or the language of the country or a third language (e.g. French for many of our Portuguese co-citizens). Yet such mastery of a language is the essential prerequisite for the learning of the much discussed 'basics'. Hence, without basics there can be no 'Back to Basics', or: '*Where there is nothing, nothing can grow*'!!)

By building upon the educational slogan of the Minister of National Education of that time ('Back to Basics'), the author of the letter develops the familiar argument of semilingualism, which claims that these children not only fail to master the national language (Luxembourgish) or a third language (such as French); they do not even acquire their home language (Portuguese) 'properly'. The sociolinguistic diversity within Portuguese is erased, and the children are simply expected to have acquired standard Portuguese. If it turns out that they do not master this particular variety, then they are branded as being linguistically deficient. In this way, the standard language ideology underlies – and distorts – the writer's view of these children as entering school with no linguistic system of any kind.

Blommaert, Creve and Willaert (2006) report on a similar situation in their study of transnational children in the Flemish school system. The authors show how the Eastern European or African languages, in which the children are competent, are dismissed as 'non-languages' in the Dutch classroom:

> Unless one speaks standard Dutch, or unless one possesses the specific literacy skills associated with Dutch ortho-graphy, one is language-less and illiterate, even if one is a proficient multilingual individual, and even if one is a sophisticated literate in a writing system different from that of Dutch.
>
> (Blommaert, Creve and Willaert 2006: 53)

In both the Flemish and the Luxembourgish school systems, the migrant children's linguistic resources are largely delegitimized, and as a result these students are sometimes even looked upon as incompetent or lazy, and exhorted to make more of an effort. This is a typical instantiation of the 'blame the victim' strategy, with a multi-dimensional issue of exclusion and inequality being reduced to a one-dimensional problem of linguistic deficiency, which can then be dealt with at the level of individual human weakness and individual human effort (for the similar process of linguistic stigmatization of Latinas/os in US society, see e.g. Urciuoli 1996 and Rosa 2016).

ACTIVITY: A SENSE OF SUPERIORITY?

The following letter to the editor was also published in the *Luxemburger Wort* in January 2002. The author argues that texts like the letter to the editor discussed in the previous section 'imply notes of Luxembourgish superiority over foreigners':

> Considérant l'exceptionelle réussite économique et sociale du Luxembourg, il n'est pas facile de digérer ces résultats scolaires nationaux qui ne mettent pas le pays au premier rang auquel il

> est habitué. Mais certaines remarques, telles que 'Auch wenn in Berlin nur knappe 15 per cent und in Paris gar nur 8 per cent Ausländer, gegenüber ca. 38 per cent in Luxemburg, den Unterricht belasten...' impliquent des notions de supériorité luxembourgeoise par rapport aux étrangers qui nous étonnent dans le cadre de la construction européenne commune et nous fait revenir les souvenirs douloureux du passé continental, pas tellement éloigné, qui s'est terminé par une déchéance culturelle et sociale générale.
> (*Luxemburger Wort*, 26 January 2002, p. 26)
>
> (Because of the extraordinary socio-economic success story of Luxembourg, it is not easy to digest these [PISA] results for national education which do not put the country in the first position to which it is accustomed. However, certain comments such as 'Even if in Berlin only 15 per cent and in Paris only 8 per cent of foreigners act as a burden upon the school system, as opposed to about 38 per cent in Luxembourg...' imply notions of Luxembourgish superiority over foreigners, which surprise us within the framework of a common European vision and which bring back painful memories of the not so remote past of the continent, which ended in a general cultural and social downfall.)

Read through the extract in the previous section again and see to what extent you agree with the author. Also read through the texts in the following sections (on the UK and the US) and discuss whether you also find evidence of a sense of superiority of British over South Asian in the UK and American over Hispanic in the US.

CONSTRUCTING THE UK AS AN ENGLISH-ONLY SPACE

Multilingualism as 'tribal'

Blackledge (2000) studies the role of political and media discourses in ideological debates about minority languages in Britain. He quotes the following extract from a newspaper article as an illustration of what he calls a 'widespread monolingual and monolingualizing ideology in multilingual Britain' (Blackledge 2000: 38). In this article entitled 'Row over Punjabi signposts: Taking the Britishness out of Brum-Tory', the *Birmingham Evening Mail* reports on a scheme to put up signs in Balsall Heath, an inner-city area of Birmingham, saying 'Welcome to Apna Town' (which means 'our [town]' in Punjabi). The article quotes a Conservative Party councillor commenting upon this scheme as follows:

> It is a step on the way to removing the Britishness from Birmingham and especially the inner city. The city is a multi racial society in which everybody is accepted as part of our British culture. To revert to individual components or tribes is not progressive.
>
> (*Birmingham Evening Mail*, 3 November 2000)

The Tory councillor presents a narrow definition of 'Britishness' as if it were commonsensical, and hence shared by everybody. In this worldview, the presence of Asian languages in the public space erodes Britishness. There is a tension in what he says between an illiberal, monolingual ideology and a more liberal, multilingual and multicultural one. The latter is foregrounded in 'The city is a multi racial society in which everybody is accepted. . .' and at the very end of the last sentence, where he implicitly refers to this position as the 'progressive' one. However, these liberal elements are interspersed with their illiberal opposites. Thus, he does not say, for instance, that in Birmingham everybody is accepted by everybody else, but 'everybody is accepted as part of our British culture'. The pronoun *our* makes clear who does the accepting, and who has the right to do it, in the councillor's eyes. It reinstates an 'us' vs. 'them' discourse, which specifically excludes Asian languages from 'British culture'. Indeed, the last sentence makes clear that using Asian languages in the public space is tantamount to 'reverting to individual components or tribes'. According to Blackledge (2000: 39), the 'apparently tolerant, "progressive", multicultural ideology of the councillor' fades into the background and leaves its place to a discourse of 'intolerance' and neo-colonialism. Implicitly, using English is equated with being civilized, and multilingualism (or using languages other than English in the public space) with being 'retrogade and tribal' (Blackledge 2000: 40).

Pathologizing immigrant minority languages

In some other publications, Blackledge (2005, 2006) presents a critical examination of policy-making on language, immigration and citizenship by the British Labour Government at the beginning of the twenty-first century. More particularly, he focuses on the discourses linking the 'race riots' in the north of England in the summer of 2001 with the Nationality, Immigration and Asylum Act of November 2002. Blackledge's case study is very much in line with Blommaert and Verschueren's (1998) analysis of the 'rhetoric of tolerance' in Belgian public discourse. Blackledge similarly shows how the liberal rhetoric of UK politicians thinly veils an illiberal discourse associating languages other than English, and hence the speakers of these languages, with social disorder and street violence, and how this illiberal claim is linked through complex chains of discourse to the new legislation concerning language testing requirements for British citizenship applicants, which in the November 2002 Act are extended to spouses of British citizens.

The text which in these debates aroused perhaps the greatest indignation (at least among sympathizers of bilingual education and multilingualism in general) was an article written by the Home Secretary at that time, David Blunkett, and published on the website of the Foreign Policy Centre in October 2002. In his article, Blunkett asserts that he never said, explicitly or implicitly, that lack of proficiency in English was 'directly responsible' for the disturbances in Bradford, Burnley and Oldham, and he continues as follows:

> However, speaking English enables parents to converse with their children in English, as well as their historic mother tongue, at home and to participate in wider modern culture. It helps overcome the schizophrenia which bedevils generational relationships.

In this text, Blunkett responds to criticisms of earlier statements he made. His claim that a lack of fluency in English is not 'directly responsible' for what happened in the summer of 2001 implies that it may have been indirectly responsible. Moreover, he contrasts 'historic mother tongue' with 'wider modern culture', thus setting up a binary opposition between the primitive past (of which Asian languages are a part) and modernity (which, presumably, is British in the same narrow sense in which the Birmingham councillor used the term in the previous extract). Finally, the sentence 'it [i.e. knowledge and/or use of English] helps overcome the schizophrenia which bedevils generational relationships' presupposes that people who use minority languages at home suffer from a form of schizophrenia while asserting that English can help them to 'overcome' this mental condition. Blackledge (2006: 38) also suggests that 'the verb "bedevils" adds a sinister note, implying evil'. In this way, Blunkett's sentence links failure to use English with mental health problems, family disharmony and (indirectly also) social disorder. In his discourse, the responsibility for social segregation and sectarian violence seems to be put on speakers of minority Asian languages in Britain.

Interestingly, Blackledge (2005) also shows how in some authoritative discourses, the emphasis shifts from the illiberal link between lack of English and social disorder to a more liberal argument linking lack of English with inability (of mostly British Asian women) to participate as equal citizens. This apparently egalitarian and emancipatory argument is then used to justify the extended requirement for testing the English language proficiency of spouses of British citizens in the new legislation of November 2002. However, what gets erased in the process is, first, a discussion of the real causes of social segregation: i.e. inequalities based on racism, economic discrimination and patriarchal social structures; and second, a full acknowledgement of the role of the far right British National Party in creating the conditions for social unrest, which finally erupted in 2001 in the Burnley–Oldham–Bradford area. Blackledge's detailed analysis of discursive and argumentative strategies thus reveals an illiberal and discriminatory ideology of monolingualism which masquerades as liberalism and which pretends to be egalitarian. The discourses informed by this ideology 'contribute to the production and reproduction of consensus which appears to be "common-sense", while in fact including discriminatory practices' (Blackledge 2005: 209). Ultimately then, such language-ideological debates constitute a struggle not over language alone but over the kind of nation that Britain imagines itself to be.

THE ENGLISH ONLY MOVEMENT IN THE US

In the US, the English Only movement is lobbying for a constitutional amendment which would designate English as the sole official language. Such a move is needed, they argue, to protect English, which is currently threatened by other languages, especially Spanish. This agenda is being pushed by associations such as US English and English First. US English was founded in 1983 by Senator Samuel Hayakawa, as well as John Tanton, who also founded the Federation for American Immigration Reform, an association aiming to limit immigration to the US. As for English First, it was founded by Larry Pratt, the director emeritus of Gun Owners of America.

While the English Only movement has not been successful at the federal level, it has achieved much better results at state level: many states have now declared English to be their sole official language. It has also been successful in its fight against bilingual education. Most bilingual programmes in the US have been of a limited, transitional type (transitioning students mostly from Spanish to English), yet the English Only movement worked hard to restrict bilingual education even further. Ron Unz, a Silicon Valley businessman, led campaigns against bilingual education in such states as California, Arizona and Massachusetts. This has entailed the passing of California's Proposition 227 in 1998 (though overturned in 2017), Arizona's Proposition 203 in 2000 and Question 2 in Massachusetts in 2002, the effect of which has been to restrict even transitional bilingual programmes and to replace them with ESL (English as a Second Language) programmes. Furthermore, a similar effect has been achieved at the federal level by former President Bush's No Child Left Behind policy, which replaced the Bilingual Education Act (see Chapter 9).

These anti-bilingual education measures have had a lot of popular support, as can be seen from the votes in California, Arizona and Massachusetts. But we may wonder why so many Americans feel that English, the dominant global language, is threatened by Spanish, and why they fear that English might actually die out and be replaced by Spanish. Undoubtedly, these fears need to be understood as a response to (biased) media coverage of an increase in the number of poor immigrants, mostly from Mexico. In other words, language is used as a proxy in what is largely an anti-immigration feeling and movement.

Clash of the titans, or: the war between English and Spanish

In this section, we discuss a text published on the website of English First and titled 'Why English is not the "official language" of the United States' (Reeves 2009). In it, the author tells a story full of contradictions. First, on the international dimension, English is referred to as the clear 'winner':

> English began its steady climb to modern world dominance in the sixteenth century with the rise of the British Empire. Riding on the waves of trade and a strong navy, English spread as the *lingua franca* of world commerce. The founding of the United States, the most successful nation in history in terms of economic and military power, caused English to supersede all previous *lingua francas*. Technology and free market world trade assure that it will continue to be the world's dominant tongue, the medium of communication, and the language of democracy that all nations must master to survive in the global economy.
>
> (Reeves 2009: 2)

This is the typical discourse about the global spread of English which Pennycook refers to as 'colonial celebration' combined with 'laissez-faire liberalism' (see discussion in Chapter 4). Those who are at a disadvantage here are clearly all the other non-English-speaking countries whose inhabitants *must* acquire English 'to survive in the global economy'.

However, at the national level a completely different story is told. Here English is seen as having been 'under attack' (Reeves 2009: 2) from 'the enemy within' (2009: 4) since the 1960s. These enemies are radicals and left-wingers, who are waging a 'guerilla war' (2009: 3) against English, and are twice referred to as 'anti-American activists' (2009: 3), in a discourse which is reminiscent of the Cold War era and of the McCarthyan witch-hunt against Communists. This happened in the 1950s when thousands of Americans were accused of having Communist links by Senator Joseph McCarthy and the House Committee on Un-American Activities. In the twenty-first century, it is using – or supporting the use of – languages other than English (especially Spanish) that is constructed as being un-American.

Both Cold War and colonial discourse tend to be informed by binary oppositions, one member of which is evaluated positively (e.g. white) and the other negatively (e.g. black). And there is 'no place for in-betweens', as one character in Michelle Cliff's novel *No Telephone to Heaven* (1987: 99) puts it. Such a Manichean world-view has been critically discussed by postcolonial thinkers such as Frantz Fanon (in *Black Skin, White Masks*) and Abdul JanMohamed (in *Manichean Aesthetics*). In the English First text, too, no middle position is allowed: being *for* Spanish implies being *against* English, and being against English implies being against America. Thus, since bilingual education is identified with the pro-Spanish and hence anti-English position, it is interpreted as a refusal to teach migrant children English:

> The movement to prevent the recent wave of immigrants, mostly from Latin America, from becoming integrated and successful citizens by not teaching them English as the foundation for their success is alive and well-funded.
>
> (Reeves 2009: 3)

Since teaching migrant children English means helping them to 'integrate' and providing them with the best possible educational and employment opportunities, it is therefore imperative to abolish bilingual education, which – it is alleged – imprisons these children within their heritage languages. On the one hand, these arguments reveal a (deliberate or not) misunderstanding of the nature of bilingual education; on the other hand, and even more worryingly, they also reveal a narrow mindset informed by an ideology of monolingualism which cannot even conceptualize the possibility of learning or using more than one language.

What is particularly interesting in the English First text is the way in which languages are anthropomorphized. In yet another binary opposition, English is described as the language of 'democracy and freedom', whereas the other side allegedly sees it as the 'language of oppression' (2009: 3), as 'racist, imperialistic, chauvinistic, and homophobic' (2009: 4). Usually, one would expect people, not languages, to be free and to act in a democratic way or, alternatively, to be racist and to oppress other people. Here, however, it is the languages which are presented as the main actors in this clash of the titans. The role of human beings is a minor, though important one, since their actions can influence the outcome of the battle. In a typical instantiation of the 'us' vs. 'them' discourse, 'they' (the 'bad' Americans) are blamed for weakening English and thus helping Spanish to win, while 'we' (the 'good' Americans) must protect and defend English by making it the sole official language of the US:

> The US needs to adopt English as *our* official language before *we* lose *our* national identity, *our* cultural heritage, and *our* system of government.
>
> (Reeves 2009: 5; italics added)

'Before we lose' suggests that there is a need to act quickly: if 'we' do nothing, Spanish will win. What will be lost includes 'our national identity' – narrowly defined and presumably limited to Anglo-Protestant values – and 'our cultural heritage', which obviously does not include the Hispanic heritage. And, as the climax of this rhetorical three-part statement, the final threat implies that if the 'language of democracy' (English) is defeated, then the future will be a dark and totalitarian one.

We conclude with the words of Schmidt (2007: 204), who points out that, on the contrary, the real danger to national unity is constituted not by the Hispanic community or by Spanish, but by the English Only movement itself:

> Seeking to *impose* English as the *sole* public language in the United States is an injustice that is bound to generate social and political conflict for years to come. Put differently, the evidence is powerful that social and economic incentives for English language shift are so strong in the laissez-faire hegemonic English-dominant environment of the US that mounting a social movement in opposition is highly unlikely *in the absence of direct English-only pressure mounted by the Official English movement*. In short, 'national unity' is undermined far more powerfully by the Official English movement than by the feeble efforts of the relatively weak political groups supporting bilingual education and other policies seeking to acknowledge and support language communities other than those speaking English in the United States. My claim, then, is that both 'justice' and the 'common good' require a pluralistic, not an assimilative English-only, language policy.

CONCLUSION: A HISTORICAL PERSPECTIVE ON THE ONE NATION–ONE LANGUAGE IDEOLOGY

In this chapter, we have looked at a number of attempts to essentialize the link between language and territory, and to construct both the UK and the US as (originally) English-only spaces. However, from a historical point of view, such claims are obviously untrue. The UK was originally a Celtic-speaking space, with the Celtic peoples pushed westwards and northwards when the Germanic and Scandinavian invaders conquered the territory. Similarly, in the US context, the 'original' American languages are the Native American languages. Moreover Spanish, which like English is a colonial language, was widely spoken in the southwest of what is now the US. Indeed, most of Texas, Arizona, New Mexico, California, Nevada and Utah was part of Mexico and it was only in 1848, after the Mexican–American war, that the US annexed these territories (Texas was already annexed in 1845, which led to the Mexican–American war of 1846–8). Hence, Spanish is just as much an American language as English; furthermore, in both the US and the UK English has to be looked upon historically as an immigrant language. It is just that, as Orwell might have put it, some immigrant languages are more equal than others!

FOR DISCUSSION: THE AMERICANO DREAM

In 'The Hispanic Challenge', Samuel Huntington takes issue with a book by Lionel Sosa entitled *The Americano Dream*:

> Sosa ends his book, *The Americano Dream*, with encouragement for aspiring Hispanic entrepreneurs. 'The Americano dream?' he asks. 'It exists, it is realistic, and it is there for all of us to share.' Sosa is wrong. There is no Americano dream. There is only the American dream created by an Anglo-Protestant society. Mexican Americans will share in that dream and in that society only if they dream in English.
>
> (Huntington 2004)

Who do you agree with, Huntington or Sosa, and why?

Note: The American Dream is the dream that the individual can find self-fulfilment, freedom, happiness – and, of course, financial success – in this land of unlimited opportunities. A typical instantiation of the American Dream is Jay Gatsby, the eponymous hero of F. Scott Fitzgerald's famous novel *The Great Gatsby*.

FOR DISCUSSION: PATHOLOGIZING PEOPLE'S LANGUAGE USE

We have seen in this chapter how former Home Secretary David Blunkett pathologized the use of immigrant minority languages by comparing it to a form of schizophrenia. Another example of how people's language use and attitudes can be pathologized is the following extract, though here the focus is not on immigrant minority languages but on English – or rather on

South African parents who prefer their children to be educated through the medium of English rather than an indigenous African language:

> I call the attitudinal malaise that afflicts the majority of African-language speakers by the name 'static maintenance syndrome'. This means no more, but also no less, than that most of these speakers are willing to maintain their languages in the primary domains of the family and of the community and also in religious contexts. They do not believe, however, that these languages have the capacity to develop into languages of power.
>
> (Alexander 2006: 242–3)

Critically analyse this passage in the same way as we discussed the Blunkett extract above.

Note: The author, Neville Alexander, was the director of PRAESA (Project for the Study of Alternative Education in South Africa), the organization advocating mother tongue education in South Africa (see Chapter 10).

PROJECT WORK: REPRESENTATIONS OF MULTILINGUALISM ON THE INTERNET

Look for some discussions of multilingualism on the Internet (e.g. on Facebook or in blogs, etc.). Focus in particular on the ways in which immigrant minority languages and their speakers are represented. Are these representations mostly positive or negative ones? What metaphors are used (if any) and what are their ideological implications?

PROJECT WORK: MULTILINGUALISM ON PUBLIC SIGNS

In this chapter we saw how a Conservative councillor objected to the use of Punjabi on public signs in Birmingham. Carry out a study of public signage in an area where large numbers of immigrants reside. Take photographs of street signs, signs in shop windows or other signs in the public space. What languages are used on these signs, and what values (local, national, global) are indexed by their use? (Before embarking on this project, read Chapter 16 on 'Linguistic landscape'.)

PROJECT WORK: US ENGLISH

US English is the largest association within the English Only movement. What are the main arguments it uses to advocate its cause? How would you go about refuting these arguments?

Its website is www.us-english.org. Also check out the website of James Crawford, an outspoken critic of the English Only movement who has written extensively about the benefits of bilingual education and multilingualism: www.languagepolicy.net/archives/engonly.htm.

REFERENCES AND SUGGESTIONS FOR FURTHER READING

Thematizing multilingualism in the media

Kelly-Holmes, Helen and Milani, Tommaso M. (eds) (2013) *Thematizing Multilingualism in the Media*, Amsterdam: Benjamins.

The cognitive benefits of multilingualism

The Atlantic (17 October 2014) Cody C. Delistraty, 'For a better brain, learn another language: The cognitive benefits of multilingualism'. http://www.theatlantic.com/health/archive/2014/10/more-languages-better-brain/381193/.

The discourse of deficit

Blommaert, Jan, Creve, Lies and Willaert, Evita (2006) 'On being declared illiterate: Language-ideological disqualification in Dutch classes for immigrants in Belgium', *Language and Communication*, 26: 34–54.

Davis, Kathryn A. (1994) *Language Planning in Multilingual Contexts: Policies, Communities, and Schools in Luxembourg*, Amsterdam: Benjamins.

Horner, Kristine (2004) *Negotiating the Language-Identity Link: Media Discourse and Nation-Building in Luxembourg*, PhD thesis, State University of New York at Buffalo, Ann Arbor, MI: UMI.

—— (2007) 'Global challenges to nationalist ideologies: Language and education in the Luxembourg press', in S. Johnson and A. Ensslin (eds) *Language in the Media: Representations, Identities, Ideologies*, London: Continuum, 130–46.

Rosa, Jonathan D. (2016) 'Standardization, racialization, languagelessness: Raciolinguistic ideologies across communicative contexts', *Journal of Linguistic Anthropology*, 26: 162–83.

Urciuoli, Bonnie (1996) *Exposing Prejudice: Puerto Rican Experiences of Language, Race and Class*, Boulder, CO: Westview Press.

Constructing the UK as an English-only space

Blackledge, Adrian (2000) 'Monolingual ideologies in multilingual states: Language, hegemony and social justice in Western liberal democracies', *Estudios de Sociolinguistica*, 1: 25–45.

—— (2005) *Discourse and Power in a Multilingual World*, Amsterdam: Benjamins.

—— (2006) 'The magical frontier between the dominant and the dominated: Sociolinguistics and social justice in a multilingual world', *Journal of Multilingual and Multicultural Development*, 27: 22–41.

Blommaert, Jan and Verschueren, Jef (1998) *Debating Diversity: Analysing the Discourse of Tolerance*, London: Routledge.

Blunkett, David (2002) 'Integration with diversity: Globalization and the renewal of democracy and civil society', *Foreign Policy Centre*. http://fpc.org.uk/articles/182.

The English Only movement in the US

Crawford, James (2008) *Advocating for English Learners: Selected Essays*, Bristol: Multilingual Matters.

Huntington, Samuel P. (2004) 'The Hispanic challenge', *Foreign Policy*. www.foreignpolicy.com/story/cms.php?story_id=2495&PHPSESSID=5e2867aff94461a7a95dd8fe49c70dc1.

Reeves, Bernie (2009) 'Why English is not the "official language" of the United States', *English First website*. http://englishfirst.org/congressc/why-english-is-not-the-qofficial-languageq-of-the-united-states.html.

Schmidt, Ronald Sr. (2007) 'Defending English in an English-dominant world: The ideology of the "Official English" movement in the United States', in A. Duchêne and M. Heller (eds) *Discourses of Endangerment: Ideology and Interest in the Defence of Languages*, London: Continuum, 197–215.

Postcolonial writings

Cliff, Michelle (1987) *No Telephone to Heaven*, London: Plume.

Fanon, Frantz (1986) *Black Skin, White Masks*, trans. C.L. Markmann, London: Pluto.

JanMohamed, Abdul R. (1983) *Manichean Aesthetics: The Politics of Literature in Colonial Africa*, Amherst, MA: University of Massachusetts Press.

Pathologizing people's language use

Alexander, Neville (2006) 'Socio-political factors in the evolution of language policy in post-Apartheid South Africa', in M. Pütz, J. Fishman and J. Neff-van Aertselaer (eds) *'Along the Routes to Power': Explorations of Empowerment through Language*, Berlin: Mouton de Gruyter, 241–60.

CHAPTER 15

Multilingualism in the new media

In this second chapter on multilingualism and the media, we focus more specifically on the sociolinguistics of the new media, which has grown into a vibrant subfield of sociolinguistics. It started with the development of the new technologies of communication and information in the second half of the twentieth century, and in the twenty-first century it has experienced exponential growth in the number of publications and researchers working in the field. Like linguistic landscape studies (discussed in the following chapter), new media sociolinguistics has come of age by developing from the more linguistic approaches of the late twentieth century to the increasingly user-based or ethnographically based approaches of the twenty-first century (Thurlow and Mroczek 2011; Androutsopoulos 2006). Early studies of computer-mediated communication (see e.g. Herring 1996) tended to explore the linguistic – often orthographic – features of new media language and the hybrid nature of new media genres. A frequent characteristic was also their monolingual focus (Androutsopoulos 2011: 279). Recently, however, researchers have become more interested in such aspects as the following:

- how online users perform particular (local or global) identities;
- how they position themselves in ideological terms;
- how they frequently refashion traditional identity positionings;
- how they adopt particular linguistic and cultural forms and mix them in creative ways;
- how they tend to draw upon all their multilingual and heteroglossic resources;
- what ideological tensions or 'heteroglossic contrasts' (Androutsopoulos 2011: 283) result from this.

In the following section, we explain what Androutsopoulos means by 'heteroglossic contrasts' and we argue that a full understanding of such positionings and tensions can only be achieved by taking an ethnographic approach. The other sections of this chapter discuss language contact phenomena in digital language, the limited multilingualism of the Internet and the policing of new media language.

DIGITAL ETHNOGRAPHY

Heteroglossia, a term coined by Bakhtin (and already mentioned in Chapter 9), refers to people's linguistic repertoires and resources in different named languages and in different registers and styles (standard and non-standard), as well as their indexical links with identity positionings and ideological values. According to Bailey (2007: 257–8), heteroglossia (a) 'encompasses both mono- and multilingual forms' and (b) addresses 'the tensions and conflicts' among those forms, 'based on the sociohistorical associations they carry with them'. Androutsopoulos (2011: 284) gives the following example of a YouTube comment to illustrate a **heteroglossic contrast** between seemingly contradictory identity positionings:

> des is doch echt so geil zefix oida
> so sama holt mia bayern
> (this is really great, mate
> that's the way we are, we Bavarians)

The text is written in Bavarian German, and the writer identifies him/herself as an ingroup member (we Bavarians), whereas his/her screen name uses English: 'BosniaStyle'. The heteroglossic contrast here is between the body of the text, which is indexical of a Bavarian identity, and the screen name, which points to another, non-local identity (Bosnia). Thus we have 'two different languages explicitly indexing two different identities, moulded together into one post yet at the same time differentiated in terms of its functional components' (Androutsopoulos 2011: 285). While Bavarian is used in the text for a communicative or instrumental purpose, the name is a largely symbolic or emblematic element and as such draws upon different linguistic and cultural resources. To find out in what ways the two identity positionings relate, the researcher would need to carry out a more fine-grained, contextualized analysis of an ethnographic nature, for instance by carrying out an online interview with the person who posted the comment.

For reasons such as the above, new media sociolinguists are increasingly adopting an ethnographic approach, which enables them to enter people's lived realities and to see the world through their eyes. In online environments, they have easy access to people's situated practices and can study them through systematic online observation. Hine (2000) and Yang (2003) refer to this as **guerilla ethnography**, with the researcher playing the double role of observer (often invisible to others) and participant (sometimes posting questions or otherwise taking part in the activities) – though the aggressiveness of the metaphor may make it a rather unfortunate choice of term.

To achieve a deep understanding and provide a fine-grained analysis (what Geertz calls a 'thick description' – see Chapter 2) of what is going on, the ethnographic researcher needs to adopt a highly contextualized approach. After all, the aim is to explore linguistic and cultural practices in specific contexts and to tie these local practices to wider social processes. In this way, the researcher attempts to gain access to participants' life-worlds, their ways of acting and thinking; what Bourdieu calls their **habitus**. Therefore it is important to establish direct contact with selected web users and, if the participants are willing, to organize (possibly online) interviews as a way of eliciting insider perspectives.

This means that it is desirable for new media sociolinguists to combine screen data and user-based data. As a result, new media sociolinguists do not limit themselves to the analysis of the online texts they are interested in, but also try to explore the contexts of production and reception of these texts. The idea is to end up with multiple data types, which can then be triangulated in a 'thick' ethnographic analysis. Just as in other kinds of ethnographic research, there may be a need here to remind all budding researchers of the importance of ethical concerns and their duty to protect their participants' privacy: therefore, it is essential to anonymize the data and, especially for private online data, to use consent forms asking participants for permission to use their data.

LANGUAGE CONTACT PHENOMENA IN DIGITAL LANGUAGE

Online environments such as texting, chatting and social networking are 'weakly regulated' (Deumert 2014: 101) and hence constitute ideal spaces for linguistic experimentation and creativity. They tend to be marked by a form of written orality, with online users drawing upon the whole of their heteroglossic resources. Blommaert (2011), for instance, has described mobile phone texting as a **supervernacular**, by which he means the wide array of semiotic (i.e. not only linguistic but multimodal) forms that circulate in this environment. Unlike other vernacular (or non-standard) linguistic varieties, the forms of such a supervernacular are not constrained by 'territorial fixedness, physical proximity, sociocultural sharedness and common backgrounds'; on the contrary, an online community is a 'loose, elastic, dynamic and deterritorialized' one (Blommaert 2011: 4). We should probably add that Blommaert's concept of supervernacular is not uncontroversial and that it has been critiqued by Makoni (2012) and Orman (2012) as being too static and 'based on conventional notions of language' (Makoni 2012: 194).

The linguistic forms of this supervernacular include at least the following, according to Deumert (2014: 131):

- acronyms, such as LOL
- consonant writing, such as swdrms (sweet dreams)
- phonetic spellings, such as guyz and gooooood
- special symbols, such as emoticons
- rebus writing, such as English be4 or German n8 (n + acht --> Nacht, night).

These are globally circulating resources which are always locally deployed in slightly different ways and therefore often involve multilingual and heteroglossic elements. Deumert (2014: 137) gives the following example to illustrate some of these strategies:

Sibo: Sori babes *kuphele umoya* talk 2 u 2moro
(Sorry baby airtime got finished talk to you tomorrow.)
Sxosh: Ok *ndisenawo* bt talk 2 u b4 *ndilale*
(OK. I still have some but talk to you before I sleep.)
(English – plain; isiXhosa – italics)

Sibo and Sxosh are a South African couple who are bilingual in English and isiXhosa. In this extract, they rely on the strategies of **rebus writing**, consonant writing and phonetic spelling (sori). Deumert points to a contrast in their use of English and isiXhosa: whereas their English is non-standard (mostly due to the application of the above strategies), they only use full and standard spelling in their isiXhosa. She argues that this might index a contrast between a transgressive English voice and a more traditional and respectful isiXhosa voice.

Another illustration of the local deployment of heteroglossic resources is the following example of rebus writing (from Blommaert 2011: 12):

U R my 3M (you are my drie-M, you are my dream)

According to Blommaert, the writer here is a Flemish-speaking person living in Antwerp, who draws upon the local (Flemish) pronunciation of 3 (drie) to creatively represent the English word 'dream'.

Because web users tend to draw upon all their heteroglossic resources, it is common to observe a wide range of **language contact** phenomena, with a language that enters into contact with another one affecting the latter's internal structure and as a result potentially giving rise to a new contact variety. Evidence of such processes can be found for instance in the online chat of young people in Hong Kong, as in the following example taken from Lim and Ansaldo (2016: 166):

Shirley: 7am. Very shit lei
([I have to work at] 7am. It's very bad.)
Ellen: ahaha ... add oil!!!! Then goodnight and sweet dreams la
([laughs] Work hard! Then goodnight and sweet dreams.)

Apart from the use of the Cantonese particles *lei* and *la*, what is interesting here from a language contact perspective is Ellen's use of the phrase 'add oil', meaning 'work hard'. This is a direct translation or **calque** of a Cantonese expression into English. In their discussion of this – and similar – phrases, Lim and Ansaldo (2016: 167) argue that the computer-mediated communication platform 'does indeed prompt the development of a contact variety of English, in this case, in the use of particular Hong Kong English phrases, here calqued from Cantonese'. They also note that such expressions as 'add oil' are gradually spreading from computer-mediated communication to spoken discourse in Hong Kong, as well as spreading from the Hong Kong community to expatriate 'Hongkongers with Hong Kong networks' (Lim and Ansaldo 2016: 168).

Another interesting illustration of language contact phenomena comes from a study of the online texts of a group of Finnish Christians who share an enthusiasm for extreme sports (Peuronen 2011; Leppänen *et al.* 2009). These young Finns' engagements with the new media refract their translocal alignments and affinities. At the global level, they draw on the English terminology of international extreme sports culture (Leppänen *et al.* 2009: 1100). But at the same time, the global is also localized, in that they change the orthography of these English terms, thus making them look more Finnish. As Leppänen *et al.* (2009: 1100) put it, by linking these terms to 'their own experiences and sporting activities, they localize both their forms and meanings'. For instance, the English word 'respect' (plural 'respects') – which is a key term in the hip-hop scene, often used as a greeting – is embedded within Finnish orthography and morphology, and is spelled as 'RISPEKTIT'. In terms of orthography, 'c' has been substituted by Finnish 'k', and in terms of morphology, word-final 'i' and the plural marker –t have been added.

In another example from the same study, a young expert in inline skating gives advice concerning the best gear set for a novice to buy:

> siin olis mun kompliitti ... smuutti ja valkoinen
>
> (Peuronen 2011: 170)
>
> (this would be my complete ... smooth and white)

Again, the English adjectives 'complete' and 'smooth' are localized and fully integrated into the Finnish sentence. Peuronen (2011: 170) emphasizes that 'kompliitti' and 'smuutti' are '(to a local Finn) foreign lexical items', but the modified spelling makes them look more Finnish. Furthermore, Peuronen notes that the addition of the Finnish –i endings makes the two words rhyme, thus highlighting the creative and playful nature of this language mixing, and ultimately also strengthening the writer's construction of her or his own expertise.

THE LIMITED MULTILINGUALISM OF THE INTERNET

In the previous section we have seen how web users draw on the whole of their heteroglossic resources, thus turning the Internet into a superdiverse space. *The Multilingual Internet* is even the title of a recent book (Danet and Herring 2007), though in fact the multilingualism of the Internet is quite limited. As Deumert (2014: 57) makes clear, many languages are not represented at all on the Internet, many other languages are only minimally represented and there is sustained use of only a small number of languages. Among the languages that dominate the Internet, there are almost only European languages. Here is Deumert's list of the dominant languages (from more dominant to less): English, Russian, German, Japanese, Spanish, French, Chinese, Portuguese, Italian and Polish. As for the languages that are only minimally represented, these are often minority languages that tend to be used in a symbolic or emblematic way, e.g. for names or in translanguaging, with the symbolic use being indexical of a particular identity.

In social media, a greater variety of languages tend to be used not only symbolically but also communicatively, so that social media could be seen as constituting what Fishman (1991: 59) refers to as 'breathing spaces' for small and minority languages. Nevertheless, there are still limitations. An example illustrating this is Phyak's (2015) study of data from a Facebook group using mostly Nepali and English for their online conversations (while the many minority languages of Nepal are largely absent). Like most of the studies discussed in this chapter, it is of a more ethnographic nature, with the author not only observing the linguistic practices and the discussion topics posted within the Facebook group, but also conducting online chats and interviews with some of the members, as well as contextualizing all this data within the socio-political context of Nepal. The following extract, which is part of an online conversation between two members of the Facebook group, has a direct bearing on the topic of this section, namely the limitations of multilingualism in social media and the reasons for this:

> LT: My problem, I can't type in Nepali in the facebook!!
> RR: Don't say like that, u r nepali u should type on nepali language not in english.
> LT: As I said I tried to use Unicode to write in Nepali but couldn't make it ... You have to learn to understand others' problem, without imposing your views!
> RR: Sister, I can understand english also, but I want to chat with u on nepali language Becoze u r nepali an me also nepali person
> (Phyak 2015: 386)

Phyak informs us that the home language of LT is Tamang, one of the many minority languages in Nepal, a highly multilingual country but which is marked by a strong Nepali-only ideology. This one nation–one language ideology informs what RR writes when in the above extract he tries to get LT to use Nepali rather than English because, as he says, 'you are Nepali'. Interestingly, there seems to be an ideological contradiction – a heteroglossic contrast, as Androutsopoulos would say – since he asks her to chat with him in Nepali though he himself uses English, in fact a non-standard variety of English in which he would appear to be quite fluent.

While Tamang is one of the many minority languages largely absent from the Internet, even Nepali, the national language of Nepal, is not very strongly represented. It is, however, used not only emblematically but also for communicative purposes (which is why RR asks LT to write to him in Nepali). However, LT continues to write in English, arguing that she finds it difficult to type in 'Nepali Unicode', which is a Romanized version of Nepali. Elsewhere she also says that she prefers to use English because she needs to communicate with her translocal network of Facebook friends. Hence, there are two reasons why she resists RR's Nepali-only ideology: first, because of the technological difficulties involved in typing in Nepali and second, because of the overall dominance of English on the Internet. However, as Phyak (2015: 386) points out, this implies that she counters RR's monolingual, Nepali-only ideology not with a multilingual ideology but with another monolingual ideology, namely an English-only one.

Phyak's study is interesting not only because it provides an insight into some of the reasons for the dominance of the English language in social media and the difficulties of writing in languages that use a script other than the Roman one (Nepali uses Devanagari script), but also because it shows how users can resent and resist the pressures of others to write in a particular language (in this case, LT tells RR to stop imposing his views). The social mediascape can thus be seen as a site of discursive struggle with different actors, perspectives, ideologies and interests or, in the words of Phyak (2015: 379), a 'contested space where dominant language ideologies are both reinforced and subverted'. In fact, RR's behaviour towards LT is a form of what has been called 'language policing', which is the topic of the following section.

THE POLICING OF NEW MEDIA LANGUAGE

Language policing can be defined as 'the production of "order" – normatively organized and policed conduct – which is infinitely detailed and regulated by a variety of actors' (Blommaert *et al.* 2009: 203). Policing takes place not only locally between Facebook friends such as RR and LT but can at times lead to veritable **moral panics** about digital language use in the media. Thurlow (2006) shows that such moral panics, ostensibly about digital language, invariably involve debates about declining standards (not only linguistic but also social ones). Parents, teachers or journalists express concern about non-standard spellings, a concern which is then blown out of all proportion so that the non-standard spellings are seen as signalling the end of language and even of the whole social and moral order. Here are a couple of examples out of the many discussed by Thurlow (2006: 678):

> Text messaging ... is posing a threat to social progress.
> The English language is being beaten up, civilization is in danger of crumbling.

In these two extracts, just as in so many of his examples, we note how a direct causal link is established between language decline and social disorder. As Thurlow (2006: 671) puts it, 'Often, it seems, adult anxieties about youth, about technology, and about language merge into a kind of "triple-whammy" panic about declining standards of morality and the unwinding of the social fabric.' In fact, however, research has shown that non-standard writing does not destroy young people's reading and writing abilities but can even enhance these abilities through greater metalinguistic awareness of how languages function (see e.g. studies by Plester, Wood and Joshi 2009 and Wood *et al.* 2011).

In the remainder of this section, we discuss several more ways in which language policing can be carried out online, without necessarily giving rise to wholesale media panics. Sherman and Svelch (2015) examine how language policing is carried out on self-styled 'Grammar Nazis' Facebook pages, in this case for the Czech language. Linguistic deviations from the norms of standard written Czech are collected, discussed, condemned and ridiculed, along with the people who committed them. The use of humour makes the criticism more acceptable and helps to avert accusations of racism or classism. The members of this Facebook group thus reproduce the standard language ideology in relation to the Czech language. However, since they are mostly concerned with orthographic deviations, it follows that their conception of grammar is a rather impoverished one; namely, grammar is understood as, or reduced to, orthography. While these constitute the huge majority of complaints, Sherman and Svelch (2015: 325) note that there are also some negative evaluations of English loanwords and translanguaging, like for example *čoko doughnut* (chocolate doughnut).

A less face-threatening and more nuanced form of language policing, also on Facebook, has been studied by Lenihan (2011). Facebook is available in a number of different languages, including minority or regional languages and even such 'ways of speaking' as Klingon (from Star Trek; Lenihan 2011: 49). It has a translations application, which can be applied by any interested users, who thus become part of the community of (self-appointed) translators for a particular language. They work collaboratively to provide the necessary translations for that language. In her study, Lenihan focuses on Irish and explores not only how the Irish language translation of Facebook is constructed but, more generally, how the Irish language itself is constructed within this new media domain.

In this Facebook group, most of the language-ideological debates about Irish take place in the discussion board, where the members of the community of translators comment on the suggested translations. Many posts insist on the importance of keeping Irish separate from English and comment negatively on any perceived anglicisms. For instance, 'fón póca' (mobile phone; literally, pocket phone) is considered too anglicized because of the loanword 'fón' (from English 'phone'), and alternative, more Irish-sounding translations are suggested such as 'guthán soghluaiste' or 'guthán póca' ('guthán' is the official Irish word for telephone; Lenihan 2011: 58).

Underlying such comments is the ideology of languages as separate, bounded entities, an ideology which, as Lenihan (2011: 56) points out, is also promoted by Facebook, the company itself. Indeed, on Facebook, each language has its own translations application and is thus kept separate from the other languages, with each additional language opening up a new market for Facebook. We note that this view of multilingualism as a set of bounded languages – and the attendant use of multilingualism as a marketing strategy – is far removed from the understanding of multilingualism as heteroglossic resources, which we discussed at the beginning of this chapter (and which we have adopted throughout this textbook).

In this section, we have examined a number of different language policing practices. It should be obvious that these practices are not uniformly accepted, but that they are frequently contested or resisted. We have already seen one example of this in the Nepali Facebook group, where one member (LT) resists another member's (RR) attempt to impose the use of the Nepali language upon her. A similar instance of resistance to language policing is analysed in Leppänen and Peuronen (2012: 394–5; see also Kytölä 2012). It concerns an online football forum based in Finland. The language norm in this forum is to use Finnish, with users posting in Swedish, English or other languages and varieties frequently being subjected to complaints or even hate discourse. Before looking at an example, we need to contextualize these attitudes and norms in relation to the current socio-political context of Finland. Finland is an officially bilingual country in Finnish and Swedish, though Swedish is a minority language in Finland and mostly only used in the southern, south-western and western coastal areas. The official bilingualism is a thorn in the side of the nationalist Finns Party, and many of its supporters and sympathizers would like to see it abolished and turn Finland into a monolingual Finnish-only country.

In the following extract, a Swedish-speaking Finn uses three languages – Swedish, Finnish and English – to contest and subvert the norms of the online football forum:

> Och ni som inte orkar läsa allt som står på svenska,
> (And those of you who don't have the patience to read everything that is said in Swedish,)
> *I don't give a fuck.*
> **Minä puhun ruotsia, ja en ymmärrä paljon suomea.**
> (I speak Swedish, and I don't understand much Finnish.)
> *That's why I write in Swedish. Simple as that.*
> Tänk på all finsk text vi måste traggla oss igenom för at ens fatta om, och hur ni jävlas med oss.
> (Think about all the Finnish text we have to try and read to at least understand, and how you make fun of us.)
>
> (Swedish – plain; Finnish – bold; English – italics; Leppänen and Peuronen 2012: 395)

The Swedish-speaking soccer fan's use of multilingualism is an act of resistance, by which he is pitting a more multilingual Finnish identity against the monolingual Finnish-only identity of the Finns Party and its supporters. In this way, we can also see how ideological – including language-ideological – conflicts in society are carried over into, and how they play out in, online environments.

CONCLUSION

This chapter has emphasized the importance of adopting an ethnographic approach to achieve a deep understanding of the links between users' heteroglossic resources and their ideological and identity positionings. We have also studied how the local deployment of globally circulating resources can give rise to language contact phenomena or even to new contact varieties. Finally, we have explored how users' heteroglossic practices are often constrained by norms and ideologies that attempt to reimpose homogeneity. Such forms of language policing tend to focus on anglicisms or orthographic deviations from the standard variety and, as such, are informed by the standard language ideology, the ideology of purism and the ideology of languages as separate, bounded entities. At the same time, we have also seen how attempts at language policing are frequently contested and resisted. To conclude with the words of Phyak (2015: 381), the Internet is a 'contested *ideospace* in which language ideologies concerning both diversity and homogeneity are discursively constructed'.

ACTIVITY: THE 'DISPLAY' OF MULTILINGUALISM

Look at the following SMS interaction between two male, English-dominant South African students, as well as a comment on the interaction made by the second speaker (Carlo) during an interview with the researcher:

> Dustin: Molloboetie, hoe gaan dit? What's the plans for tonight?
> Carlo: Shabash shabash, gildie gildie. What do you say we hit Jade.
> (molo boetie = isiXhosa, meaning 'hello brother'; hoe gaan dit? = Afrikaans, meaning 'how are you?'; shabash = Urdu, meaning 'well done'; gildie = a word most likely made up by Carlo; Jade = a local night club)

> [Dustin] uses three languages in one sentence to display his level of intelligence as well as practising his writing in all three languages. The message I sent to Dustin was to display my form of multilingualism and intelligence by saying something in Arabic.
> (Deumert 2014: 119)

Discuss the links between the two students' heteroglossic practices and their (especially Carlo's) ideological and identity positionings.

FOR DISCUSSION: LANGUAGE POLICING

Have you ever had an experience of an act of language policing in an online environment? What language ideology/ies informed this act? How did you (or other users in the online environment) react to it?

PROJECT WORK: LANGUAGE CONTACT PHENOMENA

Collect some data from a multilingual Facebook group and carry out a linguistic analysis to find out whether the languages or varieties being used influence each other. In other words, are there any language contact phenomena?

Once you have collected a number of examples, analyse in detail what is going on in each of them: which language influences which other one(s)? At what linguistic levels does the influence operate (orthographic, lexical, syntactic. . .)?

If possible, try to contact the producers of these heteroglossic texts and interview them about their reasons for writing in this way. Alternatively, you can also ask some other people about how they react to these contact features.

PROJECT WORK: THE LANGUAGE OF HIP HOP

Focus on a particular hip-hop community and their online site. To what extent do the contributions to this site draw upon multilingual resources, including the linguistic resources of African-American English? Are there any 'global' markers of hip-hop style?

For a study of the German hip-hop field (in particular, the online site webbeatz.de) along these lines, see Androutsopoulos (2007).

PROJECT WORK: EXPLORING HETEROGLOSSIC PRACTICES

Look for some heteroglossic features in your friends' status updates or wall comments on Facebook. First, make sure you ask them for permission to use their postings as data for this project. Analyse these heteroglossic practices and try to account for them in terms of ideological or identity positionings.

REFERENCES AND SUGGESTIONS FOR FURTHER READING

Computer-mediated communication

Androutsopoulos, Jannis (2006) 'Introduction: Sociolinguistics and computer-mediated communication', *Journal of Sociolinguistics*, 10: 419–38.

—— (2011) 'From variation to heteroglossia in the study of computer-mediated discourse', in C. Thurlow and K. Mroczek (eds) *Digital Discourse: Language in the New Media*, New York: Oxford University Press, 277–98.

Herring, Susan C. (1996) *Computer-Mediated Communication: Linguistic, Social and Cross-Cultural Perspectives*, Amsterdam: Benjamins.

Lee, Carmen (2017) *Multilingualism Online*, London: Routledge.

Leppänen, Sirpa, Westinen, Elina and Kytölä, Samu (eds) (2017) *Social Media Discourse, (Dis) identifications and Diversities*, London: Routledge.

Seargeant, Philip and Tagg, Caroline (eds) (2014) *The Language of Social Media: Identity and Community on the Internet*, Basingstoke: Palgrave.

Tagg, Caroline (2015) *Exploring Digital Communication: Language in Action*, London: Routledge.

Tannen, Deborah and Trester, Anna Marie (eds) (2013) *Discourse 2.0: Language and New Media*, Washington DC: Georgetown University Press.

Thurlow, Crispin and Mroczek, Kristine (2011) 'Introduction: Fresh perspectives on new media sociolinguistics', in *Digital Discourse: Language in the New Media*, New York: Oxford University Press, xix–xliv.

Digital ethnography

Bailey, Benjamin (2007) 'Heteroglossia and boundaries', in M. Heller (ed.) *Bilingualism: A Social Approach*, Basingstoke: Palgrave, 257–74.

Bourdieu, Pierre (1992) *The Logic of Practice*, London: Polity Press.

Hine, Christine (2000) *Virtual Ethnography*, London: Sage.

Varis, Piia (2016) 'Digital ethnography', in A. Georgakopoulou and T. Spilioti (eds) *The Routledge Handbook of Language and Digital Communication*, London: Routledge, 55–68.

Yang, Guobin (2003) 'The Internet and the rise of a transnational Chinese cultural sphere', *Media, Culture and Society*, 25: 469–90.

Language contact phenomena in digital language

Blommaert, Jan (2011) 'Supervernaculars and their dialects', *Tilburg Papers in Culture Studies*, 9: 54–90.

Deumert, Ana (2014) *Sociolinguistics and Mobile Communication*, Edinburgh: Edinburgh University Press.

—— and Lexander, Kristin Vold (2013) 'Texting Africa: Writing as performance', *Journal of Sociolinguistics*, 17: 522–46.

Kytölä, Samu (2012) 'Peer normativity and sanctioning of linguistic resources-in-use: On non-standard Englishes in Finnish football forums online', in J. Blommaert, S. Leppänen, P. Pahta and T. Räisänen (eds) *Dangerous Multilingualism: Northern Perspectives on Order, Purity and Normality*, Basingstoke: Palgrave, 228–60.

Leppänen, Sirpa, Pitkänen-Huhta, Anne, Piirainen-Marsh, Arja, Nikula, Tarja and Peuronen, Saija (2009) 'Young people's translocal new media uses: A multiperspective analysis of language choice and heteroglossia', *Journal of Computer-Mediated Communication*, 14: 1080–1107.

Lim, Lisa and Ansaldo, Umberto (2016) *Languages in Contact*, Cambridge: Cambridge University Press.

Makoni, Sinfree B. (2012) 'A critique of language, languaging and supervernacular', *Muitas Vozes*, 1: 189–99.

Orman, Jon (2012) 'Not so super: The ontology of supervernaculars', *Language and Communication*, 32: 349–57.

Peuronen, Saija (2011) '"Ride hard, live forever": Translocal identities in an online community of extreme sports Christians', in C. Thurlow and K. Mroczek (eds) *Digital Discourse: Language in the New Media*, New York: Oxford University Press, 154–76.

The limited multilingualism of the Internet

Danet, Brenda and Herring, Susan, S.C. (eds) (2007) *The Multilingual Internet: Language, Culture, and Communication Online*, Oxford: Oxford University Press.

Fishman, Joshua A. (1991) *Reversing Language Shift*, Clevedon: Multilingual Matters.

Phyak, Prem (2015) '(En)countering language ideologies: Language policing in the idiospace of Facebook', *Language Policy*, 14: 377–95.

The policing of new media language

Blommaert, Jan, Kelly-Holmes, Helen, Lane, Pia, Leppänen, Sirpa, Moriarty, Máiréad, Pietikäinen, Sari and Piirainen-Marsh, Arja (2009) 'Media, multilingualism and language policing', *Language Policy*, 8: 203–7.

Lenihan, Aoife (2011) '"Join our community of translators": Language ideologies and/in Facebook', in C. Thurlow and K. Mroczek (eds) *Digital Discourse: Language in the New Media*, New York: Oxford University Press, 48–64.

Leppänen, Sirpa and Peuronen, Saija (2012) 'Multilingualism on the Internet', in M. Martin-Jones, A. Blackledge and A. Creese (eds) *The Routledge Handbook of Multilingualism*, London: Routledge, 384–402.

Sherman, Tamah and Svelch, Jaroslav (2015) '"Grammar Nazis never sleep": Facebook humor and the management of standard written language', *Language Policy*, 14: 315–34.

Thurlow, Crispin (2006) 'From statistical panic to moral panic: The metadiscursive construction and popular exaggeration of new media language in the print media', *Journal of Computer-Mediated Communication*, 11: 667–701.

Text messaging and school achievement

Plester, Beverly, Wood, Clare and Joshi, Puja (2009) 'Exploring the relationship between children's knowledge of text message abbreviations and school literacy outcomes', *British Journal of Developmental Psychology*, 27: 145–61.

Wood, C., Jackson, E., Hart, L., Plester, B. and Wilde, L. (2011) 'The effect of text messaging on 9- and 10-year-old children's reading, spelling and phonological processing skills', *Journal of Computer Assisted Learning*, 27: 28–36.

The language of hip hop

Androutsopoulos, Jannis (2007) 'Style online: Doing hip-hop on the German-speaking web', in P. Auer (ed.) *Style and Social Identities: Alternative Approaches to Linguistic Heterogeneity*, Berlin: Mouton de Gruyter, 279–317.

CHAPTER 16

Linguistic landscape

This chapter moves beyond the analysis of verbal text to consider multimodal texts which combine verbal and visual elements. Such a **multimodal** discourse analysis (Kress and van Leeuwen 2006; Kress 2009) is needed to analyse, for instance, advertisements or public signs. In the last couple of decades, there has been a growing interest in studying how language is used in the public space. This new area of analysis has been variously referred to as 'linguistic landscape' (Gorter 2006), 'semiotic landscape' (Jaworski and Thurlow 2010) or 'discourses in place' (Scollon and Scollon 2003). Gorter (2006) even claims in the subtitle of his book that it constitutes 'a new approach to multilingualism'. In a seminal paper, Landry and Bourhis (1997: 25) define linguistic landscape as follows:

> The language of public road signs, advertising billboards, street names, place names, commercial shop signs, and public signs on government buildings combines to form the linguistic landscape of a given territory, region, or urban agglomeration.

As for Shohamy (2006: 58), she sees language in the public space as one of the main mechanisms affecting *de facto* language policies and practices, alongside other mechanisms such as language-in-education policy (as discussed in Chapters 9–11 of the present book) and language testing (discussed in Chapter 13).

LIMITATIONS OF SOME LINGUISTIC LANDSCAPE ANALYSES

Like some early research in computer-mediated communication, some of the early linguistic landscape studies are limited in the following two ways:

first, these studies are quantitative rather than interpretive, and largely limit themselves to counting the languages used on multilingual signs. Such studies need to be complemented by more ethnographic approaches to provide deeper understandings of the context, including the production and reception of signs. Second, the whole notion of identifying and counting the 'languages' of multilingual signs is highly problematic, as we have seen in Chapter 3. It can also be seen from a consideration of language use on the bilingual signs in Figures 1.1 and 16.1 (Figure 1.1 was part of the quiz in Chapter 1 and is reproduced here for ease of reference).

Schengen (in Figure 1.1) is the village in Luxembourg whose name has become famous because the agreement to abolish border controls between a number of EU member-states was signed there. The village is situated on the Moselle river, with Germany on the other side of the river (and the border with France also nearby). Unsurprisingly, the name 'Schengen' is rather German-sounding, like most place-names on the Luxembourgish side of the Moselle (Remich, Grevenmacher, Wasserbillig, etc.). However, official policy requires place-names to be indicated on bilingual signs with French at the top and Luxembourgish at the bottom. For instance, the capital city signs read 'Luxembourg' and, below it, 'Lëtzebuerg' (see Figure 16.1). This means that the Schengen sign is actually to be read as bilingual: the top 'Schengen' is in French, the bottom one is in Luxembourgish, and neither of them is in German!

Figure 1.1 Schengen place name

Figure 16.1 Luxembourg place name

LANGUAGE CONTACT PHENOMENA ON MULTILINGUAL SIGNS

Signs in multilingual areas frequently display language contact phenomena. One example is Figure 16.2, a sign advocating items for sale in a German-American shop in Wisconsin, USA, which shows the influence of English on German: German 'mit oder ohne' has become 'mitt or mittout' under the influence of English 'with or without'. In fact, the shop sells these sausages with or without garlic, and the fact that this instance of hybrid language use is put between quotation marks suggests that it is a fixed local phrase.

Another example is Huebner's (2006) study of language contact phenomena between Thai and English which have occurred as a result of globalization. He investigates language mixing on signs in Bangkok and explores in detail how English influences Thai. His data, collected in fifteen neighbourhoods of central and suburban Bangkok, contains both monolingual signs and multilingual signs with different combinations of languages. One pattern he notices is the large number of signs in Thai script mixed with English lexicon or syntax, whereas there are no signs in English script (or orthography) with Thai lexicon or syntax. He argues that the inclusion of English lexicon or syntax on Thai-script signs 'adds a cosmopolitan flair

Figure 16.2 Sign outside German-American shop in Kenosha, Wisconsin

to the message that isn't available in a sign using only Thai script, lexicon and syntax' (Huebner 2006: 48).

For instance, on one of these signs 'Ta Beauty' is written in Thai script. Apart from the lexical borrowing, English also influences Thai here on the syntactic level:

> The vocabulary consists of the name of (presumably) the Thai proprietor and the English word 'beauty'. And the syntax, while lacking the possessive [–s] morpheme, retains the English word order of 'adjective + noun'.
>
> (Huebner 2006: 35)

The normal Thai word order would have been 'noun + adjective'. Another interesting sign, also written in Thai script, reads 'K. L. Fashion House'. In this case, English influences Thai not only at the lexical and syntactic levels but also, according to Huebner (2006: 48–9), at the levels of orthography and pronunciation: 'Thai orthography uses no spaces between words, nor does it use punctuation such as periods for abbreviations (or for that matter, to delineate syntactic units).' Here, however, both spaces and periods (full stops) are used. In this way, Huebner's study reveals the full extent of the influence of English on Thai: it is not just a matter of lexical borrowing, as one might have expected, but the influence can also be seen at the syntactic and orthographic levels.

SOME BASIC DISTINCTIONS

Symbolic and instrumental uses of language

In his study of multilingual signs in shop windows and restaurants in two areas of the Swedish city of Malmö, Hult (2009) relies upon the important distinction between **symbolic** and **instrumental** uses of language. Contrary to his expectations, he finds that on many signs English is used symbolically and Swedish in a more instrumental or communicative way. For instance, the name of a grocery shop is SUNSHINE LIVS: the English name (SUNSHINE) communicates nothing about what is actually sold there, while the Swedish word LIVS (foodstuffs) does. He argues that English names are often used symbolically to index the values of internationalism and globalization, which contradicts 'the belief most strongly held in *de jure* language policies . . . that English serves primarily as a language of wider communication in Sweden' (Hult 2009: 100).

Top-down and bottom-up signs

Ben-Rafael *et al.* (2004) carried out a study of multilingual signs in Israel to investigate the different roles of English and of the two official languages, Hebrew and Arabic (see Chapter 5 for background information about the language situation in Israel). They collected linguistic landscape items in six areas inhabited by Jews and/or Arabs, including East Jerusalem. In their analysis, they rely upon a basic distinction between **top-down** (official signs issued by institutional actors) and **bottom-up** signs (put up by autonomous, individual social actors).

They found that in Jewish areas, the most widely used languages on both top-down and bottom-up signs are Hebrew and English, with Arabic being almost completely absent. In Arab-speaking areas, Arabic was present but usually alongside Hebrew, which was also widely used in these areas, both on top-down and bottom-up signs. This reflects the powerful position of Hebrew and the rather powerless position of Arabic in Israeli society, even though the latter is also an official language.

Concerning the Arab-speaking areas, Shohamy (2006: 121), who was one of the co-authors of the study, reports on an interesting difference between East Jerusalem and the other Israeli Palestinian areas that they surveyed. As has been mentioned above, in most of these areas, there were a lot of signs in Arabic and Hebrew – indeed, there was also a lot of Hebrew on bottom-up signs. In East Jerusalem, on the other hand, the signs were mostly in Arabic and English, with hardly any Hebrew, except on trilingual top-down signs (in Arabic, Hebrew and English). Shohamy concludes that here the choice of languages on multilingual signs is connected with the degree of political dissent and the consequent rejection of the dominant language (i.e. Hebrew, which in East Jerusalem is looked upon as the language of the oppressor, of the enemy).

CONTEXTUALIZING AND HISTORICIZING LINGUISTIC LANDSCAPES

In this section, we discuss some recent directions in the study of linguistic landscape which open up such analyses to a more fully contextualized approach. These researchers advocate an ethnographic and interdisciplinary approach, linking up with cultural geography in general and more particularly with urban planning policy. They insist on the need for a historicizing approach that takes into account the ways in which the production of particular signs has been shaped by the socio-historical context.

The first study we consider here is Leeman and Modan (2009) on signage in the newly gentrified Chinatown in Washington DC. We will see in a moment that the authors build upon the distinction between symbolic and instrumental uses of language that Hult (2009) also uses. On the other hand, they reject or at least problematize the distinction between top-down and bottom-up signs that Ben-Rafael *et al.* (2004) rely upon. They show that the redevelopment of Chinatown was a joint venture undertaken by both the state and private enterprise. This means that the top-down vs. bottom-up distinction becomes increasingly untenable, for two main reasons: first, because of the frequent public–private partnerships in urban planning policies and revitalization schemes, and second, because public policies often regulate and constrain private sector signage practices (Leeman and Modan 2009: 334). They replace the top-down vs. bottom-up distinction with another distinction, which they look upon as more useful for their analysis, namely a distinction between signs made for specific establishments and signs made for more general distribution (Leeman and Modan 2009: 335). We will see that the latter distinction also underlies the second study we will discuss later on in this section, by Stroud and Mpendukana (2009).

Leeman and Modan's (2009) analysis is structured along the historical dimension. In their account of the redevelopment of Chinatown, they distinguish between a first wave (in the 1970s and 1980s) and a second wave (in the 1990s). The establishments that opened during the first wave were mostly small, Chinese-owned businesses, which displayed signs with a mostly instrumental function. Whether English and/or Chinese was used on these signs, the primary aim was to communicate information to potential customers, both English-speaking tourists and Chinese-speaking residents. Second-wave establishments, on the other hand, are very different: they tend to be corporate-owned national or international chains. This trend was actively encouraged by the official policy in the 1990s of up-scaling and gentrifying the area. Thus companies such as Starbucks, Ann Taylor, Aveda cosmetics, Fado's Irish pub, La Tasca tapas restaurant and Matchstick Pizza opened shops and restaurants in Chinatown, and all of them display Chinese language signs on their storefronts. Bilingual English-Chinese signage was enforced by the D.C. Office of Planning. But what it means is that the English name of the establishment is used for communicative purposes, whereas the Chinese translation of the name is used for purely (or primarily) symbolic or aesthetic reasons. In this way, the Chinese language has become highly visible in the area, though mostly just as an element of design and certainly not as an indication of the vitality of this heritage language.

At the same time, the redevelopment and gentrification of Chinatown has led to a steep increase in prices, which has forced out a large number of the Chinese residents, while affluent whites have moved into the area. The consequence is a smaller number of the traditional Chinese-owned businesses, and a growing number of national and international shop and restaurant chains, all of them with their names displayed not only in English but also in Chinese characters. Leeman and Modan (2009: 356) conclude that the Washington DC Chinatown is in the process of becoming a 'Disneyfied landscape', with Chinese writing used as a mere 'ornament in the commodified landscape' (Leeman and Modan 2009: 359). The Chinese language has thus become a 'floating signifier that can be used to signify, or to sell, not just things Chinese but anything at all' (Leeman and Modan 2009: 353–4).

In the second study, Stroud and Mpendukana (2009) explore the linguistic landscape of Khayelitsha, a township on the edge of Cape Town, which in a way becomes emblematic of the new 'politics of aspiration' (Stroud and Mpendukana 2009: 363) in post-apartheid South Africa.

The authors examine in particular billboards advertising either local or global products. They notice a similar distinction to that described by Leeman and Modan (2009) between first-wave Chinese-owned signs and second-wave corporate-owned signs, but they refer to it in Bourdieuan terms as a distinction between sites of necessity and sites of luxury. Signs in sites of necessity are more instrumental and task-oriented, advertising a local shop or service provider. In sites of luxury, on the other hand, the symbolic or aesthetic dimension is foregrounded, as the billboards advertise a more global product (such as, for instance, Cadbury sweets). Sites of necessity and luxury can be distinguished along a number of further dimensions:

(a) mode of production:

Whereas signs of necessity are locally and manually produced with very low economic investment, signs of luxury have gone through high-tech modes of production with substantial economic investment.

(b) placement:

Whereas signs of necessity are tied to a particular local place, signs of luxury are to be found in economically 'up-market' places such as main squares or taxi stands.

(c) reader positioning:

Whereas signs of necessity directly address the reader as a potential customer, signs of luxury tend to position the reader more ambiguously as 'non-proximal' interactant, bystander or overhearer (Stroud and Mpendukana 2009: 369).

Moreover, these differences correlate with differences in language choice, as well as spelling and grammatical conventions. The following examples should make this clearer: an example of a luxury sign is the Cadbury advertisement mentioned above. It portrays a huge Cadbury sweet with the following text written on the sweet:

P.S. i love you.
xxxx

and the following slogan underneath:

sweet-talk
waya waya

Here standard English is combined with a pan-African variety of language (i.e. an expression common to many different African languages) to mean something like: sweet talk non-stop (Stroud and Mpendukana 2009: 369).

Local signs of necessity, on the other hand, are more strongly marked by linguistic hybridity, typically with translanguaging between English and isiXhosa (the most widely used indigenous African language in the Cape Town area), as in the following texts:

1) ISIPHO UPHOLSTERERS
   SIVA KHAVA ISOFA
2) YEBO EXHAUST
   FITTMENT
   CENTRE
   . . .
   CHEAP AND NAGOCIABLE

In the first example, English words are mixed into, and adjusted to, the isiXhosa text, with 'khava' meaning 'cover' and 'isofa' standing for 'sofa'. In the second example, *Yebo* is an isiXhosa word meaning 'yes', and 'fittment' and 'nagociable' are examples of non-standard spellings, based on what Blommaert *et al.* (2005) refer to as **peripheral normativity** (the norms of peripheral or local English, as opposed to the norms of standard British and American English).

Interestingly, Stroud and Mpendukana (2009: 376) also note the increasing presence in the township of new signs combining features of both sites of necessity and sites of luxury, thus deconstructing the traditional distinction between luxury products and quotidian products of necessity. In these 'sites of implosion', as they call them, global products are 're-represented as local products of necessity' (Stroud and Mpendukana 2009: 381). Their example is a series of three billboards advertising Kentucky Fried Chicken, a global (and hence luxury) product, but which here is embedded within the local context through a number of features more typical of sites of necessity including, for instance, translanguaging between English and isiXhosa. Stroud and Mpendukana (2009: 381) conclude that townships such as Khayelitsha are imagined in post-apartheid South Africa not only as localized places (in sites of necessity) or as places of aspiration (in sites of luxury), but also as places of ongoing social and economic transformation in the new sites of implosion.

The studies by Leeman and Modan (2009) and Stroud and Mpendukana (2009) break through many of the limitations of earlier linguistic landscape research. While Leeman and Modan insist on the importance of contextualizing and historicizing the analysis, Stroud and Mpendukana's (2009: 363) aim is to work 'towards a material ethnography of linguistic landscape', as they put it in the title of their article. At the same time, the authors of both studies know that there are further steps that still need to be taken: while they focus in detail on the context of production of the signs that they analyse, they mostly ignore the context of reception, which can be equally important. The authors are fully aware that this element is missing from their analyses; Stroud and Mpendukana (2009: 382) put it as follows:

> A limitation of our analysis is that we have only so far provided potential and possible readings that we find layered into the composition, and would need to explain how these variants are taken up or circulated among speakers.

Meanwhile, Leeman and Modan (2009: 359) say:

> The role of spaces of representation (i.e. representations as lived experience) is an important area for further research that might be fruitfully investigated through ethnographic interviews of people in Chinatown.

EXPLORING THE CONTEXT OF RECEPTION

We have seen in the previous section that recent studies in linguistic landscape have begun to incorporate the context of production of signs into their analyses but there are still only a small number that also investigate the context of reception. One of these is the study by Collins and Slembrouck (2004) on a multilingual immigrant neighbourhood in the Belgian city of Ghent. The authors showed some of the signs that they collected in this neighbourhood to a number of different people and asked them to comment upon them. It is interesting to see how different ideologies (or discourse models) led the informants to different readings of the same signs. Here is just one of the examples that they discuss:

BESTE KLANTEN WIJ ZIJN VERHUISD NAAR NR. 171
← 30 METER VERDER

SAYIN MÜSTERİLERİMİZ BİZ 171 NUMARAYA TAŞINDIK
← 30 METRE ÖTEDEYİZ

The sign, which was on the window of a shop that had recently moved, says 'Dear clients, we have moved to number 171, 30 metres away', first in Dutch (in the bigger font) and below it in Turkish. Collins and Slembrouck showed this sign to three informants:

- Meryem, Turkish, lives in Istanbul, speaks Turkish but no Dutch;
- Nezat, local Turkish-Belgian, born in Istanbul but has lived most of his life in Ghent, speaks Turkish and Dutch;
- Herman, Flemish Belgian, lives in Antwerp, speaks Dutch but no Turkish.

Meryem focuses on the word 'ötedeyiz', which in her eyes indexes a rural variety of Turkish. She contrasts it with what she considers to be the urban form: 'ilerdeyiz'. She concludes that the sign writer must be originally from a rural area of Turkey. Nezat offers two interpretations, switching from one to the other. He also focuses on the word 'ötedeyiz', hypothesizing first that it may be a translation from Dutch and that the sign was written by somebody who is more fluent in Dutch than in Turkish. But then he changes his mind and offers an alternative interpretation very similar to Meryem's: the sign writer may be from a rural part of Anatolia, where a different variety of Turkish is used. Herman, on the other hand, takes a very different interpretative direction. He focuses on two design aspects: the fact that the font for the Turkish text is smaller than that for Dutch, and that the Turkish text is written below the Dutch one. He interprets this as indexing the sign writer's successful assimilation into Flemish-Belgian society. He then generalizes this to the whole city of Ghent, which he sees as a model of harmonious community relations and integration practices, unlike – he alleges – Brussels and Antwerp (the city where he resides). In this way, we see how people's beliefs and values, assumptions and preoccupations can lead them in very different interpretative directions in their readings of (multilingual) signs.

DISCUSSION AND CONCLUSION: DISCOURSES IN PLACE

A highly promising approach to linguistic landscape that brings together the various strands discussed in this chapter and also links up with cultural geography, urban planning and other interconnected fields is Scollon and Scollon's (2003) 'discourses in place'. It explicitly builds upon Kress and van Leeuwen's multimodal discourse analysis, which we referred to in the introduction to this chapter and which provides a theoretical framework for the analysis of both verbal and visual texts. An important element included in this framework is **reader positioning**: this is a dimension that Stroud and Mpendukana (2009) also include in their analysis, when they note that in signs of necessity (e.g. the Isipho Upholsterers and Yebo Exhaust Fittment Centre signs) viewers are directly addressed as potential customers, and in signs of luxury (e.g. the Cadbury sweets billboard) they tend to be positioned as bystanders or overhearers.

Scollon and Scollon extend this approach even further by developing what they call a **place semiotics**. Place semiotics is specifically geared for the analysis of signs in the public space, and it consists of three parts: a code preference system, an inscription system and an emplacement system.

The **code preference system** applies to all multilingual signs, such that there is always a preferred code and at least one marginalized code. The preferred code is often legally enforced: for instance, we have seen that on place-name signs in Luxembourg French is the preferred code (at the top of the sign and in larger font) and Luxembourgish is the marginalized code (at the bottom, smaller font). Scollon and Scollon give some examples from Hong Kong, contrasting street signs, signs in a shopping mall and signs for the Mass Transit Railway (MTR) system. Whereas on the street signs and the shopping mall signs, English is on top and Chinese below, the MTR signs are just the inverse, with Chinese on top and English below. Scollon and Scollon argue that the street signs constitute a carryover from the era of colonialism, and the shopping mall signs refract an ideology of globalization (English as the global language, Chinese as local). On the other hand, the MTR signs are more pragmatic and instrumental, primarily addressing the users of the transport system, the huge majority of whom are Chinese-speaking. At the same time, Scollon and Scollon (2003: 124) caution that such systems of values 'cannot be "read off" simply from seeing the code choice which has been made but must be subjected to historical and ethnographic analysis'.

The **inscription system** is concerned with how the signs and their (verbal and/or visual) texts are presented in the material world, with a focus on special fonts as well as the materials on which the texts are written. This is where we would consider Stroud and Mpendukana's distinction between how signs of luxury and signs of necessity are produced: whereas the former go through expensive, high-tech modes of production, the latter are often manually produced at low cost by a painter or craftsman from the local neighbourhood.

While the inscription system deals with important aspects of the context of production, the **emplacement system** opens up the analysis to the context of reception. It attempts to understand the ways in which the meaning of signs depends on where and how they are placed in the material world. Scollon and Scollon distinguish between three main types of emplacement:

- situated
- decontextualized
- transgressive.

Thus signs exist on a continuum from more situated signs, which take on their meaning from being placed in a particular location, to more decontextualized signs, such as registered trademarks (logos, brand names), which carry more or less the same meaning wherever they are placed. Finally, there are unauthorized signs, such as graffiti, which break and transgress whatever rules there are.

An example illustrating the distinction between more situated and more decontextualized signs would be Stroud and Mpendukana's discussion of how signs of necessity are much more tied to a specific local place than signs of luxury. Another example is Leeman and Modan's (2009) distinction between the more instrumental signs of Chinese-owned businesses and the more symbolic signs of second-wave corporate-owned businesses in Washington DC Chinatown. The instrumental signs in the shop windows of the Chinese-owned establishments are highly situated: they acquire their full meaning in the particular context in which they are placed, indicating for instance the range of items for sale in *this* shop or the kinds of dishes available in *this* restaurant. On the other hand, the corporate-owned chain shops and restaurants tend to have signs placed on the storefront above the shop windows, or even higher up on the façade. The Chinese characters usually represent the name of the establishment, and they are used alongside the English name. But, as Leeman and Modan argue, the Chinese language is used here in a primarily symbolic, and hence also more decontextualized, way: rather than referring to one particular establishment, it is more part of the overall aesthetic design of the area, marking it as Chinatown.

Like Stroud and Mpendukana, Leeman and Modan, as well as Collins and Slembrouck, Scollon and Scollon also insist on the importance of contextualizing the analysis by incorporating an ethnographic and a historical dimension:

> The understanding of the visual semiotic systems at play in any particular instance relies crucially on an *ethnographic* understanding of the meanings of these systems within specific communities of practice.
>
> (Scollon and Scollon 2003: 160; our italics)

> Each of these discourses [the discourses of place semiotics] would have its own *history*, its own trajectory by which it came to be in that place, perhaps through architectural plans or municipal ordinance.
>
> (Scollon and Scollon 2003: 206; our italics)

It is therefore essential to gain a deep insight into the community of practice that one wants to investigate before one can fully understand the 'discourses in place', and this will involve both a historical study of the context of production of the signs and an ethnographic study of their context of reception.

FOR DISCUSSION: THE INTERCONNECTEDNESS OF LANGUAGE AND POLITICS

Discuss the interconnectedness between language and politics in relation to the following signs. The first sign is in Colmar, a town in Alsace, France (the text on the partly ripped-off sticker, which has been stuck onto the road sign, should read *Elsass frei*, German and Alsatian for 'Alsace free'). The second one is a sign in the window of a cheesesteak shop in Philadephia, USA (the sign has since been removed).

Figure 16.3 Sign in Colmar, Alsace

Figure 16.4 Sign in Philadelphia

FOR DISCUSSION: EXPLORING THE CONTEXT OF RECEPTION

Look at one or more of the linguistic landscape examples in this book and explore how you and your classmates react to them. Are there any significant differences between the responses?

PROJECT WORK: LINGUISTIC LANDSCAPE

Choose a multilingual site, e.g. an immigrant area in the city where you reside or perhaps the university campus (assuming that your university has a fairly international student body). Collect a large number of linguistic landscape items (if possible, use a digital camera to take photos, and do not forget to note down the emplacement of each sign that you photograph).

In your analysis, consider the following points:

- distinguish between top-down and bottom-up signs (if you find that this distinction, which has been criticized by Leeman and Modan (2009), applies to your data);
- distinguish between symbolic and instrumental uses of language;
- analyse the linguistic varieties used on the signs;
- analyse reader/viewer positioning;
- explore Scollon and Scollon's three systems of place semiotics:
    - code preference system
    - inscription system
    - emplacement system;
- try to add a historical dimension to your analysis (e.g. find out about urban planning policies or institutional language policies, if any).

PROJECT WORK: TRANSGRESSIVE SEMIOTICS

Conduct a study of transgressive signs. Take photos of graffiti and other unauthorized writings on walls, etc. Consider the same points as in the previous project work – though, obviously, not all of these will apply in the present case. You may find it useful to read through Pennycook's (2009) study of graffiti.

PROJECT WORK: THE CONTEXT OF PRODUCTION

Explore the context of production of some linguistic landscape items. Who commissioned, wrote, designed these signs? Conduct ethnographic interviews with (some of) these people. Ask questions about the choice of language(s), design, etc. on the signs, as well as about their emplacement (why in this particular location).

PROJECT WORK: THE CONTEXT OF RECEPTION

Explore the context of reception of some linguistic landscape items. Choose multilingual signs and/or monolingual signs in a minority language. Conduct ethnographic interviews with people who are the recipients (readers, viewers) of these signs: how do they interpret the signs? How do they react to the linguistic variety/ies used on the signs? etc. Make sure you interview people from both minority groups and the majority group. What differences are there between their readings? How can these differences be accounted for?

PROJECT WORK: ADVERTISING AND MULTILINGUALISM

In this project work, which brings together the media (discussed in Chapters 14 and 15) and linguistic landscape (discussed in this chapter), we invite you to explore the use of language in advertising. Collect a number of multilingual advertisements, which could be (photos of) advertising billboards, ads in newspapers or magazines, ads on the radio or TV, or on the Internet. Analyse both visual and verbal text. Try to account for language choice as well as translanguaging (if any). Analyse the linguistic varieties used in the ads, and distinguish between symbolic and instrumental uses of language. Also consider whether reader/viewer positioning is relevant. A good place to start reading is Kelly-Holmes' *Advertising as Multilingual Communication.*

REFERENCES AND SUGGESTIONS FOR FURTHER READING

Multimodal discourse analysis

de Saint-Georges, Ingrid and Weber, Jean-Jacques (eds) (2013) *Multilingualism and Multimodality: Current Challenges for Educational Studies*, Rotterdam: Sense.

Kress, Gunther (2009) *Multimodality: A Social Semiotic Approach to Contemporary Communication*, Abingdon: Routledge.

—— and van Leeuwen, Theo (2006) *Reading Images: The Grammar of Visual Design*, Abingdon: Routledge.

Linguistic landscape

Ben-Rafael, E., Shohamy, E., Amara, M. and Trumper-Hecht, N. (2004) *Linguistic Landscape and Multiculturalism: A Jewish-Arab Comparative Study*, Tel Aviv: Tami Steinmetz Center for Peace Research.

Blackwood, Robert, Lanza, Elizabeth and Woldemariam, Hirut (eds) (2016) *Negotiating and Contesting Identities in Linguistic Landscapes*, London: Bloomsbury.

Blommaert, Jan (2013) *Ethnography, Superdiversity and Linguistic Landscapes: Chronicles of Complexity*, Bristol: Multilingual Matters.

Collins, James and Slembrouck, Stef (2004) 'Reading shop windows in globalized neighbourhoods: Multilingual literacy practices and indexicality', *Working Papers on Language, Power and Identity* 21. http://bank.ugent.be/lpi.

Gorter, Durk (ed.) (2006) *Linguistic Landscape: A New Approach to Multilingualism*, Clevedon: Multilingual Matters.

Huebner, Thom (2006) 'Bangkok's linguistic landscapes: Environmental print, codemixing and language change', *International Journal of Multilingualism*, 3: 31–51.

Hult, Francis (2009) 'Language ecology and linguistic landscape analysis', in E. Shohamy and D. Gorter (eds) *Linguistic Landscape: Expanding the Scenery*, Abingdon: Routledge, 88–104.

Jaworski, Adam and Thurlow, Crispin (eds) (2010) *Semiotic Landscapes: Language, Image, Space*, London: Continuum.

Landry, Rodrigue and Bourhis, Richard Y. (1997) 'Linguistic landscape and ethnolinguistic vitality: An empirical study', *Journal of Language and Social Psychology*, 16: 23–49.

Leeman, Jennifer and Modan, Gabriella (2009) 'Commodified language in Chinatown: A contextualized approach to linguistic landscape', *Journal of Sociolinguistics*, 13: 332–62.

Lou, Jackie Jia (2016) *The Linguistic Landscape of Chinatown: A Sociolinguistic Ethnography*, Bristol: Multilingual Matters.

Pennycook, Alastair (2009) 'Linguistic landscapes and the transgressive semiotics of graffiti', in E. Shohamy and D. Gorter (eds) *Linguistic Landscape: Expanding the Scenery*, Abingdon: Routledge, 302–12.

Rubdy, Rani and Ben Said, Selim (eds) (2015) *Conflict, Exclusion and Dissent in the Linguistic Landscape*, Basingstoke: Palgrave.

Scollon, Ron and Scollon, Suzie Wong (2003) *Discourses in Place: Language in the Material World*, London: Routledge.

Shohamy, Elana (2006) *Language Policy: Hidden Agendas and New Approaches*, Abingdon: Routledge.

——, Ben-Rafael, Eliezer and Barni, Monica (eds) (2010) *Linguistic Landscape in the City*, Bristol: Multilingual Matters.

Stroud, Christopher and Mpendukana, Sibonile (2009) 'Towards a material ethnography of linguistic landscape: Multilingualism, mobility and space in a South African township', *Journal of Sociolinguistics*, 13: 363–86.

Peripheral normativity

Blommaert, Jan, Huysmans, M., Muyllaert, N. and Dyers, C. (2005) 'Peripheral normativity: Literacy and the production of locality in a South African township school', *Linguistics and Education*, 19: 374–403.

Advertising and multilingualism

Kelly-Holmes, Helen (2008) *Advertising as Multilingual Communication*, Basingstoke: Palgrave.

TEST YOURSELF QUIZ PART V*

1. Is integration something that can be measured and quantified?
2. Explain in what way the discourse of integration is informed by a deficit model and an ideology of superiority.
3. Why do many people believe that immigrants assimilated more smoothly in the 'good old days'?
4. In what sense do the language-ideological debates analysed by Blackledge constitute a struggle 'over the kind of nation that Britain imagines itself to be'?
5. What different activities have been constructed as being 'un-American', both in the past and in the present?
6. Why is there a frequent focus in attempts at language policing on such (seemingly minor) aspects as anglicisms or orthographic deviations from the standard?
7. Why is an ethnographic dimension important both for new media sociolinguistics and for linguistic landscape studies?
8. What is a multimodal discourse analysis, and why do we need it?
9. Explain why Leeman and Modan refer to the Washington DC Chinatown as a 'Disneyfied landscape'.
10. If you were teaching a pre-school or primary class, what would be your policy concerning the linguistic landscape of your classroom? Include in your answer a consideration of the roles of immigrant minority languages. Also explain why you would choose this policy.

*Suggested answers can be found on page 296.

PART VI

Further directions in the study of multilingualism

CHAPTER 17

Conclusion

Just as we started Chapter 1 with an intertextual reference to E.M. Forster's *Howards End* (did you spot it?), we now conclude this book with a quotation from another masterpiece of English literature, Henry Fielding's *Tom Jones*:

> We are now, reader, arrived at the last stage of our long journey. As we have therefore travelled together through so many pages, let us behave to one another like fellow-travellers in a stage-coach, who have passed several days in the company of each other; and who, notwithstanding any bickerings or little animosities which may have occurred on the road, generally make all up at last, and mount, for the last time, into their vehicle with chearfulness and good-humour; since, after this one stage, it may possibly happen to us, as it commonly happens to them, never to meet more.
>
> (*Tom Jones*, Penguin, 1749/1968, p. 813)

Thus reads the first paragraph of the last book of Fielding's famous eighteenth-century novel. We, too, have travelled a long way together on the road of multilingualism and have almost reached the end of our journey. We have seen many things together on the way, potentially learned to think more critically about our own language ideologies and hopefully gained a deeper understanding of numerous issues, such as:

- what a language is, and what multilingualism is;
- what the chances and pitfalls of revitalizing a language are;
- what the links between language and identity are;
- how societies attempt – and sometimes fail – to manage the multilingualism in their midst;

- how multilingual systems of education can best be organized, and how mother tongue and heritage education programmes sometimes lack the necessary flexibility;
- how policy and media discourses frequently aim to impose homogeneity and monoglossia upon societal diversity and heterogeneity.

You may not have agreed with everything we have said about these (and many other) topics and formed your own thoughts about them. But, above all, we hope you have enjoyed the journey.

This book is only a brief introduction to the social aspects of multilingualism, and has not been able to offer an exhaustive coverage of all the fascinating topics to do with multilingualism. In the following section, therefore, we list some further research directions in the study of multilingualism, and in the final section, at the risk of becoming over-pedantic, we summarize three main lessons to be kept in mind as key pointers towards a brighter multilingual future, a future without linguistic repression. For you, the reader of this book, we hope that this is the beginning of a long journey, and that the book has whetted your appetite to get involved in your own research on multilingualism.

FURTHER DIRECTIONS IN THE STUDY OF MULTILINGUALISM

Multilingualism is an exciting research topic to study because it is about people's use of language in the real world. It is people who translanguage and mix their languages, who set up fixed or flexible educational systems and who have certain ideas about how their societies should deal with multilingualism. Because human behaviour is so multifaceted, there are always new developments in the study of multilingualism and new research areas opening up: in this section, we briefly discuss four such areas which we have not been able to fully include in this short introductory textbook.

Multilingualism and sign language

The first research area is bi-/multilingualism and sign language. According to Grosjean (2008, 2010), many deaf people are bilingual in their sign language and the majority language in its written form (and sometimes also in its spoken form). He advocates this type of bilingualism (and biculturalism) as the best form of linguistic education for deaf children. Learning sign language will foster the development of the spoken language in deaf children, whereas a strictly auditory education frequently does not allow them to develop their spoken language to a high degree of fluency:

> A sign language–oral language bilingualism is the only way that Deaf children will meet their many needs, that is, communicate early on with their parents, develop their cognitive abilities, acquire knowledge of the world, communicate fully with the surrounding world, and acculturate into the world of the hearing and of the Deaf.
> (Grosjean 2008: 233)

Grosjean's views are confirmed by many studies including, for instance, Koïshi's (2010) study of deaf education in Japan. She discusses the limitations of the traditional audio-oral method (of lip-reading), and shows the importance of education through Japanese sign language for deaf children. New and highly successful bilingual and bicultural schools teaching both Japanese sign language and (written) Japanese have opened in Tokyo since the turn of the twenty-first century. This implies a positive shift in the perception of deaf children from being physically disabled to speaking a minority language (namely, Japanese sign language).

Multilingual assessment

Most child language assessments in use nowadays are based on monolingual standards and hence are unsuitable for multilingual children. Indeed, they can lead to wrong diagnoses of children as suffering from language delay or impairment, which in turn can have very serious consequences for the children concerned. In school environments marked by high-stakes testing (such as the No Child Left Behind policy in the US), monolingual assessment in the dominant language reinforces the perception of migrant or other emergent bi-/multilingual students as a 'problem'. In a revealing study, Escamilla (2006) shows how Latino students in Colorado fared in the high-stakes tests: when they were tested in Spanish, the results were highly positive, but these results were discounted and ignored in an environment that only valued monolingual English language proficiency. When, on the other hand, they were tested in English and the results were not so positive (unsurprisingly, since many of them were only in the process of acquiring the language), then the blame was put not on an inequitable testing regime but on the alleged shortcomings of bilingual education programmes: these students do too much in Spanish and not enough in English. In this way, the solutions advocated consisted mostly in abolishing bilingual education and subjecting these students to monolingual English-only instruction. Escamilla (2006: 195–6) comments upon such proposed 'remedies' in the following way:

> The notions that being poor, and speaking Spanish are explanations for low achievement are so prevalent that they go unquestioned. When counter evidence is presented, this evidence is often ignored.

> Most alarming, however, is the great potential that exists for educators and policy-makers to prescribe inappropriate educational solutions to ELL [English language learner] students because they have misdiagnosed and misunderstood the nature of perceived underachievement .... In spite of evidence of success of teaching and testing ELL students in Spanish, school districts in Colorado continue to propose to solve the 'problem of educating Spanish-speaking students' with programs that devalue Spanish and emphasize English.

Escamilla advocates just the opposite solution: more bilingual education and more bilingual testing in both English and Spanish as a way of allowing the Latino students to show their knowledge in each language. Alternatively, they could be given tests in English, but with glosses or translations provided in Spanish. While such measures would increase the reliability, validity and equitability of tests, they are still limited in their perception of bilingualism as double monolingualism: the Latino students would simply be given standard monolingual assessments in two languages (instead of just one). In this way, assessment is still based on monolingual standards.

There is therefore an urgent need to develop multilingual norms for the assessment of multilingual children (Cruz-Ferreira 2010). Such flexible bi- or multilingual tests would have to take into account the integrated nature of the students' bi-/multilingual competence. Moreover, flexible multilingual assessments need to be implemented at all levels from early childhood to adulthood: not only for early language development tests but also for integration and citizenship tests (see Chapter 13). Unfortunately, however, very little work has been done in this area so far, and thus it should constitute one of the highest priorities for future research on multilingualism (for recent work in this direction, see Gorter 2017).

What could such multilingual forms of assessment look like? A highly promising form in this respect is dynamic assessment (Lantolf and Thorne 2006: 327–57). Dynamic assessment is based on Vygotskyan sociocultural principles of learning and reserves a crucial role for performance prompts, hints and leading questions by the examiner during the assessment procedure. Of course, these prompts, hints and questions could be administered in a multilingual or translanguaging mode. In this way, dynamic assessment takes us worlds away from high-stakes testing, with the examiner becoming a mediator whose primary concern is to help children develop their sociocognitive and linguistic abilities.

Multilingualism and gender

The study of how language use and multilingualism intersect with ideologies of gender goes back at least to seminal work by Gal (1978). Recent work that builds upon Gal to explore the nexus between language, gender and political economy includes Canagarajah's (2011: 85) discussion of how Sri Lankan Tamil women living in the diaspora (Toronto, London and Lancaster, California) turn away from Tamil and embrace English 'as a way out of their unequal and restricted life conditions'. It also includes Nguyen's (2007) ethnographic investigation of the multilingual and multiethnic village of Dong Son in Northern Vietnam in 2002. In Vietnam, the majority group is the Kinh or Viet people, and the largest ethnic minority is the Tay people. The official language is Vietnamese, and the minority languages (such as Tay) are used less and less. Especially among the younger generations, there has been a marked shift from the minority languages to Vietnamese.

In Dong Son, the majority of villagers are Tay. One 'rich point' (see Chapter 2) that Nguyen came across in her ethnographic fieldwork was the following, rather unexpected and surprising, paradox: in the village, most men (both Tay and Viet) as well as Tay women prefer to use Vietnamese when interacting with unfamiliar people in public spaces. The only exception to this general pattern is a number of Viet women who moved into the village when they married local men. Even though these women are native speakers of Vietnamese (the dominant or prestige language), they seem to avoid this language and prefer to use Tay in their interactions with unfamiliar people in public spaces. How can the strange language choice of these bilingual women be accounted for?

The explanation Nguyen presents is a historical one that goes back to the American war in Vietnam (1954–75) and its effects on linguistic practices in a multilingual society. After the war, there were far more women than men (many of whom had been killed or wounded) and it was very difficult for women to find a husband. The Viet women who found a Tay husband moved into Dong Son at a time when Tay was still widely spoken, so that they quickly learnt the language. Since then, the linguistic situation has been almost completely reversed, with Vietnamese being spoken much more widely than Tay nowadays. But why do these Viet women continue to use Tay with unfamiliar people in public spaces? Here is what one of them says:

> I don't know what others [Viet women] think. But, I don't want aliens to find out that I am a Viet woman who couldn't find a Viet husband.
>
> (Nguyen 2007: 363)

Thus these women's avoidance of Vietnamese in public spaces shows, as Nguyen (2007: 363) puts it, 'how a historical event like a war interacts with local ideologies of gender to put pressure on a woman's life not only during the war but also long after that'. Nguyen (2007: 363) concludes that gendered linguistic practices can only be understood in their historical context, because they are often shaped by socio-political events.

The interplay of social and affective factors

In this section, we do not discuss so much a particular theme in the study of multilingualism as push back the borders of this book, which focuses on the social aspects. We provide a brief glimpse into the fascinating interconnectedness of social and cognitive approaches. If there is a specific theme here, it is the link between multilingualism and emotions. Readers interested in taking the leap and exploring the cognitive and emotional dimensions of multilingualism are referred to the excellent work done by Pavlenko (2006, 2008) in this area. Here we look at two other studies that illustrate particularly well the complex interplay between social, cognitive and affective factors. It is a topic that has been present though largely backgrounded in chapters such as the one on language and identity, namely the important role that all of these factors play in the processes of second language acquisition and of identity construction.

The first study we discuss is Norton (2013), who sees the process of second language learning as shaped by learners' emotional investments in new identities, and their desire to become members of particular communities. However, Norton's study also shows that affective factors such as **investment** are not sufficient to ensure language learning, but they can be blocked by issues of power and access. In particular, migrants are often, as Norton (2013: 64) puts it, caught in a Catch-22 situation: they need to have command of the dominant language to gain access to relevant social networks, but they cannot develop fluency without access to these networks.

One of the participants in Norton's study was Eva, a Polish immigrant to Canada. Eva had a high level of investment in learning English for both educational and professional reasons (hope of attending a Canadian institution of higher education and need to find a job). She was accepted on a language course where she learnt the basics of English grammar, vocabulary and pronunciation, and felt that what she needed upon completion of the course was lots of practice to gain fluency in the language. She managed to find a job in a fast food restaurant, where she worked alongside anglophone Canadians, which in theory should have provided her with the necessary opportunities to practise her English. In fact, however, Eva was given all the 'hard jobs' to do, such as cleaning the floors or taking out the trash, which involved very little interaction with either co-workers or customers. In this way, she also had very little language practice, as she had no access to the anglophone social networks in her workplace. Her co-workers looked down upon her as the 'stupid' immigrant, thus effectively silencing and marginalizing her.

The other important study that reveals the intricate interconnectedness of, on the one hand, social and, on the other hand, cognitive and emotional factors is Koven (2006, 2007). It shows how multilingual speakers can have different affective styles and repertoires, and how this influences the different ways in which they perceive themselves. Koven explores the bilingual identities of young luso-descendant women living in the Paris area, and how they experience the link between language, self and emotion. She is concerned with describing her participants' experience of being a 'different person' in their two languages, in the sense that their varieties of French are experienced as indexing the identity of young (sub)urban Parisians, whereas their varieties of Portuguese are experienced as indexing the identity of provincial villagers (reflecting their parents' rural origins).

Koven paints a detailed picture of how the women enact bilingual selves differently in each language. For instance, they make use of very colloquial or even 'vulgar' registers – including many emotional expressions – in the French-language narratives that they recount, but not in their Portuguese-language ones. An example is Teresa's use of 'vous êtes qu'un con' (you're just an asshole) in the French telling, with an equivalent expression completely missing from her Portuguese retelling of the same story. Koven (2007: 198) speculates as follows:

> Perhaps [Teresa] feels she cannot fully evoke personas of vulgar, racially marked insulters in Portuguese – because such comparable personas are not available to her, culturally, or personally. She may either not be able to or not feel comfortable making him and herself feel equally 'vulgar' in Portuguese as in French.

Teresa did not feel able or 'entitled' to enact the identity of the aggressive and assertive (sub)urban youth in the Portuguese retelling of her story. In other words, this identity of the tough Parisian youth speaking in emotional and vulgar registers is available to her in French but somehow she did not deem it appropriate for herself in Portuguese. There is thus a difference between what bilinguals such as Teresa 'can "do" and who they can "be" in each language' (Koven 2007: 72), and Koven concludes that this underlies their feeling of being a 'different person' in French and Portuguese.

NORMALIZING MULTILINGUALISM

Finally, we have selected three important themes out of many possible ones, which we think are worth flagging up once again here at the very end of the book, because together they point to the ultimate aim that we should all strive for: namely, the normalization of multilingualism.

(1) understanding the ubiquity of multilingualism

We have seen that named languages are social constructs; the linguistic reality, on the other hand, is the coexistence of a huge range of varieties which are not bounded entities but are in contact with, and influence, each other. They constantly change, moving closer to (sometimes mixing or merging with) some varieties and distancing themselves from others. What this implies is that multilingualism is ubiquitous, and it makes no real difference whether we translanguage among, say, German and Dutch or among standard German and Bavarian German.

(2) acknowledging the linguistic diversity in the world

Protecting the world's linguistic diversity should not be limited to revitalizing the standard varieties of particular languages which are perceived as being endangered. It should also involve the recognition of the new linguistic diversity emerging every day in our quickly changing and globalizing world. This refers for instance to the mixed youth languages which are spreading in many urban areas all over the world. Such varieties should not be stigmatized as 'bad' or 'inferior' (to the standard); on the contrary, if they are part of children's home language repertoires, they should be used as *additional* media of instruction in all progressive (flexible multilingual) educational systems. This leads directly to the following point.

(3) building upon the whole of students' linguistic repertoires

It is essential for teachers to respect the whole of their students' linguistic repertoires if they want to provide them with the best possible chances of educational success. This means neither simplifying the children's repertoires by reducing them to a small number of standard languages nor merely celebrating their multilingualism. On the contrary; teachers actually need to build upon all of the children's linguistic resources in a positive and constructive way. Starting from what children already know is the best way of making them aware of the differences between standard and (their own) non-standard varieties and, in this way, developing their proficiency in the standard school language(s).

In Chapter 9, we briefly referred to Cenoz's (2008: 26) continuum of more to less multilingual schools. However, what seems to us a much more useful distinction would be a continuum from more to less flexible educational systems. Indeed, multilingual educational systems can be very 'fixed' and rigid, and hence not very open to any form of linguistic diversity going beyond the traditional one (as we have seen in Chapter 9 in the case of

Luxembourg and Catalonia). In the end, it is a matter of attitudes of social actors – whether teachers, policy-makers or people in general. And the reason why it is difficult to change these attitudes is that frequently underlying them is a fear of losing one's language, identity, power or privileges, a fear of other languages and other people. In the Christian world, this attitude towards multilingualism and diversity goes back all the way to the Bible with its well-known tower of Babel metaphor, which is often popularly interpreted as presenting multilingualism in a negative way, almost as a curse or punishment meted out to human beings by god (see also Chapter 14 for analysis of negative representations of multilingualism). To counteract these negative attitudes, it is necessary to move beyond programmes of linguistic normalization focused upon one single minority language (e.g. the normalization of Catalan in Catalonia, as discussed in Chapter 9) and to work towards the normalization of multilingualism itself – of all forms of multilingualism, without any restrictions, both at school and in society as a whole. If this book has made a little contribution to this aim, then it will not have been written in vain.

REFERENCES AND SUGGESTIONS FOR FURTHER READING

Multilingualism and sign languages

Grosjean, François (2008) *Studying Bilinguals*, Oxford: Oxford University Press.

—— (2010) 'Bilingualism, biculturalism, and deafness', *International Journal of Bilingual Education and Bilingualism*, 13: 133–45.

Koïshi, Atsuko (2010) 'L'éducation des enfants sourds au Japon: ouverture d'une première école bilingue/biculturelle à Tokyo', in S. Ehrhart, C. Hélot and A. Le Nevez (eds) *Plurilinguisme et formation des enseignants*, Frankfurt/Main: Peter Lang, 145–56.

Schembri, Adam C. and Lucas, Ceil (eds) (2015) *Sociolinguistics of Deaf Communities*, Cambridge: Cambridge University Press.

Multilingual assessment

Cruz-Ferreira, Madalena (ed.) (2010) *Multilingual Norms*, Frankfurt/Main: Peter Lang.

Escamilla, Kathy (2006) 'Monolingual assessment and emerging bilinguals: A case study in the US', in O. García, T. Skutnabb-Kangas and M.E. Torres-Guzmán (eds) *Imagining Multilingual Schools*, Clevedon: Multilingual Matters, 184–99.

Gorter, Durk (ed.) (2017) *Education and Multilingualism: Navigating Policy and Assessment*, special issue of *Language and Education*, 31 (3).

Hopewell, Susan and Escamilla, Kathy (2014) 'Struggling reader or emerging biliterate student? Reevaluating the criteria for labeling emerging bilingual students as low achieving', *Journal of Literacy Research*, 46: 68–89.

Lantolf, James P. and Thorne, Steven L. (2006) *Sociocultural Theory and the Genesis of Second Language Development*, Oxford: Oxford University Press.

Multilingualism and gender

Canagarajah, A. Suresh (2011) 'Diaspora communities, language maintenance, and policy dilemmas', in T.L. McCarty (ed.) *Ethnography and Language Policy*, New York: Routledge, 77–97.

Gal, Susan (1978) 'Peasant men can't get wives: Language change and sex roles in a bilingual community', *Language and Society*, 7: 1–17.

Nguyen, Binh (2007) 'Gender, multilingualism and the American war in Vietnam', in B. McElhinny (ed.) *Words, Worlds, and Material Girls: Language, Gender, Globalization*, Berlin: Mouton de Gruyter, 349–67.

Pavlenko, Aneta, Blackledge, Adrian, Piller, Ingrid and Teutsch-Dwyer, Marya (eds) (2001) *Multilingualism, Second Language Learning, and Gender*, Berlin: Mouton de Gruyter.

Takahashi, Kimie (2012) 'Multilingualism and gender', in M. Martin-Jones, A. Blackledge and A. Creese (eds) *The Routledge Handbook of Multilingualism*, London: Routledge, 419–35.

The interplay of social and affective factors

Koven, Michèle (2006) 'Feeling in two languages: A comparative analysis of a bilingual's affective displays in French and Portuguese', in A. Pavlenko (ed.) *Bilingual Minds*, Bristol: Multilingual Matters, 84–117.

—— (2007) *Selves in Two Languages: Bilinguals' Verbal Enactments of Identity in French and Portuguese*, Amsterdam: Benjamins.

Norton, Bonny (2013) *Identity and Language Learning: Extending the Conversation* (2nd edition), Bristol: Multilingual Matters.

Pavlenko, Aneta (ed.) (2006) *Bilingual Minds: Emotional Experience, Expression and Representation*, Bristol: Multilingual Matters.

—— (2008) *Emotions and Multilingualism*, Cambridge: Cambridge University Press.

Language, multilingualism and education

Cenoz, Jasone (2008) 'Achievements and challenges in bilingual and multilingual education in the Basque Country', *AILA Review*, 21: 13–30.

TEST YOURSELF QUIZ PART VI – OVERALL REVIEW*

1. What is the problem with the terms L1, L2, L3, etc.?
2. What is the problem with the term 'code-switching'?
3. Remember Meeuwis and Blommaert's example (that we discussed in Chapter 7) of code-switching between two code-switched codes (Lingala-French and Swahili-French): how many languages are involved in this case?
4. Discuss the link between globalization and language variation.
5. Is Kven a dialect or a language?
6. Explain the difference between individual and societal multilingualism.
7. What are the main criteria for *flexible* multilingual education systems?
8. What is the main problem with mother tongue education programmes?
9. What is the main difference between mother tongue education and heritage language education?
10. What would multilingual forms of assessment look like, and what are the main difficulties in implementing them?

*Suggested answers can be found on page 297.

Notes on the activities

CHAPTER 2: THE IMPORTANCE OF BEING CRITICAL

a) As the cancer spreads
According to Fairclough (1989), this metaphor represents social problems (the 1981 'riots') as a disease ('cancer') that undermines the health of society. The choice of metaphor has ideological and social implications: it implies a certain way of dealing with events, in the sense that 'one does not arrive at a negotiated settlement with cancer .... Cancer has to be eliminated, cut out' (Fairclough 1989: 100).

b) Her family wished to secure me, because I was of good race.
In this sentence and in the whole of chapter 27 in *Jane Eyre*, from which this sentence is taken, Rochester expresses his sense of nationalist and racial superiority. Because Bertha was born in the Caribbean and is not (pure) English, he looks upon her as racially inferior.

c) *Education précoce* groups include both Luxembourgish children and children who have learnt another L1.
The text relies upon an 'us vs. them' discourse, differentiating between 'Luxembourgish children' and those using 'another L1'. The Luxembourgish children are perceived as being a homogeneous group with one and only one home language (namely Luxembourgish), thus erasing large numbers of children from mixed marriages with more than one home language. The migrant children are similarly homogenized as having an L1 other than Luxembourgish. In this way, Luxembourgish children are simply assumed to have Luxembourgish as their L1, otherwise they are categorized as 'foreign'.

CHAPTER 4: LINGUISTIC VARIABLES

(a) morphological level, variable (ly): 'serious' vs. 'seriously'. As a speaker of English, can you hypothesize what external factors this variable might be correlated with?
(b) syntactic level: genitive case (des Wetters) vs. dative case (dem Wetter). The use of the dative after the preposition 'wegen' is often considered to be more colloquial than the genitive.
(c) syntactic level: present perfect tense vs. simple past tense. In this case, the variation is more geographical, with present perfect frequently being preferred in most of Spain, while simple past tends to be more common in Galicia, León, Asturias, the Canary Islands and Hispanic America.

CHAPTER 4: LINGUISTIC VARIATION IN TIME AND SPACE

Beowulf

We have heard of the might in days of yore of the Spear-Danes, kings of the people.

The General Prologue

line 1: shoures soote = sweet showers

line 4: of which virtue the flower is engendered (i.e. whose creative power or influence brings the flowers into blossom)

line 13: palmeres = pilgrims wearing a palm leaf or branch in their hats;

strondes = shores

line 14: to far-away shrines, known in sundry lands

Wuthering Heights

I'd rather he [Heathcliff] had gone himself for the doctor! I would have taken care of the master better than him – and he wasn't dead when I left, nothing of the sort.

Sozaboy

J.J.C. = 'Johnny Just Come' (an expression the protagonist uses to refer to beautiful women) wey = who

soza = war

sozaboy = soldier

CHAPTER 5: THE DISCOURSE OF ENDANGERMENT

- The author of the letter to the editor uses a metaphor from gambling (what is at stake) to emphasize the high level of risk and danger of loss, and a metaphor from the domain of health (strengthen our endangered or dying language), evoking an image of Luxembourgish as an ailing patient who needs to be given powerful drugs to restore her or his bodily strength.
- Read Horner (2005) for a cogent argument that standardization and linguistic purism can be regarded as two sides of the same coin.

CHAPTER 7: SPATIAL REPERTOIRES

The Italian *formaggio* is part of the spatial repertoire of this restaurant; it is the word commonly used in this particular space. Pennycook and Otsuji (2014: 174) comment as follows on this extract:

> Here the Italianness of the pizza restaurant intervenes in their linguistic negotiations, as Krzysztof ... searches for their shared resource for talking about cheese. It is not of course Polish that is intervening here but the Italian *formaggio* which is a well-established 'ingredient' of the repertoire of this space.

CHAPTER 7: THE STORY OF THE DIFFICULT CUSTOMER

According to Sebba, the storyteller mostly associates London English with his own speech and actions, and London Jamaican with the customer's. Thus, in this case London Jamaican is *not* a we-code, as we might have expected; on the contrary, it is used to distance the customer and to create his 'otherness'. Sebba also notes that the impersonation of the shop manager is done in a 'posh' accent or voice – an example of what Bakhtin would call uni-directional stylization (since here it is not the manager but the difficult customer who is being evaluated negatively and laughed at). Hence, this example shows us again how important it is to analyse language use in its actual context and not to rely on stereotyped attributions.

CHAPTER 7: TRANSLANGUAGING AND STYLIZATION

Asiye tells Eda to speak Danish. Most likely, Asiye is here stylizing the voice of a teacher (i.e. this is what they have frequently been told to do by many teachers). It is a case of vari-directional (ironic) stylization, since Asiye does not follow her own stricture and switches into Turkish herself in her next turn. Jørgensen (2005: 400) comments that Asiye voices an utterance (*you must speak Danish*) which is not her own, knowing that it represents a normative attitude that neither she nor her listeners 'intend to act according to'. Jørgensen (2005: 400) adds, referring to more utterances of this kind in the rest of the adolescents' conversation:

> They repeat the words of their masters, and on the surface they may pursue these to a certain extent, but at the same time the circumstances turn the words' original meanings around (if they are not ridiculed) into humorous imitations.

CHAPTER 8: ANGLICISM OR VERNACULAR FRENCH?

According to Heller (2006: 109), this extract 'encapsulates the two fronts on which [the school's] struggles for language quality are conducted: the struggle against English and the struggle against stigmatized variants within French (however fuzzy the boundaries of that language may be)'. It is mostly the purist and standard language ideologies that inform these struggles.

CHAPTER 12: DISCURSIVE OR INTERACTIONAL STRATEGIES

The mother uses what Lanza (2009) calls the 'minimal grasp strategy', until eventually the child switches over to German, the mother's language of choice. In other words, she pretends not to understand as long as the child uses the 'wrong' language with her.

CHAPTER 13: INTEGRATED SPEECH

The adolescents distinguish between two different ways of speaking Danish: street language and integrated speech. They associate the latter with the way their teachers speak. Jørgensen (2010) comments as follows upon their use of the word 'integrated':

> 'Integration' is a buzzword for Danish politicians, particularly politicians who think of minorities as problems. There is a strong undercurrent of non-accept of minorities in the discourse, and 'integration' is often taken to mean in reality 'assimilation', i.e. the underlying expectation is that the minorities at least hide their non-mainstream cultural features, clothing, religion as well as language, etc., from the public eye. It is obvious that the girls in [this] example combine the term 'integrated' with authority and the norms of the authorities.

Notes on the quizzes

QUIZ CHAPTER 1: INTRODUCTION

1. Switzerland: French, German, Italian, Romansch; USA: no official language (at the federal level); New Zealand: English and Māori; Belgium: French, Dutch and German.
2. Nash sings in Nouchi, and Amoc in Inari Sámi, mixed with English and other languages. For further details read Chapter 4 on Nouchi and Chapter 5 on Sámi.
3. Read Chapter 4 for information about Côte d'Ivoire. Didier Drogba is a well-known Ivoirian footballer (formerly playing for Chelsea), who campaigned for the political reunification of his country during the civil war of the early twenty-first century.
4. Hindustani is the vernacular mix of Hindi and Urdu spoken by many people in India (linguistically speaking, the two languages are virtually indistinguishable). Gandhi hoped that Hindustani would bring together the Hindu and Muslim population of India. However, the Hindu elite chose to promote (a purified) Hindi as an official language of India at the expense of Urdu, because the latter is the official language of Pakistan, the neighbouring country with which India has entertained highly strained relations.
5. See the section on Scots in Chapter 3.
6. Please consult Chapters 3 and 6 for Singlish, Chapter 4 for Verlan and Chapter 10 for the Ebonics debate (the variety is usually referred to as African-American English or African-American Vernacular English).
7. Chinese in fact refers to a whole range of languages spoken in China (and other Asian countries such as Singapore), from Cantonese in Hong Kong to Mandarin in Beijing. The standard variety Putonghua is based on Beijing Mandarin (see Chapter 6).

8. Apart from English, there are about 175 Native American languages still spoken in the United States. As for Spanish, which like English is a colonial language, it would probably also need to be looked upon as a language of the United States, since it was the main language spoken in the southwest (from Texas to California, and from Arizona and New Mexico to Utah and Nevada), which used to be part of Mexico until it was annexed by the US in the middle of the nineteenth century. See the discussion in Chapter 14.
9. English Only takes a subtractive approach in that it wants immigrants to switch over to English as quickly as possible: all immigrant minority languages should be eradicated (see Chapter 14); English Plus, on the other hand, takes an additive approach: immigrants should be allowed to maintain their own languages *plus* they should acquire English as quickly as possible.
10. See the discussion of this sign in Chapter 16.

QUIZ PART I

2. The difference is between going along with the assumptions made by/in the text vs. rejecting (some of) these assumptions. A good way to try this out is to look at advertisements or political discourse.
3. Key ideas for an answer include: qualitative and contextualized approach; thick description, deep understanding, in-depth analysis of certain people's life-worlds, their ways of acting and thinking; gaining access to their lived realities and seeing the world through their eyes.
4. A small-d discourse is the individual text that we want to analyse; Big-D Discourses consist of: (a) many individual texts (e.g. the Discourse of feminism) and (b) more than language (e.g. the Discourse of punks also consists of a certain way of behaving, of dressing, etc.).
6. The difference between a language and a dialect is socio-political rather than only linguistic – see Chapter 3.
7. The link between language and identity is important but not essential. For example, Irish identity has changed over the course of history but it has not been 'destroyed' even though most of the Irish have switched from Irish Gaelic to English as their primary language.

QUIZ PART II

2. To become aware of the complex issues involved, consider whether the following count as one or two languages: Cantonese and Mandarin; Flemish and Dutch; Swiss German and German; Scots and English; Croatian and Bosnian. What about the mixed urban vernaculars which are widely used in African cities? How do they count?

3. Each variety, whether perceived as a 'language' or a 'dialect', has its own grammatical system with systematic grammatical rules. (Otherwise how could we even try to put together a meaningful sentence in this particular variety?)
4. When considering this question, there is a need to remember that all languages are involved in constant processes of change, due to social pressures and other factors, with some varieties (languages, dialects) falling out of use and other new ones developing.
6. Many youth languages such as Verlan are what has been called 'anti-languages' and as such are indexical of oppositional identities, thus constituting an act of resistance against mainstream societal values.
8. If a community wants its language to be preserved, then as linguists we have a duty to help them. One frequently heard argument in favour of revitalization is that the loss of a language leads to the loss of the culture associated with this language. However, there is a need to relativize this rather essentialist position. (Thus, for instance, Irish culture continued despite the shift from Irish to English as the primary means of communication in Ireland. It may have changed but then culture is always a process that is subject to change.)
9. Advantages: a standard variety is needed for teaching purposes (although it is possible to take a more flexible approach, as in Corsica).

   Disadvantages: if the new standard variety is seen as being too artificial, it may not be widely accepted within the community (as happened with néo-Breton in Brittany).
10. Remember that the most important factor ensuring the survival of a language is family transmission of the language.

QUIZ PART III

1. In Singapore, the 'official mother tongue' is decided upon by the state: e.g. if you are ethnically Chinese, your offical mother tongue will be Mandarin, whether you actually speak Mandarin as a home language or not.
2. In Singapore, Mandarin has not only symbolic value (as being indexical of a Chinese Singaporean identity) but also more and more instrumental value, because of the growing importance of trade with the People's Republic of China.
3. Is it people's fear of the other in their midst (other languages, other cultures, other religions, other people)?
4. A language has symbolic value in that it is indexical of a particular identity; and it has instrumental value in that it is useful in a particular society for reasons such as being educationally successful, getting a job, doing business, etc.

5. When considering this question, we need to remember that, because identity is always a process of construction and negotiation between achieved and imposed identities, we cannot help being influenced – even unconsciously – by how other people categorize us.
6. Indexicality is the process of 'pointing to' something, as in (the use of) a particular variety pointing to (being indexical of) particular values or a particular identity.
9. The key ideology informing such negative attitudes is the ideology of language purism (see Chapter 2).

QUIZ PART IV

2. Teaching some non-linguistic subjects (history, biology. . .) through the medium of a foreign language can improve both students' knowledge of the subject and their competences in the foreign language.
3. Language-in-education policies are frequently informed by the ideology of languages as separate, bounded entities (ideology of fixed or separate bi-/multilingualism), whereas the multilingual realities of life for many people in today's world of migration and superdiversity tend to be much more flexible, fluid and heteroglossic.
4. Because that is the way we all learn new things: namely, by connecting what we already know with the new things we are learning.
5. Could recognizing AAE as a language be seen as a threat to national unity?
6. The standard varieties of these languages were artificially constructed by missionaries or colonial administrators during the colonial period and can be very different from the way people actually speak. Moreover, the fact that people of many different ethnicties live together in urban areas has led to the development of new urban vernaculars, especially among young people. Therefore, the education system should probably be based on these vernaculars that young people actually use, rather than on the artificial, colonial standards that hardly anybody uses.
7. Remember that a heritage language can be an indigenous minority language or an immigrant minority language.
8. Students worked as researchers doing projects on the role of languages in their community. They also took courses to develop both their heritage and academic English abilities and identities.

QUIZ PART V

1. Some aspects of integration can be quantified (employment rates, educational success rates) but others are much more difficult to quantify (feelings of belonging, etc.).

2. If certain people are seen as not (yet) being integrated, this implies that 'they' lack something that 'we' have (i.e. they have a deficit) and hence also that 'we' are superior to 'them'.
4. The basic issue is whether England is imagined as a monolingual, English-only 'nation' or a multilingual and multicultural one.
5. Activities sometimes seen as un-American:

   - in the 1950s, during the Cold War: being a Communist
   - increasingly nowadays: speaking Spanish or, more generally, a language other than English
   - increasingly nowadays also: being a Muslim.
6. Maybe it shows the strength of language ideologies such as the standard language ideology, the ideology of purism and the ideology of languages as separate, bounded entities.
7. An ethnographic study of the contexts of production and reception is needed to achieve a deeper understanding of what is going on.
8. A multimodal discourse analysis is needed for the analysis of public signs, advertisements, etc. which contain not only verbal but also visual elements.
9. Because the use of Chinese characters in the Washington DC Chinatown is largely just decorative (rather than communicative).

QUIZ PART VI – OVERALL REVIEW

1+2+3. The main issue in all three questions is the difficulty of defining what a 'language' is, and hence of counting 'languages'.

4. Linguistic variation is inherent to all languages. As for the spread of a global language such as English, it has led to the worldwide use of standard English (especially in writing), but at the same time it has also led to the development of innumerable local varieties (often referred to as World Englishes).
5. The question can only be answered from a socio-political (rather than linguistic) perspective. Whereas Kven used to be *perceived* as a dialect of Finnish, nowadays it tends to be *perceived* as a language in its own right.
6. Read Chapters 6–8 again if you are unsure about this.
7. In Chapter 9, we suggested the following five criteria: (a) building upon all the children's home language and literacy practices; (b) working towards educational equity; (c) using translanguaging pedagogies; (d) offering a range of educational tracks with different combinations of media of instruction; and (e) providing students with access to the important local and global languages (including English). However, you may consider other criteria to be more important than these.

8. A major issue is that mother tongue education programmes often ignore the dimension of language variation. (Again, you may see other issues as more fundamental ones.)
9. The main aim of mother tongue education is or should be to build upon the children's actual home linguistic resources to help them achieve educational success, whereas heritage language education is more concerned with the preservation of a particular 'heritage' (a language and culture shared by the community).
10. First of all, there is a need to consider whether administering tests in more than one language constitutes a multilingual form of assessment; as for the second question, there is a need to consider the role played by various language ideologies and how they potentially influence the attitudes of teachers, students, parents and policy-makers.

Author index

Adegbija, E. 99–100, 101
Agar, M. 18–19
Agard, J.: 'Cowtalk' 139
Ager, D. 133
Aldridge, M. 80
Alexander, N. 238
Amoc 13, 73
Anderson, B. 108
Androutsopoulos, J. 64, 241–2, 247, 252
Ansaldo, U. 245
Appadurai, A. 8
Auer, P. 22

Backus, A. 118–19
Bailey, B.H. 111, 113–14, 242
Bailey, G. 170
Baker, C. 131
Bakhtin, M.M. 114, 242
Bannerji, H. 125
Bardtenschlager, H. 171
Barradas, O. 184–5
Barth, F. 109
Baugh, J. 170
Bejarano, C.L. 118
Bennett, L. 64
Ben Rafael, E. 259–60
Bentahila, A. 76
Berryman, M. 81
Biko, S. 97
Bilaniuk, L. 91, 101
Blackledge, A. 7, 22, 26, 78, 105, 141, 170, 179–81, 222, 230–3, 273
Bloch, C. 169–70
Block, D. 44, 153
Blom, J.P. 112, 113
Blommaert, J. 3, 7, 18, 20–1, 23, 27–8, 31, 101, 112–13, 118–19, 209, 223, 229, 231, 243–4, 248, 263, 287
Blunkett, D. 232, 237–8
Bokhorst-Heng, W. 57, 93, 101
Bourdieu, P. 131, 243, 262
Bourhis, R.Y. 255
Bourne, J. 165
Brathwaite, E.K. 52–3
Breeze, J. 'Binta' 64
Brontë, C.: *Jane Eyre* 17
Brontë, E.: *Wuthering Heights* 54
Brutt-Griffler, J. 162, 164
Bucholtz, M. 18
Budach, G. 142, 171, 211
Burnaby, B. 125
Burns, R. 13
Busch, B. 119, 169

Cabau-Lampa, B. 185–6
Canagarajah, S. 110, 281
Castells, M. 8
Cenoz, J. 147–8, 284
Chaucer, G.: *Canterbury Tales* 53
Chen, Y. 188
Chick, K. 164
Cliff, M.: *No Telephone to Heaven* 235
Codo, E. 193–5
Coetzee, J.M.: *Waiting for the Barbarians* 9
Collins, J. 264, 267

Cook, S. 162–3
Cooke, M. 222
Corona, V. 146
Coulmas, F. 24
Coupland, N. 80
Coyle, D. 155
Crawford, J. 142, 239
Creese, A. 141, 170, 178–81
Creve, L. 229
Crowley, T. 39, 81
Cruz-Ferreira, M. 280
Cummins, J. 168, 185
Curdt-Christiansen, X.-L. 196

Danet, B. 246
Davies, E. 76
Davies, W.V. 25, 31
Davis, K. 144, 151, 183–4, 187
de Fina, A. 109
de Houwer, A. 196
Delanty, G. 8
Desani, G.V.: *All About H. Hatterr* 54
Deterding, D. 56
Deumert, A. 22–3, 243–4, 246, 251
Diam's 62
Dong Jie 18, 97
Doran, M. 61
Duchêne, A. 78, 191, 200
Duff, P. 124

Eades, D. 192
Ehrhart, S. 4
Erfurt, J. 142
Escamilla, K. 152–3, 279–80
Extra, G. 217, 219

Fairclough, N. 17
Fanon, F. 235
Fasold, R. 41
Faulks, K. 216
Fetterley, J. 16
Fielding, H.: *Tom Jones* 277
Fishman, J. 246
Fitzgerald, F. Scott: *The Great Gatsby* 237
Fogle, L.196
Fong, V. 55
Forster, E.M.: *Howards End* 277

Gal, S. 280–1
Gandhi, M.K. 13, 41
García, O. 110, 117, 141, 143, 149–52, 154, 174
Garner, S. 109
Gee, J.P. 18–21, 26, 31, 35, 38, 105–6, 208, 223
Geertz, C. 18, 243
Georgakopoulou, A. 64
Gorter, D. 255, 280
Grin, F. 92, 101
Grosjean, F. 278–9
Gu, M. 63
Guibernau, M. 108
Gumperz, J.J. 111–13, 120, 121
Gupta, A.F. 185
Guzula, X. 169

Haboud, M. 177–8
Haque, E. 125
Harris, R. 24, 179
Heller, M. 78, 124, 127–32
Hélot, C. 223
Herder, J.G. von 22–3, 27, 164
Herriman, M. 69
Herring, S. 241, 246
Hine, C. 243
Hogan-Brun, G. 217
Holliday, A. 23
Hood, P. 155
Hopewell, S. 152–3
Hornberger, N. 81
Horner, K. 25, 78, 144–5, 209, 227
Hornsby, M. 79
Huebner, T. 258–9
Hult, F. 259–60
Huntington, S. 237

Igboanusi, H. 100, 101
Irvine, J. 20
Isin, E.F. 217

Jacquemet, M. 196
Jaffe, A. 25, 81, 185
JanMohamed, A. 235
Jaworski, A. 255
Jenkins, R. 108
Johnson, L. Kwesi 64–5
Johnson-Laird, P.N. 19
Jørgensen, A.M. 64
Jørgensen, J.N. 4, 37, 120, 221
Joshi, P. 248

Kamberelis, G. 46
Kang, Phua Chu 62
Kelly-Holmes, H. 271
Kennedy, W.: *Legs* 55
King, K.A. 81, 177–8, 196
Klein, C. 145–6
Koïshi, A. 279
Korth, B. 92, 101
Kotthoff, H. 114–15
Koven, M. 117, 283
Kress, G. 255, 265
Kroskrity, P. 20, 217
Kulick, D. 47
Kunkel, M. 142
Kytölä, S. 250

Labov, W. 161
Lam, A. 96
Landry, R. 255
Lane, P. 72–3
Langer, N. 25, 31
Lantolf, J.P. 280
Lanza, E. 197, 201
Lasagabaster, D. 140
Lee, E. 57–8
Leeman, J. 260–4, 267, 270, 273
Le Nevez, A. 62
Lenihan, A. 249
Leppänen, S. 245, 250
Leung, C. 24, 179
Lim, L. 101, 245
Lin, A. 95
Lippi-Green, R. 25
Li Wei 110, 117, 188
Lo Bianco, J. 69
Logan-Terry, A. 196
Luykx, A. 198
Lytra, V. 182

McCarty, T.L. 175–6, 183
McDonald, M. 76
Mackay, N. 53
McLaughlin, F. 163
McNamara, T. 218–19
McWhorter, J. 42, 160
Maher, J. 44
Makoni, S. 162, 164, 167, 244
Mandela, N. 97–8
Mar-Molinero, C. 217
Marsh, D. 155
Martin, P. 150, 169
Martin-Jones, M. 149
Marxer, V. 208, 210, 213–14
Marxer, W. 208
Maryns, K. 195–6, 202
Mashiri, P. 162, 164, 167
May, S. 23, 31, 67, 70–1, 126, 133, 153
Meeuwis, M. 112–13, 287
Mehlem, U. 168
Menken, K. 142
Milroy, J. 21–2
Milroy, L. 21–2
Modan, G. 260–4, 267, 270, 273
Montgomery, M. 16
Moore, E. 146
Moore, H. 69–70
Mortimer, K. 178
Moyer, M. 191–3, 200
Mpendukana, S. 261–7
Mroczek, K. 241
Mufwene, S. 170
Musk, N. 80

Nash 13, 62
Newell, S. 60
Ngugi wa Thiong'o 161
Nguyen, B. 281–2
Nic Craith, M. 143
Nkence, N. 169
Norton, B. 57–8, 282

Orman, J. 244
O'Rourke, B. 79
Orwell, G. 237
Otheguy, R. 110
Otsuji, E. 4, 44, 119

Pakir, A. 101
Palmer, J.D. 105
Park, M.Y. 222
Parodi, C. 183
Patrick, D. 125–6
Pavlenko, A. 7, 22, 78, 90, 101, 105, 282
Pennycook, A. 4, 40–1, 44, 56–60, 62, 64, 95, 119, 166, 234, 270
Pérez-Báez, G. 199–200, 201
Peuronen, S. 245–6, 250
Pfaff, C. 64
Phillipson, R. 23–4, 44, 57
Phyak, P. 246–8, 251

Pietikäinen, S. 73–4, 80
Plester, B. 248
Portes, A. 8
Probyn, M. 98, 101, 164
Pujolar, J. 79, 146, 153

Ramallo, F. 79
Rampton, B. 7, 24, 108, 115–16, 179
Reeves, B. 234–6
Reid, W. 110
Rhydwen, M. 69
Ricento, T. 22
Rickford, J. 170
Rihanna 64
Roberts, C. 191, 200
Rojo, L. Martin 193
Romaine, S. 41, 47, 85
Romero-Little, M.E. 175
Rubdy, R. 94, 101
Rubino, A. 197
Rumbaut, R.G. 8
Rumford, C. 8
Rushdie, S. 9, 27

Salmons, J. 221
Saro-Wiwa, K.: *Sozaboy* 55, 99
Schiffman, H. 187
Schmid, C.L. 159–60
Schmidt, R. Sr. 236
Scollon, R. 255, 265–7, 270
Scollon, S. Wong 255, 265–7, 270
Sebba, M. 46, 51, 111, 119
Sefyu 62
Selvon, S.: *The Lonely Londoners* 54
Setati, M. 98, 101
Shakespeare, W.: *Julius Caesar* 54
Sherman, T. 249
Shohamy, E. 74–5, 77, 81, 217–18, 255, 260
Singh, I. 46
Skutnabb-Kangas, T. 23–4, 57
Slembrouck, S. 264, 267
Smith, A. 121
Sosa, L. 237
Spitzmüller, J. 133
Spolsky, B. 196–7
Spotti, M. 217, 219
Stenström, A.B. 64
Stevenson, P. 217
Stotz, D. 92, 101
Stroud, C. 150, 261–7
Süssmuth, R. 208–9
Svelch, J. 249

Taeschner, T. 201
Tagliamonte, S.A. 50
Thorne, S.L. 280
Thurlow, C. 241, 248, 255
Torres, L. 221
Tosi, A. 42
Trudgill, P. 36

Unamuno, V. 146–7
Urciuoli, B. 229

Valdés, G. 182–3
Van Avermaet, P. 217–18
Van Leeuwen, T. 255, 265
Van Lier, L. 105
Verschueren, J. 20, 23, 209, 223, 231
Vertovec, S. 6
Vygotsky, L.S. 280

Wachendorff, U. 211
Walsh, M. 68
Wang, W. 96
Watts, R. 91–2
Weber, J.-J. 78, 144–5, 151, 166–7, 209
Wee, L. 56, 63, 94, 101, 150
Widdowson, H. 4
Wiese, H. 64
Wiley, T. 141, 154
Wilkerson, M. 221
Willaert, E. 229
Williams, C. 80
Williams, R. 108
Wilson, W.H. 187
Wolf, H.-G. 100, 101
Wolfram, W. 47
Wood, C. 248
Wood, P.K. 217
Wright, S. 143, 154
Wu, C.-J. 188

Yamamoto, M. 197–8
Yang, G. 243
Young, A. 223

Zaimoglu, F. 64
Zepeda, O. 175
Zhu, H. 117

Subject Index

(A page number in bold refers to the page where a key concept is first introduced or where it is explained.)

Aboriginal languages: Australian 68–70
Abruzzese 42
Afghanistan 223
African-American English (AAE) 42, 49–52, 55, 117, 158–61, 170, 204, 252
Afrikaans 64, 97–8, 162, 251
Alemannic 114
Alsatian 37, 268
anglicism 127, **128**, 131–3, 135, 249, 251, 273
Aotearoa 70; *see also* New Zealand
Arabic 75, 168, 251, 259–60
Australia 40, 68–70, 79, 97, 119, 191, 197, 217–19; *see also* Aboriginal languages
authenticity **73**, 76, 129–31, 162–3, 212
Aymara 198

backstage language **193**
Bangladesh 115, 179–81
Baoule 59
Basque 140–1, 143, 146–9, 153, 204
Bavarian 110, 242, 284
Belgium 13, 28, 109, 112, 143–4, 223
Bengali 93, 175, 179–82, 184
Beowulf 53
Berber 61, 168
Bete 59
Bolivia 81, 176, 191, 198
Bosnia, Bosnian 21, 242
bottom-up sign *see* top-down sign
breathing space 246
Breton 68, 75–7, 81
Brunei 150
Burkina Faso 59

Calabrese 42
calque **245**
Cambodia 222
Canada 97, 124–32, 217, 282
Cantonese 56, 63, 93, 95, 100, 179, 188, 245
Cape Verdean Creole 166
Caribbean 36, 49, 52–5, 64, 111, 115, 119, 139, 178
Catalan, Catalonia 90, 140–1, 143, 146–9, 153–4, 193–4, 285
categorization 7, **104–6**, 117–18, 169, 195
CEFR (Common European Framework of Reference for Languages) 142, 154, 211, 214, 217–18
China 63, 90, 94–7, 100, 153, 188
Chinese 13, 246; Modern Standard Chinese 94–7, 186; on signs 261–2, 266–7; varieties of 21, 93–7, 100, 124, 188; *see also* Mandarin and Putonghua
citizenship 6, **216–17**; policies 10, 68, 208, 231–2; test 90, 140, 211–12, 217–20, 222, 280

CLIL (Content and Language Integrated Learning) 125, 142, 154–5, 204
Cockney 116
code-mixing **110**, 118, 170
code preference system **266**
code-switching 9, 56, 98, 287; and identity **110**, 111–19; situational vs. metaphorical **112–14**, 121, 135
commodification **130**
complementary school 179–82, 184, 188
Congo (Democratic Republic of) 112, 163
Corsican 25, 68, 76–7, 81, 185
Côte d'Ivoire 13, 49, 59–60, 62, 64, 153, 163
Cree 124
creole **39–40**, 46, 68, 97, 166, 183, 187, 195; Caribbean and Jamaican creoles 49, 51–3, 111, 115–16
Croatian 21
Czech 249

Danish 21, 89, 120, 221
deficit: discourse of 212, 215–16, 220, 227–9, 273
Denmark 72, 218
diglossia **5–6**
Dioula 59–60
discourse model 15, **19**, 35, 40, 208, 220, 223, 264; language ideologies as 20, 26, 28
dogma of homogeneism **23**, 143
Dominican Republic 113–14
Dong 96
Dutch 8, 97, 219, 229, 264–5; and German 21, 37–8, 110, 284

Ebonics 13, 158–60; *see also* African-American English
Ecuador 81, 174–5, 176–8
Emilian 42
emplacement system **266**, 270
endangered language 5, 9, 58, 81, 85, 147, 174; in Canada 126, 129; discourse of 20, 25, 27, 39, **44–5**, 78–80, 284; indigenous languages 67–79, 176, 200; in USA 141, 161, 175
England 38, 41–2, 81, 115, 178–81, 184, 231–3; *see also* UK
English: in Africa 97–100, 158, 161–5, 169–70, 195, 237–8; in Asia 63, 89, 93–6, 150, 197–8; in Australia 68–70, 119; in Canada 124–32, 282; in European countries 18, 91–2, 112, 142, 145–8, 152, 186, 204; as global language 49, 56–9, 67, 101, 151; in Israel 75; killer language 44, 85; as label 37, 45; in mixed codes 61–2, 73; in New Zealand 71; on signs 257–67; in social media 242–51; standard 36–7, 159–60; in UK 13, 90, 115–16, 120, 179–81, 230–3; in USA 113, 117–18, 141–2, 152–3, 175–6, 182–4, 199, 220–1, 233–7, 279–80; varieties of 35–40, 42–3, 46, 50–6, 64, 111; World Englishes 39–40; *see also* African-American English
English Only 13, 70, 141, 233–7, 238–9
essentialist: ideologies 111, 143, 166; link language–national identity 22–3; vs. social constructivist accounts of identity 106, **107–8**
Estonia 218
ethnicity 7, 93; ethnic identity 53, 92–4, **108–9**, 115–16, 150, 163–4; metroethnicity 44; reactive **8**
ethnography 15, 18–19, 264; digital 242–3; guerilla **243**
EU (European Union): citizenship and integration policies 217–19, 222, 223; policy of multilingualism 89, 132, 140, 145, 154–5, 184–7; policy on lesser used languages 67, 90, 140, 142, 143, 154

family language policy **196–200**, 201, 202
Finnish, Finland 72–3, 245–6, 250
fixed multilingualism 139–52, **140–1**
Flemish, Flanders 27–8, 37, 223, 229, 244, 264–5
flexible multilingualism 139–52, **140–1**; in EU 141–3, 184–7; in Luxembourg 143–6, 150–2, 166–7; multilingual education 149–52, 153–4, 166–8; in South Africa 161–6, 168–70; in Spain 146–9; in USA 141–3, 152–3
Florentine 42
France 6, 59–62, 68, 75–8, 124, 133, 268
French 51, 75, 77, 117, 163, 186, 223, 283; in Canada 124–32; as global

language 49, 64, 99, 132, 142, 161; in Luxembourg 17, 25, 78, 90, 143–7, 151–2, 166–7, 227–9, 256, 266; in Switzerland 91–2; youth languages and mixed codes 59–62, 76, 112–13, 287; *see also* Nouchi and Verlan
Frisian 37–8
frontstage language **193**

Gaelic 38–9, 81, 90, 219, 249
German 24, 89, 117, 125, 172, 200–1, 210, 214; in Luxembourg 18, 25, 78, 80, 90, 144–6, 151, 166–8, 227; on signs 256–8, 268; in social media 242, 244, 252; standard vs. non-standard varieties 21, 37–8, 50, 64, 110, 114–15, 284; in Switzerland 5–6, 91–2, 153, 159–60
Germany 64, 114, 133, 143–4, 168, 207–8, 214–15, 256
globalization **7–8**, 49, 92, 101, 152, 207, 216, 287; discourse/ideology of 73, 91, 266; vs. localization 245–6; on signs 257, 259
graffiti 267, 270
Guilin 96
Guiliu 96
Gujerati 93
Gullah 46
Gyeongsang 222

habitus 169, **243**
Haiti 127, 129
Hausa 99
Hawai'i 72, 183, 187, 204
Hawaiian 72, 183, 187
Hawai'i Creole English 46, 183, 187
Hebrew 68, 74–5, 76, 259–60
heritage: language education 5, 10, **174**, 175–88, 204, 207, 235, 278, 287; tourism 131, 132, 135
heteroglossia 74, 141, 149–50, 169, 176, 179, **242–6**, 250–2; heteroglossic contrast 241, **242**
Hindi 37, 41, 89, 93
Hindustani 13, 41
hip hop *see* rap
Hiri Motu 40
Hokkien 56, 58, 93

Hong Kong 63, 90, 94–8, 100, 153, 245, 266

identity text **168**
Igbo 99
Ilokano 183
impact belief **196**, 197, 199
indexicality 44, 60, 73, **113–15**, 118, 135, 164, 176, 179, 283; and signs 259, 265; and social media 242, 244, 246
India 13, 41, 52, 89, 93–4, 150, 153; Indian English 42, 54, 55
inscription system **266**, 270
instrumental use of language 56, 67, 70, 73, 94, 104, 125, 135; vs. symbolic 193, 242, **259**, 260–2, 266–7, 270
integration: discourse of 10, 20, 139–40, **207–9**, 209–23, 273, 280; integrated speech 221; language of 145; social vs. educational 146–7, 153
Inuktitut 124–6
investment **282**
Iraq 223
Ireland 81
Isicamtho 98, 163
Israel 68, 74–5, 79, 259–60
Italian: national language vs. 'dialects' 42, 89, 197, 200–1; in other countries 18, 25, 78, 91, 119, 124, 166, 171
ius sanguinis 217
ius soli 217

Jamaican Creole English 36, 51–2; London Jamaican 111, 120
Japan, Japanese 96, 191, 197–8, 279
Javanese 93

Kanaksprak 64
Karelian 71
Kenya 64
Kiezdeutsch 64
Krio 195–6
Kriol 68
Kven 68, 71–3, 287

Ladino 74
language affiliation **24**, 31
language contact 39, 127–8, 183, 242, **245**, 251–2, 257–9, 284

language crossing 9, **115–16**, 118, 121, 135
language death **44–5**, 68
language endangerment *see* endangered language
language expertise **24**, 31, 165
language ideological debate 78, 81, **92**, 101, 145, 230–3, 249, 273
language ideology: hierarchy of languages 15, 21, 35, 45, 58, 104, 144, 182; of languages as discrete, bounded entities 4, 21, 41, 44–5, 110, 118, 149, 249, 251, 284; linguistic purism 15, 25, 27, 45, 79–80, 180, 182–4, 218, 251; mother tongue ideology 15, 23–5, 158, 162, 198; one nation–one language 15, 22–3, 27–8, 38, 97, 139, 164, 207, 228, 236–7, 247; standard language ideology 15, 21–2, 49, 51, 77, 182–4, 229, 249, 251
language inheritance **24**, 31, 165
language maintenance **44**, 69, 73, 76, 80, 176–83, 196
language nest **71**
language policing 242, 248–52, 273
language revitalization 9, 45, 67–81, **68**, 85, 186; human costs of 74–5, 133; of indigenous languages 176, 177–8, 183, 187
language shift **44**, 67, 69, 72–6, 175–6, 201, 236
language testing 139, 207, 216–22, 232, 255; high-stakes 142, 178, 279; multilingual 279–80; *see also* citizenship
language variation awareness programme **43**, 47
Latin 42, 168
Liechtenstein 207–8, 213–14
Ligurian 42
Lingala 112–13, 163, 287
linguistic continuum **37–8**, 41–2, 45, 53, 55, 111
literacy bridge 10, **166–8**, 171
Lithuania 218
Lombard 42
Luxembourg 23, 25, 27, 90, 141, 166, 227–30; language-in-education policy in 17–18, 143–53, 285
Luxembourgish 17, 23, 37–8, 90, 167; as endangered language 25, 27, 68, 77–80; on signs 13, 256–7, 266

Malay 56–7, 63, 92–4, 150
Mali 59
Malinke 59
Mandarin 63, 95, 100, 179, 188; in Singapore 57–8, 90, 92–4, 101, 135, 150, 185–6; *see also* Chinese and Putonghua
Manichean 58, 235
Māori 68, 70–1, 81
metrolingualism 4, **44**
Mexico 191, 199–200, 234, 237
minimal grasp strategy **197**
minority vs. majority: definition of **7**, 78
moral panic **248**, 249
Morocco 28, 168
mother tongue education 5, 60, 89, 150, **158**, 170–1; AAE 158–61; in Africa 97–9, 101, 161–4, 168–70, 238; problems with 10, 44, 95, 165–6, 175, 184, 278, 287
multimodality 10, 168, 243, **255**, 265, 273

national identity **108–9**, 117; and language 22–3, 26–7, 79, 89, 94, 97, 110, 121, 145, 236
native monolingualism **196**
Native American languages 71, 174–6, 187, 237
Navajo 174–6, 183, 184
Ndebele 98
Neapolitan 42
near-balanced bilingual *see* receptive bilingual
Nepal, Nepali 246–8, 250
new speakers **79**
New Zealand 13, 68, 70–1, 79
Nigeria 6, 90, 99–100, 101; Nigerian Pidgin English 40, 46, 55, 99–100
Njala 195–6
Northern Ireland 39, 109
Norwegian, Norway 21, 68, 70–3
Nouchi 49, 59–60, 62, 85, 163

OPOL (one parent one language) **196–8**, 201
Otomanguean 199

Pakistan 41, 181, 192–3
Papua New Guinea 40–1, 47, 68
Paraguay 178
peripheral normativity **263**
Peru 81, 176
pidgin **39–40**, 46, 68, 99–100, 183, 187
Piedmontese 42
place semiotics **266–7**, 270
Polish 119, 282
polynomic language 76, **77**, 81
Portuguese 18, 78, 143, 151, 166–7, 228–9, 283
prestige: covert **56**
Pugliese 42
Punjabi 93, 192–3, 230, 238
Putonghua 63, 95–7, 100–1, 188; *see also* Chinese and Mandarin

Quechua (Kechwa) 81, 176, 198
Quichua (Kichwa) 81, 176–8

racial identity **109–10**
rap and hip hop music 50, 62, 73, 85, 129, 245, 252
reader positioning 262, **265**, 270, 271
rebus writing **244**
receptive bilingual **197**
regimes of language 217
repertoire: heteroglossic/mixed 176, 195–6, 242; of identities 107; linguistic 3–5, 27, 42–4, 57, 61, 100, **118–19**, 121, 160, 163, 167–9, 197, 283–4; spatial **119**; and translanguaging 110
rich points **18–19**, 28, 281
Romansch 91
Russian/Russia 73, 90–1

Sámi 68, 70–4
Samoan 71, 183
Scots 13, 38–9, 117
Senegal 161, 163
Senufo 59
Sepedi 98
Serbian 21
Sesotho 64, 98
Setswana 76, 8, 148, 162–3, 166
Sheng 64
Shona 162
Sicilian 42, 197
Sierra Leone 195–6
Singapore 55–9, 62–4, 90, 92–4, 97, 99–100, 153; language-in-education policy in 135, 150, 185–6; Speak Good English and Mandarin campaigns 56, 93–4, 101
Singlish 49, 55–60, 62–3, 90, 92–4, 99
site: of control **191**, 200; of resistance 200
social constructivism 105–6, **107–8**
Somalia 127, 129–30
South Africa 7, 64, 90, 97–100, 109, 132, 153, 217; English medium vs. mother tongue education 76, 98, 101, 148–9, 158, 161–71, 238; signs in 261–4; and social media 244, 251
South Korea 222
Spain 90, 140–1, 147, 153, 177
Spanglish 118
Spanish 7, 50, 62, 146, 148, 166, 184, 204; Castilian 90, 140, 147; in Latin America 118, 176–8, 198–200; in state bureaucracy in Catalonia 193–5; in USA 79, 113–14, 118, 141–2, 152–3, 176, 182–3, 187, 199–201, 233–7, 279–80
standardization **21–2**, 41, 51, 76, 78–81, 85
structure of feeling **108**, 117
stylization 9, 114, 118; uni- vs. vari-directional **114–15**, 116–17, 120–1
superdiversity 6, **7**, 119, 148, 167, 191, 246
superiority: ideology of 28, 181, 211, **212**, 229–30, 273
supervernacular **243–4**
Swahili 37, 64, 112–13, 287
Swati 98
Swedish, Sweden 21, 72–3, 186, 250, 259
Swiss German (Schwyzertüütsch) 6, 91–2, 159–60
Switzerland 5–6, 13, 90–2, 100–1, 153, 159
Sylheti 180–2, 184, 186
symbolic use of language *see* instrumental
Syria 223

Taiwan 188
Tamang 247
Tamazight 168
Tamil 57, 92–4, 281

Tay 281–2
Teochew 93
Thai, Thailand 257–9
they-code vs. we-code **111**, 114, 120, 135
thick description **18**, 243
third space **22**, 61
Tok Pisin 40
Tongan 71
top-down vs. bottom-up sign **259–60**, 270
Torres Strait Creole 68–9
translanguaging **110–11**, 119–20, 127, 135, 149, 152, 191, 196–8, 202, 271; identities 117–18; pedagogies 151, 169–70, 280; on signs 263; in social media 249
translingual practice 110
Tsonga 98
Tsotsitaal 64, 98, 162
Turkish: migrants in EU 28, 64, 120, 168, 208, 215–16; migrants in UK 179, 182; on signs 264–5

UK 90, 99, 109, 174–5, 179, 185, 222, 227, 230–3, 236–7; *see also* England
Ukrainian, Ukraine 90–1, 101
Ulster Scots 38–9, 78
Urdu 41, 93, 181, 193, 251
USA 8, 57, 109, 125, 177, 191; heritage language education in 152–3, 175–6, 182–4; high-stakes testing in 142, 279–80; language-in-education policy in 141–3, 149, 154–5, 187; languages in 13, 113–14, 118, 187, 199, 201, 220–1; signs in 257–8, 260–1, 268–9; *see also* African-American English and English Only
us vs. them discourse **111**, 209, 215, 231, 235

variable: linguistic 50, 77
variation: linguistic 42–3, 45, 49–65, 77, 187, 287; inter-language vs. intra-language **43**, 158, 171
Venda 98
Venetian 42
Verlan 13, 49, 60–2, 85
Vietnamese, Vietnam 222, 281
voice **114–15**, 120

we-code *see* they-code
Welsh, Wales 80, 90
Wolof 163

Xhosa 64, 98, 148, 169–70, 244, 251, 263

Yao 96
Yiddish 74
Yoruba 99

Zapotec 199–200, 201
Zhuang 96
Zimbabwe 162
Zulu 64, 98, 148, 162